Independence Edition

VOLUME IX

THE PAGEANT OF AMERICA

A PICTORIAL HISTORY OF THE UNITED STATES

RALPH HENRY GABRIEL

EDITOR

PETER GUILDAY   HARRY MORGAN AYRES

ASSOCIATE EDITORS

OLIVER McKEE   EDWIN MIMS JR.

ASSISTANT EDITORS

CHARLES M. ANDREWS   ALLEN JOHNSON
HERBERT E. BOLTON   WILLIAM BENNETT MUNRO
IRVING N. COUNTRYMAN   VICTOR H. PALTSITS
WILLIAM E. DODD   ARTHUR M. SCHLESINGER
DIXON RYAN FOX   NATHANIEL WRIGHT STEPHENSON

ADVISORY EDITORS

DAVID M. MATTESON

INDEXER

From the portrait by Douglas Volk (1856–) in the Albright Art Gallery, Buffalo, N. Y., reproduced by permission of the Medici Society, Boston

ABRAHAM LINCOLN

THE PAGEANT OF AMERICA

MAKERS OF A NEW NATION

BY

JOHN SPENCER BASSETT

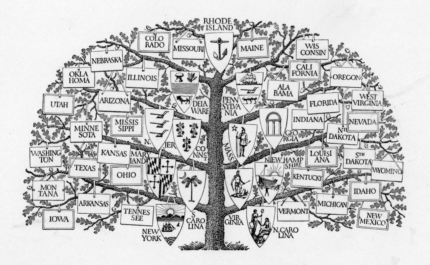

NEW HAVEN · YALE UNIVERSITY PRESS

TORONTO · GLASGOW, BROOK & CO.

LONDON · HUMPHREY MILFORD

OXFORD UNIVERSITY PRESS

1928

TABLE OF CONTENTS

THE POLITICAL FOLKWAYS OF INDUSTRIAL AMERICA

IN the spring of 1865 Generals Lee and Grant sat down together at Appomattox to arrange the terms of that document which, in effect, brought the Confederacy to an end. On that day when the firing ceased few men, either of North or South, would have believed it possible that thirty-three years later one of the junior officers who wore the Confederate gray would be a general in the Army of the United States, leading American troops against a foreign foe, or that fifty-two years later the sons or grandsons of Lee's veterans would answer the call of the nation as readily and in the same spirit of sacrifice as their fathers had met the summons of the Confederacy. Four years of bloody, desperate war had engendered what seemed to be unforgettable hatreds. The South had fought to exhaustion for independence. When the smoke of battle lifted from their fields, the Confederacy still remained for large numbers of the southern people a beautiful and glorious dream. Peoples conquered by superior force have been wont to chafe under the heel of the victor and to bide their time awaiting a favorable moment to strike again for freedom. So Ireland waited through the centuries. The southerners were a conquered people, whose bitterness was magnified by the vindictive reconstruction policy of a radical group in Congress. In 1865 the Union was, in fact, pinned together with bayonets. With the passing years, however, the wounds of war slowly healed and the ugly scars which the conflict left were effaced. The Confederates accepted the results of the war. The dream of independence faded.

The rival sections were bound together by common blood and a common heritage. The great deeds and the great figures of the young United States belonged to the South as much as to the North. Washington was a Virginian whose mantle fell upon the shoulders of Lee. Yet such ties of blood, language, and tradition had failed to prevent the splitting of the British Empire in 1776 or the fratricidal strife of 1861. Such factors would keep the southern people from feeling after the Civil War that theirs was in a sense a *terra irredenta*, but need not necessarily check the spirit of independence. When other powerful forces were at work, however, they served to make the reconciliation complete.

The primary reason for the passing of the dream of independence was the change which the war brought in the economic foundation of the South. President Lincoln's Emancipation Proclamation and the Thirteenth Amendment destroyed the peculiar labor institution of the South. On slavery was based the plantation system of the Cotton Kingdom and out of these two grew naturally the southern practice and ideals of aristocracy. The war brought crashing down the whole structure of southern social life. The conflict proved a ruthless and at times a terrible leveler. It raised the slave to the status of a free man. It practically wiped out capital in the South, which was not

1

expressed in land and buildings, and the value of these was sadly diminished. Almost universally the southern officer and enlisted man returned from the army to poverty, a poverty which in certain of its aspects was hard indeed to bear. The returning father looked into the faces of children who for four years had had inadequate schooling or none at all, and the future held out little hope. During the ten dread years of reconstruction proper schools were impossible and, when at last the ex-Confederate regained control of his own destinies, he found his states, torn by war and looted by carpet-baggers and scalawags, too poor to provide suitable educational facilities for the oncoming generation. Thus in a tragic way that democratic equality which was the expressed ideal of the North came to the South. The southern people were bound together by the fraternity of a common misfortune. Out of the common mass arose, as a result of their own activities and abilities, the leaders of the new day. The making universal throughout the United States of the principle of free labor and the passing of the aristocracy of the Old South meant that the primary reason for the divergence between the sections had been brought to an end. This, however, was not the only factor to be considered.

One of the reasons why the southern man had been willing to fight to make his section free was the haunting fear of the domination of the free negro in those numerous areas in the South where the blacks outnumbered the whites. In Hayti, whose rugged mountains rise from tropical waters not far from the shores of the United States, could be seen at any time after the opening of the nineteenth century the results of a successful slave uprising. In an orgy of pillage, rapine, and blood the French planters had been destroyed or driven from the island. The old order vanished and a new and much more primitive order took its place. In the days when men like Robert Toombs and Jefferson Davis were opposing the agitation of the abolitionists with every argument and every political device they could muster, the southerners did not see how the negro race could be controlled in regions where it was numerous without the institution of slavery. The southern man of 1861 who shouldered his musket and tramped off to war did so to preserve from serious impairment, if not destruction, the civilization which the white man had inherited. After the Thirteenth Amendment, some solution of the race problem satisfactory to the whites must be achieved before the defeated southerners could be reconciled to being held by force within the Union. When Federal troops were finally withdrawn from the defeated section by President Hayes in 1877, such a solution was found. Without losing that friendship for the negro which had for generations characterized the representative southerner, the white man below the Mason and Dixon line excluded the colored man from political life and brought about the segregation of the races. With the accomplishment of this one of the important motives for secession passed. So it came about that the war gave to the Constitution wrought in 1787 and to the nation of which it is the fundamental law a strength which had never before been achieved. The union of the warring sections was made complete by the extension into the South of that economic revolution which industrialism brought to the United States in the last third of the nineteenth century. This revolution was fraught with important consequences for the political habits of the American people. Industrialism brought into being the great corporation, the huge city, and a new material civilization; and it brought lessons in coöperation and organization which were promptly applied to political parties. The modern type of party organization had appeared in the days of the ascendancy of Andrew Jackson. Political management is a specialty and, in the North, had tended to pass into the hands of the professional politician, who derived his reward from the spoils system. In the South before the war the great planter had carried forward that concept of aristocratic political leadership which had characterized the parties in the days of Hamilton and Jefferson. After the Civil War the efficiency of party organizations in both North and South steadily increased. The development was reflected by the coining of the term "party machine" to describe the effectiveness of the new arrangements. An increasing tendency manifested itself to center power and responsibility in the hands of a single individual, the "boss." Significant, however, is the fact that, though the city and the state boss came sometimes into possession of vast power, no national boss ever appeared. The Republican party extended from Maine to California and numbered millions of adherents; no individual could direct effectively the destinies of an organization so vast. Instead, a national committee was developed, an adjustment to the size and diversity of interests of the nation. In the quadrennial battles for the Presidency, however, resort was had to the leadership of a single campaign manager. The party organization, like the business corporation, did not spring fully developed into being. Both were the results of the growth of many decades. And their evolution brought about inevitably a closer and closer relationship between them. This was in part due to more or less conscious imitation on the part of the political organization but more particularly to the need of the parties for funds.

In the years immediately following the struggle between the North and the South, the war chests of the parties were habitually replenished by contributions from officeholders such as postmasters or customs collectors, who owed their positions to the success of the party. While in theory always voluntary, these contributions were, in reality, assessments. The practice emphasized the worst aspect of the spoils system. The business of both state and nation was carried on by individuals whose primary claims to the offices they held was neither character nor efficiency but party service, and who sought to retain their positions by contributing money to the party to enable it to carry on its battles more effectively. Such practices were so patently against the public interest that a demand for reform arose. During the 'eighties the assessment evil was practically stopped. It was the more easily brought to an end because political leaders could turn elsewhere for their funds with every prospect of success. "Big Business," as it came to be called in the latter years of the century, was willing to contribute to the party because of the influence of that organization over the acts of the Federal and state governments. Railroads sought franchises or aid from legislatures; other enterprises asked for privileges or protection against hostile legislation. The managers of the political party which controlled a given legislative body were the obvious persons to approach to bring about the desired results. Under the circumstances the more party managers there were, the greater was the difficulty of transacting business between the economic and political organizations. The system of the political boss was the logical and inevitable outcome of the situation.

The Civil War laid a heavy burden upon the Democratic party. Within its ranks were to be found the secessionists of the South and the Copperheads of the North. The passions aroused by the struggle were long in subsiding. For years the northern dema-gogue urged his hearers to vote as they had shot. For years the bogey of the return of the leaders of secession to a position of dominance in the nation was paraded through the North. Moreover, the South, a former stronghold of the Democratic party, lay for a decade prostrate before the Congressional group of radical Republicans. When these gentlemen in the 'sixties and 'seventies forced negro domination upon the white South, they accomplished two things. They ensured for at least two presidential elections a substantial bloc of votes in the Electoral College for the Republican nominee, and they welded the southern whites into the "Solid South." Even the least astute reader of the political barometer in the years following the Civil War could predict the strong proba-bility of Republican ascendancy for a considerable period of time in the councils of the nation. Inevitably the relations of the business interests with the Republican party were closer than with their Democratic opponents. Not without significance also is the fact that the Republicans also tended to control those northeastern states where in-dustrialism was developing most conspicuously. This "alliance" between business and politics brought both strength and weakness to the party organization; strength in increased financial resources and weakness in the opposition which the arrangement called forth.

As the nineteenth century drew to a close, many citizens of the United States observed that in other ways industrialism was profoundly modifying the practice of American democracy. Millions of immigrants, more and more of them from southern Europe, were seeking the shores of the United States. Ignorant of American traditions and ideals, they created in the larger cities important blocs of votes which the political manager could control. On such a foundation rested the power of Tammany Hall during the régime of the notorious "Boss" Tweed. The purchasing of votes became a well-nigh universal practice and party managers sat at the polls to see that the recipients of the bribe money voted as instructed. In the larger cities these men were frequently voted in gangs, sometimes visiting several polling places before their day's work was done. Such practices reduced the significance of the individual voter. The methods of the highly organized party machine were seriously impairing the frontier ideal of democracy. The spread of industrialism itself brought further modifications of this ideal. On the frontier, democracy had been the outgrowth of a rough economic equality. Industrialism brought about increasing inequalities in wealth and its concentration into a relatively few hands. The captain of industry and his employee had each but one vote, but the financial power of the former gave him vastly more political influence. Such modifica-tions of principle which had been almost a fetish to the early nineteenth-century Americans were not permitted to go without challenge.

Between 1865 and 1900 occurred no less than five political movements which were the outgrowth of protests against the changed conditions of the new era. In parts of the United States frontier conditions persisted until very near the end of the century. Large areas in the South, in the Mississippi valley, and on the Pacific coast remained dominantly agricultural. Nor did agriculture disappear as an important interest in the industrial region itself. In these agricultural communities the folkways and the ideals of early nineteenth-century America persisted tenaciously. It is not surprising, therefore, that three of the five movements of protest were agrarian in their origin. Economic suffering, however, more than outraged ideals, goaded the farmers into action. In the late 'sixties and early 'seventies the agricultural population of the upper Mississippi valley revolted against the dominant position of the new railroad in the economic and political life of their communities. Abandoning both the old parties they attempted independent political action. The legislation which this Granger movement wrote on the statute books of several states marks the beginning of the abandonment of that policy of *laissez faire* which had always characterized the relation between government and business in the United States. Practically contemporaneous with the Grange was the Liberal Republican movement of 1872. Among the changes advocated by these reformers, many of whom were representative of the best thought of the industrial section, was the abolition of the spoils system. This, their most important issue, was a direct assault upon the party machine. They failed but, after the passing of several decades, civil service reform has been widely, though not universally, adopted. Its victory, however, was not so much the result of a desire to weaken the party machine as of the conviction that the spoils system made for dangerous governmental inefficiency and corruption. When the interests of the party and government collided, the former, though reluctantly, had to give way and adjust itself to the changed circumstances.

Hard upon the heels of the Liberal Republican movement came a second agrarian rising which finally took form in the Greenback party. Where the Grangers had carried out local forays against particular railroads, the Greenbackers attempted a general assault upon the moneyed interests of the East. Their demand was for a cheap and depreciated paper currency, which would in appearance, if not in fact, improve their economic condition relative to that of the industrial section. They failed, however, to prevent the resumption of specie payments for the Civil War greenbacks or to bring about a return to "fiat" money. But the protest continued. The Greenback party of the late 'seventies and early 'eighties merged into the Populist party of the 'nineties. In the Presidential election of 1896 the business interests of the East found themselves combating an agrarian West which was suffering from hard times and which was determined, if possible, to reduce the great power of the industrial and financial magnate. With the disappearance in the years immediately following 1896 of the hard times which had brought it into being the Populist movement collapsed. Before the crisis of the last agrarian movement the fifth protest against the new conditions had occurred. This took the form of the rapid adoption in the late 'eighties and early 'nineties of the secret or Australian ballot. When the voter cast his ballot in secret he could not be intimidated. Moreover, the former practice by party managers of checking the delivery of purchased votes was abolished. Yet, in spite of many positive accomplishments, the reform movements and the political revolts of the last third of the nineteenth century did not halt the increase in power and efficiency of the party organization.

Matthew Stanley Quay symbolizes the almost complete dictatorship which the state boss sometimes achieved and which he cynically used to further his own ends. In the 'nineties many of these state bosses were members of that powerful legislative body, the Senate of the United States. In the seats beside them were many persons of great wealth. The Senate gained the nickname of the "millionaires' club." The closing decade of the nineteenth century seems to mark the nearest approach of the American people to a plutocracy. The power of the party machine and its influence over legislative bodies resulted in a loss of confidence in representative government. As a result the opening years of the twentieth century saw a new wave of democracy come out of the frontier and agricultural West. In that region the people were seeking to take power into their own hands. In the direct primary they attempted to make the will of the rank and file of the party supreme in the nominating of candidates. The initiative and referendum checked the state legislatures by a direct expression of the will of the people. The direct primary has been widely adopted but the spread of the practice of direct legislation has not been great. This new democratic movement found its culmination in two amendments to the Constitution of the United States, one providing for the popular election of Senators and the other extending the franchise to women. These changes of the twentieth century, while they have modified somewhat party practices, have not affected greatly the power of the party organization. In city and state it retains, in general, the strength of former years. Such an outcome is a demonstration primarily of the fact that party organization is an indispensable part of the political life of the American people.

Closely following this twentieth-century wave of democracy has appeared a contrasting phenomenon. Since the election of 1896 the apathy of the American electorate has been increasing. In that year eighty-two per cent in round numbers of those Americans eligible to vote cast ballots. This sank to sixty-two per cent in 1912, to forty-nine in 1920, and rose only to fifty-one in 1924. The phenomenon is not limited to any particular section though it is naturally most pronounced in the South where the negro population is large. Closely related to this political attitude is that widespread disinclination of the natural leaders of communities either to participate regularly in the work of party organizations or to hold public office. There is no space here for an analysis of the factors which have produced these ominous phenomena. One only can be mentioned. Both the Democrats and Republicans have come to include a vast aggregation of individuals representing a great variety of interests and points of view. Each includes what has sometimes been called a "conservative" and a "liberal" wing. No issue except, perhaps, that of the protective tariff has separated them for any period of years. In fact insistent issues present dangers to the parties themselves and the practice of "straddling" has become common in order to avoid party schisms. Party platforms have become little more than bundles of compromises. Under such circumstances the weakening of the ties of party loyalty and the increase of independent voting have been inevitable. The parties have tended to become organizations whose primary function is to put men into office and to compel, so far as possible, the officials of the same party to work together for common ends. The advocacy of issues has tended to pass to other than party organizations.

These organizations of the twentieth century should be set against the background of the nineteenth. By the time of the eighteen thirties several semi-isolated geographical sections had become marked within the boundaries of the United States. Each of these sections sought to further its peculiar interests by bringing pressure to bear upon both of the dominant political parties of the time. With the development of transportation, isolation has largely disappeared, but geographic sectionalism still persists. Industrialism, however, has modified its importance. The political prominence once enjoyed by the three great sections, the North, the South, and the West, has tended to pass to three main economic groups — the business interests, the labor interests, and the agricultural interests. Each of these groups, ignoring partisanship, seeks to secure either from the Democrats or the Republicans those things which will further its particular ends. In addition to these three economic groups a number of organizations, like the Anti-Saloon League, either ephemeral or more or less permanent, have come into being to pursue definite objectives. The result has been the development of what is sometimes loosely called the "bloc" system in American political life. There have been occasions when one of these groups has become for a time sufficiently powerful to impair the discipline or even to threaten the cohesion of one or both of the national political parties. The development is only at its beginning. What the end will be the future alone can determine.

Side by side with the increased effectiveness of the advocacy of particular interests has gone the development of a counter-balancing influence. In the first quarter of the twentieth century was definitely abandoned the governmental policy of *laissez faire* with respect to the development of industrial or business enterprises within the nation. Early nineteenth-century Americans had trusted to competition to correct economic evils and abuses. When competition began to break down with the development of great and sometimes monopolistic corporations, it became obvious that measures must be taken to control the new forces which had been created within the state. The extensive development of regulative machinery within both national and state governments has been based upon the principle of the paramountcy of the public over private interest and of the general over local welfare. An unpremeditated and partly unconscious corollary to the growth of this concept has been the development of the power of the central government at the expense of the states. As the first quarter of the twentieth century came to an end, Americans began to realize that year by year they were saddling the Federal Government with increasing burdens so great, at times, as to make for inefficiency. The result has been a reaction and another appeal to the doctrine of states rights. In the years before the Civil War that doctrine had been invoked more than once to protect a minority against the power of the majority. In the twentieth century it is advocated in the interests of efficiency. The pendulum swings again toward Jefferson's position that only in the state governments can the people make their will easily effective. This tendency does not, however, imply a diminution in the sentiment of nationalism.

One of the most striking aspects of twentieth-century America has been the growth and development of nationalist sentiment. Before the Civil War the nationalist ideals of Clay, Webster and Marshall clashed with the sectionalist loyalties of Calhoun and Josiah Quincy. At that time nationalism was thought of in domestic terms and was set against the background of self-conscious states, the oldest of which had traditions running back more than a century before the beginning of the national period. After the war between North and South the old type of state loyalty passed away and the foundations were laid for a new nationalism of the twentieth century. This is set against the background of the society of nations. From the Spanish-American War of 1898 throughout the World War the citizens of the United States became increasingly conscious of the existence and characteristics of other peoples. Armed conflict brought them into contact not only with the Spaniard but with the Filipino, the Chinese, and finally in 1917 with nations the world over. The last of these wars in particular developed immensely what might be called the group consciousness of the American people. War, however, was not the first agency to bring about a manifestation of the new nationalist spirit.

The immigrants who came flooding to the shores of the United States in thousands and even millions in the late nineteenth and early twentieth centuries presented a menace of major importance to the solidarity of the American group. The result was "Americanization," a conscious and deliberate attempt to transmit to the newcomers the ideals and folkways of the American people. Apparently the German Government estimated in 1917 that this intrusion of foreign elements into the United States had rendered the western republic largely impotent in a military sense. That America was able to make a telling effort in the World War was evidence that the policy of Americanization had been surprisingly successful. On the other hand certain aspects of the conflict demonstrated the danger to the national group to be found in the unrestricted admittance of foreigners to the American population. The instinctive reaction of Americans, once they saw the problem clearly, was one of self-preservation. In the epoch-making Immigration Act of 1924 the intense nationalism which had grown out of the war manifested itself. In it America opposed a barrier to what was perhaps the greatest population movement the world had ever known, and either completely or largely excluded all immigrants from countries other than those of northern Europe, the blending of whose blood in the New World had created the "old American stock." Probably no act in the legislative history of the United States is destined to have an influence so important as this one upon the destiny of the American people. In this new national consciousness, which has been largely responsible for the failure of the United States to become a member of the League of Nations, and which has had such offensive manifestations as the recent Ku-Klux-Klan, may be summed up the political folkways of the American people of the second quarter of the twentieth century. With disruptive forces at home largely eliminated America faces the society of nations conscious of the power which comes from unity.

RALPH H. GABRIEL

CHAPTER I

LINCOLN AND THE IMPERILED UNION

THE victory of the North in the Civil War cannot be accounted for without Abraham Lincoln. Next to the operations of the army and navy it was the political genius of Lincoln which finally decided that there should be one and not two nations in the vast region between Canada and Mexico.

Lincoln's political career was founded on his character. Extraordinarily honest, he had also the gift of persuasion and of personal influence. In origin a plain man of the people, he understood the masses and knew how to win their complete confidence. His calm judgment enabled him to keep his poise in crises. When panic fell upon his associates, it was Lincoln who brought them back to a state of confidence. His love of all mankind made all mankind love him — even the Confederates when they came to know him. He was one of those few men whose greatness cannot be measured by their vices. His genius dwelt apart in an atmosphere of its own in which such faults as he possessed did not appear.

Coming to the White House a relatively unknown statesman — a "dark horse" accepted by the leaders of the new Republican party as a compromise candidate — he had either to become a mere figurehead, or to establish a personal ascendancy that would gradually weld the jarring factions of the new party into an aggressive harmony capable of sustaining a great war. To accomplish this he had only his tact, good sense, insight, and genius. He began without any personal following on which to rely and with no definite faction committed to his support. Gradually he built up a following so powerful and so loyal to him that in the last stage of the war he dominated the nation.

Lincoln's fixed purpose was always to preserve the Union. When at the opening of his administration the majority of his Cabinet would have let the South go in peace he held fast to the ideal of unity and refused to compromise. He accepted the challenge of the South and opened the gates of war. Thereafter all his policies were controlled by his steadfast devotion to his ultimate object — a restored Union. It was for this that he followed his cautious course in regard to emancipation, restraining the too impetuous abolitionists as long as their program would embarrass the Union cause. It was for this that he compromised in the Trent affair, smoothed over the angry surface of diplomacy, and kept Great Britain and France from giving aid to the South. It was for this that late in 1863 he inaugurated a course of reconstruction which would call out the sincere coöperation of the most reasonable element of the southern population. It was for this that he carried through the election of 1864 and contemplated cordial coöperation with his rival in the event of his own defeat. If it is fortunate for the world to-day that we have a unified country it is largely to Lincoln that we owe thanks.

1 Lincoln at the time of his Cooper Union speech, Feb. 27, 1860, from a photograph by Brady

LINCOLN IN 1860

IN 1860 Abraham Lincoln was elected President of the United States. Less than six months after that autumn day when the voters went to the polls the North and South were at war (see Vol. VII). The man who more than any other individual held the destinies of the nation in his hand was a frontier lawyer from Illinois, with but the slightest training in national office. A few months before his election the people of New York city had looked curiously upon the westerner, already popular in his own section of the country, as he spoke at Cooper Union. Lincoln used to say that this portrait, with his Cooper Union speech, made him President. On March 4, 1861, the people of the whole North fixed their gaze intently upon this same man, but this time their interest was mingled with doubt and apprehension. To them he was unknown, and his outward uncouthness prejudiced their views of his capacity. Lincoln's philosophy at this time was quite simple. He had taken an oath to preserve the Union and he stood by his oath. His sincere soul knew no way of making that oath square with disunion. He waited patiently for public opinion to form on this point.

LINCOLN IN 1863

LINCOLN had been President almost two years when this photograph was taken. The features in their repose lack the traces of anxiety that the long struggle with the South was to bring. To many contemporary observers it seemed a strange destiny that had elevated this man to the office of chief executive at a time of national crisis.

THE SPIRIT OF CALHOUN

To Calhoun more than anyone else was due the attempt of the South to establish a separate government in which not only slavery, but taxation, commerce and all other affairs, might be directed according to the desires of the majority of the southern voters. His speeches abound in the belief that the South was at the mercy of the more populous North. The election of Lincoln in 1860, ten years after Calhoun's death, gave the southern people a confirmation of this idea. Remembering what Calhoun had said, they believed that the time had come for a separation. Calhoun symbolized the sectional loyalties of the South but he, like the leaders of secession who followed him, was driven by forces over which he had little control. American civilization in the South was developing in a somewhat different direction from that in the North. When the ascendancy of the North in the councils of the

2　　　From a photograph by Brady, Feb. 23, 1863

nation threatened to modify the growth of the South the latter section sought independence. Its people had been trained to believe in the right of a state to secede when it concluded that its interests were no longer protected by the Union, and they believed that the time had come to exercise that right.

4　The Palmetto Flag of South Carolina, from *Harper's Weekly*, Nov. 24, 1860

3　　Tomb of John C. Calhoun at Charleston, S. C., from *Harper's Weeky*, Nov. 24, 1860

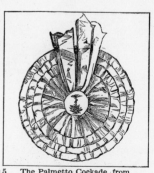

5　The Palmetto Cockade, from *Harper's Weekly*, Nov. 24, 1860

6   Southern students raising a secession flag on Alumni Hall, Yale College, January 20, 1861, from *Frank Leslie's Illustrated Newspaper*, February 2, 1861

THE SENTIMENT OF THE NORTH

In the early weeks of 1861 it did not seem likely that the North would go to war to preserve the Union. Horace Greeley in the *New York Daily Tribune* denounced the idea of a Union "pinned together by bayonets." Many northerners wished to see the "erring sisters go in peace."

8   Jefferson Davis, from a photograph taken at Richmond, during the war, by Vannerson & Jones. © H. P. Cook

THE "CONFEDERATE STATES OF AMERICA"

Other states followed South Carolina's lead and by February 4 five more were in secession; Georgia, Alabama, Mississippi, Louisiana and Florida. On this day representatives from these states in session at Montgomery, Alabama, organized the "Confederate States of America" and chose Jefferson Davis of Mississippi for President; Texas did not secede until February 23, after which it joined the Confederacy.

7   Inauguration of Jefferson Davis at Montgomery, Ala., Feb. 18, 1861, from a chromo-lithograph, 1878, of a painting by James Massalon based on a contemporary photograph, in the Kentucky State Historical Society, Frankfort, Ky.

JEFFERSON DAVIS, 1808–89

Seven other states had slavery: North Carolina, Virginia, Maryland, Delaware, Tennessee, Kentucky, Arkansas and Missouri. They were not so ready to secede as the first seven. Four of them did not join the Confederacy until war had actually begun. The three "border states," Maryland, Kentucky and Missouri, were kept in the Union by the skillful and energetic action of Lincoln. Delaware though a slave state was strongly opposed to secession. The North looked upon Jefferson Davis as the archconspirator among a band of rebels. Time has placed him before us in another light. He was not a radical secessionist. His selection as President was a victory for the moderates over the extremists in the Montgomery convention. In attempting to give unity to the Confederate movement, while each state claimed sovereign authority, his task was very delicate; in attempting to sustain a great war on an economic basis wholly inadequate the task proved impossible. But it is doubtful whether there was any other man in the Confederacy better fitted to undertake it.

9   Lincoln on the way to the Capitol to be inaugurated, from *Frank Leslie's Illustrated Newspaper*, March 16, 1861

INAUGURATION

WHEN Lincoln drove up Pennsylvania Avenue on his way to the inauguration, high above him towered the unfinished dome of the Capitol — a symbol of the unfinished structure of the Union which he was to bring to completion. The situation was tense. Seven states, organized as a Confederacy, were in open defiance of the Government. The last efforts at compromise had failed, Lincoln himself having refused to give his assent to the terms of the proposed Crittenden compromise. The atmosphere of the time was filled with uncertainty. The President-elect for fear of secret enemies had been compelled to enter the National Capital secretly. As he took the oath of office, threatening Confederate batteries confronted the Federal forces which still held Fort Sumter in Charleston harbor. All eyes turned to the new President to see what his attitude would be, and the reply was found in his inaugural address, in which he showed a fixed determination to preserve the Union. From that time he stood squarely upon the oath of office which he took on that fateful fourth of March, pledging himself to preserve the Constitution and to enforce the laws of the land. These two things he would do to the best of his ability, come what might. But he added an earnest appeal urging the seceding states to return to their old allegiance.

> You can have no conflict, without being yourselves the aggressors. You have no oath registered in Heaven to destroy the government, while I shall have the most solemn one to "preserve, protect and defend" it.
>
> ☞ I am loth to close. We are not enemies, but friends— We must not be enemies. Though passion may have strained, it must not break our bonds of affection. The mystic chords of memory, stretching from every battle-field, and patriot grave, to every living heart and hearth-stone, all over this broad land, will yet swell the chorus of the Union, when again touched, as surely they will be, by the better angels of our nature.

10   Facsimile of peroration of Lincoln's first inaugural address, original in the Lincoln Papers, estate of Robert T. Lincoln

11   William H. Seward, 1801–72, from a photograph by Brady

SEWARD'S ATTITUDE

WILLIAM H. SEWARD, Lincoln's Secretary of State, had been his chief rival for the nomination in 1860. Seward was not in favor of precipitating war and believed that the southern states if left alone would presently return to the Union. He tried to persuade Lincoln not to send supplies to Fort Sumter, which was on the point of starvation. Lincoln believed that Sumter must be held as an indication of policy. He notified the Governor of South Carolina that he would send supplies. This was construed by the Confederates as an act of war. They opened fire on Sumter, April 12, and forced it to surrender on the following day (see Vol. VII). War having been begun, Seward gave Lincoln faithful support. Seward's policy of delay would inevitably have played into the hands of the Confederacy. Time would be given to strengthen and perfect the organization of the government that was being set up in great haste. Delay would doubtless have been interpreted in European capitals as weakness on the part of the Government of the United States and might have resulted in early recognition of the Confederacy; and probably European action of that kind would have made it difficult to enforce the blockade of the southern ports.

A FIRM STAND AGAINST SECESSION

PRESIDENT JEFFERSON DAVIS had sent three commissioners to Washington to demand the transfer of forts and other property within the limits of the newly proclaimed Confederacy. Lincoln would not receive them, since a reception would imply acquiescence in secession. At that time Seward was still confident he could direct Lincoln's policy. He sent word indirectly to the commissioners that they might count on the eventual surrender of the forts. But Seward had not spoken with authority. When Lincoln announced his policy with regard to Sumter the commissioners regarded it as a breach of faith and left Washington. Lincoln had not had the least intention of negotiating, but he was waiting for an overt act by the South before employing actual force. Meanwhile he took no effective military measures to defend the Government and the Constitution. Two days after Lincoln's inauguration President Davis had called for one hundred thousand volunteers for one year's service. After the attack on Sumter, Lincoln called out seventy-five thousand militia.

12   Contemporary broadside, April 20, 1861, in the New York Historical Society

CONFEDERATE SECRETARY OF STATE

WHEN the Confederate Cabinet debated firing upon Sumter, the Secretary of State, Robert Toombs, urged delay in the hope of still reaching an amicable understanding with the North. Later, Toombs withdrew from the Cabinet to enter the army. His most noted successor as Secretary of State was Judah P. Benjamin. A distinguished lawyer, Benjamin after the fall of the Confederacy went to England, where he attained great renown in the practice of his profession.

LINCOLN'S SECRETARY OF WAR

THE war could hardly have been won but for the efforts of Stanton, whom Lincoln made Secretary of War in January, 1862. He was a strong-willed man and became a terror to fraudulent army contractors and inefficient generals. He frequently and severely criticized Lincoln, who nevertheless had the generosity to keep him in office on account of his zeal and executive ability. It is told of Lincoln that he once remarked, "Did Stanton say I was a d—— fool? Then I dare say I must be one, for Stanton is generally right and he always says what he means." Lincoln thus showed his ability to continue amicably with a Cabinet member whose brusque personality was only redeemed by his executive capacity. He had a rare faculty of doing the necessary thing and directing those whose spirits chafed under a superior.

13 Robert Toombs, 1810–85, from a photograph by H. P. Cook, Richmond, Va.

14 Edwin M. Stanton, 1814–69, from a photograph by Brady

A STANTON CARICATURE

As Secretary of War, despite his passionate energy, Stanton proved to be something of a martinet; he was also excitable and unforgiving. He was guilty, at times, of undue interference with military commanders in the field. He made many enemies. Nast, the celebrated cartoonist of the time, represented him as a stern-faced man riding a hobbyhorse.

15 From a caricature of Secretary Stanton by Thomas Nast (1840–1902), in the Albert Davis collection, New York

16 Salmon P. Chase, 1808–73, from a photograph by Brady

LINCOLN'S SECRETARY OF THE TREASURY

ONE of the most distinguished figures in Lincoln's Cabinet was Chase, Secretary of the Treasury. His greatest service was the passage of the National Banking Act of 1863, which created a series of national banks with notes secured by Government bonds deposited with the United States Treasury. These notes replaced the notes of the state banks, thus giving the country a safe currency for the first time since the destruction of the Bank of the United States in Jackson's day. The Act also provided a market for the bonds which the Government issued to support the war. In 1864 Chase allowed a dissatisfied faction inside the Republican party to use his name as a rival of Lincoln's for the Presidential nomination. When this came to light and Chase in confusion offered to resign Lincoln replied: "Whether you shall remain at the head of the Treasury Department is a question which I will not allow myself to consider from any standpoint other than my judgment of the public service, and in that view I do not perceive occasion for a change." Again he had shown how to deal with a crisis in his own Cabinet. Chase was too good a Secretary to lose.

ATTITUDE OF THE SOUTH

THE secession movement divided the South in two. The upper South wished to remain in the Union but was resolved not to admit the right of the Federal Government to coerce a state. Sumter and Lincoln's call for volunteers decided the matter. Virginia, North Carolina, Arkansas and Tennessee joined the Confederacy.

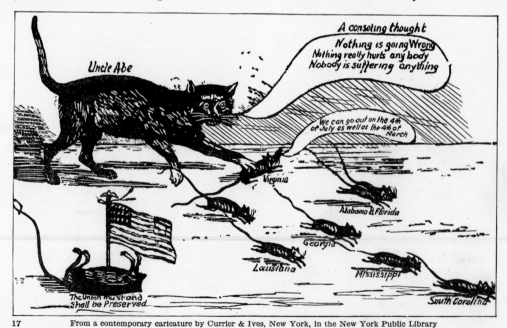

17 From a contemporary caricature by Currier & Ives, New York, in the New York Public Library

THE CREATION OF WEST VIRGINIA

IN the western counties of Virginia there were few slaves and the majority of the inhabitants were loyal to the Union. Early in the war these counties were occupied by Union armies, under whose protection a separate state government was organized. The new government applied for admission to the Union and Congress granted it, regardless of the clause in the Constitution saying that no state can be divided without its consent. It was held in Washington that the state government at Richmond was tainted with treason and its protest against division was not binding. Lincoln set up a rump government at Alexandria, composed of delegates from the parts

18   The Virginia Convention at Wheeling which organized a new state, June 1861, from *Harper's Weekly*, July 6, 1861

of Virginia occupied by Federal troops, and it went through the form of consenting to the division of the state. Congress completed the process by admitting to its fold Senators and Representatives from West Virginia.

THE PROGRESS OF EMANCIPATION

WHEN Virginia seceded, May 23, 1861, General Benjamin F. Butler commanded a Union army at Fortress Monroe. Many slaves escaped from their masters and took refuge inside the Federal lines. When their owners demanded their surrender Butler refused. He said that while slaves were "property" in Virginia they were a sort of property that might be used to build Confederate fortifications and therefore he would consider them contraband of war. The term in this application aroused much merriment in the North. Butler put the refugees to work on military fortifications and other kinds of service in his camp.

19   The "Contraband" at Fortress Monroe, under the pay and direction of the United States, from *Frank Leslie's Illustrated Newspaper*, Nov. 2, 1861

GEN. FREMONT'S PROCLAMATION.

MARTIAL LAW IN MISSOURI

ALL REBELS TAKEN IN ARMS TO BE SHOT.

REBELS' PROPERTY CONFISCATED.

Slaves of Rebels Declared Free.

PROCLAMATION OF GEN. FREMONT.
St. Louis, Saturday, Aug. 31, 1861.
The following Proclamation was issued this morning:

"Headquarters of the Western Department, St. Louis, Aug. 31, 1861.

"Circumstances, in my judgment of sufficient urgency, render it necessary that the Commanding General of this Department should assume the administrative powers of the State. Its disorganized condition, the helplessness of the civil authority, the total insecurity of life, and the devastation of property by bands of murderers and marauders who infest nearly every county in the State and avail themselves of the public misfortunes and the vicinity of a hostile force to gratify private and neighborhood vengeance, and who find an enemy wherever they find plunder, finally demand the severest measures to repress the daily increasing crimes and outrages which are driving off the inhabitants and ruining the State. In this condition the public safety and the success of our arms require unity of purpose, without let or hindrance, to the prompt administration of affairs.

"In order, therefore, to suppress disorders, to maintain as far as now practicable the public peace, and to give security and protection to the persons and property of loyal citizens, I do hereby extend, and declare established, martial law throughout the State of Missouri. The lines of the army of occupation in this State are for the present declared to extend from Leavenworth by way of the posts of Jefferson City, Rolla, and Ironton, to Cape Girardeau on the Mississippi River.

"All persons who shall be taken with arms in their hands within these lines shall be tried by court-martial, and, if found guilty, will be shot. The property, real and personal, of all persons in the State of Missouri who shall take up arms against the United States, and who shall be directly proven to have taken active part with their enemies in the field, is declared to be confiscated to the public use; and their slaves, if any they have, are hereby declared free.

"All persons who shall be proven to have destroyed, after the publication of this order, railroad tracks, bridges or telegraphs, shall suffer the extreme penalty of the law.

"All persons engaged in treasonable correspondence, in giving or procuring aid to the enemies of the United States, in disturbing the public tranquillity, by creating and circulating false reports or incendiary documents, are in their own interest warned that they are exposing themselves.

"All persons who have been led away from their allegiance are required to return to their homes forthwith; any such absence without sufficient cause will be held to be presumptive evidence against them.

"The object of this declaration is to place in the hands of the military authorities the power to give instantaneous effect to existing laws, and to supply such deficiencies as the conditions of war demand. But it is not intended to suspend the ordinary tribunals of the country where the law will be administered by the civil officers in the usual manner, and with their customary authority while the same can be peaceably exercised.

"The Commanding General will labor vigilantly for the public welfare, and in his efforts for their safety, hopes to obtain not only the acquiescence, but the active support of the people of the country.   "J. C. FREMONT,
"Major-General Commanding"

20

From the *New York Daily Tribune*, Sept. 1, 1861

SLAVERY IN THE BORDER STATES

The Abolitionists clamored for a declaration from the Government in favor of unconditional emancipation. The slave owners in the border states became alarmed, particularly when General Fremont, commanding in Missouri, issued an order for the emancipation of all slaves under his jurisdiction. Lincoln promptly reversed his order. He did the same when General Hunter, commanding on the coast of South Carolina, followed Fremont's example. He then took occasion to appeal to the border states "not to be blind to the signs of the times," but to coöperate with him for the purpose of effecting emancipation with compensation for slaves through an act of Congress.

POLITICAL FACTIONS AND THE WAR

Lincoln's political situation was very difficult. Though a great proportion of the Democrats supported his government, the remainder formed an active and hostile opposition party. The Republicans were divided into several factions. A very powerful group, hostile to Lincoln, induced Congress to create the inquisitorial Committee on the Conduct of the War. Dominant in this committee were the anti-Lincoln Republican Senators, Chandler of Michigan and Wade of Ohio. They led a group of bitter extremists who wished to wage war with relentless severity on southern slaveholders. John Hay called this group "the Jacobin club." To this group the southerners were very wicked people for whom a policy of punishment ought to be pursued when the war should have been won. It was a favorite saying among them that rebellion should be made odious. In refusing to share these views Lincoln aroused their opposition and became the object of the attacks of newspapers that supported them. It was one of their favorite doctrines that the Government should use the opportunity of the war to emancipate the slaves.

21 Zachariah Chandler, 1813–79, from a photograph in possession of the publishers

WHAT THE TYRANTS OF THE OLD WORLD THINK OF SECESSION.
"Oh! ain't we Sorry!!!"

22   From a cartoon in *Harper's Weekly*, Dec. 1, 1860

EUROPEAN INTEREST IN AMERICAN AFFAIRS

ALL Europe took vivid interest in the American struggle. Sympathy was divided. In England while the masses were on the side of the North the aristocracy and the government at first favored the South. Alexander II of Russia took the northern side while Napoleon III, with his Mexican schemes in mind, hoped to see the American republic broken in two. Early in the war Napoleon tried in vain to persuade England and

Russia to intervene. Pope Pius IX wrote to the Archbishops of New Orleans and New York in 1863, urging them to use all their efforts to restore peace to the United States. President Davis then sent Dudley Mann as a special envoy of the Confederacy to Pius IX with a letter thanking the Pope for his efforts. On December 3, 1863, Pius IX acknowledged Davis' courtesy. The publication of the correspondence caused considerable feeling in the North.

FEELING IN ENGLAND

THE ruling class in England felt drawn to the South, partly because they thought the South more aristocratic than the North, and partly because they remembered past struggles and were not averse to seeing the United States divided. The English cotton manufacturers and exporters also wanted to see a free-trade, cotton-raising South set up independently, for it would yield them a free market for their commerce and give them the opportunity to obtain cotton unrestricted. The London *Times* summed up these points of view by saying: "The contest is really for empire on the side of the North and for independence on that of the South." The existence of slavery, however, in the South tended to divide English sentiment and materially lessened sympathy for the Confederate cause.

LATEST FROM SPIRIT-LAND.

GHOST OF KING GEORGE III. "WELL, MR. WASHINGTON, WHAT DO YOU THINK OF YOUR FINE REPUBLIC NOW, EH?—WHAT D'YE THINK? WHAT D'YE THINK, EH?"
GHOST OF MR. WASHINGTON. "HUMPH!"

23   From a cartoon by John Tenniel (1820–1914), in *Punch*, London, Jan. 10, 1863

24   Charles Francis Adams, from a photograph by
Warren, Boston

CHARLES FRANCIS ADAMS, 1807–86

LINCOLN had sent Charles Francis Adams to London as our minister. On the eve of his arrival the British Government gave the Confederacy the status of a belligerent, with the right to buy supplies. This action displeased the Union Government which held that the Confederates were only a group of insurgents, or rebels, and entitled to no recognition under the rules of war. Adams protested strongly against the haste with which belligerency had been extended, but without avail. Until the very end of hostilities the Confederacy hoped against hope that England would recognize it as an independent power. President Davis finally was willing to have slavery abolished in the Confederacy if this would bring recognition.

THE BLOCKADE AND INTERNATIONAL LAW

THE immediate purpose of Confederate diplomacy was to induce European nations to break the Federal blockade. British merchants shipped goods to Bermuda or Nassau where they were transhipped and started for Atlantic or Gulf ports in small swift ships. Nassau became a great port overnight. Lincoln struck at blockade running by evoking the doctrine of "continuous voyage." Ships bound for Nassau were arrested on the high seas and if they could not prove the destination of their cargoes they were held to be subject to the law of contraband.

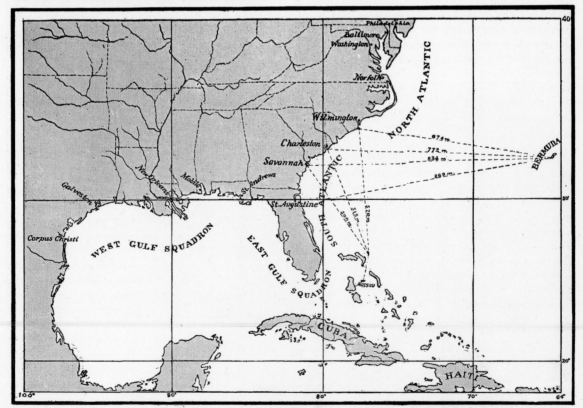

25   Blockade of the Atlantic Coast of the Confederacy, from J. P. Soley, *The Blockade and the Cruiser*, Charles Scribner's Sons, New York, 1883

26   James Murray Mason, 1798–1871, from a photograph by L. C. Handy

27   John Slidell, 1793–1871, from a photograph by L. C. Handy

THE MISSION OF MASON AND SLIDELL

WITH the hope of securing recognition of the Confederacy and perhaps bringing about armed intervention in the termination of the blockade, President Davis in the autumn of 1861 sent James M. Mason and John Slidell to Europe. The first was accredited as Confederate minister to Great Britain and the second to France. The Confederate envoys ran the blockade and reached Havana. As they made no secret of their business, the news that they were *en route* caused much indignation in the North. It also reached England, where it was the cause of much expectant speculation.

28   The *San Jacinto* stopping the *Trent*, from *The Illustrated London News*, December 7. 1861

SEIZURE OF THE *TRENT*

AT Havana, Mason and Slidell took passage on the British ship *Trent* for Halifax, whence they intended to sail on another British ship for England. On November 8, 1861, the *Trent* was intercepted by the United States ship-of-war *San Jacinto*, Captain Charles Wilkes, and the Confederate envoys were taken prisoners against the protest of the captain of the *Trent* and carried to the United States. The incident caused high feeling on both sides of the Atlantic.

LOOK OUT FOR SQUALLS.

Jack Bull. "YOU DO WHAT'S RIGHT, MY SON, OR I'LL BLOW YOU OUT OF THE WATER."

29   From a cartoon in *Punch*, London, Dec. 7, 1861

RECEPTION OF THE NEWS IN LONDON

News of the seizure of Mason and Slidell caused great resentment in Great Britain. Wilkes' action was clearly a violation of the rules of neutrality. It also violated the position the United States had long taken with respect to the right of search at sea. Lincoln and one member of his Cabinet, Montgomery Blair, saw that a mistake had been made. For a moment, however, the North rang with praise of Captain Wilkes of the *San Jacinto*.

THE PRINCE CONSORT

The British Government lost no time in stating its position. It assembled a large fleet ready for action and ordered eight thousand troops sent to Canada. As the troops embarked, a band played *I Wish I Was in Dixie*. The Government also prepared a severe note to be sent to Washington. This dispatch came under the eye of Prince Albert, husband of Queen Victoria, and in the interest of peace he had its terms softened so that the Government of the United States might find it acceptable. The Prince was at that time suffering from the illness which soon after ended his life. This man of good sense who held his temper in a time of difficulty found a counterpart in the President of the United States. Lincoln estimated the diplomatic situation detached from the passion that stirred the northern crowds. He displayed both judgment and courage in his decision. He avoided war and did so without an appearance of weakness. He said that the British protest in this case pleased him, since it admitted the illegality of searching neutral ships.

30   Embarkation of British troops for Canada, from *The Illustrated London News*, Dec. 14, 1861

THE RELEASE OF THE ENVOYS

LINCOLN accepted the situation and ordered Mason and Slidell to be surrendered and placed on a British ship, so that they might continue their journey to England; but he offered no apology. In the note sent by Secretary Seward to the British Government it was admitted that Wilkes had gone beyond his authority in exercising the right of search. But it was added that he would have been within his right if, instead of taking the Confederate agents off the *Trent*, he had seized the ship itself and sent her before an Admiralty court for adjudication.

SIGNIFICANCE OF THE *TRENT* AFFAIR

THOUGH Mason and Slidell reached their destinations they found that Europe was not likely to intervene unless the South should win some great victory unaided. The blockade continued to be the key to the situation. Among their few achievements was the floating of a speculative loan to be discharged by cotton that might be brought through the blockade. The Confederacy had opened its cotton policy with a great mistake. Believing that the manufacturers of England and France would be ruined if the supply of American cotton was interrupted the southerners confidently asserted "Cotton is King." Acting on

COLUMBIA'S FIX.

COLUMBIA. "WHICH ANSWER SHALL I SEND?"

31   From a cartoon in *Punch*, London, Dec. 28, 1861

this belief the Richmond Government early in the war forbade the exportation of cotton, hoping thus to force Europe to intervene. The result was that southern planters lost the cotton market in the months during which the blockade was thinly established. When the Confederacy relaxed its embargo, in 1862, the blockade was so effective that very little could be sent out. The cotton bonds sold in Europe soon became valueless and the British and French speculators who bought them lost much money as a result of their confidence.

32   The Confederate steamer *Nashville* running the blockade at Beaufort, N. C., from *Harper's Weekly*, Apr. 5, 1862

KING COTTON BOUND;
Or, The Modern Prometheus.

33   From a cartoon in *Punch*, London, Nov. 2, 1861

34   Giving provisions to idle cotton workers at Manchester, England, from *The Illustrated London News*, Nov. 29, 1862

SUFFERING AMONG THE BRITISH COTTON WORKERS

THE distress caused by the blockade brought out the sharp division of sentiment in England on the subject of the American war. The operatives in the manufacturing towns were thrown out of employment and had it not been for the relief distributed by philanthropic societies would have come near to starvation. Nevertheless, because the working people were opposed to slavery, their conviction that the war was being fought to put an end to it nerved them to endure their suffering until victory came to the cause of liberty.

FRANCE CRITICIZES ENGLISH MEASURES TO GET COTTON

THE failure of the cotton supply was a blow to French industry also, but not to the same extent as to British industry. There was a considerable party in France that sympathized with the North, and though they were cautious in criticizing Napoleon III, at least they could sneer at the desires of the British manufacturers, which were much the same as those of the Imperial Government that ruled France.

35   From a caricature *John Bull Steps on His Former Protégé, Uncle Tom, to Seize a Bale of Cotton*, in *Actualités*, Paris, 1862

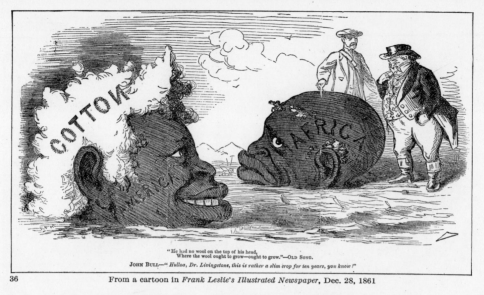

"He had no wool on the top of his head,
Where the wool ought to grow—ought to grow."—OLD SONG.

JOHN BULL—"*Hulloa, Dr. Livingstone, this is rather a slim crop for ten years, you know!*"

36   From a cartoon in *Frank Leslie's Illustrated Newspaper*, Dec. 28, 1861

COTTON GROWING IN AFRICA

THE cotton famine in England caused the Government to look elsewhere for a supply. Efforts were made to raise the staple in Africa. But African cotton was not so good as southern cotton and it was not possible to organize the natives into a laboring class sufficiently large to produce an appreciably large supply. So far as Africa is concerned, southern cotton still remains "King," despite the many efforts made during the war and down to this day to supply the world from Africa.

OVER THE WAY.

MR. BULL. "OH! IF YOU TWO LIKE FIGHTING BETTER THAN BUSINESS, I SHALL DEAL AT **THE OTHER SHOP**."

37   From a cartoon in *Punch*, London, Nov. 16, 1861

COTTON FROM INDIA

GREAT BRITAIN also tried to stimulate the growth of cotton in India where for ages it has been in constant use. However, the short-fibered Indian cotton was not as well adapted as American cotton to the machinery then in use, and it could not make as good cloth.

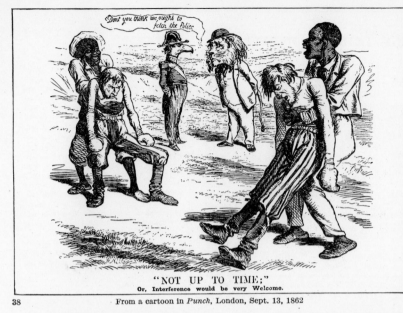

"NOT UP TO TIME;"
Or, Interference would be very Welcome.

38   From a cartoon in *Punch*, London, Sept. 13, 1862

AWAITING EXHAUSTION

THE impression prevailed in Europe that North and South would wear themselves out fighting. In such a process, however, the North had the advantage. Her resources were greater than her rival's. Throughout the war her population was replenished by immigration and her mineral resources were better worked than the South's. Her credit was better, and her superior railroad system, with her command of the ocean, enabled her to move troops at will. The South had in her favor the fact that she fought at home with inside lines; but this advantage did not outweigh her tremendous loss in man power, with the consequent breaking of confidence in ultimate victory. Despite these facts her resistance continued until her resources were exhausted.

39   From the painting *The Proclamation of Emancipation* by Francis B. Carpenter (1830–1900), in the Capitol, Washington

THE TENTATIVE EMANCIPATION PROCLAMATION

EARLY in the war it became plain that what Lincoln called "the Liberal party throughout the World" would side with the North on the issue of emancipation but not on the issue of nationality. In the grim days of the summer of 1862 the Abolitionists took practically the same position. Lincoln felt that the cause was desperate. On July 22, he read to his Cabinet a draft emancipation proclamation, justifying it as a military measure. All the Cabinet but Blair, Postmaster-General, approved it; but at the suggestion of Seward its announcement was postponed until the Union armies had won a victory. Otherwise, said Seward, it might seem that the Government was "stretching forth its hands to Ethiopia" in confession of weakness.

NEW YORK DAILY TRIBUNE WEDNESDAY AUGUST 20, 1862.

THE PRAYER OF TWENTY MILLIONS.

To Abraham Lincoln, President of the U. States:

DEAR SIR: I do not intrude to tell you—for you must know already—that a great proportion of those who triumphed in your election, and of all who desire the unqualified suppression of the Rebellion now desolating our country, are sorely disappointed and deeply pained by the policy you seem to be pursuing with regard to the slaves of Rebels. I write only to set succinctly and unmistakably before you what we require, what we think we have a right to expect, and of what we complain.

I. We require of you, as the first servant of the Republic, charged especially and preëminently with this duty, that you EXECUTE the LAWS. Most emphatically do we demand that such laws as have been recently enacted, which therefore may fairly be presumed to embody the *present* will and to be dictated by the *present* needs of the Republic, and which, after due consideration have received your personal sanction, shall by you be carried into full effect, and that you publicly and decisively instruct your subordinates that such laws exist, that they are binding on all functionaries and citizens, and that they are to be obeyed to the letter.

II. We think you are strangely and disastrously remiss in the discharge of your official and imperative duty with regard to the emancipating provisions of the new Confiscation Act. Those provisions were designed to fight Slavery with Liberty. They prescribe that men loyal to the Union, and willing to shed their blood in her behalf, shall no longer be held, with the Nation's consent, in bondage to persistent, malignant traitors, who for twenty years have been plotting and for sixteen months have been fighting to divide and destroy our country. Why these traitors should be treated with tenderness by you, to the prejudice of the dearest rights of loyal men, we cannot conceive.

III. We think you are unduly influenced by the counsels, the representations, the menaces, of certain fossil politicians hailing from the Border Slave States. Knowing well that the heartily, unconditionally loyal portion of the White citizens of those States do not expect nor desire that Slavery shall be upheld to the prejudice of the Union—(for the truth of which we appeal not only to every Republican residing in those States, but to such eminent loyalists as H. Winter Davis, Parson Brownlow, the Union Central Committee of Baltimore, and to *The Nashville Union*)—we ask you to consider that Slavery is everywhere the inciting cause and sustaining base of treason: the most slaveholding sections of Maryland and Delaware being this day, though under the Union flag, in full sympathy with the Rebellion, while the Free-Labor portions of Tennessee and of Texas, though writhing under the bloody heel of Treason, are unconquerably loyal to the Union. ...

IV. We think timid counsels in such a crisis calculated to prove perilous, and probably disastrous. It is the duty of a Government so wantonly, wickedly assailed by Rebellion as ours has been to oppose force to force in a defiant, dauntless spirit. It cannot afford to temporize with traitors nor with semi-traitors. It must not bribe them to behave themselves, nor make them fair promises in the hope of disarming their causeless hostility. Representing a brave and high-spirited people, it can afford to forfeit anything else better than its own self-respect, or their admiring confidence. For our Government even to seek, after war has been made on it, to dispel the affected apprehensions of armed traitors that their cherished privileges may be assailed by it, is to invite insult and encourage hopes of its own downfall. The rush to arms of Ohio, Indiana, Illinois, is the true answer at once to the Rebel raids of John Morgan and the traitorous sophistries of Beriah Magoffin.

V. We complain that the Union cause has suffered, and is now suffering immensely, from mistaken deference to Rebel Slavery. Had you, Sir, in your Inaugural Address, unmistakably given notice that, in case the Rebellion already commenced were persisted in, and your efforts to preserve the Union and enforce the laws should be resisted by armed force, you would recognize no loyal person as rightfully held in Slavery by a traitor, we believe the Rebellion would therein have received a staggering if not fatal blow. At that moment, according to the returns of the most recent elections, the Unionists were a large majority of the voters of the Slave States. But they were composed in good part of the aged, the feeble, the wealthy, the timid—the young, the reckless, the aspiring, the adventurous, had already been largely lured by the gamblers and negro-traders, the politicians by trade and the conspirators by instinct, into the toils of Treason.

VI. We complain that the Confiscation Act which you approved is habitually disregarded by your Generals, and that no word of rebuke for them from you has yet reached the public ear. Fremont's Proclamation and Hunter's Order favoring Emancipation were promptly annulled by you; while Halleck's No. 3, forbidding fugitives from Slavery to Rebels to come within its lines—an order as unmilitary as inhuman, and which received the hearty approbation of every traitor in America—with scores of like tendency, have never provoked even your remonstrance. We complain that the officers of your Armies have habitually repelled rather than invited the approach of slaves who would have gladly taken the risks of escaping from their Rebel masters to our camps, bringing intelligence often of inestimable value to the Union cause. We complain that those who have thus escaped to us, avowing a willingness to do for us whatever might be required, have been brutally and madly repulsed, and often surrendered to be scourged, maimed and tortured by the ruffian traitors, who pretend to own them. We complain that a large proportion of our regular Army Officers, with many of the Volunteers, evince far more solicitude to uphold Slavery than to put down the Rebellion. And finally, we complain that you, Mr. President, elected as a Republican, knowing well what an abomination Slavery is, and how emphatically it is the core and essence of this atrocious Rebellion, seem never to interfere with these atrocities, and never give a direction to your Military subordinates, which does not appear to have been conceived in the interest of Slavery rather than of Freedom.

* * * * *

IX. I close as I began with the statement that what an immense majority of the Loyal Millions of your countrymen require of you is a frank, declared, unqualified, ungrudging execution of the laws of the land, more especially of the Confiscation Act. That Act gives freedom to the slaves of Rebels coming within our lines, or whom those lines may at any time inclose—we ask you to render it due obedience by publicly requiring all your subordinates to recognize and obey it. The Rebels are everywhere using the late anti-negro riots in the North, as they have long used your officers' treatment of negroes in the South, to convince the slaves that they have nothing to hope from a Union success—that we mean in that case to sell them into a bitterer bondage to defray the cost of the war. Let them impress this as a truth on the great mass of their ignorant and credulous bondmen, and the Union will never be restored—never. We cannot conquer Ten Millions of People united in solid phalanx against us, powerfully aided by Northern sympathizers and European allies. We must have scouts, guides, spies, cooks, teamsters, diggers and choppers from the Blacks of the South, whether we allow them to fight for us or not, or we shall be baffled and repelled. As one of the millions who would gladly have avoided this struggle at any sacrifice but that of Principle and Honor, but who now feel that the triumph of the Union is indispensable not only to the existence of our country but to the well-being of mankind, I entreat you to render a hearty and unequivocal obedience to the law of the land.

Yours, HORACE GREELEY.

New York, August 19, 1862.

40   Extract from an open letter to Lincoln in the *New York Daily Tribune*, New York, August 20, 1862

"THE PRAYER OF TWENTY MILLIONS"

IN August Horace Greeley in *The Tribune* published the Abolition ultimatum under the title "The Prayer of Twenty Millions." It gave Lincoln a chance to feel the country while waiting for a turn of the tide. In an open letter he replied — "My paramount object in this struggle is to save the Union, and it is not either to save or destroy slavery. . . . What I do about slavery and the colored race I do because I believe it will help to save the Union; and if I forbear, I forbear because I do not believe it would help to save the Union." Thus President Lincoln made the preservation of the Union the paramount issue.

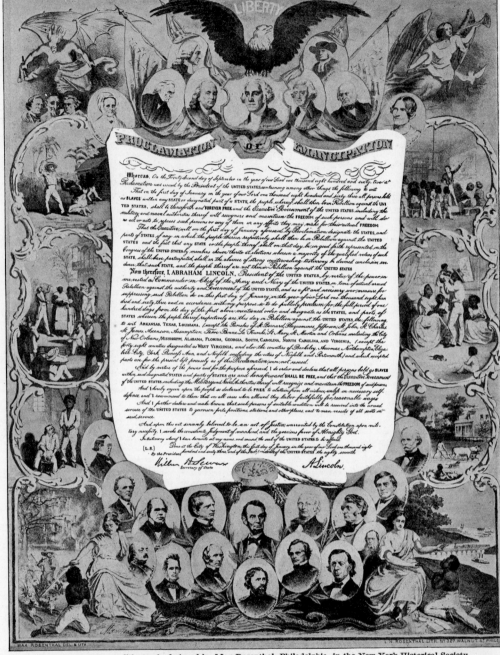

41   From a contemporary lithograph, designed by Max Rosenthal, Philadelphia, in the New York Historical Society

EMANCIPATION IS PROCLAIMED ON JANUARY 1, 1863

THE Union success in driving Lee from Maryland, as a result of the battle of Antietam, September 17, 1862 (see Vol. VII), was the victory for which Lincoln had waited. On September 23 he issued a preliminary statement warning the South that he would declare free all slaves held on January 1, 1863, in territory resisting the authority of the Union. This statement was made good in the Emancipation Proclamation published to the world on the following New Year's Day. It was not observed in the South, but thenceforth the war was waged for two objects, to preserve the Union and to put an end to slavery. The proclamation did not apply to Tennessee, mostly in Union hands, and to the parts of Louisiana that were held by Union troops.

COMPENSATED EMANCIPATION

THE Emancipation Proclamation did not apply to slavery in loyal states in which Lincoln wished to see emancipation with compensation by the Government. On March 2, 1862, he had suggested this idea to Congress, saying that at four hundred dollars on an average for each slave, slavery might be wiped out in Maryland, Kentucky, Missouri and Delaware. Congress took no action, but he renewed the suggestion in his annual message of December 1, 1863. Congress now manifested some interest and a bill for compensated emancipation in Missouri passed the House and had a conditional approval in the Senate. It was opposed by the Democrats in the border states who did not think the South would be subdued. The measure was not popular with the radical Republicans who objected to giving so much money to slaveholders. It has been thought that Lincoln would have extended his offer to the other southern states as a condition of submission to the Union. It should be remembered that it was only Lincoln that made this offer to the South, and that it is not certain that he could have induced the North or the South to accept it. Probably the matter had to be fought out to the end. If the North had offered compensated emancipation in 1862 the South would probably have rejected it at that time; but the offer still standing would have been a powerful appeal to the

42 From the statue *Emancipation* in Washington, by Thomas Ball (1819–1911), courtesy of the Commission of Fine Arts, Washington

South and it may well have produced a crumbling of southern resistance as the fortunes of war ebbed. That is the way that Lincoln thought it would affect the situation.

ABE LINCOLN'S LAST CARD: OR. ROUGE-ET-NOIR.

43 From a cartoon *Abe Lincoln's Last Card; or Rouge-et-Noir*, in *Punch*, London, Oct. 18, 1862

EFFECTS OF EMANCIPATION ON EUROPE

THE South, which had been generally successful in the field up to January 1, 1863, jeered at the proclamation. In Europe it was regarded as Lincoln's last card on which all was staked. It proved to be a great stroke of diplomacy because of which the European liberals became enthusiastic propagandists on the side of the North. In England their influence put an end to the possibility of intervention.

Thirty-Eighth   Congress of the United States of America;

At the Second Session,

Begun and held at the City of Washington, on Monday, the fifth day of December, one thousand eight hundred and sixty-four.

A RESOLUTION

Submitting to the legislatures of the several States a proposition to amend the Constitution of the United States.

Resolved by the Senate and House of Representatives of the United States of America in Congress assembled, (two-thirds of both Houses concurring), that the following article be proposed to the legislatures of the several States as an amendment to the Constitution of the United States, which, when ratified by three-fourths of said Legislatures shall be valid, to all intents and purposes, as a part of the said Constitution, namely: Article XIII. Section 1. Neither slavery nor involuntary servitude, except as a punishment for crime whereof the party shall have been duly convicted, shall exist within the United States, or any place subject to their jurisdiction. Section 2. Congress shall have power to enforce this article by appropriate legislation.

Schuyler Colfax
Speaker of the House of Representatives
H. Hamlin
Vice President of the United States
and President of the Senate

Approved, February 1, 1865.

Abraham Lincoln

44   From the original in the Department of State, Washington

THE THIRTEENTH AMENDMENT

SPEAKING of the Proclamation of Emancipation Lincoln said: "I conceive that I may in emergency do things on military grounds which cannot constitutionally be done by Congress." He denied that Congress had power to free slaves in a state. Nevertheless, he wished emancipation to rest on a firmer mandate than military necessity, and was not sure that the Supreme Court would sustain it on the return of peace. With his approval the Thirteenth Amendment was introduced into Congress March 28, 1864, and was duly ratified by the requisite number of states. It was promulgated February 1, 1865, and accepted by the conquered states after the war ended.

A BRITISH FRIEND OF THE UNITED STATES

SECOND to none in influence among the friends of the North abroad was John Bright, a great leader of the English and Scotch middle class. Though an ardent free trader and opposed to the high tariff policy of the Republicans, he was nevertheless consistently on the side of the Union, because of his opposition to slavery. From the beginning of the Civil War he saw that the chief issue was the destruction of that institution. He used his influence to keep the English people from demanding that their Government break the blockade of southern ports to get cotton for British mills. In June, 1863, Bright made what Lord Morley calls "perhaps the most powerful and noblest speech of his life" in opposition to a motion in the British Parliament for the recognition of the Confederacy.

45 John Bright, 1811–89, from a photograph by
William Luks, London

NAPOLEON III AND THE CONFEDERACY

AN indirect effect of emancipation was the final breakdown of the schemes of Napoleon III for intervention in the war. His Mexican project required the dissolution of the American republic. In October, 1862, he had suggested to Great Britain and Russia a joint note to the United States proposing an armistice of six months to consider the terms of a compromise. The other powers declined to coöperate with him. Then Napoleon, having heard of the disastrous battle at Fredericksburg, offered the United States his good offices for making peace. This was declined pointedly with a sharp protest against intermeddling. Still another of Napoleon's plans lay behind the movement in the British Parliament which Bright helped defeat in 1863. He gave Slidell permission to construct ships secretly in France, but withdrew it to prevent diplomatic complications with the United States.

THE "COPPERHEADS"

A COMPLICATED political situation had developed in America. When the war began, many Democrats, among them Stephen A. Douglas, gave Lincoln their earnest support. Many others were lukewarm. They believed that the war had resulted from the

ONE HEAD BETTER THAN TWO.

Louis Napoleon. "I SAY, HADN'T WE BETTER TELL OUR FRIEND THERE TO LEAVE OFF MAKING A FOOL OF HIMSELF?"

Lord Pam. "H'M, WELL, SUPPOSE YOU TALK TO HIM YOURSELF. HE'S A GREAT ADMIRER OF YOURS, YOU KNOW."

46   From a cartoon by John Tenniel in *Punch*, London, Nov. 22, 1862

election of a Republican President and that it would not have occurred if a Democrat had been chosen. In the elections of 1862 they appealed to the country on this line. The Union men denounced them as supporters of the South and declared their course treason. These opposition Democrats were given the name "Copperhead," in allusion probably to the copperhead snake.

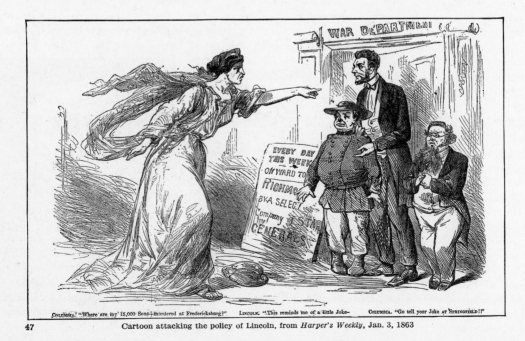

Columbia. "Where are my 15,000 Sons—murdered at Fredericksburg?"   Lincoln. "This reminds me of a little Joke—   Columbia. "Go tell your joke at Springfield!!"

47   Cartoon attacking the policy of Lincoln, from *Harper's Weekly*, Jan. 3, 1863

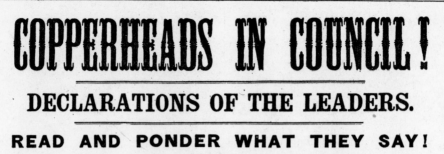

COPPERHEADS IN COUNCIL!

DECLARATIONS OF THE LEADERS.

READ AND PONDER WHAT THEY SAY!

THESE DECLARATIONS
Show the spirit of the Traitors who are now attempting to gain ascendency in New-Hampshire for the encouragement of the Rebels in their attempt to subvert our noble and beneficent Government.

"*I do not believe aggression by arms is a suitable or possible remedy for existing evils.*" FRANKLIN PIERCE, *Chief Sachem of the "Knights of the Golden Circle" in New-Hampshire, in a Speech from balcony of Eagle Hotel, Concord, April 19, 1861.*

"*What are to be the ultimate fruits of having first wronged and then conquered and humiliated a spirited and gallant people, whose fathers were the loved friends and co-laborers with our fathers in the Revolution, and who have nobly stood with us, as companions and fellow-soldiers, in every war with foreign foes since that period, remains to be seen.—PIERCE. Published in the N. H. Patriot after the capture of Fort Donelson.*

"Gentlemen, radical *abolitionism must be put down.* This great and glorious country will be shattered into fragments if it is not, or else we shall find ourselves at last brought under the iron rule of military despotism.—*IRA A. EASTMAN, Copperhead candidate for Governor, in speech of acceptance.*

If the South need any assistance, *I will go out and assist them. . . . I won't do a thing to sustain the President, the Administration, Congress, or any of the piratical crew that have control of this government. I won't do any thing that can be interpreted in in any way supporting this war. . . . I am personally acquainted with* Jefferson Davis. I have seen letters from him. He is a man of *wonderful executive power and firmness of will, and the only one who could have successfully conducted the South through her present struggle. . . .* President Lincoln is a *knave, an imbecile, a usurper and a tyrant, who curses the country with his administration. . . . Poor, miserable, ignorant, lousy negro. . . . The bloodthirsty followers of beasts, the clergy.*—JOHN H. GEORGE, *Copperhead candidate for Congress in 2d District.*

" The abolitionists were a more insidious and dangerous foe than the Southern rebels. *The war has been brought on by the clamor of abolitionists.* The question now at issue was, *whether the President's proclamation should be carried out in the emancipation of slaves, or abolitionism should be put down.* The Democratic party was for putting down the abolitionists, *and maintaining the institution of slavery undisturbed.* He (Minot) was personally opposed to abolition, and in *favor of the perpetuity of slavery. A convention should be called after proclaiming an armistice, for arranging a peace satisfactory to both parties by mutual compromise.*"—JOSIAH MINOT, *intimate personal and political friend of Pierce, and the chief manager of the Copperhead Party, in a recent speech at Canterbury.*

"I am a REBEL. I was locked up forty days in a jail, I never saw the inside of before, because I am

Knights of the Golden Circle in Secret Session.

in favor of a free government for white people and not for niggers. SLAVERY IS RIGHT. It can not be proved that Slavery is a sin. Any physician can disprove that position. The forearms of negroes are four inches longer than those of a white man's. They never sprung from Adam. God never made an animal, except a skunk, that smells half so bad. I AM DEATH ON MINISTERS. They have been preaching the negro twenty-five years, but I haven't heard them for ten years, because I haven't been inside of a church for that period. They are always preaching the negro, and in my town they haven't converted any souls for a good many years. Niggers are their breakfast, dinner, supper, and lodging. Go home and vote the democratic ticket.—Dr NAT. BATCHELDER, *a leading Copperhead, and member of the Rockingham County Democratic Committee, in a Speech at the Democratic State Convention.*

" The *Wolfborough News* publishes a communication, in which it is asserted that nineteen twentieths of the ministers, and four fifths of those who attend church regularly, vote the Republican ticket; and the writer inquires why this is so. Admitting the facts to be as stated, one of them accounts for the other—the first for the last. The ministers not only vote the Republican ticket, but they are *active political fuglers* (on the sly), and preach far more politics than religion from their so-called "*sacred desks.*" The consequence is, Democrats will not go to hear them; they first became disgusted with this shameful and dishonest conduct of the priests, and then as their treachery to duty, principle, and country became more apparent, the great mass of Democrats instinctively resolved to give them no countenance or support. Here we have the reason for one of the facts stated by the *News* writer—and ample reason it is. As to the reason for the other—the fact that the mass of the ministers are Republicans, we account for it upon the principle of natural affinity. A class of men who are ever *meddlesome, scheming, and disposed to rule,* are naturally attracted to a corrupt, unscrupulous, and revolutionary party, which delights in turmoil and public peril, and labors to destroy the institutions of our fathers, in order to insure their own lease of power, which they use only for the promotion of their own private interests."—*N. H. Patriot, February 16, 1863.*

The draft must be resisted at all hazards. *I should prefer to live under the administration of JEFFERSON DAVIS than that of Abraham Lincoln.*—THOMAS P. TREADWELL, *in a speech at Concord, March 7.*

Said a Concord democrat, within the last three months : "*The happiest day I ever had in my life ; yes, let me repeat it, the happiest day I ever had in my life, was when I heard of the first battle at Bull Run ; and I hope every man who goes South to fight will meet the same fate as those killed there !*" Shocking and even brutal as is this declaration, the feeling which prompted it lies in the hearts of more men calling themselves democrats than is dreamed of in the philosophy of people who suppose all the world as honest as themselves.

The "Knights of the Golden Circle" are doing a good work in this State. *FRANKLIN PIERCE, to a gentleman in the cars.*

The most startling political crime, the most stupid political blunder yet known in American history, has now been consummated. The promised proclamation of Abraham Lincoln to decree the abolition of negro slavery, is laid before the reader this morning.—*RICHMOND EXAMINER, Jan. 1.*

"The greatest crime ever committed by a Chief Magistrate of a free people has been perpetrated by the President, in the promulgation of the Emancipation Proclamation. *N. H. PATRIOT, Jan. 7.*

It is time for a separation of the country. I have a mind to sell my property and go South.—*DANIEL MARCY, Copperhead candidate for Congress in the 1st District.*

Rather than that the *Emancipation Proclamation should be enforced, and SLAVERY be ABOLISHED, I would prefer that the GOVERNMENT should be DESTROYED.*—WILLIAM BURNS, *Copperhead candidate for Congress in 3d District, in recent speeches.*

At a Democratic meeting in Laconia, addressed by Col. T. J. Whipple and G. W. Stevens, Esq., the following plan of settlement was broached: An *immediate armistice and a speedy peace*—the reunited States to assume all the expenditures of the War: those of the South and those of the North alike. *Slavery to be as it was before the Rebellion, and agitation of that topic to be deemed worthy of the death of all offenders.*

Slavery is a Divine Institution, and I will defy ministers enough to fill a church to prove it to the contrary.—GEORGE W. STEVENS, *in a speech at New-Hampton, and other places.*

The Republicans must be put down at THE POINT OF THE BAYONET.—WM. A. RICHARDSON, *U. S. Senator from Illinois—particular friend of John H. George, and stumping his Cong. District for him—in a speech at Concord, March 6, 1863, at which IRA A. EASTMAN presided.*

In contrast with the above, read the following words of Stephen A. Douglas:

"There can be no *neutrals* in this war; only *patriots and traitors.*"

MEN OF NEW-HAMPSHIRE!
WILL YOU VOTE THE TICKET MADE UP BY SUCH MEN?
PLEASE PASTE UP IN A CONSPICUOUS PLACE.

48 From a New Hampshire election poster, 1864, in the New York Historical Society

THE "SONS OF LIBERTY"

THE activities of the Copperheads led to the organization of the secret "Knights of the Golden Circle," later called the "Sons of Liberty." Their object was to stir up popular feeling against the Republicans, and, while criticizing the way in which the war had been conducted, gain control of the Government and make some kind of compromise with the South. The more extreme leaders had a plan for a union of the northwestern states which might separate from the North, at least until peace could be obtained. Most of the Democrats discountenanced this movement, and it is certain that the majority would not have gone so far as to fight for the South.

THE ELECTION OF HORATIO SEYMOUR

THE feeling against the Republicans for having brought on the war continued strong in New York. In the autumn of 1862 the Democrats elected as Governor Horatio Seymour, a man of marked ability and patriotism, later nominated for President (No. 128). His election over General James Samuel Wadsworth, a radical on the slavery question and a military supporter of the President's, was taken as a severe blow at the Washington Government and gave new hope to the Democrats.

49   New York's celebration of Governor Seymour's election, from *The Illustrated London News*, Dec. 20, 1862

DRAFT RIOTS IN 1862

THE opposition made an issue with the Government on conscription. At first the North relied on volunteers to form the armies, but in 1863 it was necessary to order a draft. This was bitterly resisted in many places. In New York, where the Democrats were strong, it occasioned rioting; the drafting was broken up, stores and residences were looted, negroes were beaten and killed, and the population terrorized until troops were brought to the city. Seward asked Archbishop Hughes of New York to aid in stopping the riot and the Archbishop made a spiritual appeal to the mob.

50   Rioters sacking brownstone houses in New York, from *The New York Illustrated News*, July 25, 1863

51   Clement L. Vallandingham, 1820–71, from
a photograph by Brady

A NORTHERN DEMOCRAT IS BANISHED TO THE CONFEDERACY

VALLANDINGHAM, of Ohio, was one of the most outspoken of the peace Democrats. Smarting under the contempt of his enemies, he flung moderation to the winds. In 1863, while a candidate for the nomination for Governor, he was arrested under an order given by General Burnside and tried by a military commission. He was found guilty of "declaring disloyal sentiments" and sentenced to prison for the remainder of the war. His detention made him a martyr to his followers, and Lincoln, realizing that his punishment would have a bad political effect, commuted the sentence to banishment into the Confederacy. The prisoner was sent to the Confederate lines, whence he went to Canada and carried on his propaganda to disconcert the actions of the Republicans. The Democrats made him their candidate for Governor, but the Republicans defeated him by supporting Brough, a war Democrat. The incident was notable because Vallandingham had been tried by military law for an offence that was not military. It raised a serious question about the extent to which martial law should apply and it was not settled until after the war.

THE ELECTION OF 1864

THE Republicans in 1864 renominated Lincoln. To have done otherwise would have been confession that his war policy was a failure. The Democrats nominated General George B. McClellan, popular with the soldiers. He had not been associated with the Copperheads and was in favor of carrying on the war. From the party standpoint the nomination was as good as could be made. George B. Pendleton was nominated for Vice-President. McClellan's candidacy was destined to injure his standing with the American people. During the early phases of the campaign it seemed at times that he might be elected. In the end, however, he was crushed by the triumphant majority which returned Lincoln to office. After the war had been won and Lincoln slain, the martyred President came into a place in the affections of the American people held by no other figure of their history. Then McClellan was remembered not only as an unsuccessful general but as the man who had tried to defeat Lincoln.

52   The Democratic National Convention nominating McClellan, from an illustration by W. T. Crane in *Harper's Weekly*

A BRITISH VIEW OF THE ELECTION

THE year 1864 opened with gloomy prospects for the North. From Gettysburg until the spring, an interval of nine months, no considerable military success occurred in Virginia. The spring operations in the East and the West only resulted in heavy losses. Lincoln in the early autumn considered his reelection improbable. In Europe it was generally believed that the end was approaching and that intervention in the interests of humanity would soon come about. This gloomy situation was relieved by Farragut's brilliant victory at Mobile in August and by Sherman's capture of Atlanta, September 4, 1864. Pessimism in the North now was being dispersed by feats of arms that presaged ultimate victory for the Union.

MRS. NORTH AND HER ATTORNEY.

MRS. NORTH. "YOU SEE, MR. LINCOLN, WE HAVE FAILED UTTERLY IN OUR COURSE OF ACTION; I WANT PEACE, AND SO, IF YOU CANNOT EFFECT AN AMICABLE ARRANGEMENT, I MUST PUT THE CASE INTO OTHER HANDS."

53   From a cartoon in *Punch*, London, Sept. 24, 1864

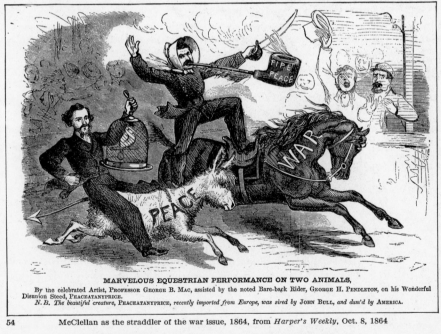

MARVELOUS EQUESTRIAN PERFORMANCE ON TWO ANIMALS,

By the celebrated Artist, PROFESSOR GEORGE B. MAC, assisted by the noted Bare-back Rider, GEORGE H. PENDLETON, on his Wonderful Disunion Steed, PEACEATANYPRICE.

N.B. *The beautiful creature,* PEACEATANYPRICE, *recently imported from Europe, was sired by* JOHN BULL, *and dam'd by* AMERICA.

54   McClellan as the straddler of the war issue, 1864, from *Harper's Weekly*, Oct. 8, 1864

REPUBLICAN VIEW OF THE DEMOCRATS

DURING the Presidential campaign the Republicans refused to make a distinction between McClellan, who declared himself for a vigorous prosecution of the war, and the Democratic platform which contained most of the assertions made in recent months by Vallandingham and his friends. Pendleton, candidate for Vice-President, was said to run on a peace platform. In this way the Democrats were not allowed to evade the program of submission.

55 Shipyard of the Lairds at Liverpool, from *Frank Leslie's Illustrated Newspaper,*
April 30, 1864

ENGLAND BUILDS WAR SHIPS FOR THE CONFEDERACY

As the war drew toward an end American diplomacy insisted that it had grievances against the British Government. The Confederates had ordered a number of cruisers, followed by "rams," which the Lairds, of Liverpool, agreed to build. The first cruiser was the *Florida*. She got out to sea but was captured before great damage had been done. A more powerful ship was the *Alabama*, built by the same firm. As she neared completion Adams, our minister in London, made emphatic protest and asked that she be seized before she could leave British waters. The English Government made a perfunctory investigation and replied that no evidence was found that the *Alabama* was intended for the Confederacy. Adams renewed his efforts and handed in such overwhelming evidence that an order was given to detain her. But the British acted so tardily that the *Alabama* got to sea before the order reached Liverpool.

Long ABRAHAM LINCOLN a Little Longer.

57 From a cartoon *Long Abraham Lincoln a Little Longer* in *Harper's Weekly,* Nov. 26, 1864

THE TRUE ISSUE OR "THAT'S WHAT'S THE MATTER".

56   From a campaign cartoon, 1864, published by Currier & Ives, New York

A DEMOCRATIC RETORT

THE Democrats minimized their previous utterances for peace and stressed McClellan's declaration for preserving the Union. Their conduct in this respect shows that they found Union sentiment too strong to be ignored in the canvas.

LINCOLN IS REËLECTED BY A STRONG MAJORITY

THERE were some bitter quarrels within the Union party. In the summer a determined effort was made to force Lincoln to withdraw as a candidate. For a time a third ticket was headed by Fremont. A strong rally of the friends of Lincoln was helped on at a critical moment by Sherman's success in Georgia; also by Lincoln's firmness in refusing to give up conscription to win doubtful votes. The election resulted in giving two hundred and twelve electoral votes for Lincoln against twenty-one for McClellan.

58   From a Brady photograph of Lincoln taken in 1864, in the United States Signal Corps, War Department, Washington

LINCOLN'S SECOND INAUGURAL

LINCOLN explained his second election by saying that the country did not think it wise to swap horses while crossing a river. He had shown his astonishing freedom from personal enmity by appointing Chase as Chief Justice and it was Chase who administered the oath of office at Lincoln's second inauguration. His second inaugural address is one of his most effective utterances. It closed with the following beautiful words: "With malice toward none, with charity for all, with firmness in the right, as God gives us to see the right, let us strive on to finish the work we are in; to bind up the nation's wounds; to care for him who shall have borne the battle, and for his widow, and his orphan — to do all which may achieve and cherish a just and lasting peace among ourselves and with all nations."

59   From a cartoon in *Harper's Weekly*, April 25, 1863

60 From an illustration, *The Approach of the British Pirate Alabama*, by Winslow Homer in *Harper's Weekly*

THE *ALABAMA* AS A COMMERCE DESTROYER

UNDER the command of the Confederate Admiral Semmes the *Alabama* had a brief but destructive career. She appeared suddenly in remote parts of the sea, destroying many United States merchantmen, taking off the crews and passengers, but sinking ships and cargoes (see Vol. VII for chart of her career). Finally, Semmes offered battle to the ship *Kearsage* off Cherbourg and was defeated. Other "rams" being built by the Lairds were detained by the British Government. The United States filed claims for the damage done by the *Florida*, *Alabama* and other similar ships, contending that it was a violation of neutrality to permit such vessels to go forth from British harbors. The fact that orders were given to hold the *Alabama* and that the dreaded "rams" were actually held seemed to support the American position. These claims for damages were laid before the British Government and payment demanded.

THE FRENCH GOVERN MEXICO, 1861–67

WHILE the North had its hands full in suppressing secession, Napoleon III of France established authority in Mexico, making Maximilian Emperor and supporting him with a French army. The Confederacy hoped to secure a virtual ally in Maximilian. By the time he reached Mexico, Napoleon had decided to make an end of his anti-Northern policy and Maximilian refused to receive a minister and envoy from Richmond.

61   Maximilian's reception in Mexico, from *Frank Leslie's Illustrated Newspaper*, Sept. 3, 1864

THE PEACE MOVEMENT

A CONSIDERABLE group of people in the. North steadily maintained that the war could be ended by negotiation. Though ridiculed by the more aggressive northerners the peace advocates continued to insist that if Lincoln would only extend a friendly hand the South would accept it. Lincoln consented to make a test. A conference was arranged between him and Confederate commissioners at Hampton Roads, Virginia, February 3, 1865. He offered to end the war if the South would accept emancipation and recognize the authority of the Union. The southerners would accept nothing that did not concede southern independence, and so the conference ended in failure.

THE COPPERHEAD PLAN FOR SUBJUGATING THE SOUTH.

War and Argument—Cold Steel and Cool Reason—having failed to restore the Union, it is supposed that the South may be *bored* into coming back.
Our Picture represents the successful operation of this exceedingly humane and ingenious device.

62 From a cartoon, *The Copperhead Plan for Subjugating the South,* in *Harper's Weekly,* Oct. 22, 1864

THE CONFEDERATE CAPITAL EVACUATED

On April 3, the Confederates evacuated Richmond, pressed by Grant's irresistible blows on Lee's weakened army. On April 4, Lincoln entered the city, much of which was a smoking ruin. He was at the culmination of his career. The task he set for himself four years and one month earlier, in his first inaugural address, was accomplished. Disunion was forever put beyond the range of the possible, and, incidentally, slavery had been banished from the nation. For this achievement thanks were due to the army of the North and the support the northern portion of the Union gave to the war. Nor should we forget the devotion and courage of the South. Its people had put the utmost of their faith and devotion into the war for the Confederacy.

63 The Confederate capitol, Richmond, from a photograph

64 Lincoln entering Richmond, from a drawing by Thomas Nast in *Harper's Weekly,* Feb. 24, 1866

65 Jefferson Davis signing Confederate documents by the roadside, from a drawing published in *The Illustrated London News*, Dec. 14, 1885, immediately after his death

THE CONFEDERACY COLLAPSES

IF Jefferson Davis had yielded at the Hampton Roads Conference, February 3, 1865, the South would not have been entirely ruined. Lincoln was willing to accord payment for the slaves, though it is doubtful if Congress would have agreed. But it was not in Davis to submit. The exhaustion of his government was, however, near at hand. As Lee gave up Richmond, Davis fled to the westward and southward, taking his Cabinet along and sending out orders from the roadside. In Georgia he was taken prisoner by Lincoln's soldiers and placed in confinement. His capture ended the civil arm of the Confederate States. To the people of the North in the days of the war Jefferson Davis symbolized the rebellion against which they were fighting. His fate at the hands of posterity has not been the same. Lee, rather than the President of the Confederacy, has come to typify the Lost Cause.

BACK TO PEACE

WHEN the Confederate armies surrendered, their soldiers accepted paroles and swore allegiance to the Union, then turned their steps homeward to take up the labor of rebuilding southern society. The whole economic and financial system was reduced to chaos. No form of safe investment remained. The values of shares of stock, notes in hand and railroad bonds, all fell to nothing, or next to nothing, in this day of calamity. So great was the confusion that valuable land sold for a song. The war plunged the South into abject poverty.

66   Confederate soldiers taking the oath of allegiance, from *Harper's Weekly*, June 17, 1865

67 Lincoln in 1865, from a photograph in the United States Signal Corps, War Department, Washington

LINCOLN'S HUMANITY

SECRETARY STANTON criticized Lincoln's habit of freely pardoning soldiers condemned by court-martial. Among the objects of his clemency often were southern prisoners. One of his last official acts was such a pardon, issued at the request of a woman, by which he liberated a prisoner on condition that the recipient of the pardon should take the oath of allegiance. Many of the convictions were for desertion. Lincoln in refusing to apply the full penalty of military law showed sound judgment as well as humanity. The Federal armies were made up largely of volunteer troops. The regulars among them were so few as to be negligible. The method of recruiting was customarily the organizing and raising of new regiments instead of sending new men as replacements to old regiments that had been depleted in battle. Such a system interfered with discipline and extensive desertion was one of the results. The military measures of the Government were probably as much at fault as the deserters themselves. Under such circumstances numerous executions would have been both unjust and bad policy, and Lincoln's good sense recognized the fact.

68   Booth fleeing after he shot Lincoln, from *Harper's Weekly*, April 29, 1865

ASSASSINATION AND DEATH OF LINCOLN

On April 14, 1865, Lincoln was speaking to his Cabinet about the situation before them. "I hope," he said, "there will be no persecution, no bloody work after the war is over. No one need expect me to take any part in hanging or killing those men, even the worst of them. . . . We must extinguish our resentments if we expect harmony and union." That night while he sat in his box at Ford's Theatre, John Wilkes Booth, an actor who was a demented southern sympathizer, shot him through the head. Lincoln died at 7:22 A.M. April 15, 1865. His heroic life was a sacrifice to the political fury which is so often generated by war.

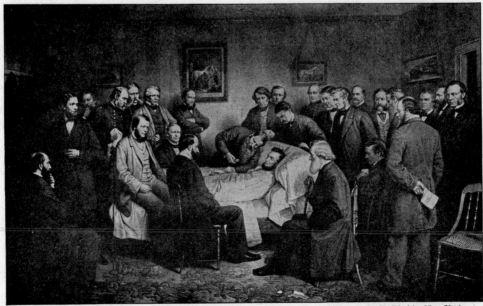

69   After the painting *The Death of Lincoln* by Alexander H. Ritchie (1822–95), owned by G. W. H. Ritchie, New York

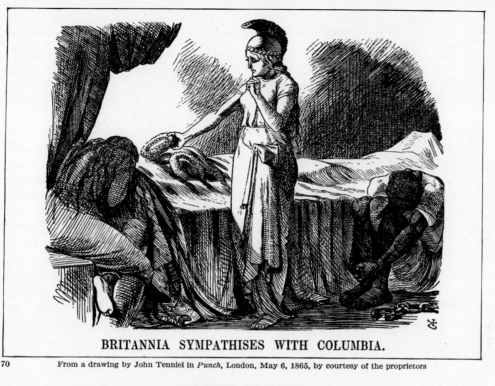

BRITANNIA SYMPATHISES WITH COLUMBIA.

70   From a drawing by John Tenniel in *Punch*, London, May 6, 1865, by courtesy of the proprietors

BRITISH FEELING

THROUGHOUT the war *Punch*, representing the point of view of the English upper classes, had been distinguished for its sneers at Lincoln. Now that his great task was done, *Punch* was struck with contrition. The editors had a meeting and declared a change in their policy. On May 6, 1865, this attitude was announced in a beautiful picture by John Tenniel and in a poem by Tom Taylor of which the following is a part:

You lay a wreath on murdered LINCOLN's bier,
  You, who with mocking pencil wont to trace,
Broad for the self-complacent British sneer,
  His length of shambling limb, his furrowed face,

His gaunt, gnarled hands, his unkempt, bristling hair,
  His garb uncouth, his bearing ill at ease,
His lack of all we prize as debonair,
  Of power or will to shine, of art to please.

You, whose smart pen backed up the pencil's laugh,
  Judging each step, as though the way were plain:
Reckless, so it could point its paragraph,
  Of chief's perplexity, or people's pain.

Beside this corpse, that bears for winding-sheet
  The Stars and Stripes he lived to rear anew,
Between the mourners at his head and feet,
  Say, scurril-jester, is there room for *you?*

Yes, he had lived to shame me from my sneer,
  To lame my pencil, and confute my pen —
To make me own this hind of princes peer,
  This rail-splitter a true-born king of men.

My shallow judgment I had learnt to rue,
  Noting how to occasion's height he rose,
How his quaint wit made home-truth seem more true,
  How, iron-like, his temper grew by blows.

How humble yet how hopeful he could be:
  How in good fortune and in ill the same:
Nor bitter in success, nor boastful he,
  Thirsty for gold, nor feverish for fame.

He went about his work — such work as few
  Ever had laid on head and heart and hand —
As one who knows, where there's a task to do,
  Man's honest will must Heaven's good grace command.

Who trusts the strength will with the burden grow,
  That God makes instruments to work his will,
If but that will we can arrive to know,
  Nor tamper with the weights of good and ill.

So he went forth to battle, on the side
  That he felt clear was Liberty's and Right's,
As in his peasant boyhood he had plied
  His warfare with rude Nature's thwarting mights—

 .   .   .   .

So he grew up, a destined work to do,
  And lived to do it: four long-suffering years'
Ill-fate, ill-feeling, ill-report, lived through,
  And then he heard the hisses change to cheers,

The taunts to tribute, the abuse to praise,
  And took both with the same unwavering mood:
Till, as he came on light, from darkling days,
  And seemed to touch the goal from where he stood,

A felon hand, between the goal and him,
  Reached from behind his back, a trigger prest, —
And those perplexed and patient eyes were dim,
  Those gaunt, long-labouring limbs were laid to rest!

 .   .   .   .

The Old World and the New, from sea to sea,
  Utter one voice of sympathy and shame!
Sore heart, so stopped when it at last beat high,
  Sad life, cut short just as its triumph came.

IX—4

CHAPTER II

RECONSTRUCTING THE UNION

RECONSTRUCTION was the last phase of the struggle to abolish slavery. It was worked out in the midst of a controversy at the heart of which was the prevalent northern belief that if the troops were withdrawn from the South the negroes would be forced back into some form of partial slavery and a large part of the fruits of the horrible war would be lost. Lincoln and his successor, Johnson, were willing to trust the South to accept emancipation fairly. They believed the southern whites would not deny to the black men the opportunity to advance under the new conditions as fast as they proved able to use them. They wished to bring the southern states back into the Union with the least friction possible. A majority in Congress thought this too lenient a position. They wished to impose severe conditions before permitting the states that had fought against the Union to resume all the functions they had enjoyed before the war.

The Constitution did not indicate how a seceded state could be restored to its place in the Union. Lincoln thought that the matter lay in his hands because, as commander in chief of the army and navy, he could withdraw the troops occupying a southern state whenever he saw fit. He announced that he would do this as soon as the southern states had accepted their defeat and had set up state governments loyal to the Union. He was not supported by a majority in Congress. His opponents, known at the time as the Radicals, wished to exclude from the suffrage a large part of the southern whites until the work of restoration was completed. Some of them desired to confiscate a large portion of the property of the former slaveholders, and thus, as they said, "make treason odious." Between these two views no compromise was possible.

It was unfortunate that the controversy was joined when most of the people, North and South, were filled with anger and suspicion still inflamed by the bitterness and the fury of a time of war. These feelings, however, were natural. War always engenders bitterness and much time is needed for it to die out. In 1865 the slavery controversy had been acute for more than thirty years. No citizen who was under fifteen when the war began had ever known the older days when the people of either section did not in the main regard the other with suspicion. Thus it happened that few Americans were in a frame of mind to treat restoration in a calm spirit.

The Civil War ended in April, 1865, and Congress did not meet in regular session until the following December. The President therefore had seven and one half months in which he could, unless he called an extra session, do what he chose about reconstruction. His efforts during this interval are spoken of as Presidential Reconstruction. When at last Congress assembled, the Radicals were in complete control of each house; they ignored the work of the President and set out to get bills passed which would, as they put it, save the fruits of the war. Their program is called Congressional Reconstruction. Congress proved to be stronger than the Executive. Its program was enacted into law. The result included two amendments to the Federal Constitution, the Fourteenth and the Fifteenth, and a series of acts destined to overthrow the temporary governments created under Presidential authority. This done, the former Confederate states one after another were given all their former rights and by 1877 reconstruction was accomplished.

THE FIRST MOVEMENT
OF THE NEW ERA

THE first general impression immediately after the close of hostilities was that the spirit of Lincoln would prevail and there would be, to use his own words, "A union of heart and hands as well as of States."

JOHNSON LACKS COMMON–SCHOOL
EDUCATION

LINCOLN's death had brought a strange figure to the Presidency. Among the many self-made men who have risen to eminence in the United States, few were more humbly born than Andrew Johnson. He had no formal education. Starting as a tailor, his force and courage raised him to the United States Senate. As a Unionist he became the man of the hour in the turbulent politics of war-ridden Tennessee. Finally Lincoln had appointed him Governor of the conquered state. He was a good Governor, but his work in Nashville gave him little training for the difficult post of President. The political problems of Tennessee in time of war were vastly different from those of the national capital just after war had come to an end. Johnson had been engrossed with local

THE RE-UNITED STATES.

COLONEL NORTH (TO COLONEL SOUTH) "WAL, BROTHER, GUESS WE COULDN'T BOTH WIN. SO LET'S SHAKE HANDS, AND JUST LIQUOR UP"

71   From a cartoon in *Punch*, London, Oct. 7, 1865

affairs. As a result he had no wide acquaintance with national figures and very little perspective in his outlook upon national questions. Scarcely a month after he was inducted into office responsibilities devolved upon him for which he was quite unprepared. The incident made clear an important weakness in the organization of the Government of the United States. Johnson was the unfortunate victim of a system. Though he cannot avoid responsibility for his acts, this fact should always be remembered.

72   Andrew Johnson's tailor shop, Greenville, Tenn., from a photograph in the possession of the United
States Department of Roads, Washington

73   Andrew Johnson, 1808–75, from a photograph by Brady

JOHNSON'S COURSE ON RECONSTRUCTION

JOHNSON kept Lincoln's Cabinet and on its advice tried to carry out Lincoln's plan of reconstruction. He proceeded to set up civil governments in the southern states, and these governments elected assemblies which adopted the Thirteenth Amendment, abolishing slavery, and made other laws to meet the industrial crisis due to the final disappearance of slavery. Because the President was a southerner the significance of whatever he did in favor of mild treatment of the South was distorted by the Radicals.

LINCOLN'S PLAN OF RECONSTRUCTION

THE difficulties which Johnson had to meet date back to December 8, 1863, when Lincoln issued a "Proclamation of Amnesty and Reconstruction." All but a few of the higher officers of the Confederacy were to be pardoned upon taking an oath of loyalty to the Union. When enough men had complied in any state to equal one tenth of its vote in 1860 he would order elections to be held, and when state officials thus chosen should be installed he would withdraw the military government. This plan, which made restoration easy, was applied in Louisiana with success. It was begun also in Arkansas and Tennessee. But before Lincoln's death Congress had intervened. It refused under the leadership of Thaddeus Stevens to seat the Senators and Republicans who came to it from the reconstructed states. This fact would have warned a man of political insight that care must be taken to avoid a split between the executive and legislative branches of the government. Lincoln seems to have sensed the dangers ahead. Johnson failed to do so. He also failed to note that a reaction against the excessive powers which the President had held in war time was inevitable.

74   Inauguration of Hon. Michael Hahn as Governor of Louisiana, March 4, 1864, from an illustration
by C. E. H. Bonwill, in *Frank Leslie's Illustrated Newspaper*, April 2, 1864

THE WADE–DAVIS BILL

THE opposition of the Radicals in Congress began before Johnson became President. They were determined not to let Lincoln take reconstruction out of their control. They gave notice of their chagrin by passing the Wade-Davis Bill, disfranchising for the time all who had borne voluntary allegiance to the Confederacy. Lincoln gave this bill a "pocket veto." His amnesty was well received by the country; for at that time reconciliation was popular. If Lincoln had lived he might have kept this spirit alive and carried out the main features of his plan. When Johnson succeeded him a great task fell into less skillful hands.

THE NEGRO'S STATUS IN A STATE OF FREEDOM

THE passing of slavery left the negro in a singular condition. He was a free man, but not a citizen; for citizenship had been looked on as an affair of the state. Whether or not a man was recognized as a citizen depended on the state in which he lived. It was for the state to define his rights. When the northern friends of the negro thought of these things they realized that the fate of the negro might still be very far short of absolute freedom, for by

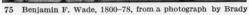

75 Benjamin F. Wade, 1800–78, from a photograph by Brady

state law he could be denied rights of travel, ownership of property, and many other essentials of liberty. To Lincoln, however, such suggestions had not seemed weighty. He trusted the southerners to carry out emancipation in good faith. He did not expect them to give the freedmen the vote, but he thought they should be given limited suffrage when they proved capable of using it intelligently. Lincoln's attitude toward the white southerners was one of unusual magnanimity and trust. But the passions which the long war had aroused made difficult its general acceptance. Had he lived, Lincoln must have encountered great obstacles in bringing about a reconstruction policy based on faith in the men who had so recently fought in the Confederate ranks.

CUTTING HIS OLD ASSOCIATES.
MAN OF COLOR: "Ugh! Get out. I ain't one ob you no more. *I'se a Man, I is!*"

From a cartoon by Frank Bellew in *Harper's Weekly*, Jan. 17, 1863

77 Vagrant negroes in New Orleans being taken up by the provost guard, from an illustration by F. H. Schell, in
Frank Leslie's Illustrated Newspaper, May 21, 1864

THE "NEW BLACK CODE"

BEFORE the war the black population of the South was restricted in all its movements by rigid laws. It was a firm conviction in the South that if negroes were free and came, went and lived as they chose, they would be a menace to the white people. After the war the restrictive codes were revised to meet the new conditions. But still the negro was expected to live under close restraint. In some states the restraint was severe. One law declared that any man without visible means of existence might be fined for vagrancy and if the fine was not paid his service would be sold to the highest bidder. This act was taken in the North as a subterfuge for the reëstablishment of slavery; and it brought much odium on Presidential Reconstruction under Johnson.

THE FREE NEGRO

THE NORTH took emancipation and enfranchisement lightly. Few negroes lived within its borders, and it did not have to face the problem of sharing responsibilities, political and social, with this great mass of ignorant people. Illiteracy was only one of the negro's deficiencies. His moral standards were low, and neither his African past nor his two centuries in America had prepared him for the duties of citizenship in a modern civilized community. Of the two problems which had previously faced the country, one, slavery, was solved; the other, the negro problem, was impending.

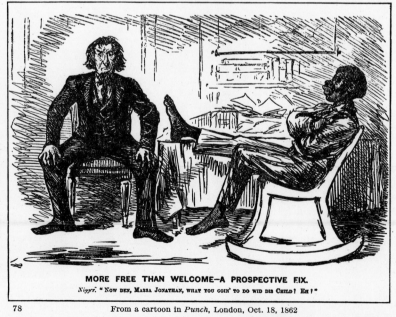

MORE FREE THAN WELCOME—A PROSPECTIVE FIX.
Nigger. "Now den, Massa Jonathan, what you goin' to do wid dis Child! Eh !"

78 From a cartoon in *Punch*, London, Oct. 18, 1862

79   From the painting *The Lost Cause* by Henry Mosler (1841–1920), courtesy of Dr. Shaler Berry, Newport, Ky.

THE SMITTEN SOUTH FACES THE TASK OF UPBUILDING

THE fall of the Confederacy had left the South in general bankruptcy. The slaves were freed, which meant a loss to their former owners of three billions of dollars. Land values were temporarily destroyed. Confederate bonds and money were now worthless paper; almost as valueless were most of the notes and mortgages which had previously rested on undoubted credit. Everywhere the task of upbuilding had to be begun at the bottom. In many places battles and the maneuvering of armies had caused widespread destruction. For four years the railroads had had very few repairs, many miles of track had been torn up and the rolling stock was practically worn out. Bridges were broken down. Factories had been destroyed. The southern people, dispirited by this calamity, were not prepared to look with tolerance upon the policy of the Radicals. They were faithful to the oath of allegiance, but they were not submissive to harsh terms of reconstruction. Their attitude in this respect only made the Radicals more determined.

DISTRIBUTING RATIONS

THE exhaustion of the South is shown by the necessity for the distribution of rations by the Union army. Whites as well as blacks were the recipients, and the process was still going on in some parts of the South a year after the surrender at Appomattox.

80   From an illustration by A. R. Waud, in *Harper's Weekly*, Aug. 11, 1866

81   Thaddeus Stevens, from a photograph by Brady

THADDEUS STEVENS, 1792–1868

STEVENS of Pennsylvania was the leader of the House of Representatives and the most influential man among the Radicals. He felt no sympathy for the southern whites and wished to confiscate a part of their property in order to distribute it among the freedmen. A strong party man, he accepted negro suffrage in the belief that it would build up the power of the Republicans in the South. The relentless hostility of Stevens and his immediate supporters had resulted in their being dubbed the Vindictives. It was their bitter spirit that carried through Congress the stern policy by which the South was at last reconstructed.

CHARLES SUMNER, 1811–74

CHARLES SUMNER of Massachusetts was so bent on doing something for the negro that he seemed to forget to do anything for the good of the white man. He was passionately in earnest and took the right side of most questions. On the relation of the government to the freedmen he acted from the standpoint of theory alone. He thought that the backwardness of the race was due to slavery and that if the negro were given freedom it would be remedied.

82   From a cartoon on Sumner. *I'm not to blame for being white, Sir,* in the possession of the Massachusetts Historical Society, Boston

SUMNER'S DREAM

SUMNER held a theory that was characteristic of America in the middle of the nineteenth century. He believed that the mere possession of the right of citizenship would teach any one how to use it wisely. Many northerners rejected this view, thinking it would be foolish to place the ballot in the hands of the negro in his existing state of progress; but Sumner would not take their advice. He was the most conspicuous and constant member of the Senate who advocated the extension of suffrage to the negro race.

83   Charles Sumner, from a photograph by J. W. Black & Co., Boston, in the collection of the Bostonian Society

THE CIVIL RIGHTS ACT SUPPLEMENTS THE THIRTEENTH AMENDMENT

THE northern Radicals led by Stevens and Sumner determined to reinforce the Thirteenth Amendment. They believed that the freedmen might suffer oppression in the state courts of the South. The Freedmen's Bureau Bill of 1866 gave the Bureau authority over cases in which one party was a freedman. Johnson vetoed it, believing that it created an

84   From an illustration *The Lobby of the House of Representatives*, Washington, during the passage of the Civil Rights Bill, in *Harper's Weekly*, April 28, 1866

unconstitutional tribunal in opposition to state courts. His opponents could not carry the bill over his veto. In the same year they also passed a bill to define the civil rights of citizens. Johnson vetoed this bill also; he held that it took from the states a function long possessed by them. The Radicals cried out that Johnson was bent on leaving the freedmen at the mercy of the southern legislatures and won enough support in Congress to carry the bill over his veto. From this time forward Johnson was not able to prevent his opponents from carrying measures over his veto. He did not show resentment and although he thought the reconstruction policy of the majority wrong and unconstitutional, once it was adopted he carried it out faithfully.

> ### Article XIV.
>
> Section 1. All persons born or naturalized in the United States, and subject to the jurisdiction thereof, are citizens of the United States and of the State wherein they reside. No State shall make or enforce any law which shall abridge the privileges or immunities of citizens of the United States; nor shall any State deprive any person of life, liberty, or property, without due process of law; nor deny to any person within its jurisdiction the equal protection of the laws.

85   From the original engrossed text of the Fourteenth Amendment, in the Department of State, Washington

THE FOURTEENTH AMENDMENT

THE next step of the Radicals was to introduce an amendment to the Constitution dealing with negro suffrage. The ballot was not granted outright, but if any state denied it to any part of its male adult population its representation in Congress was to be diminished in the same ratio. This was done because, with emancipation accomplished, southern states would gain in representation equal to two fifths of their freedmen. Sumner thought that the measure did not go far enough. He insisted on incorporating in it the substance of the Civil Rights Act. The Fourteenth Amendment fixed Federal citizenship and guaranteed the personal and property rights of the Federal citizens. It put a penalty on a state that withheld the ballot from the negro. It also pledged the payment of the Union, and forbade payment of the Confederate debts. When Congress passed the Amendment, a majority were willing to go no further if the South accepted it. To accept the Fourteenth Amendment seemed to the southerners an act of humiliation. One after another the states with reconstructed governments rejected it. Ratification of the Amendment was thus postponed until those governments were overthrown as the result of drastic Congressional action in 1867. Eventually southern governments helped create the three fourths majority of the states necessary for ratification of an amendment.

86   A race conflict at Charleston, S. C., June 24, 1866, from an illustration by A. R. Waud,
in *Harper's Weekly*, August 4, 1866

ACTS OF VIOLENCE

UNDER existing circumstances it was natural that acts of violence should occur in the South. The blacks, exuberant over their freedom, would express themselves in offensive ways; white men would undertake to make them desist; casual encounters would grow into riots and often lives would be lost before the police restored order. The Charleston affair of June 24, 1866, began on the fashionable Battery when some white men tried to quiet a group of boisterous negroes. Accounts of affairs were carefully gathered by the Radical press and published with some exaggeration for the effect on northern public opinion.

87   A secret meeting of Southern Unionists, from an illustration by A. R. Waud, in *Harper's Weekly*, Aug. 4, 1866

SOUTHERN UNIONISTS MEET

SOUTHERN Republicans often found it safer to organize their local committees in secret. Like most men in that region they went armed, as did the white conservatives. Frequently a party caucus would be broken up when passers-by fired into it through the thin walls of a house. These affairs were described in the northern papers as more "southern outrages." Deplorable as they were they were generally exaggerated.

88   Struggle for the flag during the attack on freedmen marching to Mechanics Institute, New Orleans, July 30, 1865, from an illustration by Theodore R. Davis, in *Harper's Weekly*, Aug. 25, 1866

RESENTMENT OF THE WHITES

THE southern whites saw with bitter anger the advance of the freedmen toward political power, and resented deeply the course of those whites who were inducing them to assert themselves. In one way or another they interfered to check the negro advance. The intensity of feeling, inescapable at the moment, often produced tragic results. In the race riots thus produced the whites were usually victorious.

89   Interior of Mechanics Institute, New Orleans, during the riot of July 30, 1866, from an illustration by Theodore R. Davis, in *Harper's Weekly*, Aug. 25, 1866

RACE RIOTS

OCCASIONALLY there were outbreaks in which the loss of life was considerable. Such an affair was the riot in New Orleans, July 30, 1866, in which thirty-seven negroes and three white friends were slain with the loss of only one of their opponents. Previously, a large negro procession on its way to a political meeting at Mechanics Institute had been attacked by white men without serious results. Later, while the negroes were in the hall, the police, on some unknown provocation, opened an attack and shot them down without restraint. In Memphis, Tennessee, on May 1, 2, and 3 of the same year, a riot occurred in which one white man and twenty-four negroes were killed. In most of these affairs the blacks suffered in overwhelming proportion to their opponents. Vicksburg was also the scene of rioting. People in the North gained the impression that the southerner was wreaking vengeance upon the freedman.

90 Johnson making his fatal Washington Birthday speech, Feb. 22, 1866, from *Harper's Weekly*, March 10, 1866

BITTER ATTACKS ON JOHNSON

PRESIDENT JOHNSON was a man of honorable principles but he had acquired in early life rough-and-tumble habits that were not appropriate to the office of Chief Executive. In his speeches he was sometimes coarsely abusive of his enemies. One, made at the White House, February 22, 1866, was widely resented; he was accused of being under the influence of liquor; and the same charge was made later when he delivered a series of speeches in "a swing around the circle" in the West. His enemies seized quickly upon his weaknesses. They painted him as habitually drunk, ignorant and of violent passions. A large majority of the people of the North accepted this view, and Johnson had no way of enlightening them. His personal unpopularity was an asset to his opponents. They built up a solid sentiment against him in Congress and carried their measures over his veto by a two-thirds majority.

JOHNSON APPEALS TO MODERATE MEN

JOHNSON hoped to unite moderate men North and South in a new party with liberal views. In keeping with that idea, the Philadelphia Convention of August 14, 1866, was attended by Republicans and Democrats from the North and men of known moderation from the South. The Radicals pronounced the event a blind to deceive the North and pictured it as dominated by the former Confederates. The Convention did not accomplish the results aimed at. The tide for coercion of the South was running too strong for such a result. Many men had hoped that some such movement would lead to a political party in which the best people of the North and the South would act together. It was never to be accomplished.

OTHELLO. DOST THOU MOCK ME?
IAGO.   I MOCK YOU! NO, BY HEAVEN:
WOULD YOU WOULD BEAR YOUR FORTUNES LIKE A MAN.
                                            SHAKSPEARE.

91   From a cartoon by Thomas Nast in *Harper's Weekly*, Sept. 1, 1866

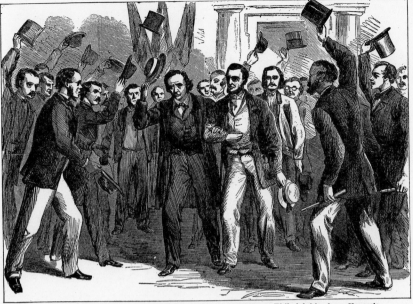

92   "Parson" Brownlow at the Southern Loyalists Convention at Philadelphia, from *Harper's*
Weekly, Sept. 22, 1866

LOYAL SOUTHERNERS

Much sympathy was shown in the North for the white Republicans of the South and they were referred to as "southern loyalists," or "the truly loyal." As an offset to the conventions called by Johnson's friends, a convention of these southerners met in Philadelphia, September 3, 1866. A large majority of those who attended were officeholders, and practically all were representatives of the unfortunate poorer class in southern society. Reverend W. G. Brownlow, of Tennessee, was a striking example of this class. The affair made a sorry impression on the country.

THE SOLDIERS AND SAILORS HOLD CONVENTIONS

Johnson's supporters called a convention of soldiers and sailors at Cleveland, September 17, 1866. It was enthusiastically attended and had the support of so notable a leader of the former Abolitionists as Henry Ward Beecher. Nevertheless, it had little influence on northern opinion. The Radicals also called a "Soldiers' and Sailors' Convention" at Pittsburgh, September 26, 1866. The conventions helped to make clear that the tide was setting against the President. Vigorous measures on his part became necessary.

93   The Convention at Pittsburgh, from an illustration by John Donaghy, in *Frank Leslie's*
Illustrated Newspaper, Oct. 20, 1866

94   From *Harper's Weekly*, Oct. 27, 1866   95   From *Harper's Weekly*, Oct. 27, 1866

JOHNSON "SWINGS AROUND THE CIRCLE"

In the autumn of 1866 President Johnson made a speaking tour of some of the leading northern and western cities, trying to rally public opinion against the program of the Radicals. He was not a good speaker without preparation. His violent denunciation of opponents and his rather boastful defense of his own conduct brought down on him merciless ridicule from the Republican papers. They insisted that often while speaking he was intoxicated, and the net result of the tour was unfortunate. It exhibited this crude son of the mountains in his most unfavorable phase. Perhaps its most unfortunate aspect was the fact that some of the incidents of this much advertised journey impaired the dignity of the high office of President. The episode prepared the way for that assault upon the prerogatives of the President which was later made in the Tenure of Office Act. In this experience Johnson learned a lesson: he did not appear again in so unseemly a condition, but the damage to his reputation had been done irreparably.

96.   From *Harper's Weekly*, Oct. 27, 1866

97   Union commanders assigned to southern states, from *Harper's Weekly*, April 6, 1867
LEFT TO RIGHT: Maj.-Gen. Daniel E. Sickles, Maj.-Gen. John Pope, Maj.-Gen. George H. Thomas, Gen. Ulysses S. Grant, Brevet Maj.-Gen. John M. Schofield, Maj.-Gen. Philip H. Sheridan, Brevet Maj.-Gen. E. O. C. Ord.

MILITARY GOVERNMENT IN THE SOUTH

THE reply of the Radicals was expressed in three acts passed respectively March 2, March 23, and July 19, 1867. By these acts Johnson's reconstructed state governments in the South were swept aside and military governments were reëstablished in all the southern states except Tennessee under the control of Union generals. The new authorities were directed to set up civil government in the southern states elected by all the male citizens, regardless of race, except unpardoned Confederates. When such governments should be accepted by the people and the Fourteenth Amendment had been adopted, the states would be re-admitted fully to the Union. In taking the franchise each voter was required to swear that he had not served the Confederacy voluntarily. At first it was held that the officials must accept this statement, but the act of July 19 permitted them to decide whether or not they should do so. The meaning of this procedure was that since the South would not accept the Fourteenth Amendment she was forced to see armed men take charge of her polls, and permit the negro to vote for state conventions called to determine whether or not he should vote. That is, he voted on the question of his own enfranchisement. It was this supreme humiliation that united the vast majority of the whites into a "Solid South" and led them to believe that any measure would justify them in trying to undo the wrong they had received.

CONGRESSIONAL RECONSTRUCTION IN OPERATION

WHILE this new scheme of reconstruction was being got under way, the South was divided into five military districts, each ruled by a Union general. The five military Governors acted promptly, and in the autumn of 1867 the southern states were busy holding elections. In view of the circumstances under which they were held these elections were travesties on popular government. Then came constitutional conventions and the elections of Governors and assemblies. In the latter were a large number of colored members, the result of enfranchisement. A great many of the whites were not yet pardoned for resisting the Union and took no part in these elections. In 1868, seven states thus returned to normal relations with the Union, and in 1870 three more came back. The remaining one, Tennessee, had accepted the Fourteenth Amendment and returned in 1866.

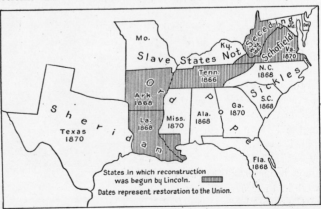

98   Administrative divisions of the South under military governors, drawn from data in N. W. Stephenson, *An American History*, New York, 1919

THE RECONSTRUCTION DOSE.

NAUGHTY ANDY—"*Don't take that physic, Sis, it's nasty—kick his shins.*"
MRS. COLUMBIA—"*My dear Andy, don't be a bad boy, don't interfere—Dr. Congress knows what's best for Sissy.*"

99   From a cartoon in *Frank Leslie's Illustrated Newspaper,*
July 13, 1867

THE SOUTH AND ITS MEDICINE

CONGRESSIONAL Reconstruction was a bitter dose for the South, which made no pretext of taking it voluntarily. The North took the view that the medicine would do as much good taken unwillingly as taken willingly. The sense of wrong that remained in the South has been a long time subsiding.

NEGRO REGISTRATION IS UNDER MILITARY CONTROL

WHERE the Radicals were in control in a southern state, the freedmen came in large numbers to register as qualified voters. Army officers and other officials under the military governments of 1867 and 1868 were ordered to read to the illiterate negroes explanations of their new privileges. The whites resented these efforts to bring out the negro votes, which they looked upon as open participation of the government officials in behalf of the Republican party.

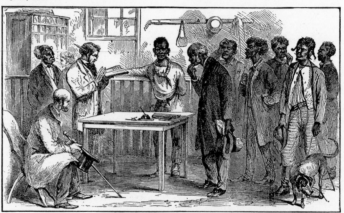

100   Scene in a Registration Office, Macon, Ga., from *Frank Leslie's
Illustrated Newspaper,* Nov. 30, 1867

AT THE POLLS, 1867

THE freedmen flocked to the polls. They rarely understood the meaning of party platforms and accepted any Republican candidate as a friend. As a result, many unfit persons were placed in office. In this class were a large number of northern whites who used the opportunity to have political careers in the South. Such men were called "carpet-baggers," because it was said that all the possessions they brought South with them were in their carpet-bags. Some of the carpet-baggers amassed fortunes out of their offices.

101   Freedmen voting in New Orleans, from *Frank Leslie's Illustrated Newspaper,* Nov. 30, 1867

102   A jury of whites and blacks, from an illustration in *Frank Leslie's Illustrated Newspaper*, Nov. 30, 1867

NEGROES AS JURORS

THE Radicals insisted that the negro should have all the civil rights of white men. Sumner in his theoretical way believed that the exercise of these rights would teach the freedman how to use them. He did not reflect that the process of learning would cover many years. One demand was that negroes should be admitted to the jury without discrimination of race. It was insisted that they had such a right by the Fourteenth Amendment. But in 1880 the United States Supreme Court held that if a state in its law denied negroes admission to a jury the law was unconstitutional; however, if an official, acting in his discretion, failed to put a negro name on the jury list the act was not unconstitutional, since the act of discrimination was not committed by a state. By taking advantage of this decision it was posssible to prevent negroes from serving as jurors.

KEEPING THE NEGROES FROM VOTING

THE whites used various means to keep the negroes from voting. One method was to order them to work on election day and to discharge those who did not obey. Such action created a great deal of resentment among the negroes who usually voted the Republican ticket, and sometimes they retaliated by burning barns, fodder stocks, and other property. The whites felt justified in what they did, and they frequently replied to the violence of their former slaves with whippings or other acts of physical punishment. A racial point of view, the result of generations of slavery, could not be changed overnight. The southern whites had, also, the argument that the negroes were incompetent, that they voted for dishonest white men and that they had been given the vote by unconstitutional means.

103   Freedmen discharged for voting the Radical Ticket, from *Frank Leslie's Illustrated Newspaper*, Nov. 30, 1867

104 Registration in the South, from an illustration by Alfred W. Thompson (1840–96),
in *Harper's Weekly*, Sept. 28, 1867

THE "SCALAWAGS"

THE southern whites were of two classes. Besides the old ruling class there were a number of poor men, owning little or no land and few if any slaves, who had not become accustomed to a part in the government. When the Congressional plan was put into operation ambitious men of this second class began to join the Republican party and to run for office. In the regions near the Appalachian mountains these men were numerous enough to make a majority. The leaders of this movement were denounced by the old group of politicians. Many of them were ignorant and some were dishonest. They were nicknamed "scalawags."

105 Electioneering in the South, from an illustration by W. L. Sheppard (1833–1912),
in *Harper's Weekly*, July 25, 1868

THE NEGRO AS A POLITICIAN

AMONG the negroes were a few individuals who developed capacity as political leaders of their race. They proved striking figures in the political life of the South at that time. But they fell easy prey to the more capable white politicians. In many of the southern legislatures the negro members were induced for trifling bribes to support schemes of fraud designed for the benefit of the white carpet-baggers and scalawags.

THE FREEDMEN'S BUREAU

THE Freedmen's Bureau was established to act as a protective and helpful agency for the freedmen in their new state of living. It supervised educational and hospital efforts in behalf of the freedmen, undertook to clothe them and put them to work, and heard disputes between negroes and their employers. Action in this last-mentioned capacity caused much irritation. The whites resented being summoned before the Freedmen's Bureau on complaint of

106   An office of the Freedmen's Bureau, from *Frank Leslie's Illustrated Newspaper*, Feb. 2, 1867

their former slaves. Often the agents were men of tact and good sense and lived in harmony with the former slave owners. But some were zealously prejudiced in favor of the negroes and aroused bitter resentment. The bill gave the bureau a judicial authority which was left to the courts in states not in the South. It was intended for a temporary expedient merely and efforts were made to make its operations as mild as possible.

107   St. Philip's Church, Richmond, Va., a school for colored children, from *Harper's Weekly*, May 25, 1867

EDUCATING THE BLACKS

PHILANTHROPIC people in the North lost no time in beginning work to help the freedmen. They opened schools, set up hospitals and found preachers for negro churches. The blacks responded eagerly. They were disposed to live peaceably with their old masters; but their teachers and preachers thought they would not develop as long as they effaced themselves in the presence of white people. They taught the negroes to be self-assertive. As a consequence the northerners who accepted positions in negro schools were ostracized by the southern whites. The schools for blacks were attended by old as well as young. These schools undoubtedly did good, but the negroes did not absorb learning as fast as was expected.

108   Statue in memory of Booker T. Washington, *Removing the Veil of Ig-
norance and Superstition*, by Charles Keck (1859–) at Tuskegee Normal
and Industrial Institute, Tuskegee, Ala.

THE ADVANCEMENT OF THE NEGRO

THE most ardent northern friends of the negro in 1865 expected him to make a quick advance in culture. Their mistake was in not knowing that the negro's mind would not cast off the effect of ages in Africa except through generations of training. Through much disappointment the process of education was carried on. At last came the idea that the hand of the negro should be educated as well as his mind. The best exponent of this idea was Booker T. Washington, a colored man, founder and president of Tuskegee Institute, in Alabama. His splendid task was to give hope and confidence to his own race and to win the coöperation of southern as well as northern whites.

THE FIFTEENTH AMENDMENT

THE turn of events in 1867 enfranchised the negro in the states concerned; but he was still denied the ballot in many of the states that had not left the Union. To remedy this condition and to make surer the gain in the South, Congress in 1869 passed the Fifteenth Amendment which was ratified the next year. The grounds on which it was declared that the franchise should not be denied were "race, color, or previous condition of servitude." Congress considered an educational basis also but refused to include it in the Fifteenth Amendment. The final phraseology of the Amendment was agreed upon by a committee of conference after the House had adopted one form and the Senate another.

109

THE TENURE OF OFFICE ACT

THE Radicals relied on Stanton, Secretary of War, to see that their reconstruction plan was executed. Fearing that Johnson might remove him and appoint another, they passed the Tenure of Office Act, March 2, 1867. This Act took from the President the power of dismissing officials but permitted him to suspend them, subject to the approval of the Senate. It made an exception of his Cabinet members who were to "hold their offices respectively for and during the term of the President by whom they have been appointed, and for one month thereafter, subject to removal by and with the advice of the Senate." The Radicals thought they were protecting Stanton from removal. Subsequently, it was held that the Act did not protect him, since he was appointed by Lincoln.

Sec. 2. And be it further enacted, That when any officer appointed as aforesaid, excepting judges of the United States courts, shall, during a recess of the Senate, be shown, by evidence satisfactory to the President, to be guilty of misconduct in office, or crime, or for any reason shall become incapable or legally disqualified to perform its duties, in such case, and in no other, the President may suspend such officer and designate some suitable person to perform temporarily the duties of such office until the next meeting of the Senate and until the case shall be acted upon by the Senate; and such person so designated shall take the oaths and give the bonds required by law to be taken and given by the person duly appointed to fill such office; and in such case it shall be the duty of the President, within twenty days after the first day of such next meeting of the Senate, to report to the Senate such suspension, with the evidence and reasons for his action in the case and the name of the person so designated to perform the duties of such office. And if the Senate shall concur in such suspension and advise and consent to the removal of such officer, they shall so certify to the President, who may thereupon remove such officer, and by and with the advice and consent of the Senate, appoint another person to such office. But if the Senate shall refuse to concur in such suspension, such officer so suspended shall forthwith resume the functions of his office, and the powers of the person so performing its duties in his stead shall cease; and the official salary and emoluments of such officer shall, during such suspension, belong to the person so performing the duties thereof; and not to the officer so suspended: Provided, however, That the President, in case he shall become satisfied that such suspension was made on insufficient grounds, shall be authorized, at any time before reporting such suspension to the Senate as above provided, to revoke such suspension and reinstate such officer in the performance of the duties of his office.

110   Section 2 of the Tenure of Office Act, from the original in the Department of State, Washington

REMOVAL OF STANTON

STANTON opposed the President at every point and finally Johnson asked him to resign. Stanton replied that the interests of the country made it necessary for him to stay in office and refused to resign. Then he was dismissed. The Radicals had long been seeking grounds on which they could get rid of Johnson and now they thought they had found them. A committee of the House of Representatives took up the matter and prepared impeachment charges, in order that a trial might occur before the Senate, in accordance with the Constitution.

111   Impeachment Committee preparing the indictment against Johnson, from *Harper's Weekly,*
March 14, 1868

112   The Johnson Impeachment Committee, from a photograph by Brady in the United States
Signal Corps, War Department, Washington
LEFT TO RIGHT, *Seated:* Benjamin F. Butler, Thaddeus Stevens, Thomas Williams, John A. Bingham.
Standing: James F. Wilson, George S. Boutwell, John A. Logan

THE CHARGES AGAINST JOHNSON

THE indictment contained eleven specifications, but the most important was the dismissal of Secretary Stanton. The President was charged with violating the Tenure of Office Act, which had been passed to protect the Secretary. Public opinion at the time was certain that the case against Johnson was strong. At the suggestion of Thaddeus Stevens, an "omnibus" article was included in the charges, by which it was possible to include most of the objectionable things Johnson had done while President. The House appointed seven managers to conduct the case before the Senate. At the head was Stevens, and among the others was Benjamin F. Butler. So began the assault upon an individual and inevitably at the same time upon the power of the office which he held. At the opening of the attack public attention was focused largely upon the personal issues. But the constitutional implications began to be recognized before the trial was completed.

THE INDICTMENT PRESENTED

No more dramatic moment has occurred in United States history than when the committee of managers chosen by the House presented to the Senate, sitting as a high court, the charges against the President. Thaddeus Stevens, who more than anyone else was responsible for the trial, was conspicuous among the managers. He was seventy-six years old, and this was the last notable act in his stern career. Five months later he lay on his deathbed. The indictment of Johnson is now considered ill-advised and partisan; but in 1868 it was indorsed by the northern Republicans generally. His enemies had laid the foundation of general contempt for the President and on that basis it was not hard to build up the belief that he had criminally violated the Tenure of Office Act. Stanton's removal was an action that could not be disputed, but there was the further question of criminal intent.

113   Impeachment Committee entering the Senate Chamber to present the articles of impeachment,
from an illustration by James E. Taylor, in *Frank Leslie's Illustrated Newspaper*, March 21, 1868

THE WRIT OF INDICTMENT IS SERVED ON JOHNSON

JOHNSON's defense was that he believed the Tenure of Office Act was unconstitutional and violated it so that a case might go to the Supreme Court for a test. He also contended that the act (see No. 110) did not protect Stanton, since he was appointed by Lincoln. The reply of the Radicals to these two points was that a man who violates a law, even if he regards it as unconstitutional, does so at his peril and has no right to decry the penalty. They also said that when Johnson asked Stanton to continue in office, after Lincoln's death, it was equivalent to an appointment. They considered Johnson's defense a lawyer's quibble. Such were the legal aspects of the case. Unfortunately, however, the situation was such that political considerations made a decision of the merits of the question impossible. The Radicals wished to control the Presidency in order to carry out their plans in the South and they hoped to do this by putting Senator Wade in Johnson's place.

114 George T. Brown, Sergeant-at-Arms of the Senate, serving the summons on President Johnson, from a sketch by Theodore R. Davis, in *Harper's Weekly*, March 28, 1868

115 Judge Nelson administering the oath to Chief Justice Chase as presiding officer of the Court of Impeachment, from an illustration by James E. Taylor, in *Frank Leslie's Illustrated Newspaper*, March 28, 1868

CHASE PRESIDES AT THE COURT OF IMPEACHMENT

By the Constitution the Chief Justice of the Supreme Court presides over the Senate when the President is impeached, and thus Chief Justice Chase presided in this important trial. The initial form of procedure was that of a court, but when a vital point arose, the decision of the Chief Justice was appealed to the floor and a vote taken. When Chase ruled that Johnson might introduce evidence to show that his intent was merely to test the act, the Senators overruled him by vote. Thus the members of the Senate exercised functions which in an ordinary court belong to both judge and jury. This vote created the impression among some persons that the President was not being given an entirely fair trial. It helped to modify to some extent the popular opposition to him. The clamor for conviction, however, remained loud. By the Constitution a two-thirds vote was necessary to convict.

116   Facsimile of card of admission to the Impeachment Trial, from *Harper's Weekly*,
April 4, 1868

THE COUNSEL FOR THE DEFENSE

IN selecting his lawyers Johnson had the advantage of his opponents who had to take their counsel from the House, which was composed of politicians rather than of distinguished lawyers. Among those who defended the indictment, the most conspicuous were Stevens, Butler and Boutwell, not one of them a first-rate lawyer. Johnson, however, could draw from the best lawyers in the country. At the head of his counsel was William M. Evarts, unexcelled in powerful pleading. At his side stood Benjamin R. Curtis, formerly a Justice of the Supreme Court, Henry Stanbery, who had resigned the position of Federal Attorney-General to defend the President, Thomas A. R. Nelson and William S. Groesbeck. The trial attracted much attention in the country and there was a great demand for admission to the sessions of the court. It was the first time a President of the United States had been impeached and curiosity seekers were keen to witness the spectacle, so that cards of admission were in great demand.

117   The scene of Johnson's trial, from *Frank Leslie's Illustrated Newspaper*, March 28, 1868

THE TRIAL

THE trial continued from March 30 to May 16. There was much talking by the lawyers and much evidence was introduced. Men like Butler, whose ideas never rose above the level of practical politics, made a poor showing. The voting began on May 16, thirty-six votes being necessary for conviction. The Radicals believed they had just that many. As the name of one doubtful member after another was called, everybody present held his breath to catch the response. At the end of this excruciating hour the result was announced, thirty-five for conviction and nineteen against. This vote was on the eleventh article only, but it indicated that all the charges would probably be voted down.

THE DOUBTFUL VOTES

In the excited last days of the trial, the Radicals did their best to win over the Senators who had not yet decided how they would vote. Every possible argument was brought to bear. Senator Ross of Kansas was probably most beset. He received a telegram reading: "Kansas has heard the evidence and demands the conviction of the President." He replied: "I do not recognize your right to demand that I shall vote either for or against conviction. I have taken an oath to do impartial justice." He

118   From a cartoon of the impeachment trial, published by Currier & Ives, New York

was not to be coerced by political threats and his persistence proved to be the salvation of Johnson.

THE RADICALS IN DEFEAT

The managers of impeachment were dumbfounded when the first ballot was taken. Overruling Chase, they voted to adjourn for ten days. Their purpose was to see whether something could not be done to save the day before ballots were taken on the other articles. In this turn of the affair Benjamin Butler was prominent. He insisted that the doubtful Senators had been bribed. He sent spies to the homes of prominent men; he had Evarts' waste-paper basket searched; he inspected the files in the telegraph office. Nowhere did he find evidence of fraud. Butler's assiduity in the matter disgusted many people, for he was a popular man.

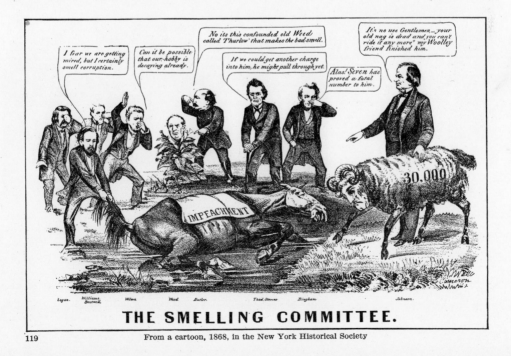

THE SMELLING COMMITTEE.

119   From a cartoon, 1868, in the New York Historical Society

120   President Johnson's last levee at the White House, from an illustration by James E. Taylor, in
Frank Leslie's Illustrated Newspaper, June 6, 1868

JOHNSON AND PUBLIC OPINION

JOHNSON received the congratulations of his friends with a grateful heart. Long before the final vote was taken it was evident that public opinion was turning against the persecutors. Their exhibition of prejudice caused disgust in many people. The election of President and Congress was drawing near and astute men began to fear that if Johnson were put out of office the effect on the elections would be bad. Moreover, some people objected to Wade, President *pro tem* of the Senate, who would succeed if Johnson were removed. He was an extreme Radical and a very positive man. It was feared that if he got power in his hands he would produce confusion anew in the South, now showing signs of settling into normal conditions. This perceptible softening of opinion helped to reconcile the public to acquittal, but it did not mean that the rank and file of the Republicans in the North were less hostile to Johnson in a general way. He withdrew from office under a great cloud of hatred which time has gradually dispelled. He had the misfortune to be in high office at a great crisis, and he was not fitted either by nature or by training to come off successfully.

THE FRENCH ARE EXPELLED FROM MEXICO

IMPORTANT foreign affairs were included in Johnson's administration. His purchase of Alaska is dealt with in Volume II. A more difficult problem inherited from Lincoln concerned the French army in Mexico (see page 38). Negotiations with a view to forcing the French out of Mexico by diplomatic means were begun soon after the close of the Civil War in 1865. Napoleon III realized that France would not support a war for Mexico, and after some months of negotiation he promised to withdraw his troops. Maximilian was too honorable to abandon the Mexican faction that had upheld his government. He remained in Mexico after the French troops had been withdrawn, was defeated by the National Mexican army, and was executed June 19, 1867.

121   From the painting *The Last Moments of Maximilian*, by Jean Paul Laurens

RADICAL MEMBERS
OF THE Sº. Cᴬ. LEGISLATURE,

122   Radical members of the South Carolina legislature, 1868, from a photograph in the Confederate Museum, Richmond, Va.

RADICALS CONTROL A SOUTHERN LEGISLATURE

THE success of Johnson's enemies in their reconstruction policy was typified in the results of negro suffrage as seen in the composition of the South Carolina legislature of 1868. Of the one hundred and forty-six members ninety were colored men. In 1870 the proportions were about the same. In 1872 ninety-four colored and thirty white men made up the Lower House. All the colored and some of the white men were Republicans. The intellectual status is shown by the fact that of the Radical members of the legislature in 1868, fifty colored and thirteen white men, twenty-two could read and write; nineteen were taxpayers, with an aggregate amount of one hundred and forty-six dollars and ten cents; the remainder, forty-four, paid no taxes. Yet this group of men laid on the property owners of the state a burden of four million dollars. Increased taxation, however, was not all. By 1873 the public debt of South Carolina had risen from seven to twenty-nine million dollars. That of North Carolina was increased from sixteen to thirty-two million. By 1874 the obligations of Alabama had mounted from seven to thirty-two million. In Louisiana the peak was reached when in three years, from 1868 to 1871, the indebtedness of the state was increased from fourteen to forty-eight million. Southern bonds sold below par, even as low as ten to twenty-five cents on the dollar.

123   South Carolina state officers and legislators under the Moses Administration,
1872–74, from Edward King, *The Great South*, Hartford, 1874

FRAUDS IN SOUTH CAROLINA

Two governors, Scott, a carpet-bagger, and Moses, a scalawag, ruled South Carolina from 1868 to 1874. No more unblushing friends of corruption ever sat in high office, but the native southerner was the worse of the two. Frauds, petty and great, abounded. In two years one million two hundred thousand dollars were spent for which no vouchers could be found. Money voted to aid the building of railroads was largely absorbed by the committees appointed to spend it. The same was true of a large sum voted to buy land to distribute to the freedmen. The State House was refurnished at a vast expense, and many things bought for this purpose went into the hands of the members. Liquor was freely served to the legislature and paid for by the public. Among the votaries of corruption arose an able and honest man, D. H. Chamberlain, a carpet-bagger. He was elected Governor in 1874 and was able to check the worst frauds. When the whites recovered control in South Carolina they followed the example of many other southern states and repudiated the bonds on which had been raised the money for this era of plunder.

A COLORED REPRESENTATIVE

On December 21, 1868, John W. Menard, a colored man, who had been elected to fill a vacancy created by the death of a Louisiana member, appeared on the floor of the House before the Speaker called it to order and received an ovation from his political friends. He was not able to take his seat at that time because of a contest pending before the committee on election. The appearance of a negro in Congress was a striking event in a time full of unexpected happenings. He was warmly welcomed by the Radical leaders who had said so much for negro suffrage.

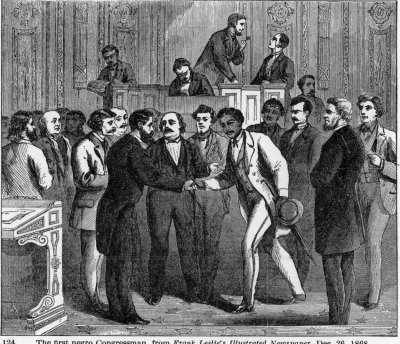

124   The first negro Congressman, from *Frank Leslie's Illustrated Newspaper*, Dec. 26, 1868

125   Dress of the Ku-Klux-Klan, from *Harper's Weekly*, Dec. 19, 1868

THE KU–KLUX–KLAN TAKES THE LAW INTO ITS OWN HANDS

THIS secret organization sprang up because the southern whites were determined to have some means of keeping the freedmen peaceable and of restraining the white men who were their leaders. At first the method was to visit the victims with a view to frightening them. Later, resort was had to whipping or tar and feathers. In time these punishments lost their effect on the negroes, and it came about that now and then life was taken. In general, the victims of the Ku-Klux, black or white, were believed to have incited the negroes to violence. The Klan acquired a political influence, which brought Congress to take action. In 1871 it passed the Ku-Klux Act, giving the President authority to suspend the writ of *habeas corpus* and put down the organization by force. The South did not wish the old days to return and the Klan was disbanded. Its activities had restrained the negroes and had shown the whites how they could lessen the burden of Congressional Reconstruction. The Klan was an inevitable phase of the struggle to regain white supremacy.

GRANT, THE REPUBLICAN NOMINEE

IN the Presidential campaign of 1868 the Republicans chose their candidate well. Before the Civil War Ulysses S. Grant was a Democrat; after the war, in the early days of reconstruction, he showed a leaning in that direction. But in 1867 Johnson quarreled with him over a minor matter which tended to throw him into the ranks of the Radicals. The Republicans were quick to seize the opportunity and soon got Grant to agree to accept their nomination for the Presidency. He was the strongest man of the country and his election was certain as soon as he entered the field.

126   John A. Logan nominating Grant in Chicago, 1868, from an illustration by James E. Taylor, in *Frank Leslie's Illustrated Newspaper*, June 13, 1868

127   George H. Pendleton, 1825–89, from a photo-
        graph by J. Gurney & Son, New York

THE DEMOCRATIC PARTY IN 1868

THE war broke the prestige of the Democratic party, which had supported the opposition to the war and had opposed Radical reconstruction. Its leaders in 1868 did not dare break entirely with their own past. They stood by their position on reconstruction but to it they added new issues which seemed to be popular. One of them was a demand for the payment of the war debt in paper money issued for that purpose. This proposal was fathered by George H. Pendleton of Cincinnati. It was popular in the agricultural West where it was generally believed that the East was determined to have the debt paid in gold. This "Ohio Idea" was summed up in the words, "One money for the bond-holder and the plow-holder." It was a demand for inflation and was to appear again in the "Greenbacks" and "Free Silver" movements. A great many western farmers continue to feel that the financial policies of the Government work to their disadvantage.

SEYMOUR AND BLAIR

THE leading New York Democrat was Horatio Seymour. He was opposed to the "Ohio Idea" but could not keep it out of the Democratic platform in 1868. He fought also against the nomination of Pendleton, defender of the "Ohio Idea," and this fight was won with the aid of the two-thirds rule. Seymour wished to see Chase, of Ohio, nominated, but the convention would not agree. After many ballots and some confusion it turned to him and nominated him over his serious protests. General Francis P. Blair was his running mate.

128   Horatio Seymour, 1810–86, from a photograph

129   From a cartoon by Thomas Nast, in *Harper's Weekly*,
        Sept. 5, 1868

SECTIONAL DIFFERENCES ARE EMPHASIZED BY POLITICIANS

WHEN we look back to 1868 we think of the "Ohio Idea" as the chief issue of the campaign. But that issue was so popular with the people at large that the Republicans were afraid to attack it with energy. The Republican press of the time gave its chief attention to matters connected with the recent struggle, appealing to popular resentment. An astounding cartoon by Nast shows the Democrats as a trio of thuggery, Confederate violence and bribery standing on a prostrate Union flag and a negro soldier while a negro school and a negro orphan asylum were burning in the background. The activities of the Ku-Klux in the South added fuel to this conflagration. Between the two sections the fires, kindled by the Abolitionists thirty-seven years earlier and raised to fever heat by war and attempted secession, were still burning and the politicians on each side did not mean to let them go out. By continuing to fan the blazes they incited their respective followers and maintained their political majorities.

GRANT ELECTED PRESIDENT

THE most telling appeal of the Republicans was their candidate. Grant was not a politician and his frank soldier ways pleased the country. He closed his letter accepting the nomination with the words: "Let us have peace." On the other hand nine days before his nomination Blair had said that the only thing for the next President to do was to declare null all the reconstruction acts of Congress and compel the army to undo the work it had done in the South in 1867 and 1868. Thus Grant appeared as the man of peace and Blair, Democratic partner of Seymour, as the man of revolution. Grant received two hundred and fourteen electoral votes and carried twenty-four states, six of them in the South. Seymour had eighty electoral votes and carried eight states, two of them in the South. Three southern states did not vote because they were not yet re-admitted to the Union with full rights. Grant's election checked the Radicals and quieted the fears of the South.

130   From an election cartoon *Victory*, in *Harper's Weekly*, Nov. 14, 1868

THE SOUTH PERMITS FREE SPEECH

IN the excitement of the campaign the northern people came to believe that the southern Democrats terrorized Republicans, beating and killing their opponents until as a party they disappeared. The fact that six of the eight restored states went Republican made this assertion seem doubtful. To this must be added the testimony of General Oliver Otis Howard, head of the Freedmen's Bureau, who made a political speaking tour through the South at this time. He said: "I did not receive a personal affront or incivility." In the heat of the campaign it was natural for trivial affairs to be written up large. But the sensational occurrences reported in the newspapers, though they usually had some truth at the bottom, resembled but slightly the real facts.

131   General Oliver Otis Howard, 1830–1909, from a photograph by Brady in the United States Signal Corps, War Department, Washington

GENERAL LEE IN RETIREMENT

LEE won the love of the South and the respect of the world. After the war he applied for a pardon and became president of Washington College in Virginia (Washington and Lee University). It was his belief that duty required him to accept defeat and to do what he could to repair the broken life of the South.

132   Robert E. Lee, 1807–70, from a pastel portrait, 1870, by John Dabour (1837–1905), owned by W. H. Taylor III, Norfolk, Va., courtesy of the Frick Art Reference Library, New York

133   Casemate at Fortress Monroe where Jefferson Davis was confined, from a photograph, 1865,
by George S. Cook, Richmond

IMPRISONMENT OF JEFFERSON DAVIS

AMID the furies of the time appeared a few signs of a new and better spirit. One of these was a movement among northerners to secure generous treatment for the President of the Confederacy; Davis was captured by Union troops in May, 1865. He was sent to Fortress Monroe where the commander, Nelson A. Miles, later a distinguished general, ordered him put in irons. This indignity caused an outburst of disapproval. It was regarded by many people as a cruel and useless attempt to humiliate a defeated man. After a time superiors intervened and Miles had to remove the shackles from his prisoner. But Davis was kept in confine-

ment, despite his hope of release on a *habeas corpus* writ. He was alleged to have had a share in Booth's conspiracy to murder Lincoln, a false charge which few sensible people believed.

RELEASE OF JEFFERSON DAVIS

AT length public opinion began to turn in favor of Davis' release. Some of the stoutest leaders of the old fight against the South, among them Greeley, editor of the *New York Daily Tribune*, urged it as an act of justice. Then the Government yielded. Davis was taken before a Federal judge in Richmond on a writ of *habeas corpus* and released on bail pending a future trial, which was never called. The former head of the Confederacy, who had lain in prison two years without an opportunity to face his accusers, walked out, now a free man. He had not been popular in the South during the war, but from his arrest to his death in 1889 his people looked upon him as a martyr. He had led the "Lost Cause" as well as it could have been led, and he had suffered in prison for its sake. Until his death he was for the South the embodiment of their lost hopes.

134   Jefferson Davis leaving the Court House at Richmond, from
Harper's Weekly, June 1, 1867

135 George Peabody and Trustees of the Peabody Educational Fund, from a photograph by
Brady in the possession of the United States Signal Corps, War Department, Washington

LEFT TO RIGHT, *Seated:* George Peabody, George P. Russell, Samuel Wetmore. *Standing:* David
Farragut, Hamilton Fish, Ulysses S. Grant, William Aiken, Charles P. McIlvaine, William C.
Rives

EDUCATION

OUT of the humiliation of the South came the conviction that the future belonged to the educated class.
The first impulse upward was toward the organization of schools. While General Lee was at work as a college
president, thousands of men and women of the former upper class became the teachers of the young. In
1867, George Peabody, a New Englander by birth, and a merchant and banker of Washington and London,
created a fund of three and a half millions of dollars, the proceeds of which were to go toward education
in the South. Before this the rich had established schools for their children. Now when all were poor it came
to be seen that the best type of education for the new day was public education.

COTTON

IN the work of restoration the South's best friend
was cotton. Though no
longer "King Cotton," as
in the days before the
Civil War, it has never
lost its leadership in
southern economy. It
has remained the chief
staple product of the
southern section though
other crops have been
introduced. The high
price of cotton in the first
years of peace enabled
the farmer to command
money. Although the
time came when it sold
for a trifle, it always

136   Cotton pickers at work, from a photograph by H. P. Cook, Richmond

brought enough money to furnish necessaries. At last, with the coming of the World War, cotton returned
to its old preëminence and the South enjoyed its greatest period of prosperity since the Civil War.

CHAPTER III

READJUSTMENT UNDER GRANT

ALTHOUGH most of the Radical Reconstructionists acted from party motives their popular support rested on the conviction that the freedmen must be protected in the South and that the negro's enfranchisement alone would make his future secure. This idea was widely held in the North and, true or false, it was a part of the reform impulse that is always present in healthy democratic government. The politicians utilized this confidence, and when it began to flag they sought to restore it by recounting with exaggeration the "outrages" committed on negroes in the South. In order to hold office and dole out corrupt privileges they found it necessary to keep alive doubts and fears about the future of the negro. It was inevitable that this situation should break after a time, and, in fact it did break about the end of Grant's second administration. It resulted, therefore, that within these eight years reconstruction problems receded while the ordinary political and economic problems of a government began to assume more prominence. And as these problems came into view it was more and more apparent that the ordinary political life of the nation was badly impaired.

The responsibility lay fundamentally in the condition of the times. In their absorption in war and its aftermath the people had forgotten to keep their eyes on ordinary government. They had come to tolerate questionable appointments, bad contracts, and debased citizenship on the ground that the supreme necessity lay elsewhere. At the same time there was a vast increase in great fortunes. A host of men who had made large sums out of war contracts crowded the lobbies of Congress seeking new favors. Grant did not create this situation but he was not the man to block it. His ideals of public life were not high, and he was easily led by his associates. At first a friend of reform he came to accept the view that reform was impracticable.

The process of recovery was difficult and proved to be slow. Corrupt government was local as well as national and deep-rooted in each sphere. Its opponents struggled to bring back *ante bellum* habits, and they demanded civil service reform and the appointment of better officials in high places. They formed a definite organization known as the Liberal Republican party and hoped that it would be the decisive factor in the election of 1872. The Radical politicians, still fighting under Grant's mantle, carried the election and exultingly gave notice that political life would have to wait at least four years more for its purification.

In one field the restoration was, in fact, accomplished with fair success. The war had left a clouded condition in the nation's foreign relations. Against Great Britain a large number of claims impended, but by using good sense the two nations were brought to settle their differences by arbitration. Another cloud was in the French dabbling in Mexico, but here again reason was used and Napoleon III was induced to withdraw his troops peacefully.

In the field of finance the restoration was also slow. It became complicated with the fatuous theory of inflation and *fiat* money. In the three fields here mentioned — public ideals, foreign affairs, and financial measures — lie the facts treated in this chapter.

137 Grant's Inauguration, from a photograph by Brady in the United States Signal Corps, War Department, Washington

GRANT BECOMES PRESIDENT ON A POPULAR WAVE

THE country loved Grant and looked kindly upon his entry into political life, but there was much wonder as to how well he would succeed in a civil office. He had no special training to qualify him for his new rôle. His political standards were the ideals of the farmers of 1840. To keep faith with friends, to disbelieve charges without proof, to steal nothing from the public, and to keep conscientiously at the post of duty — all these quiet virtues were reflected in his inaugural address. Time was to show that despite excellent purposes he was too easy going in government and yielded himself too readily to designing men. In the eyes of his countrymen he was the man who had emerged as the last of a long list of commanders of the Union troops on the eastern front, the man who had received the surrender of Lee.

GRANT AND THE POLITICIANS

RECONSTRUCTION had produced a new kind of politician. So completely were the people of the North committed to the task of reconstruction that they forgot to observe the conduct of their representatives in other matters. At the same time Washington swarmed with adventurers in search of government favor and willing to pay for it. The result was a powerful conspiracy whose members, standing together and sharing profits, were able to carry through Congress many a bill for private benefit. Public opinion was forming against this situation and it was hoped that Grant, who was essentially honest, would clear it up. The future was to show that Grant, with the best of intentions, was not a political reformer.

138 Ulysses S. Grant, 1822–85, from a photograph by Brady in the United States Signal Corps, War Department, Washington

139   From an illustration by W. S. L. Jewett in *Harper's Weekly*, April 3, 1869

LEFT TO RIGHT: Jacob D. Cox, Secretary of the Interior; Hamilton Fish, Secretary of State; John A. Rawlins, Secretary of War; John A. J. Cresswell, Postmaster-General; President Grant; George S. Boutwell, Secretary of the Treasury; Adolph E. Borie, Secretary of the Navy; Ebenezer R. Hoar, Attorney-General.

GRANT'S CABINET

THE Grant Cabinet was a disappointment to those who hoped for reforms. As at first announced, it contained Alexander T. Stewart, a rich merchant of New York, whose appointment the Senate refused to confirm because the law forbade a merchant to be Secretary of the Treasury; also Elihu B. Washburne, whom Grant soon appointed Minister to France. As finally constituted, the Cabinet contained three men who were excellent: Hamilton Fish, Secretary of State; Jacob D. Cox, Secretary of the Interior; and E. Rockwood Hoar, Attorney-General. These were known to stand for the better ideals in government. George S. Boutwell, of the Treasury, was a man of ability, but he had grown accustomed to corrupt politics. The others in the Cabinet had no distinction. Grant's inexperience in political affairs made thoughtful people anxious about his advisers. However, it was not from anyone in his Cabinet that the bad influence of his Presidency came, but from the knot of unscrupulous schemers who stood at the head of the corruption in Washington.

140   Lucius Q. C. Lamar, 1825–93, from a photograph

GRANT AND AMNESTY

BY the Fourteenth Amendment, the extending of amnesty to the Confederates was left to Congress. By March 4, 1871, Congress had pardoned only four thousand six hundred and sixteen persons. The principle followed was to grant amnesty to all who would ask for it, excepting the prominent Confederates. Most of those who applied were Republicans. The Republican control in southern states had "resulted," says Rhodes, "in the worst government ever known in the United States." Realization of this fact in the North created sympathy for the South and there was a demand in 1871 for milder measures. Grant met this by recommending an act of Congress for granting general amnesty except to a very few high Confederates. The bill passed in 1872. It readmitted to civil rights about one hundred and sixty thousand southerners, leaving about five hundred unpardoned. But not until 1898, when southerners were fighting against Spain, did Congress remove the last vestige of disability.

141   Grant signing the Ku-Klux "Force Bill," from *Frank Leslie's Illustrated Newspaper*, May 13, 1871

GRANT'S SOUTHERN POLICY

GRANT did many things in times of crisis to make the southerners esteem him. But in general he yielded to the political tide. In 1870 the Republican majority in Congress was reduced, and prospects for the elections of 1872 seemed even more unfavorable. The Washington leaders became anxious and aimed to build up their strength through control of the southern district. The southern policy of the administration now became pitilessly partisan. Grant at no time in his administration tried to stem the tide of partisanship. His conduct offers a strange combination of personal acts of great kindness to the South and an attitude of cynical expediency on matters relating to the southern policy championed by Radicals.

SOUTHERN WHITES RECOVER POWER

THE wounds of the South were healing slowly, and southerners felt justified in overcoming negro rule by any means that would work. There sprang up a wide system of "neutralizing the negro vote," and step by step the whites regained control of affairs. By the middle of 1877 they had got control of all the southern state governments, and the Congressional districts had been so arranged that all but a few of the Congressmen from the South were not Democrats. Most of the whites stood together solidly.

142   Conflict between the police and a negro mob in New Orleans, from *Harper's Weekly*, Oct. 26, 1874

POLITICAL MORALS

THE redemption of the South was a slow and painful process. Meanwhile, Washington swarmed with lobbyists, at their head genial Sam Ward, known as the "King of the Lobby." It was asserted that he had put many a railroad bill through Congress with the aid of terrapin and champagne. Grant's failure to clean out this mass of evil disappointed a large part of the nation, but the responsibility was not entirely his.

143   Sam Ward, 1814–84, from *Harper's Weekly*, May 31, 1884, after a photograph by Gambier

144   William M. Tweed, 1823–78, from an engraving after a photograph

LOCAL AND STATE CORRUPTION

WHILE the carpet-baggers and scalawags were reveling in fraud in the southern legislature, a wide area of misrule was found in local and state government in the North. Its most striking example was in New York, where reigned a group of politicians under William M. Tweed. By a system of slightly concealed frauds, protected by official corruption, Tweed took public money in a total amount estimated at from forty-five million to two hundred million dollars. Most people realized what was going on, but neither political party would make it an issue. Tweed had the city officials in his power, and the state legislature was bought so that it ate out of his hand. The Tweed scandal, like the corruption at Washington, was evidence of the moral let-down that followed the war.

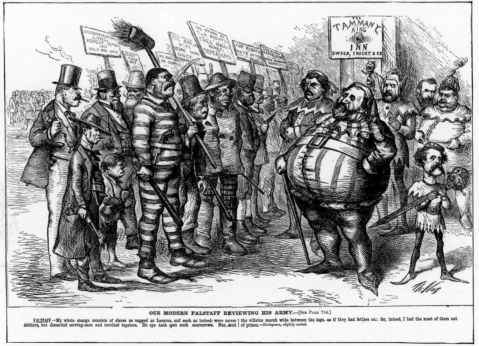

OUR MODERN FALSTAFF REVIEWING HIS ARMY.—[SEE PAGE 714.]

FALSTAFF.—My whole charge consists of slaves as ragged as Lazarus, and such as indeed: were never | the villains march wide between the legs, as if they had fetters on: for, indeed, I had the most of them out soldiers, but discarded serving-men and revolted tapsters. No eye hath seen such scarecrows. Nay, and | of prison.—*Shakspeare, slightly varied.*

145   From the cartoon *Our Modern Falstaff Reviewing his Army*, by Thomas Nast in *Harper's Weekly*, Nov. 5, 1870

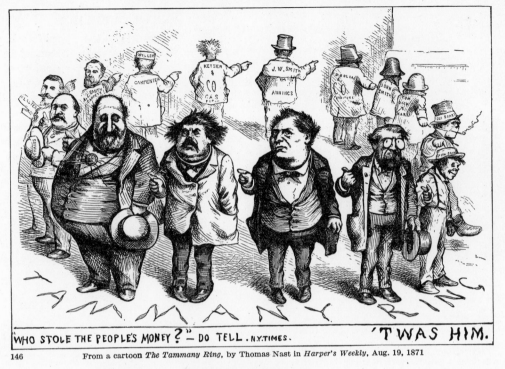

WHO STOLE THE PEOPLE'S MONEY?" — DO TELL . N.Y.TIMES.　'TWAS HIM.

146　From a cartoon *The Tammany Ring*, by Thomas Nast in *Harper's Weekly*, Aug. 19, 1871

TWEED ATTACKED

At last the cause of the people was taken up by the *New York Times* and supported by Thomas Nast, a brilliant cartoonist on *Harper's Weekly*. Their first blows caused Tweed to laugh in derision; but public opinion was aroused. Then Tweed thought it worth while to try to bribe his tormentors. He found this useless. At the critical moment, the *Times* obtained from a disappointed fellow-conspirator transcripts of the crooked accounts of the city and published them.

TWEED CONVICTED

Two brilliant lawyers, Charles O'Conor and Samuel J. Tilden, now came forward to aid the assailants of the grafters. A mass of facts furnished the basis for indictments. Some of the accused escaped to Europe with enough money to enable them to live in luxury. Tweed faced trial, expecting to be able to buy acquittal: the jury disagreed. Tried again, he was convicted and given twelve years in prison. After a year he was released on bail through a technicality. Later he was arrested again and held in bail for three million dollars. He got away and reached Spain after many wanderings but was taken and brought back to New York. His wealth gone, he could not escape; he died in prison after lingering there three years. He had operated with the aid of Tammany Hall.

147　From a cartoon *The Sacred Ermine*, by Frank Bellew in
Harper's Weekly, Feb. 17, 1872

148   Schuyler Colfax, 1823–85, from a photograph by L. C. Handy

THE CREDIT MOBILIER

WHILE the country was still intent upon the Tweed frauds, reports were circulated asserting that a huge railroad scandal had been discovered in Congressional circles involving the conduct of prominent Representatives. Investigation followed. It was found that directors of the Union Pacific Railroad had used the Crédit Mobilier (see Vol. IV), a construction company owned by themselves, as a blind for acquiring personally a large portion of the funds of the railroad. To keep their transactions from being known they had admitted prominent leaders of the House to a share in the proceeds of the fraud. Scenting danger, most of these leaders got out of their peril by handing back their profits. Others, among them Schuyler Colfax, Vice-President, escaped impeachment through the early expiration of their terms of office. The best that could be said for the guilty Congressmen was that such practices were common in politics at that time, a fact which is a severe condemnation of the existing standard of public morals.

THE SPOILS SYSTEM

SINCE about 1825 the spoils system had been fixed in our politics. It was based on the idea that some reward had to be given to a man who worked in a political campaign; and the practice of using public offices as such rewards had become habitual. The result was that after every election the President appointed many officials solely to gratify members of Congress and party leaders. This pernicious system pervaded politics, lessened the efficiency of the civil service, and led politicians to assume the attitude of petty tyrants. To uproot it was by many people considered a hopeless task and while they recognized its evils they did not try to change it.

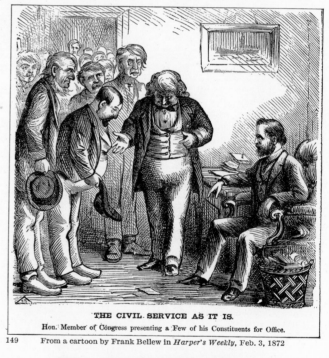

THE CIVIL SERVICE AS IT IS.
Hon. Member of Congress presenting a Few of his Constituents for Office.

149   From a cartoon by Frank Bellew in *Harper's Weekly*, Feb. 3, 1872

CIVIL SERVICE REFORMERS

IN protest against the spoils system efforts at reform began to be made as early as 1864. In 1868, Thomas Jenckes of Rhode Island made an extensive report in the House recommending the adoption of a merit system in the appointments to office. Public opinion took up the suggestion and in the campaign then in progress Grant declared for civil service reform. It was ardently advocated by such men as George William Curtis, William Cullen Bryant, and Carl Schurz. One of the main motives of the reformers was to reduce the inefficiency in the conduct of Government business which was the inevitable result of putting spoilsmen into the Government offices and discharging them whenever there was a political overturn.

150   Thomas A. Jenckes, 1818–75, from the original portrait in the possession of Thomas A. Jenckes, Jr., Providence, R. I.

THE REFORM PRESS

At this time the feeling for reform found a strong support in a section of the press. Papers like the New York *Evening Post*, the Springfield *Republican* and *The Nation* fought valiantly to purify political life. They met bitter contempt from "practical" politicians, who believed that the reformers were theoretical and eccentric. Nevertheless, it is to such leaders that we owe some of the forward steps in our national career. The power of the press in the eighteen-seventies was not to be compared to that which it has achieved in the twentieth century. The newspaper activities in the years immediately following the Civil War mark a beginning of the modern type of influence of the public print, an influence which from that time has steadily developed until it is now perhaps the strongest political force of our era.

151 William Cullen Bryant, 1794–1878, Editor of the *Evening Post*, New York, from a photograph, 1875, by Sarony

ATTITUDE OF THE PARTIES

Neither party dared oppose civil service reform, yet neither was sincerely for it. The spoils system had built up powerful party organizations which acted with the firmness and certainty of a regular army. The politicians of that day did not believe they could compensate for this efficiency through voluntary service.

CAN A MAN BE A NURSE?
U. S. G. "Both parties say they love it. But —"

152 From a cartoon *Can a Man be a Nurse?*, by Thomas Nast in *Harper's Weekly*, April 3, 1875

THE CIVIL SERVICE COMMISSION

The reformers counted on Grant, because of his personal honesty. In 1871, Congress gave him authority to make rules governing appointments. He created the Civil Service Commission to see that the rules were put into execution and faithfully observed. Very soon Congressmen saw that they had thrown away a strong instrument of personal power, and they set out to recover it. By many kinds of innuendo and false charges they attacked the Commission, and finally refused to renew the appropriation which supported it. The result was a halt in the progress of the movement. Though Grant had faithfully supported the commission when first instituted, he did nothing to save it from the vengeance of its enemies.

NO SURRENDER.
U. S. G. "I am Determined to Enforce those Regulations."

153 From a cartoon *No Surrender*, by Thomas Nast in *Harper's Weekly*, Dec. 7, 1872

154   Benjamin F. Butler, 1818–1893, from a photograph, 1884, by Falk

155   From a cartoon by J. A. Wales in *Puck*, March 26, 1879

POLITICAL ASSOCIATES OF THE PRESIDENT

GRANT's weakest point was his choice of friends. The three men in the Cabinet who had the confidence of the country, Fish, Hoar and Cox, were steadily undermined in their influence on the President by his intimate advisers, who finally managed things so that Cox resigned and Hoar was, in effect, dismissed. This was done to please the carpet-bag Senators from the South. Among the men who served to warp the mind of the straightforward general, the most conspicuous was Benjamin F. Butler of Massachusetts. His baneful influence made of public life an opportunity to line the pockets of friends. It taught the average man to believe that good government was a will-o'-the-wisp and its champions hypocrites.

156   B. Gratz Brown, 1826–85, from a photograph by Gurney & Son, New York

THE LIBERAL REPUBLICAN MOVEMENT

AN effort to purge the Republican party of this state of corruption, to introduce civil service reform, and to adopt a less severe policy toward the South began in Missouri in 1870, with the election of a Governor. A group of independent Republicans, opposing the regulars, nominated B. Gratz Brown, a reformer, and with the aid of the Democrats, elected him. In its origin the Liberal Republican movement was a reaction against two things; the severe reconstruction policy of the Radical Republicans and the growing power of the machine of the Republican party. Already long tenure of power at a time when the country was suffering a moral reaction after the idealism which marked the Civil War period had brought corruption into the administration of the dominant party. The worst aspects of this phase of our life were yet to be disclosed; but these original Liberal Republicans sniffed the tainted breeze and prepared to make an attempt to eradicate the disease. They were courageous and high-minded but they had much to learn concerning the arts of political management and warfare. They had a brief career in the nation's political life, but it was of great significance.

LIBERAL REPUBLICAN REFORMERS

CARL SCHURZ, elected Senator from Missouri in 1869, was heartily in favor of the Liberal Republican demands and became their exponent in Congress. The movement attracted attention throughout the country; prominent liberal statesmen and newspapers took it up; it became a national affair when the Missouri men in January, 1872, issued a call for a national convention to be held at Cincinnati the following May. It was to represent all who were opposed to Grant's administration and were favorable to reform.

THE CINCINNATI CONVENTION

THE country appeared to respond vigorously to the call of the Missouri reformers. The Cincinnati convention was, in reality, little more than a mass meeting. There were practically no local organizations in the various states with the result that the state delegations varied considerably in size, and even more in principles. In drawing up their platform the convention members criticized the President for his appointments and for his political friendships. They declared him unfit for the Presidency. The party demanded complete amnesty for the South and urged civil service reform. The reformers split on the tariff question. This issue they left to the voters for

157   Carl Schurz, 1829–1906, from a photograph by Gutekunst, Philadelphia

decision in the election of members of Congress. On the whole the platform was well conceived. The liberals believed that by obtaining the aid of the Democrats they could defeat Grant. Everyone was looking for the possible candidate on whom all could unite. Charles Francis Adams, formerly minister to Great Britain, was the most logical selection, but his cold New England manner repelled the men of other parts of the country.

158   Carl Schurz announcing the nomination of Horace Greeley for President at the Liberal Republican Convention, Cincinnati, from a drawing by James E. Taylor in *Frank Leslie's Illustrated Newspaper*, May 12, 1872

159   Horace Greeley, 1811–72, from a photograph by Sarony,
New York

GREELEY THE NOMINEE

ANOTHER suggested nominee was Horace Greeley, editor of the *New York Daily Tribune*, and long a defender of abolition and a castigator of the South and the Democratic party. His newspaper had made him widely known. He was exalted by his friends as a farmer, as a champion of reconciliation, as a man of simple honesty. The time was full of dramatic happenings, and it was assumed that the country would observe with approval the spectacle of Greeley coming to the aid of his former enemies, despite the fact that criticism of them, up to that time, had been his bread and meat. Consequently the Liberal Republicans nominated Greeley, with Gratz Brown for his running mate, and the Democrats indorsed the nomination. The regular Republicans renominated Grant.

GREELEY APPEARS INCONSISTENT

GREELEY seems to have been put forward by the professional politicians who for one or another reason had attached themselves to the new party. They preferred him to Adams because they thought that the impulsive editor of the *Tribune* would be more easy to manage than the hard-headed Adams who could not be depended on "to play with the boys." Greeley, moreover, was not so ardent a civil service reformer as some of his associates. Greeley's past had been filled with the bitterest attacks on most of the things he now advocated; but the other Liberal Republicans were in the same situation. Though Greeley tried to force the fighting on the new issues that had come up, his rash partisans indulged in reckless abuse of the President. This was called "mud-slinging" by his opponents and Greeley was held to be responsible for it. Try as he might, he never got the initiative in the battle; and his opponents, with the weaker issues and the stronger press, kept him under throughout the campaign.

160   From a cartoon *What I Know About Horace Greeley*, by Thomas Nast in *Harper's Weekly*, Jan. 20, 1872

161   From a cartoon *Cincinnatus*, by Thomas Nast in *Harper's Weekly*, Feb. 10, 1872

GREELEY'S ECCENTRIC FIGURE

ALTHOUGH Greeley was a man of great business success, there was something simple and childlike in his character. One of his traits was a fondness for farming, and through his *Tribune* he had been able to win the confidence of the farmers. This characteristic was strikingly caricatured by the inveterate Nast, whose lead was followed in all parts of the country. A favorite idea was to depict Greeley of the day in opposition to Greeley of the past.

"LET US CLASP HANDS OVER THE BLOODY CHASM."—HORACE GREELEY.

162   From a cartoon by Thomas Nast in *Harper's Weekly*, Sept. 21, 1872

POLITICS AND WAR HATREDS

GREELEY'S liberality toward the South was one of his best points, but his opponents used it against him with telling effect. In one of his speeches he spoke of shaking hands across the "bloody chasm." The phrase was repeated to his disadvantage in many ways. It aroused the sleeping anger of the northern people, and gave them visions of a triumphant South again dominating public life as in the *ante bellum* days.

IT IS ONLY A TRUCE TO REGAIN POWER ("PLAYING POSSUM")
H. G. "Clasp hands over the bloody chasm."
C. S. "Freely accept the hand that is offered, and reach forth thine own in friendly grasp."

163   From a cartoon by Thomas Nast, in *Harper's Weekly*, Aug. 24, 1872

GREELEY AND THE SOUTH

THE opponents of Greeley tried to turn the South against him by dwelling on his former hostility to that section. Charles Sumner, now a Liberal Republican and opposing Grant bitterly, was in the same situation. To see these two men appealing to the southern Democrat for support was a strange and unexpected turn of Fortune's wheel.

GREELEY AND TAMMANY

IT was also passing strange to see Greeley acting in close coöperation with Tammany, freshly stained with the Tweed corruption. The reformers, by accepting Democratic support, had become associated with the Tammany influence, and their opponents lost no time in making use of it. Greeley, whom his admirers called "Old Honesty," was represented as the confederate of "Boss" Tweed, whose misdeeds were not yet forgotten. This connection with Tammany seems to have been one of the reasons why that ardent cartoonist of reform, Thomas Nast, threw his powerful influence against the Liberal Republican nominee. Nast apparently failed to discern the larger issues involved in the campaign. He was, at the time, at the height of his career and any man might well fear his pencil. That he injured Greeley by his merciless ridicule there can be no doubt. That his cartoons were frequently unfair there can also be no doubt. It is generally conceded that Greeley's speeches were good and his conduct was creditable.

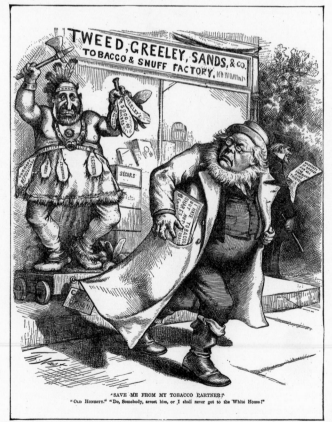

"SAVE ME FROM MY TOBACCO PARTNER!"
"OLD HONESTY." "Do, Somebody, arrest him, or I shall never get to the White House!"

164   From a cartoon by Thomas Nast, in *Harper's Weekly*, Nov. 2, 1872

RELATION OF THE DEMOCRATS TO GREELEY

IT was impossible to deny that Greeley had no logical place in the Democratic party. For a long time he had denounced it severely, and the cartoonists did not allow the country to forget his past course. With that biting style which was peculiarly his own, he had denounced the Democrats on the editorial page of the *Tribune*. For years he had held up to the public gaze what he was pleased to call their rottenness. "Not all Democrats are horse-thieves," said he, "but all horse-thieves are Democrats." His endorsement by the Democratic party as their candidate for President is one of the curiosities in the annals of American party politics. For all that, the Democrats gave him faithful support. Weak as they were in the good will of the nation, they had no political hope except through the aid of the Liberal Republican group in the North. It was going to be a long time before they could carry an election by their unaided efforts. Their weakness was not a good thing for the political life of the nation.

WHAT H. G. KNOWS ABOUT THRESHING

And now—"He comes among us to ask that we adopt *Him* as our Party Chief!"—*New York World*, June 6, 1872.

165   From a cartoon by Thomas Nast in *Harper's Weekly*, July 13, 1872

THE RETURN OF ULYSSES.

BRITANNIA. "AH, MY DEAR! I WAS CERTAIN YOU WOULDN'T TURN AWAY THE GENERAL. HE MAY SMOKE TOO MUCH, AND BE TOO FOND OF HIS RELATIONS; BUT, AT ANY RATE, HE'S BEEN A GOOD AND FAITHFUL SERVANT TO *YOU!*"

166   From a cartoon by John Tenniel in *Punch*, Nov. 16, 1872

GRANT REËLECTED

THE popularity of Grant, like that of Jackson in 1832, was too great to be overcome. With public attention trained upon Greeley's whimsicalities, little thought was given to the political shadows that had gathered around Grant, who received two hundred and seventy-two electoral votes against sixty-six for his opponent. In the popular vote Grant received 3,597,132 to 2,834,125 for Greeley. The Republicans carried all the states but Georgia, Maryland, Missouri, Louisiana, Tennessee and Texas. The reformers had not even made a good showing. All but a few irreconcilables hastened back into the fold of the Republican party and carried on their fight within its ranks. Their defeat was the first of a long series of catastrophies which brought budding third-party movements to an end. The two-party system was destined to remain as unshakable after the Civil War as it had proved to be before that conflict. It seems inherent in American politics. Reformers were to learn that their greatest chance for success lay in staying within the party organization rather than in conducting a guerilla warfare against it from the outside.

THE NEW "CONFEDERATE CRUISER."

167   From a cartoon for the campaign of 1872, published by Currier & Ives, New York

LIBERAL REPUBLICAN PRINCIPLES IGNORED

THE merciless ridicule showered upon Greeley was a new and unforeseen experience which proved to be a greater strain than he could endure. Despite his honest and simple heart and his many speeches, for the most part in excellent form and substance, the people had refused to take him seriously. His defeat was a severe blow to a nature extremely sensitive, and it was believed to have been a contributory cause to his death which occurred twenty-four days after the election.

THE *ALABAMA* CLAIMS

IN the year of Grant's reëlection occurred an important settlement with England. For the damages done during the Civil War by the *Alabama* and other British-built Confederate cruisers (see Vol. VII), the United States had presented claims, urging that England violated neutrality when she permitted her territory to be used for organizing attacks on American property. At first the British Government refused to take the demands seriously. In 1868, President Johnson directed Reverdy Johnson, American minister in London, to press the matter. Very anxious to clear it up, Johnson accepted a plan for referring it to the decision of five persons, two of them to be selected by each side. If the four could not agree, a fifth choice was to be made by lot. This plan practically left the decision to chance and was so unpopular that when it went before the Senate, April 13, 1868, only one vote was for it. It was known as the Johnson-Clarendon Convention. It was an improper agreement, but the contempt hurled at it was partly due to a desire to damage the President.

168   From a cartoon *The British Lion Disarmed*, by Thomas Nast in *Harper's Weekly*,
Aug. 1, 1868

169   From a caricature of Charles Sumner in *Vanity Fair*, London, May 25, 1872

SUMNER'S SPEECH ON THE CLAIMS

SENATOR SUMNER, who was at that time Chairman of the Committee on Foreign Relations, undertook to dispel the trivial spirit with which the British viewed the *Alabama* claims. He made a striking speech demanding payment for all losses attributed to the action of the British. These losses as he summed them up included direct damages to the amount of fifteen million dollars, in-

170   From a caricature of Hamilton Fish in *Vanity Fair*, London, May 18, 1872

flicted by the Confederate ships; losses due to driving Union commerce from the seas, one hundred and ten million dollars; and expenditures due to the continuance of the war longer than it would otherwise have lasted, two billion dollars. This staggering statement of what Sumner called "our massive grievance" increased the mirthful contempt of the British, but it showed them how serious the matter had become. It was also a challenge to public interest in America which up to this time had proved sluggish.

THE TREATY OF WASHINGTON

SECRETARY FISH was a skillful diplomat. Seeing that the air had cleared he brought about a series of conferences which resulted in the Treaty of Washington, 1871. It provided for clearing away all causes of distrust between the two nations. A controversy over fishing rights in Newfoundland was to be arbitrated, a controversy over the boundary line in Puget Sound was to be settled by a Joint High Commission, and the *Alabama* controversy was to be arranged through arbitration by a committee of five members. The treaty also laid down a general rule for determining damages in cases like that of the *Alabama*. This concession was a triumph for Fish. It took time for the British public to awaken on the subject of the claims. Though their resentment was high at first it soon gave place to the recognition that an irritating incident was standing in the way of the friendly feeling the two powers should have for one another. There followed the determination to settle it amicably. Probably the British shift of opinion was due in part to Sumner's explosive speech.

HUMBLE PIE (?)

JONATHAN (as INTERPRETED BY MR. SUMNER). "WAAL, REVERDY! GUESS THIS LOT 'LL ABOUT DU FOR YOUR FRIEND JOHN BULL THAR."

REVERDY JOHNSON. "HA! I'VE DINED WITH HIM A GOOD DEAL LATELY, AND HE WON'T EAT *THAT*, I PROMISE YOU."

171   From a cartoon by John Tenniel in *Punch*, London, May 15, 1869

172   English Members of the Joint High Commission (Puget Sound), from *Harper's Weekly*, April 1, 1871

THE *ALABAMA* ARBITRATION TRIBUNAL

THE plan was for one member of the tribunal to be named by each of five nations, Great Britain, the United States, Italy, Switzerland and Brazil. Britain's great facilities in shipbuilding made it likely that she would be called on in future wars to do for any other belligerent what she had done for the Confederacy. Americans felt that it was to the interest of every small state to have the rights and rules of neutrality strictly defined. It was hoped, therefore, that the three small powers on the tribunal would feel a moderate interest in having the United States win its case. The very bigness of British sea power made it desirable for that power to be bound by definite rules.

173   American Members of the Joint High Commission (Puget Sound), from *Harper's Weekly*, April 1, 1871

A STILL BIGGER "CLAIMANT."

174   From a cartoon by John Tenniel in *Punch*, London, Jan. 20, 1872

"BUSTED UP!"

Mr. Bull. "HA! I THOUGHT YOU'D BURST HIM AT LAST!"
Jonathan. "WA-AL, OLD HOSS! GUESS, IT'S JIST WHAT WE MEANT TO DEW—STRAIGHT THRE-EW! LET'S LIQUOR UP."

175   From a cartoon by John Tenniel in *Punch*, London, May 11, 1872

INDIRECT DAMAGES

THE Tribunal of Arbitration met at Geneva and held a brief first session in December, 1871, directed each side to file its briefs, and adjourned until June, 1872. The announcement of the position of the United States in its brief caused great excitement in Great Britain. The Treaty of Washington had been made on the assumption that we should not urge the indirect claims; but the American statement showed that they were retained and enlarged. We demanded payment for the cost of the war after the Battle of Gettysburg, July 3, 1863. So profound was the irritation in Great Britain that the ministry hardly dared permit the arbitration to proceed. Fish effected a skillful compromise by informing the British that he would be satisfied if the tribunal merely gave a ruling on indirect damages in general to be applied to cases coming up in the future.

THE POLITICAL CAMPAIGN

GIVING up indirect damages to soothe England roused a belligerent spirit in the United States. This occurred in the midst of the Presidential campaign when Sumner was opposing Grant in favor of Greeley. Had he been disposed to play the demagogue he might have made effective use of it against the administration. But Sumner was too sincere to make foreign relations the football of politics. Fearful that Sumner might turn national pride against the President, Grant announced that no more concessions should be made to England.

176   From a cartoon *Our President Puts His Foot Down*, by Thomas Nast in *Harper's Weekly*, July 6, 1872

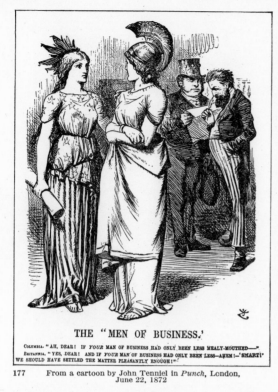

THE "MEN OF BUSINESS."

COLUMBIA. "AH, DEAR! IF *YOUR* MAN OF BUSINESS HAD ONLY BEEN LESS MEALY-MOUTHED——"
BRITANNIA. "YES, DEAR! AND IF *YOUR* MAN OF BUSINESS HAD ONLY BEEN LESS—AHEM!—'SMART!'
WE SHOULD HAVE SETTLED THE MATTER PLEASANTLY ENOUGH!"

177   From a cartoon by John Tenniel in *Punch*, London,
June 22, 1872

THE GENEVA AWARD

THE gist of the question before the court was, did Great Britain use due diligence to prevent the escape of ships like the *Alabama* out of British ports? The decision lay with the neutral arbitrators, all of whom voted for the United States. Great Britain was ordered to hand over to our Government the sum of fifteen million five hundred thousand dollars in gold to be paid to the individual claimants, August 21, 1872. At the end of two years two fifths of this sum remained unexpended, and it was not allocated until in 1882 a new court of claims was created to dispose of it. The Geneva award and the acceptance of it by the British Government was an episode of major importance. Americans had inherited from the Revolution and the War of 1812 a tendency to be hostile to Great Britain. The events which occurred during the Civil War had aroused in the American people intense emotion. To bring this to an end and to reëstablish cordial relations between the two great English-speaking peoples was indeed a victory for peaceful living. It proved to be one of the most successful cases in which international disputes were settled by arbitration in modern times.

CUBA

ANOTHER foreign complication arose over Cuba. In 1869 Grant had been induced to promise rights of belligerency to the Cuban insurgents then engaged in the Ten Years' War against Spain. Secretary Fish, knowing that the insurgents had no territorial government, was able to hold up the proclamation of recognition and to prevent its promulgation. Four years later the *Virginius*, carrying volunteers and supplies to the insurgents and flying the United States flag, was taken by Spain and a number of persons on board were executed. A great commotion occurred, and although it was not certain that the ship had a right to our flag, impetuous Americans demanded war at once. In this crisis Grant did not interfere. Fish was able to steer things safely through the period of excitement. Spain agreed to make reparation and formally salute our flag if, on investigation, the *Virginius* proved to be a United States ship. But it proved that she had no right to our flag. Sober reflection showed that we had narrowly missed entrance on a war for which we had no sound legal justification. Fish's course in this matter was generally approved despite the criticism of the jingoists and the emotional people in whom the suggestion of a free Cuba aroused enthusiasm. Twenty-five years more of Spanish misrule passed before circumstances forced us into a conflict that resulted in Cuban independence.

THE SPANISH BULL IN CUBA GONE MAD.
It must be stopped. If Spain can't do it, WE MUST!

178   From a cartoon *The Spanish Bull in Cuba Gone Mad*, by
Thomas Nast in *Harper's Weekly*, Nov. 29, 1873

179   The Santo Domingo Commission, from *Frank Leslie's Illustrated Newspaper*, Mar. 11, 1871

SANTO DOMINGO

SOON after Grant became President, he was informed that the President of the Dominican Republic would sell that nation to the United States. Grant did not detect the jobbery that was undoubtedly behind the offer but was pleased at the opportunity to acquire rich territory. He sent an agent to investigate, and suddenly laid before his Cabinet a treaty of annexation. The Cabinet, surprised at the quiet negotiations, would not accept the treaty. The matter was discussed in public, where its true nature was divined. Grant tried hard to get his treaty adopted, but in the Senate Sumner, Chairman of the Foreign Relations Committee, interposed his powerful opposition, and the project failed.

GRANT AND SUMNER QUARREL

SUMNER'S opposition to the annexation of Santo Domingo was very bitter, and he made cutting thrusts against Grant, who concluded that Sumner should be removed from the chairmanship of the Senate Committee on Foreign Relations. The Senator fought back with great vigor. For weeks this contest overshadowed all else in domestic politics. By marshaling all his influence in Congress, and with the aid of the political cliques among Congressmen, Grant prevailed. Sumner never forgot the incident and found striking ways to show his resentment.

THE LAST SHOT OF THE HONORABLE SENATOR FROM MASSACHUSETTS.—HE PULLED THE LONG BOW ONCE TOO OFTEN.

180   From a cartoon *The Last Shot of the Honorable Senator from Massachusetts*, by Thomas Nast in *Harper's Weekly*, June 22, 1872

181   Hugh McCulloch, 1808–95, from a
            photograph by Brady

THE FINANCES OF RECONSTRUCTION

ONE of the most serious problems of the time was how to restore national finances to normal soundness after the difficulties of war were past. Three main problems existed. 1. There was an enormous debt of nearly three billion dollars, created during the war at high interest rates; the obvious thing to do was to refund this debt in long-term bonds at lower interest. 2. Taxes had been raised during the war; the country looked to the government to lower them. 3. The quick demand for money in war time had been met by issuing Treasury notes or "greenbacks" (see Vol. IV) which the law made legal tender for all debts, with the result that they exchanged for gold at a fluctuating premium. There was pressing need to reduce the volume of this currency and to accumulate enough gold for the Government to be able to give specie for paper on demand. These problems were taken up by Hugh McCulloch, Secretary of the Treasury under Johnson.

REFUNDING THE DEBT

REFUNDING the debt fell into two stages. The first consisted in gathering up a large amount of floating or unfunded debt left over from war contracts, etc., paying it with short-time bonds, or out of the revenue, and through thus improving the nation's credit bringing down the rate of interest for which bonds could be issued. The second stage comprised the issue of long-term bonds at low interest to replace the high-interest bonds. The work of the first stage was successfully accomplished by Secretary McCulloch. George S. Boutwell, Secretary of the Treasury under Grant, solved the problem of the second stage. Thus the interest was lowered from six per cent to four per cent and the total amount of the war debt was reduced from three billion dollars in 1865 to two billion two hundred and five thousand dollars in 1877.

182   George S. Boutwell, 1818–1905, Secretary of
            the Treasury, 1869–79, from a photograph by
            L. C. Handy

LEGAL TENDER NOTES

THE most troublesome phase of the financial problem was the reduction of the amount of the outstanding legal-tender notes. They had been issued recklessly during the war. In all a total of some four hundred and thirty-three millions of dollars in paper money had been issued in the course of the conflict. The issue was

183   John Sherman, 1823–1900, from a
            photograph by Ritzman

due to the emergency and the Government planned to retire the notes as soon as possible. Congress in 1866 began to recall them from circulation. Soon after, there was an alarming decrease in the prices of agricultural products, due in part to general oversupply throughout the world. The American farmers attributed the falling prices largely to the contraction of the volume of paper money. So strong was their resentment that Congress in 1868 decreed that contraction should stop. McCulloch had expected to begin specie payment when the legal-tender notes were reduced to three hundred million dollars. When the act of 1868 was passed the amount outstanding was three hundred and fifty-six million dollars. John Sherman took an active part in passing the law of 1868. He believed that the expansion of business would soon be so great that three hundred and fifty-six million dollars in legal-tender notes would not be too much for the business needs of the country, and he said it was better to wait a while than to arouse the opposition of the farmers. John Sherman understood finance, but in this matter he spoke as a politician.

LET WELL ENOUGH ALONE, AND DON'T MAKE IT WORSE.

Money is *tight*, but let it recover itself naturally, and then it will stand on a *Sounder Basis.*   Stimulants or *Inflation* only bring *final collapse.*

184   From a cartoon by Thomas Nast in *Harper's Weekly*, Dec. 20, 1873

FIAT MONEY

THE dissatisfaction of the farmers now crystallized into a demand for fiat money. They wished the government to issue large amounts of paper notes without regard to specie payment. They charged that McCulloch's plans were made in the interest of the capitalists. These ideas went so far that they became a political issue in the election of 1868. This proposal to issue great quantities of currency was called inflation, but its advocates called themselves "Greenbackers," because the legal-tender notes were printed in green and were called "greenbacks."

"BLACK FRIDAY"

THE failure to resume specie payment led to a demand for gold to discharge obligations made payable specifically in that kind of money. The result was that speculators bought gold and held it to sell at a higher price when borrowers should have pressing need of it. In 1869, Jay Gould and his partner, James Fisk, Jr., had a corner in gold and put up the price with a view to making an enormous profit. They got President Grant to refuse to sell Government gold by persuading him that their plan would raise the price of wheat and thus help the farmer. The day on which Gould played his game saw many bankruptcies in New York and was called "Black Friday." The bubble burst when Grant ordered Government gold sold in the market. Grant did not share in the profits of this scheme, as he was accused of doing, but his brother-in-law was not so innocent as he, and the incident damaged the reputation of the President. It was only one of several conspicuous incidents in which Grant, through not understanding politics, was made the unconscious tool of a group of men who gathered around him to promote their own interests.

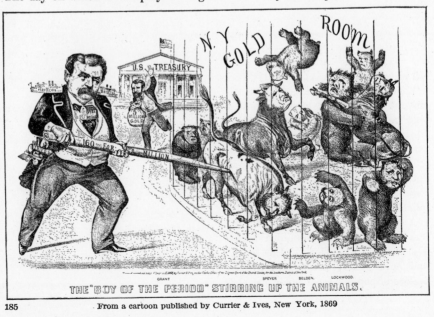

THE "BOY OF THE PERIOD" STIRRING UP THE ANIMALS.

185   From a cartoon published by Currier & Ives, New York, 1869

186   David A. Wells, 1828–98, from a photograph by W. Kurtz, New York, in the Public Library, Springfield, Mass.

TARIFF REDUCTION

An extensive form of war taxation was the tariff. The need for money to reduce the war debt led Congress to keep up the war rates for a time; but as the years passed a cry was heard for reduction, in the hope that the prices of commodities might be lowered. In reality, the protected manufacturers wished the high rates maintained, but they did not wish to confess their purpose openly lest it create opposition to protection. Acts for tariff "readjustment" were passed in 1867 and 1870. As public opinion demanded further reduction, Congress passed an act in 1872 for a general reduction of ten per cent on all rates. This method of lowering the tariff was called "horizontal reduction." Then followed the "Panic of 1873," which caused a shrinkage of the revenues, and an act was passed in 1875 by which Congress restored the ten per cent reduction of 1872. David A. Wells was the man most prominently associated with tariff reform at this time. The manufacturers were well organized and had so much political influence that the Congressmen from the manufacturing districts reflected their will. At this time the tariff was not strictly speaking a party matter; but in general the Republicans were for it and the Democrats against it.

INFLATION IN 1874

The panic of 1873 led the debtor class, strong in the West and South, to turn to inflation. The legal-tender notes had been reduced by McCulloch to three hundred and fifty-six million dollars. Richardson, who now held the office of Secretary of the Treasury, suddenly issued twenty-six million dollars on his own authority and with the approval of Grant. His action brought forth so much criticism that he dared not go on. Then Congress took a hand. A bill passed both houses to issue eighteen million dollars more, bringing the whole amount up to four hundred million dollars. The opponents were alarmed. They did not know where the process would stop. Then suddenly Grant intervened with a veto. As the inflationists could not override this veto their movement was checked. When inflation was stopped, the amount of greenbacks outstanding stood at three hundred and eighty-two million dollars. The work of McCulloch in this respect had been largely neutralized by this upflare of popular financing.

KEEPING THE MONEY WHERE IT WILL DO MOST GOOD.
Uncle Sam. "Look out, boys, they say he's a Cæsar (seiz-er)."

187   From a cartoon by Thomas Nast in *Harper's Weekly*, Oct. 11, 1873

THE RESUMPTION ACT OF 1875

DURING this period the paper money of the Government, greenbacks, was below par. The sentiment for inflation was so strong that Congress had not dared to take the steps necessary for the resumption of specie payment. Finally, in the short session of 1875, after a large number of Republicans had been defeated in the election of 1874, a law was passed authorizing the Secretary of the Treasury to resume paying out gold dollars in exchange for paper dollars on January 1, 1879. To make this possible he was to accumulate meanwhile a reserve of gold; later it was decided that this reserve must be not less than one hundred million dollars. This act, so valuable in its results, came to be called "the death-bed repentance of the Republican party," because it was passed by a Congress a large portion of which faced a political death.

188   From a cartoon *Substance and Shadow* in *Harper's Weekly*, Dec. 11, 1875

189   Peter Cooper, 1791–1883, from a photograph by Underwood & Underwood

THE GREENBACK PARTY

IN 1876, the inflationists organized what was popularly called the Greenback party and nominated Peter Cooper for President. He received no electoral vote and only eighty thousand popular votes. For the time the question of the currency was overshadowed by the need of political reform. In the Congressional elections of 1878 the Greenbackers cast a million votes, but fell to one third of that number in 1880. Peter Cooper, who led the movement in 1876, was a wealthy inventor, manufacturer, and philanthropist.

IN THE MATRIMONIAL MARKET AGAIN.
WILL MASSACHUSETTS ACCEPT THIS ENCUMBRANCE?

190   From a cartoon by Thomas Nast in *Harper's Weekly*, Oct. 26, 1878

THE RAG BABY

THE opponents of inflation dubbed it the "rag baby" in the campaign, and it was held up to scorn in a most bitter spirit. The fashion of the time was for extreme denunciation upon all political questions, and no classes of society were backward in that respect. The Nast cartoon (No. 190) refers to Butler's attempt to win the Governorship of Massachusetts as a Greenbacker with Democratic support. In 1882 he won the Governorship of that state, but with this effort Benjamin F. Butler disappears from the stage of American politics. His career typifies some of the worst aspects of the political life of the mid-nineteenth century. His political maneuvering before the Civil War secured him a general's commission though he was without military training. After the conflict his war service aided him greatly in furthering his political ends. These were unfortunately too often directed to the securing of personal profit. That he should so long be a prominent figure in national life is a significant commentary on the times.

THE BLAND–ALLISON ACT

THE Greenbackers were never very numerous and their movement ended quickly. The reason for this was the fact that the Greenbackers merged themselves with another inflationist group which emphasized silver rather than paper for the currency of the nation. More formidable were these advocates of the free and unlimited coinage of silver dollars. By an act of 1873 these coins had been dropped from the list of coins for domestic use. Since the silver advocates could not get entire inflation through irredeemable paper they were willing to have partial inflation by stamping as a dollar a piece of silver worth only eighty cents. So strong were these men in 1878 that Congress passed the Bland-Allison Act, ordering the Secretary of the Treasury to buy each month from two to four million dollars worth of silver, and coin it in silver dollars. This act was a compromise to avert an act for free and unlimited silver coinage, which was very popular in the House. The country soon realized that its effects were very unfortunate.

CAN HE?
"Now pull him over the Falls, and see if he can reach the Point again."

191   From a cartoon by Thomas Nast in *Harper's Weekly*, Feb. 23, 1878

RESUMPTION OF SPECIE PAYMENT

As the time for resumption under the act of 1875 approached, John Sherman, Secretary of the Treasury under President Hayes, made ready to meet the demands that he expected would be made on the Department. The required sum of gold was in the Treasury, and the transition to specie payment was so smooth that no one noticed any shock. The situation was helped by the fact that 1879 was a wonder year of prosperity. On account of crop failures in Europe, wheat rose to a high price, and most other commodities commanded good prices. The people had a tendency to think that this prosperity was due to resumption, although there were some who gave the credit to the Bland-Allison Act of 1878. This improvement in agricultural prices caused a recession of the discontent in the farming states and reduced materially the political unrest that had been apparent in that region.

Forty-Third Congress of the United States of America;

At the Second Session,

Begun and held at the City of Washington on Monday, the seventh day of December, one thousand eight hundred and seventy-four.

AN ACT

To provide for the resumption of specie payments.

Be it enacted by the Senate and House of Representatives of the United States of America in Congress assembled,

That the Secretary of the Treasury is hereby authorized and required, as rapidly as practicable, to cause to be coined at the mints of the United States, silver coins of the denominations of ten, twenty-five, and fifty cents, of standard value, and to issue them in redemption of an equal number and amount of fractional currency of similar denominations, or, at his discretion, he may issue such silver coins through the mints, the subtreasuries, public depositories, and post-offices of the United States; and, upon such issue, he is hereby authorized and required to redeem an equal amount of such fractional currency until the whole amount of such fractional currency outstanding shall be redeemed. Sec. 2. That so much of section three thousand five hundred and twenty-four of the Revised Statutes of the United States as provides for a charge of one-fifth of one percentum for converting standard gold bullion into coin is hereby repealed, and hereafter no charge shall be made for that service. Sec. 3. That section five thousand one hundred and seventy-seven of the Revised Statutes of the United States, limiting the aggregate amount of circulating-notes of national banking-associations, be, and is hereby repealed; and each existing banking-association may increase its circulating-notes in accordance with existing law without respect to said aggregate limit; and new banking-associations may be organized in accordance with existing law without respect to said aggregate limit; and the provisions of law for the withdrawal and redistribution of national-bank currency among the several States and Territories are hereby repealed. And whenever, and so often, as circulating-notes shall be issued to any such banking association, so increasing its capital or circulating-notes, or so newly organized as aforesaid, it shall be the duty of the Secretary of the Treasury to redeem.

192   From the original in the Department of State, Washington

GRANT IN THE HANDS OF CORRUPTIONISTS

THE separation of the Liberal Republicans from Grant threw him more emphatically into the hands of the "regulars," whose chief idea in politics was to keep satisfied a large group of men who threatened to oppose the party if their schemes were blocked. Tricking politicians practically controlled the political situation and became an offense in the eyes of good citizens. But the leaders, carried away by their success in 1872, paid no attention to the criticisms of the reformers. They felt that Grant's great popularity would shield them in anything, however bad. They defied those who insisted on political reforms and encouraged the worst kinds of corruption. Grant's original liking for good government paled as he fell under these influences. He stood by the corruptionists so firmly that it was evident that it was necessary to defeat his reëlection in order to save the political life of the country.

ALL SMOKE.

193   From a cartoon by Thomas Nast in *Harper's Weekly*, May 11, 1872

194   From a cartoon by Thomas Nast in *Harper's Weekly*, May 23, 1874

THE SANBORN CONTRACTS

IN May, 1874, a committee of the House reported the facts in the corrupt Sanborn contracts. By a law of 1872, Congress permitted the employment at a high fee of agents to collect bad debts due the Government. In this case, Sanborn, a tool of Benjamin F. Butler, had been assigned a commission of fifty per cent for collecting good debts due the Government to the amount of four hundred and thirteen thousand five hundred dollars. It was discovered that he had given a large part of his receipts to the Butler leaders in Massachusetts for party services. The public was shocked; and as Butler was one of the leaders of the group that assumed to protect and lead Grant, the incident had a serious effect on Grant's prestige.

THE "TIDAL WAVE"

IN 1873, just before the close of the session, the Congress voted to raise the salaries of its members to five thousand dollars and made the act apply to present incumbents where terms were about to expire. This "back pay steal," or "salary grab," as it was called,

caused much irritation and the effect was seen in the election of 1874. The Democrats carried the House with one hundred and sixty-eight to one hundred and eight Republican and fourteen "Liberal Republican" votes. The Republicans retained the Senate, but by a diminished majority. Among the defeated ones was Benjamin F. Butler. In this election Samuel J. Tilden, reformer and Democrat, was elected Governor of New York by a majority of fifty thousand.

195   From a cartoon *Awfully Riled*, by Joseph Keppler in *Frank Leslie's Illustrated Newspaper*, Nov. 28, 1874

THE WHISKY RING

It was generally believed that through the connivance of unfaithful officials the Government had been defrauded of a large part of the revenue that should have come from the tax on whisky. Investigation was made in 1875 by Bristow, Secretary of the Treasury, and it was shown that a ring existed in St. Louis composed of Government officials who permitted distillers, for a consideration, to escape the taxes in large amounts. This ring had made powerful friends at Washington. It was even alleged that Babcock, Grant's private secretary, was implicated. At first Grant said: "Let no guilty man escape." But after a time he cooled toward the investigation and gave a deposition of good character and integrity to Babcock, who was acquitted on technicalities, though there was evidence that he had received large sums from the ring. Grant took Babcock back as private secretary, but public opinion was too strong for this and in a short time the secretary resigned.

CALLING IN FRAUDS.
"Step up, Gentlemen. (?) Don't be Bashful!"

196   From a cartoon by Thomas Nast in *Harper's Weekly*, Nov. 20, 1875

Even then Grant's confidence in his assistant remained unshaken. The American people were amazed at this exhibition on the part of their soldier-President.

IN FOR IT.
U. S. "I hope I shall get to the bottom soon."

197   From a cartoon by Thomas Nast in *Harper's Weekly*, March 25, 1876

THE BELKNAP SCANDAL

In 1876 it was discovered that the Indian agent at Fort Sill had for several years been paying twelve thousand dollars a year to one Marsh, who had turned over half the sum to Mrs. Belknap, wife of the Secretary of War, payments after her death being made to Belknap himself. The money given to Marsh and thus divided was virtually a bribe to get Marsh to abandon an attempt to be appointed to the agency. This revelation led Belknap to resign hoping to escape impeachment, and Grant accepted the resignation "with great regret." Congress went on with the impeachment, but the Senate dismissed it because Belknap was no longer in office. Grant was severely criticized for accepting Belknap's resignation and thus permitting the guilty to escape punishment. The only plausible explanation was that the thick fog of corruption around him had blinded him to the principles of good administration.

198   From a cartoon *Blaine's Letter of Acceptance*, by F. Opper in *Puck*, July 30, 1884

THE "MULLIGAN LETTERS"

IN 1876, James G. Blaine was a candidate for the Presidential nomination. Reports were circulated of his implication in a doubtful railroad transaction, and he asked for an investigation which was granted. Then he made a clear denial of the charges, and as he was popular and magnetic there was a general disposition to believe him. However a man by the name of Mulligan, clerk for a Boston broker who had been concerned in the railroad affair, produced compromising letters written by Blaine in 1869. These letters Blaine managed to obtain. He refused to return them and read them to the House in a dramatic manner with a manipulation of emphasis which satisfied his admirers that they were innocuous. But the public was not satisfied when it saw the letters in cold type in the *Congressional Record*. They were instrumental in depriving Blaine of the Republican nomination.

GRANT AND A THIRD TERM

THE beneficiaries of corruption would have been glad to see Grant have a third term; but there was so much disgust in the country over the scandals in public life that his true friends did not wish his prestige put to the test of a campaign. They were relieved when he wrote a letter saying he would not be a candidate. Its tone was thought to indicate that he was willing to be urged to change his mind, but the country accepted the letter at its face value. He was not dishonest himself but he had an easy tolerance for corruption in others and the country demanded a President who would make reforms.

199   From a cartoon *Will the Cat do It?*, by Joseph Keppler in *Puck*, Feb. 18, 1880

CHAPTER IV

HAYES AND THE SPOILSMEN

THREE Republican Presidents sat in the White House from 1877 to 1885, Hayes, Garfield and Arthur. Hayes was a man of plain integrity and opposed to the spoilsmen, who gave him much trouble. When he withdrew the Federal garrisons from the South, thus allowing the whites there to establish the Governors they had declared elected in South Carolina and Louisiana, party extremists denounced him as a party traitor. He replied that the Government could not rule the South through military force indefinitely. The "Stalwarts" also resisted his efforts to introduce reform in the patronage. They attacked Carl Schurz, Secretary of the Interior, when he adopted civil service reform in his department, and they resisted the President when he removed Chester A. Arthur, collector of the port of New York. A majority of the Senate, led by Conkling, refused to confirm a successor to Arthur. But Hayes persisted, public opinion came to his aid, and after a fifteen-months fight Conkling was defeated.

From 1877 to 1881 the Democrats controlled one or both Houses of Congress. They used their power by trying to repeal the laws which were designed to enforce negro suffrage by giving Federal courts authority over Federal elections. By persistent filibusters they forced Hayes to consent that soldiers should not be used at the polls, but they were unable to go further. At the same time great interest was felt in the currency question. The fiat money movement of 1868 still persisted and found expression in the Greenback party, a weak but vociferous organization. Less radical inflation was demanded by many Republicans and Democrats in urging the free and unlimited coinage of silver. A bill to that effect was carried in the House in 1878 by a large majority; but it was modified by the Senate in a law providing for the purchase and coinage of not less than two and not more than four million dollars of silver each month. This law, the Bland-Allison Act, did not satisfy the silverites, but a sudden prosperity and the resumption of specie payment in 1879 removed the economic discontent which was the chief cause of the silver cry.

The "Stalwarts" failed in their efforts to nominate Grant in 1880 and the party took Garfield and Arthur for leaders. Prosperity favored them. They defeated the Democrats, who had nominated General Winfield Scott Hancock. The assassination of Garfield by a disappointed office seeker made Arthur President, September 19, 1881. Stunned by this result of the spoils system, the country turned to civil service reform, and Congress in 1883 passed the Pendleton Act, establishing a merit system in appointments.

200   President Hayes taking the oath of office, March 4, 1877, from a drawing by I. P. Pranishnikoff, after a photograph by Brady, in *Harper's Weekly*, March 24, 1877

201   Rutherford B. Hayes, 1822–93, from a photograph by Anthony & Co.,
New York

HAYES AND TILDEN

In 1876 the Republicans shrewdly shifted public opinion from the
scandals clustering around Grant's Presidency to what was called
"waving the bloody shirt" — that is, denunciation of the South
and its means of "neutralizing" the negro vote. After a hard contest the party convention nominated Rutherford B. Hayes of Ohio.
He was a "dark horse," supported by a combination of several
minor factions against Blaine, who seemed at first to be on the way
to a nomination. Blaine's bitter enemy, Roscoe Conkling, was
among those who acted at last for the success of Hayes.

TILDEN THE REFORM CANDIDATE

The Democratic candidate was Samuel J. Tilden. In 1874 he
had been elected Governor of New York as a reformer, receiving the
support of many Liberal Republicans. He made a good Governor.
Many people believed that if elected President he would establish
reforms in national politics, and overthrow the group of politicians
whose sinister influence had been responsible for the scandals under
Grant. It was also thought that a defeat at this time would be of
considerable benefit to the Republican party.

202   Samuel J. Tilden, 1814–86, from a photograph by Sarony, New York

A BITTER CAMPAIGN

THE campaign was very bitter. To turn the attention of the public from the situation at Washington the Republicans continually cited stories of brutal treatment of negroes in the South. A few outrageous occurrences there were portrayed as ordinary events, and Tilden, the reformer, was held up as facing one way in the North and another in the South. By this means the Republicans were able to hold the bulk of their voters loyal to the party. This process of "waving the bloody shirt" was in reality a phase of the dying feeling engendered by the Civil War. Politicians were quick to take advantage of this unfortunate sectional prejudice.

203   From a cartoon *S. J. T. as "Mr. Facing-Both-Ways,"* by A. B. Frost in *Harper's Weekly*, Aug. 26, 1876

204   From a cartoon *Adam's Fall*, by Thomas Nast in *Harper's Weekly*, Nov. 4, 1876

CHARLES FRANCIS ADAMS, 1807–86

CHARLES FRANCIS ADAMS, a leading Liberal Republican in 1872, supported Tilden in 1876. This brought out the denunciation of the regular Republicans. He was accused of being won over by the offer of the nomination for Governorship in Massachusetts. Adams' support was one of Tilden's most important elements of strength, and it had a powerful influence in the elections in New York and some other northern states.

A DISPUTED ELECTION — RETURNS AND CLAIMS

THE returns on election night showed that Tilden had one hundred and eighty-four undisputed votes, one less than necessary for a choice, and that Hayes had one hundred and sixty-five. The votes of Florida, Louisiana and South Carolina were for Tilden on the face of the returns, but were claimed for Hayes; and on a technicality one vote in Oregon was claimed by each side. If the Democrats got only one of the disputed votes Tilden would become President. To elect Hayes the Republicans had to have all the disputed votes. The three doubtful southern states were in Republican hands, but they had been the scenes of hard campaigning and the Democrats insisted they had carried them. The Republican officials in these states had the counting of the votes and asserted that the election returns were vitiated by fraud and crime.

"IN SELF-DEFENSE."
SOUTHERN CHIV. "Ef I hadn't-er killed you, you would her growed up to rule me."

205   From a cartoon *In Self Defense*, by A. B. Frost in *Harper's Weekly*, Oct. 28, 1876

IX—8

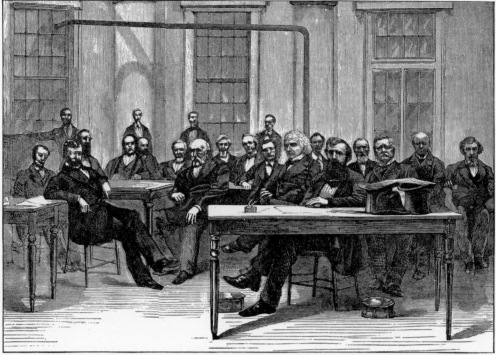

206   The Louisiana Returning Board, from an engraving after a photograph by W. W. Washburn, in *Harper's Weekly*, Dec. 16, 1876

VISITING STATESMEN

EACH of these states proceeded to count the votes by a board before whom went the returns sent in from the counties. Each party suspected fraud, and prominent northern politicans repaired to the doubtful states to watch the counting, offer aid of various kinds, and use what influence they could to have the counts favor their respective sides. These men were called "Visiting Statesmen," and dark rumors ran that they used money and promises of offices freely in order to have the counts made as they wished. Whatever the decision it was disputed, so that two sets of returns from each commonwealth went to the United States Senate, the body appointed to count the vote and declare the choice for President.

THREATS OF CIVIL WAR

THE contest was now transferred to Congress. The Republicans had a majority in the Senate, the Democrats in the House. Each side was highly excited and seemed ready to use force to have its way. Threats of armed resistance were heard, and the people became alarmed lest civil war should flare up again from the smoking embers of the past. Moderate people began to seek a way of effecting a compromise.

207   From the cartoon *A Truce — Not a Compromise, etc.*, by Thomas Nast in *Harper's Weekly*, Feb. 17, 1877

208   Mr. Ferry announcing the result of the count, from a sketch by Theodore R. Davis in
Harper's Weekly, Mar. 17, 1877

THE ELECTORAL COMMISSION

AT length Congress created the Electoral Commission, consisting of five Senators, five Representatives and five Supreme Court Justices, eight of whom, as it turned out, were Republicans and seven Democrats. The Commission was directed to pass on the conflicting returns and to say which set from each of the doubtful states, including Oregon, was to be received.

THE DECISION

EACH case was decided by a partisan vote, so that Hayes received all the disputed votes, and was declared by Congress to have been rightfully elected. The Electoral Commission reached its verdict by holding that when returns came from the actual officers of a state government they were to be taken as final, on the ground that the Federal Government had no right to "go behind the returns" and decide whether or not a state had held the election for Presidential electors in a proper way. This decision disappointed the Democrats sorely, but they submitted. For the southern wing of the party there was comfort in the announcement that the Federal Government would not interfere with the control of a state in its own affairs. This principle might be applied in a wide field of local government.

209   From the painting *The Electoral Commission in session in the Supreme Court Chamber*, by
Cornelia Adele Fassett, in the Senate Chamber, Washington

210   Inauguration of Rutherford B. Hayes, March 4, 1877, from a sketch by Theodore R. Davis in
                                        Harper's Weekly, Mar. 24, 1877

THE INAUGURATION OF HAYES

IT was Hayes' distinction that he did not have the regular politician's contempt for those who wished to improve political standards. He was fair-minded and of stubborn integrity. He took the oath of office with the intention of reforming the Government.

211   President Hayes and his Cabinet, from a photograph, 1879, by Pach, New York
      LEFT TO RIGHT: President Hayes; John Sherman, Secretary of the Treasury; Richard W. Thompson, Secretary
of the Navy; Charles Devens, Attorney-General; William M. Evarts, Secretary of State; Carl Schurz, Secretary
of the Interior; George W. McCrary, Secretary of War; David M. Key, Postmaster-General

A STRONG CABINET

THREE unusually strong men sat in Hayes' Cabinet: William M. Evarts, Secretary of State; John Sherman, Secretary of the Treasury; and Carl Schurz, Secretary of the Interior. The Postmaster-General, David M. Key, of Tennessee, had been a Confederate general and Hayes hoped that his selection would draw southerners into harmony with his party. The whole Cabinet supported his policy of conciliation and civil service reform, and Evarts, Schurz and Sherman gave him valuable aid in carrying it forward.

CARL SCHURZ, REFORMER

CARL SCHURZ, Secretary of the Interior under Hayes, was an active reformer. He checked a large amount of evil in his department, such as depredations on the public timber lands and frauds in Indian agencies. This was an important service to a defeated population who had been compelled to assume the status of wards of the nation and who had too frequently been shamelessly treated by the Government officials who were immediately in charge of them. An effort was made to checkmate Schurz by transferring the Indian Bureau to the War Department but the active opposition of Schurz himself prevented the move. In addition to his other public services he had the distinction of being one of the first public officials to call to the attention of the American people the need for the preservation of forests. He also introduced civil service reform into the management of his department, requiring competitive examinations for candidates for clerkships and permitting the removal of no one except for cause. He was denounced by the "Stalwarts," who created the opinion that he was theoretical and impractical. Hayes supported him steadily.

212 From a cartoon *Patience Until the Indian is Civilized — So to Speak*, by Thomas Nast in *Harper's Weekly*, Dec. 28, 1878

213 From a cartoon *Come Down with the Cash*, by J. A. Wales in *Puck*, July 21, 1880

THE SPOILS SYSTEM

THE state of political morality was never lower in our country than when Hayes became President, and the worst feature was the extent to which the spoils system had grown. Campaign contributions were demanded of officeholders under threat of dismissal, and of prospective applicants for offices under the expectation that appointments would be distributed among the workers for the winning side. By this means many incompetent officials had come into power and the parties tended to fall into the hands of men who cared nothing for good government. The condition of affairs in the departments and offices of the Government is almost beyond the comprehension of the man of the twentieth century accustomed to the efficiency in the management of public business which results from the merit system. The corruption and inefficiency of the 'seventies and 'eighties seem to have been necessary before the modern practice could be developed. But the spoils system, even in the second quarter of the twentieth century, has not been entirely removed from public life.

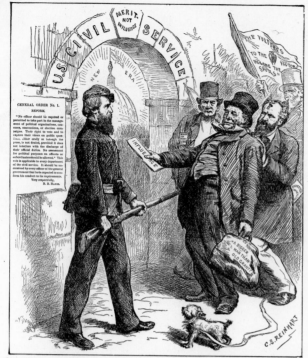

214 From a cartoon *Sentinel Hayes: "You can't come in here, Gentlemen, with that Flag!,"* by C. S. Reinhart (1844–96) in *Harper's Weekly,* Oct. 20, 1877

"STALWARTS" AND "HALF–BREEDS"

AGAINST Hayes' reforms the older leaders were in revolt. They believed him ungrateful to those who had made him President and his approaches to the moderate southerners as in the appointment of General Key, they pronounced party treason. In allusion to this feature of Hayes' policy they gave him and his followers the name "Half-Breeds"; they spoke of themselves as "Stalwarts." Roscoe A. Conkling, Senator from New York, was one of the leading Stalwarts.

216 From a cartoon *Borrowed Plumes — Mr. Jackdaw Conkling,* by Thomas Nast in *Harper's Weekly,* Dec. 20, 1879

CIVIL SERVICE REFORM

HAYES stood out for reform and in so doing had the support of his Cabinet. He issued an order forbidding officials to become partisan campaign workers, and he promised them that none should be dismissed for refusing to pay party assessments. By standing in the way of the spoilsmen he gained their bitter hatred; but he was firm and patient and received the approbation of the best citizens.

CONKLING, THE CURLED CONGRESSIONAL CÆSAR.

Though the Custom House founder in politics whirl,
He still keeps his neat back and Hyperion curl.

215 From a caricature of Conkling by J. A. Wales in *Puck,* April 30, 1879

CONKLING'S CHALLENGE TO HAYES

CONKLING, arrogant by nature, was very powerful by reason of his political ability and his position as leader in the greatest state in the Union. Resenting the order to officeholders, he encouraged the collector and the naval officer at New York to defy it. Hayes gave them due warning and when they persisted in opposition he dismissed them. Conkling tried to prevent the Senate from confirming the men the President named as their successors. At first he succeeded, but Hayes' quiet persistence at length made the country see that Conkling's opposition was factious. Senators gradually deserted him, and after fifteen months of bitter contest he stood in the minority in the Senate and Hayes had his way. Conkling's prestige was permanently lowered by this defeat.

HAYES HOPES FOR COÖPERATION IN THE SOUTH

Soon after becoming President, Hayes withdrew the garrisons from South Carolina, Louisiana, Florida and other southern states where the last vestige of Republican ascendency promptly disappeared. He hoped that he might build up a southern following which would unite with a reform element in the North, and thus establish better government. But the forces arrayed against him were more powerful than those he led.

217   From a cartoon *Saved from its Friend (?)*, by C. S. Reinhart in *Harper's Weekly*,
Oct. 20, 1877

THE END OF CARPETBAGGERY

Before he withdrew the troops from South Carolina, Hayes called Wade Hampton, Democratic claimant of the office of Governor, to Washington. It is probable that promises were exchanged with the assurance that the troops would go and Hampton be allowed to rule as Governor. Louisiana soon went through a similar process. The return of white home rule caused great joy to the South. It was the end of ten weary years of the rule of incompetents and outsiders. Carpetbaggery became a thing of the past. Those Republicans who had been in charge of the destiny of the party in that heated struggle in 1877 which ended with the final vote of the Electoral Commission declared that Hayes was surrendering unnecessarily eighteen sure electoral votes. To them he appeared to be undermining the foundation on which the party stood.

218   Demonstration of the citizens of Columbia, S. C., upon the return of Governor Hampton, from a sketch in
Frank Leslie's Illustrated Newspaper, Apr. 21, 1877

219   From a cartoon "*We Have Come to Stay*," by Thomas Nast in *Harper's Weekly*, April 19, 1879

"THE SOLID SOUTH"

THE southern people had suffered too much at the hands of Republicans to accept any party having that name, and Hayes' hopes were futile. They stood "solidly" for the Democratic party and gave it so strong a vote in Congress that it controlled the House of Representatives in 1877 and both Houses in 1879. The recovery of power by the Democrats was greeted by renewed waving of the "bloody shirt." The fears of its opponents were expressed in the phrase, "The Confederacy is in the saddle again."

SOUTHERN SELF–GOVERNMENT

ALTHOUGH Hayes failed to build up a new party, his policy had a happy effect in the South. With the carpet-bag régime buried in oblivion the people, feeling safe from outside interference, turned confidently to the task of industrial upbuilding. The white government in these states proved honest in financial affairs, but in general they repudiated the debts imposed on the states by the carpet-baggers.

220   From a cartoon The "*Strong*" *Government, 1869–1877 — The "Weak" Government, 1877–1881*, by J. A. Wales in *Puck*, May 12, 1880

A "NEW SOUTH"

NORTHERN distrust of the South and the bitter
experiences of reconstruction gave way when the
North accepted the theory, which underlay the
decision of the Electoral Commission of 1877 —
that the southern states should be supreme
within their own province. The dawn of a new
era of industry brought more harmony between
the races. It was the beginning of a "New South"
with diversified industries. There arose also a
determination to make over southern ideals on
the basis of democratic society.

POLITICAL CHARACTER OF THE
SOLID SOUTH

THE control of the House of Representatives by
the Democrats during Hayes' administration
caused the North to take notice of political conditions in the South. The map (No. 222) shows
how completely the whites had combined to overcome the negro vote. In the Forty-Fifth Congress (1877–79), to which this map refers, the
Republican districts are indicated by black areas,
the extent of Congressional districts by dotted
lines, and the numbers of the district by the
numerals in squares. In the next Congress (1879–
81) the same map will serve with the following

221   From the cartoon *The Queen of Industry, or The New South*, by
Thomas Nast in *Harper's Weekly*, Jan. 14, 1882

changes: in Maryland the sixth district is added to the Republican area; in Missouri the first, second and
third districts (St. Louis county) and the tenth district becomes Democratic, while the ninth becomes Republican; in Tennessee the first district becomes Democratic; in North Carolina the second becomes Democratic and the third Republican; and in South Carolina the entire state is Democratic. The map is based
on the votes in the dispute over Federal control of elections.

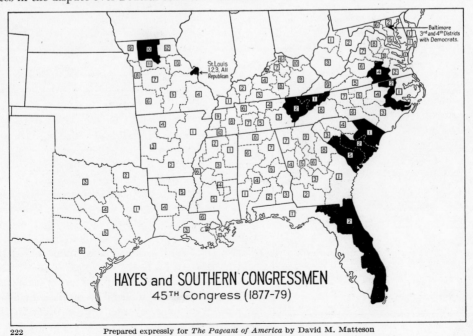

HAYES and SOUTHERN CONGRESSMEN
45TH Congress (1877-79)

222   Prepared expressly for *The Pageant of America* by David M. Matteson

223   Wade Hampton, 1818–1902, from a photograph by Brady

DEMOCRATIC GAINS, 1878

THE Democrats, in 1878, had carried each House of Congress, but they could do little against the President's veto. It was noticed that thirty members of the Senate had been connected with the Confederacy, which gave occasion for renewed appeals to the spirit of war times. The Republicans claimed that they lost their hold in Congress through Hayes' policy of giving the South up to its own control. Because he would not play the game desired by the Stalwart faction of the Republicans President Hayes was, in effect, repudiated by the very party that had put him into power. This dissension in the ranks of their opponents coupled with Democratic resentment at the outcome of the election of 1876 helped materially to bring about the victory of the Democrats in 1878.

REVIVED STRENGTH OF THE DEMOCRATS — FEDERAL TROOPS AT ELECTIONS

UNDER the leadership of Abram S. Hewitt, the Democratic House undertook to force the repeal of laws authorizing the use of Federal troops in elections. They passed a rider to the army appropriation bill making such use of troops unlawful. The Senate did not concur, and the session adjourned with no provision made for paying the army.

224   From a cartoon *Death at the Polls, and Free from Federal Interference*, by Thomas Nast in *Harper's Weekly*, Oct. 18, 1879

225   From a cartoon *The Unprotected Female*, by Thomas Nast in *Harper's Weekly*, Feb. 21, 1880

INDIFFERENCE TO THE ARMY

HAYES called an extra session at which the Democrats gave way to save the army, but they renewed their tactics in the next session; whereupon their opponents yielded and a law was passed against the use of troops in elections.

In the midst of these domestic quarrels American interests abroad began to receive new attention. There was much talk about our relative weakness among the nations and our need of a stronger army and better system of national defense. In 1880 the regular army numbered only twenty-five thousand, and it seeemed impossible to get Congress to take the situation seriously. During this period the problems of national defense were virtually ignored and the shadow of an army was kept on duty in the Indian country, for which its numbers were hardly adequate.

FEDERAL SUPERVISORS
OF ELECTIONS

THE Democrats now attacked the law permitting the appointment of Federal supervisors of elections, which had made it possible to take the elections of Congressmen and Presidential electors out of state hands. They carried bills to repeal the law but Hayes vetoed the bills and they could not overcome him. They hoped the country would rally to their support in 1880, but when that time came other forces ruled in politics.

THE DEMOCRATS AND THE
CIPHER DISPATCHES

THE Democrats believed that Tilden had been defrauded of the Presidency, and they expected to make a strong effort in his behalf in 1880 as a vindication. In order to carry out this program they said much about the fraud of 1876–77. The House ordered

226   From a cartoon *The Democrats and Their Elephant* in *Puck,* May 7, 1879

an investigation by the "Potter Committee," which reported in a partisan manner. At the same time the Republican faction in the Senate got possession of some cipher telegrams showing that an offer had been made to sell one Oregon vote to Tilden. He had refused it positively, but it seemed that his agents had considered the proposal. The incident served to take off the edge of the Democratic charges, and it made Tilden ineligible for nomination in 1880.

227   Meeting of the Potter Committee, from an illustration by W. A. Rogers in *Harper's Weekly,* June 29, 1878

PRESIDENTIAL CAMPAIGN OF 1880 — GRANT'S TRIP ABROAD

THE scandals that hung around Grant's second term were so great that his nomination for a third term was successfully prevented in 1876; but after years of Hayes' attempts at reform the Stalwarts were anxious to have Grant again. Following his retirement from the White House in 1877, Grant took a journey around the world. Full accounts of his reception abroad were supplied to the home newspapers, and his friends arranged a great welcome for him when he again reached his native soil. The political effect of this journey was great.

HAYES IGNORED BY THE POLITICIANS

ALTHOUGH Hayes had made a good President and the country had enjoyed prosperity under his leadership, nobody thought of making him President again. He was completely out of harmony with the controlling elements in his party. Conkling, who was accepted as leader of the Stalwarts, busied himself in bringing forward Grant, and several other aspirants for the honor were brought forward by their respective friends. Hayes had announced that he would not be a candidate to succeed himself.

229   From a cartoon *The Cinderella of the Republican Party and Her Haughty Sisters,* by Joseph Keppler in *Puck,* Oct. 13, 1880

STAMPEDING FOR GRANT

THE first suggestion of Grant as Republican candidate found a vast support. The glory of his military career and the organized praises of the Stalwarts seemed to carry everything before them. Conkling was jubilant.

230 From a cartoon *The Worship of the Golden Calf*, by Joseph Keppler in *Puck*, April 21, 1880

231 From a cartoon *The Modern Wandering Jew*, by Joseph Keppler in *Puck*, May 19, 1880

"A THIRD TERM"

THE prospect of the return of the Stalwarts under Grant's careless eyes alarmed those who loved reform. It was not sufficient to oppose Grant on the ground of his record in 1873–77, so an appeal was made to the traditional opposition to a third term. This was used with marked effect.

THE COURSE OF BLAINE

JAMES G. BLAINE, of Maine, described by his friends as "the magnetic statesman," was a strong opponent of Conkling. He knew that if Grant became President, Conkling would be the distributor of patronage and this made him an opponent of Grant. When the nominating convention met he had a considerable following, but not enough to get the nomination.

232 From a cartoon *The "Magnetic" Blaine; or, a very heavy "Load"-stone for the Republican Party to carry*, by Thomas Nast in *Harper's Weekly*, May 8, 1880

233   James A. Garfield, from a photograph by Sarony, New York

JAMES A. GARFIELD, 1831–81

IN order to keep the convention from going to Grant, Blaine effected a combination of the reformers with his own followers and some others and obtained the nomination of James A. Garfield. Conkling's defeat made him furious, for he believed it had been brought about by his personal enemies. It was feared by the Republican leaders that he would be unwilling to help carry New York for Garfield. To propitiate him his close friend, Chester A. Arthur, victim of Hayes' reforms, was named to run with Garfield. Arthur, however, was not a man whom any Republican in the convention would care to see President. Nevertheless he made a good President when, by the tragic death of Garfield, he was elevated to that post. Garfield's nomination had resulted from a veritable stampede on the thirty-sixth ballot.

FREE SILVER AND THE PARTIES

HAYES was opposed to free silver and his party had supported him, on the whole; some Republicans, however, notably William McKinley, were silver men. In the Democratic party were many influential men who stood for the free coinage of silver. This element gathered around Senator Allen G. Thurman, of Ohio, and tried to make him the candidate for President in 1880.

234   From a cartoon *Out of the Financial Graveyard*, by Thomas Nast in *Harper's Weekly*, Sept. 27, 1879

235   From a cartoon *Democratic Platform.   The Financial Teachings of the Democratic Leaders.   Isn't It a Little Mixed?*
by Joseph Keppler in *Puck*, Sept. 4, 1878

THE DEMOCRATS AND THE CURRENCY

THOUGH the Democrats on the whole were more favorable to inflation policies than the Republicans, a strong portion of the party stood for "sound money." As the election of 1880 approached, the money question began to be pushed into the background, partly because the Bland-Allison Act of 1878 had satisfied the more conservative friends of silver, and partly because the prosperity of 1879 had turned the minds of most people to other things. Thurman, the most prominent champion of inflation, was cast into the shade as other issues came to the front.

NOMINATION OF GENERAL WINFIELD S. HANCOCK

WITH the reform issue and the currency issue discredited, the Democratic leaders had much ado to find grounds on which to conduct a promising campaign. At last they nominated General Hancock, a prominent soldier in the Civil War, a lifelong Democrat and a man of handsome personal appearance. It was believed that he would be a popular candidate, but he had never been associated with any of the political issues of the day.

236   Winfield Scott Hancock, 1824–86, from a photograph by R. A. Lewis, New York

237   From a cartoon *The Democrats Finding their Moses*, by Joseph Keppler in *Puck*, Aug. 18, 1880

HANCOCK A POPULAR CANDIDATE

THE conservative Democrats were greatly encouraged by the nomination of Hancock. They looked upon him as the prophet who would lead them out of the wilderness of inflation and southern irregularities to a sound-money basis, with a distinctly national policy.

238   From a cartoon *Just the Difference,* by Joseph Keppler in *Puck*, July 28, 1880

PERPLEXITIES OF THE CAMPAIGN

THE record of the Democrats was a handicap to Hancock, and it taxed his efforts to carry it. On the other hand, Garfield, who had been charged with a part in the Crédit Mobilier episode, was a source of anxiety to his party managers, and Arthur, who had been removed from the New York collectorship because he had refused to carry out Hayes' civil service rules, was unpopular with the reformers. Garfield tried to overcome this feeling by renewing his avowal for civil service reform.

CONKLING'S DISAFFECTION

CONKLING'S wrath over his defeat in the nominating convention endured well into the campaign, so that the New York vote began to be doubtful. Urged to make some speeches in that state, he unwillingly complied, but the coolness with which he spoke of the candidate alarmed the Republican managers.

HANCOCK AND THE TARIFF

HANCOCK was not experienced in political campaigning. His unblemished personal record, military accomplishments, and fine appearance drew favorable comment, although Republican sarcasm described him as "a good man weighing two hundred and forty pounds." This was a campaign between generals in which Garfield, who owed his commis-

239   From a cartoon *Asking too Much*, by J. A. Wales in *Puck*, Sept. 8, 1880

sion to his political prominence, had a great advantage over his opponent from the regular army. Hancock made a blunder on the tariff question which cost him dearly. When his views were demanded he undertook to push the inquiry aside by saying: "The tariff question is a local question." The remark was taken to show how little he knew of politics.

240   From a cartoon *The Republican Delilah stealthily deprives the Democratic Samson of his strength*, by Joseph Keppler in
Puck, Nov. 10, 1880

241 From a cartoon *Positively Last Awakening of the Democratic Rip Van Winkle — "Don't leave me here for another twenty years!"* by Joseph Keppler in *Puck*, Oct. 27, 1880

THE DEFEAT OF THE DEMOCRATS

The result of the election was the defeat of the Democrats by an electoral vote of one hundred and fifty-five for Hancock to two hundred and fourteen for Garfield, and by a popular vote of four million four hundred and fifty-four thousand four hundred and sixteen to four million four hundred and forty-four thousand nine hundred and fifty-two. For twenty years fate had been against the Democrats. Most of the time they had followed a policy of expediency, trying to get into power by taking advantage of the errors of the Republicans.

GARFIELD'S SHORT PRESIDENCY — GARFIELD AND BLAINE

At Garfield's inauguration Blaine appeared as a prominent personage. He became Secretary of State in the new cabinet and the horde of office seekers in Washington turned their eyes to him as the man most influential with the President. During a brief term of two hundred days, Garfield, although he had declared for civil service reform, removed eighty-nine officials, which was fifteen more than Hayes removed in four years.

242 Inauguration of President Garfield, March 4. 1881, from a photograph by Clinedinst, Washington

GARFIELD AND CONKLING

THE rising fortunes of Blaine caused Conkling to writhe in anger. He felt that his enemy was using his position at the side of the President to break the Conkling influence. At last Garfield dealt a hard blow when he appointed as collector at New York, Robertson, a strong opponent of Conkling, to replace Merritt, Conkling's friend. Conkling naturally took the act as a thrust at his political prestige, and when he saw that the Senate would accept the nomination he resigned, thinking the New York legislature would send him back to the National Senate. His colleague Platt followed his action; but the legislature disappointed both of them and sent other men to Washington. Thus ended Conkling's political career.

GARFIELD ASSASSINATED

WHILE the fight with Conkling was at white heat, Garfield was shot by a disappointed office seeker, who was one of Conkling's followers. The assassin, Charles J. Guiteau, cried out that he was a Stalwart and that Arthur would now be President.

243   From a cartoon *New York and Her Spoiled Sons*, by Thomas Nast in *Harper's Weekly*, June 11, 1881

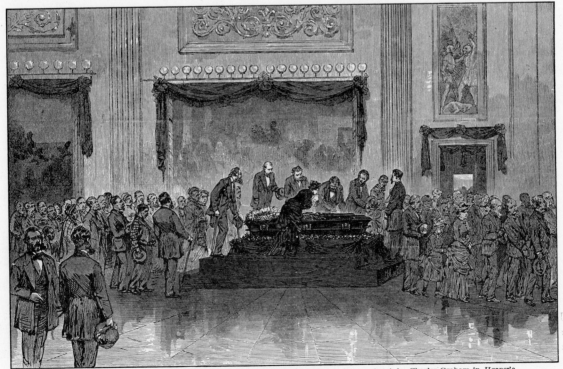

244   Garfield lying in state in the rotunda of the National Capitol, Washington, from a sketch by Charles Graham in *Harper's Weekly*, Oct. 1, 1881

245   The Night-Watch before the Executive Mansion, from a drawing by T. de Thulstrup after a sketch
by W. A. Rogers in *Harper's Weekly*, July 8, 1881

GARFIELD'S PATIENT SUFFERING

FROM July 2 to September 19 the wounded President lay between life and death, the whole country watching his fight in sympathetic awe. At last he succumbed. His administration had begun in wrangling, but its tragic termination softened the hearts of the people and put them into a frame of mind for gentler things.

246   Chester Alan Arthur, 1830–86, from a photograph

GOOD GOVERNMENT UNDER ARTHUR

BEFORE he became President, Arthur was a typical partisan of the Conkling group, a friend of the spoilsman and an opponent of reform. Called to the Presidency by the tragedy of July, 1881, he seemed to pass through a transformation and stood out as another kind of man. He took up the reins of office quietly, he managed them with fairness, and he went through the period of his power to the general satisfaction even of the reformers.

Second. And, among other things said rules shall provide and declare, as nearly as the conditions of good administration will warrant, as follows:

First, for open competitive examinations for testing the fitness of applicants for the public service now classified or to be classified hereunder. Such examinations shall be practical in their character, and so far as may be shall relate to those matters which will fairly test the relative capacity and fitness of the persons examined to discharge the duties of the service into which they seek to be appointed.

Second, that all the offices, places, and employments so arranged or to be arranged in classes shall be filled by selections according to grade from among those graded highest as the results of such competitive examinations.

Third, appointments to the public service aforesaid in the departments at Washington shall be apportioned among the several States and Territories and the District of Columbia upon the basis of population as ascertained at the last preceding census. Every application for an examination shall contain, among other things, a statement, under oath, setting forth his or her actual bona fide residence at the time of making the application, as well as how long he or she has been a resident of such place.

Fourth, that there shall be a period of probation before any absolute appointment or employment aforesaid.

Fifth, that no person in the public service is for that reason under any obligation to contribute to any political fund, or to render any political service, and that he will not be removed or otherwise prejudiced for refusing to do so.

Sixth, that no person in said service has any right to use his official authority or influence to coerce the political action of any person or body.

Seventh, there shall be non-competitive examinations in all proper cases before the commission, when competent persons do not compete, after notice has been given of the existence of the vacancy, under such rules as may be prescribed by the commissioners as to the manner of giving notice.

Eighth, that notice shall be given in writing by the appointing power to said commission of the persons selected for appointment or employment from among those who have been examined, of the place of residence of such persons, of the rejection of any such persons after probation, of transfers, resignations, and removals, and of the date thereof, and a record of the same shall be kept by said commission. And any necessary exceptions from said eight fundamental provisions of the rules shall be set forth in connection with such rules, and the reasons therefor shall be stated in the annual reports of the commission.

247   Facsimile of a page from the Pendleton Civil Service Act, original in the Department of State, Washington

THE PENDLETON CIVIL SERVICE ACT OF 1883

THE death of a President by the act of a disappointed office seeker called popular attention to the evil effects of the spoils system. Suddenly it became possible to pass a bill for reform. The Pendleton Act provided for competitive examinations, a Civil Service Commission to supervise the execution of the law, and the elimination of partisan appointments in what was known as the "classified service." As passed, the law applied to clerks in the departments in Washington, and in the larger custom houses and post offices. The President was given the power to enlarge the number within this "classified service." In 1883 the number was thirteen thousand nine hundred and twenty-four, or about one eleventh of the whole civil service of the nation.

248   From a cartoon *The Democrats after waiting for twenty years to clean out the Republican "Augean Stables,"*
see themselves fenced out, by F. Opper in *Puck,* Aug. 15, 1883

EXECUTING THE CIVIL SERVICE ACT

ALTHOUGH Pendleton was a Democrat, the Pendleton Act had the support of more Republicans than Democrats. By making it impossible to remove officials without cause, the persons then in office, chiefly Republicans, would be protected if the party lost the next election. As the Democrats carried the Congressional

elections of 1882, they had hopes of winning in 1884 and made many threats against the Pendleton Act. In this situation Arthur stood steadily by the act. During his administration, he upheld the Civil Service Commission and placed nearly two thousand employees under the protection of the rules.

CHINESE EXCLUSION ACT

IT was left for Arthur to adjust a violent controversy over the admission of Chinese labor. The Burlingame Treaty, 1868, granted the Chinese free right of entrance to the United States and in 1882 the Pacific coast contained one hundred and thirty-two thousand of them. As they underbid white labor and could not become assimilated in the population, a great outcry arose against their further admission. Hayes vetoed a bill to prohibit their entrance, but got China to accept a treaty by which Congress could suspend but not permanently prohibit immigration from China. Under this agreement Congress passed in 1882 a law suspending immigration for ten years, and in 1892 it was renewed for ten years more. In 1902 it was made indefinitely continuous.

249   From a cartoon *Chinese Immigrants at the San Francisco Custom House,* by
P. Frenzeny in *Harper's Weekly,* Feb. 3, 1877

CHAPTER V

POLITICAL AND ECONOMIC REFORM
UNDER CLEVELAND

ALTHOUGH Cleveland was a Democrat and was strong in the faith of the old Democratic party, he was elected by a combination of his own party and a large number of Republicans who believed in reform. Without the aid of these liberals he could not have been President. They were bent on rescuing politics from the cynical regulars and in overthrowing, to some extent, the predominance of the high protectionists, who, under cover of paying the national debt, desired to continue indefinitely the high tariff that had been imposed in war time.

Cleveland was true at heart to the pledges he had made for civil service reform, but his own party was not of the same opinion. Kept out of public offices for years, they did not relish a policy which left their opponents in office. "Turn the rascals out!" became their watchword. Against their demands Cleveland held back as far as he dared, incurring thereby a vast deal of dislike from professional politicians. In general, he did not remove clerks within the "classified service." But he did not observe the principles of reform with respect to the offices not thus protected. Here he aroused the wrath of some of the reformers, who held that he should keep not only the letter but the spirit of the civil service law of 1883. A calm review of his course, taking into consideration the conditions before him, shows that he met the situation as well as could have been expected of him.

At the time, the tariff had not become a strictly party question. The Democrats were traditionally against protection as such, but they were strong in some of the manufacturing states, such as Pennsylvania and New Jersey, and their Representatives and Senators from such states were unwilling to vote for low tariffs. When, therefore, the subject came before Congress it was impossible to hold the party together for reduction. The Republicans were in control in general in the manufacturing states, but they were also strong in the agricultural states of the West, where the sentiment was not in favor of protection. To hold these states in line for protection was a difficult matter. At this time the fires of sectional bitterness had not gone out and each party made them minister to its ends, the Democrats by keeping the South "solid" and the Republicans by "waving the bloody shirt" as occasion offered. Such were some of the oddities of party rivalry!

The triumph of the Democrats in 1884 had the effect of raising that party out of the stage of mere opportunism in which it had been since 1865. Cleveland's rugged character gave it a positive policy, in which, however, were the seeds of its own defeat. The opportunists who preceded him did not support his ideas. They voted for him in the election because he was their only hope of victory, but when he was in office they discovered that he "was not a Democrat" and they did not accept his leadership. They wanted to follow a man who believed in rewarding his supporters with public offices, and they denounced a President who tried to enforce the Civil Service law as then applying. Had Cleveland run on such a platform he could not have been elected. The success of the party also had an important effect on the South. It gave that section the feeling that it was again a constituent part of the nation which went far to obliterate the feeling of helplessness that the bitter experiences of reconstruction had imposed upon it.

250   The Republican Convention at Chicago in 1884, from a drawing by Schell and Graham in *Harper's Weekly*, June 14, 1884

BLAINE NOMINATED BY THE REPUBLICANS

JAMES G. BLAINE was now the most popular man in his party at least with the regular politicians. It is true that he had incurred the opposition of the reformers by his connection with several shady transactions and by ill-disguised contempt for those who preached better politics, but in 1884 he was master of his party. Blaine carried the convention with him on the third ballot, and John A. Logan was named for Vice-President.

BLAINE'S WEAKNESS AS A CANDIDATE

BLAINE'S association with the scandal of the Little Rock Railroad bonds, his alleged profits in certain guano concessions of Chile, his friendship with the lobbyists of Washington, and his scoffing attempts to capture public opinion despite the weight of adverse evidence by means of his histrionic ability, were things that could not be forgotten. They gave rise to the term, "the tattooed man." Gillam's famous cartoon is one of the bitterest and most effective of its day. The "Mulligan Letters" of 1869 were spread before the people

and their incriminating character alienated hundreds of voters who stood for decent government. All these characteristics were brought out with great emphasis in the campaign, so that Blaine was made to appear a dangerous leader. The reform element, largely associated with the old Liberal Republican movement, was for the most part led to support Cleveland. Although Cleveland was the leading Democratic reformer, he was not as well known nationally as Blaine.

PHRYNE BEFORE THE CHICAGO TRIBUNAL
ARDENT ADVOCATE—"Now, Gentlemen, don't make any mistake in your decision! Here's Purity and Magnetism for you—can't be beat!"

251   From a cartoon *Phryne before the Chicago Tribunal*, by Bernard Gillam in *Puck*, June 4, 1884

252   Stephen Grover Cleveland, from the portrait, 1871, by Eastman Johnson, in the City Hall, New York, courtesy of
the Art Commission of the City of New York

GROVER CLEVELAND, 1837–1908

CLEVELAND'S solid character was the basis of his popularity.   It brought him to the front in Buffalo, where he
was successively sheriff and mayor.   He had been elected Governor of New York in 1882 by the large majority of almost one hundred and ninety-three thousand.   This success placed him in the list of Presidential possibilities.   He had the support of the reformers, and after the Republicans had taken Blaine, whom the reformers
distrusted, it was logical for the Democrats to nominate Cleveland.   Cleveland did not bow to the dictation
of the professional politician.   In office he was fearless, independent and outspoken.   His supporters saw in him
a man capable of humbling the party machine and of making it subservient to the public interest.   And at the
time of Cleveland's nomination for the Presidency the party machine was in considerable disfavor.   This advantage tended to counterbalance the weakness under which the Democratic party had struggled since the Civil War.

From a cartoon "A Unit," by F. Opper in *Puck*, June 25, 1884

THE MUGWUMP MOVEMENT

SOME of the reformers who opposed Blaine's nomination accepted him with reluctance. They thought that a bolt would imperil the future chances of their cause which they believed to be tied up with their own party. Others disregarded the future and announced a revolt. In New York and Boston, important meetings were held and all reformers were urged to support Cleveland. Thus was launched what came to be known as "the Mugwump Movement," from the use of the ancient Algonquin term *mugquomp*, a chief, applied to the independents in a *Tribune* editorial. It was led by a small group of intellectuals, but their earnestness gave it weight out of proportion to its numbers. The Mugwumps threw their votes to Cleveland in defiance of the tradition of party regularity which in this period still exercised a powerful influence in American political life. The "regulars" in both parties treated them as a group of impractical politicians, but the Mugwumps held stoutly to their purpose.

"RUM, ROMANISM AND REBELLION."

Religion, Without Regard to Sect, Rises in Indignation.

PROTESTANTS, HEBREWS AND CATHOLICS.

Sharp Denunciation of the Blaine Ecclesiastical Ovation.

The HERALD has received numerous communications denouncing as indecorous and injudicious the remarks made by Rev. Dr. Burchard at the Blaine ecclesiastical reception on Wednesday. They come alike from laymen and from clergymen, from Roman Catholics, Protestants and Hebrews. They agree in characterizing Dr. Burchard's definition of the democratic party—as a party devoted to "rum, Romanism and rebellion"—as an insult to a whole religion, and an outrageous attack upon thousands of patriots. "Probably no other expression during this entire campaign," said one

eminent republican clergyman yesterday to a HERALD reporter, "will have carried with it the important results which will follow this one; it will withdraw many thousand votes from Mr. Blaine and give them to Mr. Cleveland." With a view to obtaining the prevailing opinion among leading divines and religious teachers of all sects the HERALD has interviewed the following well known gentlemen:—

Vicar General Keegan, of Brooklyn, said that he had read the remarks made by Mr. Burchard, but did not know whether to believe he had made use of them. In a heated discussion like this many things were published that were not true. His attention was called to the fact that the speech had been reported in a republican paper, which would not be at all likely to publish an untruth about its Presidential candidate.

"Well, all that I care to say," added Vicar General Keegan, "is that, if the clergyman said anything like that, he must be an idiot. No one but an idiot would say such a thing. It was an extraordinary speech to make to Mr. Blaine, who had just returned from a visit to relatives in a Catholic institution and whose mother was a Catholic."

HE SHOOK HIS HEAD.

The Rev. Alford A. Butler, rector of Epiphany Church, smiled and shook his head when asked what he thought of the Rev. Dr. Burchard's allusion to 'rum, Romanism and rebellion.'

"I don't care to criticise anybody else," he said, but his manner showed that he had a very decided opinion on the subject.

"Do you approve of bringing a religious issue

into politics?" asked the reporter.

Mr. Butler shook his head again. "I am in a new field which requires all my attention," he replied, as if he did not like the job of laboring with the Rev. Dr. Burchard. Then he added, very emphatically, "Although I don't care to criticise anybody else, I don't mind saying that it is a remark which I would not make myself. I don't mind saying that much."

"What do you think of the propriety of a preacher endeavoring to assist a political cause by trying to excite one denomination against another?" a reporter asked the Rev. George F. Nelson, assistant rector of Grace Church.

"I have an opinion on that subject," Mr. Nelson replied, "and personally I have no objection to expressing it. In the absence of the rector of this church I would give it to the public without hesitation. But as the rector is here you will understand that it would be improper for me to express any opinion. All expressions of opinion should, of course, come from the rector."

"Do you approve of the cry of 'Romanism, rum and rebellion?'" asked the reporter.

"I do not see what connection there is between 'Romanism' and 'rum and rebellion,'" said Mr. Nelson. "Protestants and Catholics were found on both sides during the civil war, and that is also true of 'rum.'"

"They are alliterative."

"Yes, that may be it—the three R's."

"THAT OUTRAGEOUS SENTENCE."

"Yes, I read that outrageous sentence in Dr. Burchard's speech, in the papers," said the Rev. Arthur J. Donnelly, of St. Michael's Church, "and until I saw that its authenticity was not denied I supposed it was made out of whole cloth and gotten up for effect. I can hardly believe that a minister of the holy Gospel could say such a thing in his sober senses.

"But let them talk of 'rum, Romanism and rebellion' if they want to. It will have very little effect, except to strengthen the regard for Mr.

From the *New York Herald*, Nov. 1, 1884

"RUM, ROMANISM, AND REBELLION"

A FAMOUS incident in this campaign was the use of the expression above by Dr. Samuel D. Burchard, a Protestant clergyman, in expressing to Blaine the congratulations of a group of ministers at the Fifth Avenue Hotel in New York. The candidate failed to take notice of these words and his opponents assailed him for accepting by his silence what they called an insult to the Roman Catholic church. Since the vote proved to be very close in New York, which was the decisive state, it has been argued that Dr. Burchard's incautious remark was responsible for Blaine's defeat. There was no little irony in the situation; for the Republicans had staged this reception by the divines with great care in order to counteract the attacks upon Blaine's character. The meeting reacted on the Republicans in a way that they neither desired nor expected.

255   From a cartoon "*He can't beat his own record*," by Joseph Keppler in *Puck* July 30, 1884

CAUSE OF BLAINE'S DEFEAT

THE real cause of Blaine's failure was his record. He had lived in a time when most public men tolerated any deeds by their associates short of actually taking money out of the Treasury, and he had yielded to the influences around him. In 1884 the reformers represented a new spirit in public life and Blaine was its victim. A man of great personal ability, though unfortified with heroic integrity, he ran too close to the line dividing good from bad and was never able to undo the errors of his early life. But for all this, we must not forget that he was a man of great power in public affairs and an orator of no mean ability.

256   Thomas F. Bayard, 1828–98, from a photograph

THE "NEW DEMOCRATIC" PARTY

AT the time one heard much about a "new" Democratic party; and Cleveland's Cabinet appointments showed that he believed in its existence. He allotted three places to the South and filled them with prominent members of the Senate — Thomas F. Bayard, of Delaware, Secretary of State; Lucius Q. C. Lamar, of Mississippi, Secretary of the Interior; and Augustus H. Garland, of Arkansas, Attorney-General. The others — Daniel Manning, of New York, Secretary of the Treasury;

257   Thomas A. Hendricks, 1819–85, elected Vice-President in 1884, from a photograph

William C. Endicott, of Massachusetts, Secretary of War; William C. Whitney, of New York, Secretary of the Navy, and William F. Vilas, of Wisconsin, Postmaster-General — were new men in national politics. In choosing them a group of mid-western men were ignored, who felt that they had a right to consideration.

258   From a cartoon *No Welcome for the Little Stranger*, by Zimmerman in *Puck*, Oct. 21, 1885

CLEVELAND AND THE PATRONAGE

THE first indication that he would stand by civil service reform brought the President trouble in his own party. He was besought to turn the offices over to the Democratic spoilsmen but refused steadily. Heavy denunciations were his reward. Republicans as well as Democrats united in making his course hard, and a number of influential Democratic newspapers lost no opportunity of criticizing him. Cleveland yielded, however, somewhat to the demands of Democrats for the public offices from which their party members had been excluded since 1862. In the first ten months of his administration he removed some six hundred

and fifty-three officeholders and replaced them with Democrats. But these appointments had to be confirmed by the Senate and that body was still in the control of the Republicans. Near the end of the first year of Cleveland's term the Senate had confirmed only fifteen of Cleveland's appointees. But then the Senators gave way and let the Democrats have the offices.

INTERNAL WEAKNESS OF THE DEMOCRATS

THE Democrats depended on New York and in New York they depended on Tammany, whose leader, John Kelly, was determined to have his power recognized. He feared reform, lest it be turned against his own practices. He opposed the nomination of Cleveland, and the campaign was fairly under way before he agreed to support the nominee. His alliance with the reformers was welcomed as a means of lessening the influence of Tammany and of bringing about the adoption of a higher standard within the party. Though Tammany was recovering from the debaucheries of Tweed and his friends, it was still in a distressful state of political morals.

259   John Kelly, 1822–86, from an engraving after a photograph, in
Harper's Weekly, June 12, 1886

THE CIVIL SERVICE COMMISSIONERS

THE ordinary function of the Commission was to hold examinations, make out the list of persons who passed, and see that they received justice when appointments were made. But its most important task at this time was to watch for infringements of the act by division and bureau chiefs, and to take steps to correct such action. The greatest vigilance was necessary to render the act effective. Cleveland gave his general support to the Commission, composed on the whole of able and fearless men without political bias.

THE APPEAL TO THE PEOPLE

IN these circumstances it was necessary to build up support through organized public opinion. To that end, the reformers throughout the country coöperated in the National Civil Service Reform League, of which George William Curtis was the leading spirit. This organization held meetings, published information, and in other ways counteracted the

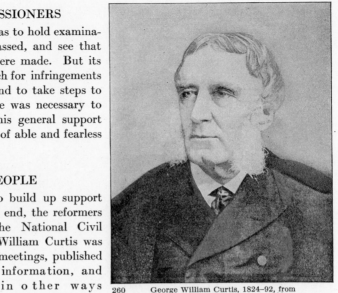

260   George William Curtis, 1824–92, from
Harper's Weekly, Sept. 10, 1892

work of the foes of reform. Its services were very important. Former President Hayes, with Theodore Roosevelt and W. D. Foulke, were also very active in support of the League, but its chief source of strength was the interest and courage with which its efforts were supported by a great mass of good citizens.

261   Dorman B. Eaton, Civil Service Commissioner, from a photograph reproduced in *Dorman B. Eaton*, New York, 1900

CIVIL SERVICE EXAMINATIONS

THE examinations were ridiculed on the ground that the questions asked were of a general character and had no relation to the work the employees were to perform. The reply was: (*a*) they were a test of education and intelligence, and (*b*) they furnished an infinitely better basis of appointment than party service, which was the alternative. Scoffers also asserted that the officials used favoritism in arranging the ranking of successful candidates. A few such cases may have occurred, but they were not typical. In general, the examinations worked well and the quality of the service was improved.

262   The beginning of civil service in New York, from a drawing in *Frank Leslie's Illustrated Newspaper*, May 10, 1879

263   The Australian ballot system in Boston, from a drawing by C. Upham in *Frank Leslie's Illustrated Newspaper*, Nov. 23, 1889

To vote for a Person, mark a Cross X in the Square at the right of the name.

GOVERNOR.	· · · ·	Vote for ONE.
JOHN BLACKMER—of Springfield	Prohibition	
JOHN Q. A. BRACKETT—of Arlington	Republican	X
WILLIAM E. RUSSELL—of Cambridge	Democratic	

LIEUTENANT-GOVERNOR,	· · · ·	Vote for ONE.
JOHN W. CORCORAN—of Clinton	Democratic	
WILLIAM H. HAILE—of Springfield	Republican	X
BENJAMIN F. STURTEVANT—of Boston	Prohibition	

264   A Ballot, from a drawing by C. Upham in *Frank Leslie's Illustrated Newspaper*, Nov. 23, 1889

BALLOT REFORM

THE progress of civil service reform stimulated the efforts of those who wished to introduce the secret ballot. Under the old system of voting in public employers could exercise pressure on their employees, and party managers could intimidate certain kinds of voters. Ballot reform depended on the action of state legislatures. Beginning with Massachusetts in 1889, state after state reformed its election laws. The secret ballot proved a severe blow to vote-purchasing, and it worked the destruction of the "black list" by which large sections of voters had been terrorized. One of its results, however, was to increase the cost of holding elections. When party managers found old methods would no longer work they turned to vote-buying, which promoted larger campaign funds.

A CHANGE IN POLITICS

THE advent of a Democratic administration showed that the country was no longer willing to entrust the Republican party with power merely on the strength of its war service; and this fact made it necessary for the party to assume a new attitude. Thenceforth its pleas for confidence tended to be based on existing conditions; its direction fell increasingly into the hands of a group of young men who took up practical issues and fought them out aggressively. Economic interest became the central appeal around which voters were to be rallied. This process was aided by the gradual disappearance of the old leaders through their death.

265   From a cartoon *The Four Rips; or Twenty Years Behind the Age*, by Bernard Gillam in *Puck*, Sept. 16, 1885

HERBERT SPENCER'S VIEWS

HIS IMPRESSIONS OF AMERICA

HIS EXPECTATIONS FAR SURPASSED—RESULTS OF FIRST IMPRESSIONS—SUCCESS OF REPUBLICAN INSTITUTIONS—TWO AMERICAN TRAITS—A BRILLIANT OUTLOOK.

Herbert Spencer recently returned to this city in a somewhat improved condition of health. When asked whether what he had seen in this country equalled his expectations, he replied:

"It has far exceeded them. Such books about America as I had looked into, had given me no adequate idea of the immense developments of material civilization which I have everywhere found. The extent, wealth, and magnificence of your cities, and especially the splendor of New-York, have altogether astonished me. Though I have not visited the wonder of the West, Chicago, yet some of your minor modern places, such as Cleveland, have sufficiently amazed me, by the marvellous results of one generation's activity. Occasionally, when I have been in places of some ten thousand inhabitants, where the telephone is in general use, I have felt somewhat ashamed of our own unenterprising towns; many of which, of fifty thousand inhabitants and more, make no use of it. From my first impressions I may say that, though free institutions have been partly the cause of these things, I think they have not been the chief cause. In the first place, the American people have come into possession of an unparalleled fortune—the mineral wealth and the vast tracts of virgin soil producing abundantly with small cost of culture. Then they have profited by inheriting all the arts, appliances, methods, developed by older societies, while leaving behind the obstructions existing in them. They have been

able to pick and choose from the products of all past experience; appropriating the good and rejecting the bad. Then, besides these favors of fortune, there are factors proper to themselves. I perceive in American faces generally a great amount of determination—a kind of 'do or die' expression; and this trait of character, joined with a power of work exceeding that of any other people, of course produces an unparalleled rapidity of progress. Once more, there is the inventiveness, which, stimulated by the need for economizing labor, has been so wisely fostered. Among us, in England, there are many foolish people who, while thinking that a man who toils with his hands has an equitable claim to the product and, if he has special skill, may rightly have the advantage of it, also hold that if a man toils with his brain, perhaps for years, and, uniting genius with perseverance, evolves some valuable invention, the public may rightly claim the benefit. The Americans have been more far-seeing. The enormous museum of patents which I saw at Washington, is significant of the attention paid to inventors' claims; and the Nation profits immensely from having, in this direction (though not in all others), recognized property in mental products. Beyond question, in respect of mechanical appliances, the Americans are ahead of all Nations. If, along with your material progress, there went equal progress of a higher kind, there would remain nothing to be wished.

"It is true that those who rule you do not do it by means of retainers armed with swords; but they do it through regiments of men armed with voting-papers, who obey the word of command as loyally as did the dependants of the old feudal nobles, and who thus enable their leaders to override the general will and make the community submit to their exactions as effectually as their prototypes of old. It is doubtless true that each of your citizens votes for the candidate he chooses for this or that office, from President downward, but his hand is guided by a power behind, which leaves him

scarcely any choice. 'Use your political power as we tell you, or else throw it away,' is the alternative offered to the citizen. The political machinery as it is now worked has little resemblance to that contemplated at the outset of your political life. Manifestly, those who framed your constitution never dreamed that twenty thousand citizens would go to the polls led by a 'boss.' America exemplifies, at the other end of the social scale, a change analogous to that which has taken place under sundry despotisms. It seems to me that the 'sovereign people' is fast becoming a puppet which moves and speaks as wire-pullers determine."

REPUBLICAN INSTITUTIONS NOT A FAILURE.

"Then you think that Republican institutions are a failure?"

"By no means! I imply no such conclusion. Thirty years ago, when often discussing politics with an English friend and defending republican institutions, as I always have done and do still, and when he urged against me the ill working of such institutions over here, I habitually replied that the Americans got their form of government by a happy accident, not by normal progress, and that they would have to go back before they could go forward. What has since happened seems to me to have justified that view, and what I see now confirms me in it. America is showing on a larger scale than ever before that 'paper constitutions' will not work as they are intended to work. The truth that 'constitutions are not made, but grow,' which is part of the larger truth that societies throughout their whole organizations are not made but grow, at once, when accepted, disposes of the notion that you can work as you hope an artificially devised system of government. It becomes an inference that if your political structure has been manufactured, and not grown, it will forthwith begin to grow into something different from that intended—something in harmony with the natures of citizens and the condition under which the society exists. And it evidently has been so with you. Within the forms of your Constitution there has grown up this organization of professional politicians, altogether uncontemplated at the outset, which has become in large measure the ruling power."

266   From *The New York Times*, Oct. 20, 1882

A FOREIGNER'S OPINION OF OUR POLITICS

IN 1882, Herbert Spencer made a brief visit to the United States. He shunned newspaper reporters but was at last prevailed upon to give his view of America. The candor with which it was uttered took away the breath of many complacent people. The electorate, he said, was "fast becoming a puppet which moves and speaks as wire-pullers determine." He struck at the American hope that education will cure evils due in reality to the decay of public character. The worst menace, he thought, was the "easy-going readiness" to endure small wrongs rather than take the trouble to combat them.

NATIONAL SYMPATHY FOR GENERAL GRANT

WHEN in 1880 ex-President Grant allowed himself to be brought out for a third term he lost much of the affection felt for him by a large part of the people. No one doubted his honesty and kindness of heart, but it was impossible to deny that he had a low sense of political morals. In May, 1884, he was reduced to poverty by the failure of the firm of Grant & Ward, in which he was a partner. With characteristic honesty he gave up his property to his creditors and stood before the world penniless but clean. His predicament brought forth an outburst of popular sorrow, and in 1885 Congress restored him to the active rank of general in the army with the regular salary attached. The unhappy political events of Grant's administrations had |in no way clouded the affections |of the people for Grant personally. In contemplating his misfortunes they thought no more of his political errors.

267   From a cartoon *Just Before the Curtain Went Down*, in *Harper's Weekly*, Mar. 14, 1885

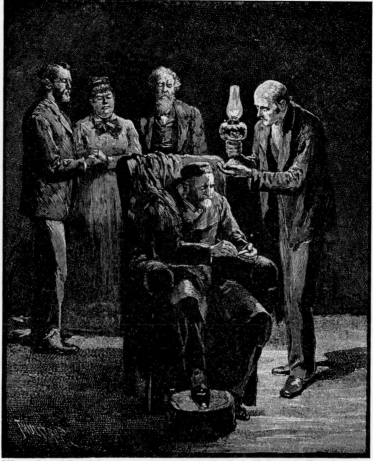

268   General Grant's last message, from a drawing by T. de Thulstrup in *Harper's Weekly*, Aug. 1, 1885

GRANT'S LAST MESSAGE TO THE NATION

In the early days of his financial troubles Grant began to write his *Personal Memoirs* dealing for the most part with his military activities. To this task he gave himself with great diligence, striving to complete it before he died so that its sale might yield enough money to support his family. The last page was written three weeks before the end of his life, and contained expressions of his gratification that former Confederate soldiers should have joined with Union men in attesting their esteem and respect. The removal of the faithful leader of the northern armies from the political scene was another evidence of how fast the days of disunion were passing into remote history, and a reminder that new problems were to be met and solved. They arose from the advent of a new day, in which self-government was to be a vital issue.

269   Grant's Tomb, Riverside Drive, New York, from a photograph

GRANT'S ILLNESS

In the summer of 1884, Grant began to have pains in the throat and the examination of experts showed that he was suffering from a malignant cancer of the tongue, supposed to have been brought on by excessive smoking. All through the winter and spring he fought the disease but without hope of cure. With the approach of summer he was moved from his home in New York to a house on the top of Mount McGregor, near Saratoga, and here he died on July 23, 1885.

THE RAILROAD BUILDERS AND THE POWER

THE two decades following the Civil War covered a period of rapid railroad building, especially in the interior. (See Vol. IV.) Lines beginning at the seacoast were extended into the grain-growing areas of the West. Chicago was the usual objective, and the result was several competing lines from that great shipping center to deep water. To get business these roads did many unfair things. They gave low rates to large shippers, low rates for long hauls, and the small shippers had to pay enough to make up any deficiency due to this kind of competition. Along these roads settled a flock of small business enterprises, usually owned privately by officers of the roads, which got special rates for shipping and were able to take business away from their local rivals. A favorite thing was for such enterprises to control the grain elevators and to become purchasers of grain at such prices as they agreed to give. In many ways the people of the interior believed themselves in bondage to the railroads.

270 Thomas A. Scott, 1824–81, who extended the Pennsylvania Railroad System into the West, from a photograph by L. C. Handy

271 Thomas M. Cooley, 1824–98, from a photograph in possession of the Library of the University of Michigan

THE INTERSTATE COMMERCE COMMISSION

THE conduct of the railroads was resented by the people living along their lines and led to state laws to restrain them, popularly known as "Granger laws." The roads tested them in the courts. In an important decision, the Wabash Case, 1886, it was held that a state law fixing charges on interstate shipments was unconstitutional. The opponents of the railroads turned to the national Government, with the result that Congress passed in 1887 an act creating the Interstate Commerce Commission, sometimes called the Federal Railroad Commission. It contained five members, Judge Thomas M. Cooley of Michigan being the chairman.

PROVISIONS OF THE ACT OF 1887

THIS Act prohibited discriminations and made pools illegal. It forbade long and short hauls, and required the roads to file their rates with the Commission. It did not give the Commission power to fix rates but permitted it to investigate the conduct of the roads, publish the results, and impose fines for actual violations of the Act. The carrier was allowed to appeal from the Commission to the courts. In executing the law the Commission encountered many difficulties. The roads found various means of evasion, and the courts showed a willingness to reverse the rulings of the Commission. Through years of confusion the Commission kept at its difficult task while public opinion slowly rallied to its support.

272 From a cartoon Uncle Sam's "Wild West" (East and South) Show — The Interstate Commissioners Moving on the Animals, by W. A. Rogers in Harper's Weekly, April 9, 1887

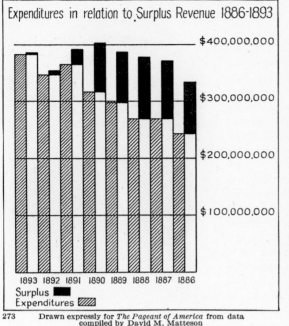

Expenditures in relation to Surplus Revenue 1886-1893

$400,000,000

$300,000,000

$200,000,000

$100,000,000

1893 1892 1891 1890 1889 1888 1887 1886
Surplus ■
Expenditures ▨

273   Drawn expressly for *The Pageant of America* from data
compiled by David M. Matteson

SURPLUS FINANCIERING

THE tariff was so high that the revenues greatly exceeded the expenditures; during the eleven years from 1880 to 1891 the average annual surplus was one hundred and three million nine hundred thousand dollars. It was unwise to keep this money out of circulation and part of it was used to buy up national bonds in the open market, thus producing a rapid reduction of the national debt. The presence of so much money in the Treasury was a temptation to extravagance, and many bills were brought into Congress which the public considered corrupt efforts to divert public money into private hands. Although some of these proposals were good, the general effect of the surplus was to promote jobbery. The surplus had unmistakably a demoralizing effect upon American public life. The obvious way to solve the problem was tax reduction. But the most important taxes to be reduced were those of the tariff. The surplus, therefore, brought into politics this question which had proved annoying before and now vexed professional politicians in the Democratic party.

THE SURPLUS AND TARIFF REDUCTION

IN spite of the professional politicians there were many people who thought that the best way to deal with the surplus was to lower the tariff. This idea spread rapidly and found a strong response among the Democrats, most of whom were traditionally against protection. In 1882, they carried the House of Representatives by a large majority. Even before that their opponents had begun to make concessions. The first step, taken in anticipation of the election, was to create the tariff commission of 1882 with authority to recommend changes in the rates. In the short session after the election the protectionists passed the tariff of 1883, making slight reductions. By this means they hoped to take off the edge of the demand for lower rates. The tariff of 1883 was, in reality, a back fire. Its sponsors sensed the growing animosity to the great business corporations that were deriving large profits from the protective rates. They were unwilling, however, to yield any material part of the benefits derived from the high tariff. Their move was a purely political one, but it found much support in those parts of the country in which there were few protected industries. The South and the agricultural portions of the North and West were naturally opposed to paying high prices for commodities to benefit the manufacturers.

274   From a cartoon *Division of Labor*, by C. J. Taylor in *Puck*, Feb. 1, 1888

CLEVELAND AND THE TARIFF

THE tariff act of 1883 satisfied few people and the Democrats undertook to carry through the House a lower tariff measure. The bill, named after Morrison, chairman of the Ways and Means Committee, placed certain articles on the free list and made a twenty per cent reduction on all other rates, on the principle that a horizontal reduction is approximately fair to all interests and can be adopted without pernicious lobbying. The bill was killed in the House by Randall, of Pennsylvania, who with forty other Democrats joined the Republicans for that purpose. Randall was bitterly denounced by most of his party, but this had no effect upon him. He showed his spirit by making a tour through the country in behalf of protection. After Randall's bolt for protection the Democrats became discouraged over the tariff, and they refused to take up the matter when called to it by Morrison in 1886. This situation appealed to Cleveland, who was earnestly in favor of reduction. In his annual message of 1886 he sent forth a clear call for action, but his words made no impression on the Randall group. His reply was to devote the entire message of

275   William R. Morrison, 1825–1909, after a photograph by Pach Brothers, New York

1887 to the tariff issue, thus forcing the party to consider the matter. He had rescued tariff reform from the lumber room where Randall had thrown it, but to carry it through Congress was another thing.

In the controversy over the tariff, Cleveland and his supporters were called "free traders," but the charge was undeserved. No doubt, many reformers believed in free trade; but most of the leaders of the movement demanded nothing more than the reduction as far as possible without their ceasing to be protective. Free trade was made a bogey to frighten the working people. The protectionist had been relying on the argument that high rates must be retained to pay the war debt; but that argument could no longer be used and he turned to the working people, with the argument that local business depended on guarding the home market against foreign competition. In their enthusiasm the Democrats claimed too much. They argued as though tariff reduction would injure no business and produce immediate prosperity. Such a result was not to be expected in the well-rooted industries that had grown up under Government protection. It was well worth arguing that reduction would lead to better conditions eventually, but it was going too far to say that the immediate shock of readjustment would be negligible. In fact, to reduce the profits of manufacturers would cause distress to those manufacturers who were making the least profit and loss of income to those making good returns. To disturb a large portion of the country's capital and labor would produce suffering, and the persons most affected would be likely to ask for speedy restoration of the discarded tariffs.

276   From a cartoon *The Free Trade Bugaboo*, by C. J. Taylor in *Puck*, May 5, 1886

277   From a cartoon *The Old Hose Won't Work*, by Bernard Gillam in *Puck*, Feb. 13, 1884

TARIFF REFORM REPLACES THE "BLOODY SHIRT"

THE Republicans had now come to a turning point in their history. Their older leaders wished to go on, as previously, denouncing the Democrats for sympathy with secession and opposition to reconstruction. One of their weaknesses in the election of 1884 was the attempt of these "elder statesmen" to continue the old tradition. It was now plain that this policy was outworn. About 1886 a group of new men began to be influential in party council; it was made up of such men as Thomas B. Reed of Maine, William McKinley, Jr., of Ohio, and Theodore Roosevelt of New York. Taking the places of the old men, who were dropping off yearly, they accepted the challenge of the Democrats and made the tariff the leading issue.

THE MILLS BILL, 1888

THE result was another tariff reform bill, taking its name from Roger Q. Mills, of Texas, the new chairman of the Ways and Means Committee. It proposed a general though slight reduction of rates; and although Randall opposed it, the President's influence was enough to rob him of his followers, so that the bill passed the House with only four Democrats voting "nay." It had no chance in the Republican Senate. It committed the Democrats to the tariff as the issue of the Presidential campaign of 1888 and on that issue the two parties were sharply and clearly ranged. The President was able to get the bill through the House only by using patronage without stint. The Mills Bill was primarily a campaign document. It clarified the issue for the voters and had the effect of committing the Democratic party to a policy of material reduction of the tariff. Many Democratic leaders, however, who did not have Cleveland's faith in tariff reform, looked forward to the coming Presidential election with grave misgivings.

278   Roger Q. Mills, 1832–1911, from a drawing by
Paul Renouard in *Harper's Weekly*, May 19, 1888

GROWTH OF CIVIL WAR PENSIONS

PENSIONS for disabilities on account of service in the army were granted liberally by Congress during or just after the war. In 1878, when twenty-seven million dollars were paid out in pensions it seemed that the annual expenditure for this purpose had reached its highest point and would soon begin to recede. This prospect was bad for the pension agents, whose prosperity depended upon getting pensions for new claimants. To improve their business they raised

279   From a cartoon *After the Mexican War Veterans are Pensioned*, by F. Opper in *Puck*, Jan. 7, 1885

a demand for arrears of pensions and the cry was quickly taken up by politicians who had become noted for their friendliness toward the old-soldier vote. The result was the passage of the arrears act of 1879, which in two years added thirty million dollars to the annual pension payment. Now followed a concerted movement to carry pensions still farther. While the sum paid for arrears mounted ever higher, the custom spread of passing private acts in Congress to gratify claims that had been disallowed by the Pension Office. A great deal of fraud was believed to lie behind such acts. Cleveland investigated them patiently and vetoed two hundred and twenty-eight of them, only one of which was passed over his disapproval. "The frauds about which Cleveland and the reformers complained were of almost every conceivable kind. Pension attorneys connived at fraud, and often participated in it. The charges brought against them ranged from the collection of illegal fees to the falsification of certificates, perjury, and forgery. The special pension acts varied. Some 'corrected' the records of veterans, to the extent of expunging charges of desertion, and giving deserters honorable discharges. Some laws were passed creating military records for men who had never served in the army, so that they might draw pensions. Then there were numerous cases on record where one man was drawing a number of pensions, in one case as many as nineteen. Medical examiners approved applications of men who were thoroughly sound. Sometimes, for reasons never explained, physicians approved pension petitions on the ground that the applicant had a 'normal heart,' or 'normal liver'; in one case, on account of a 'protuberant abdomen.'" — RALPH HARLOW, *The Growth of the United States*, pp. 635–36.

280   From a cartoon *Bidding for His Vote*, by Joseph Keppler in *Puck*, April 25, 1888

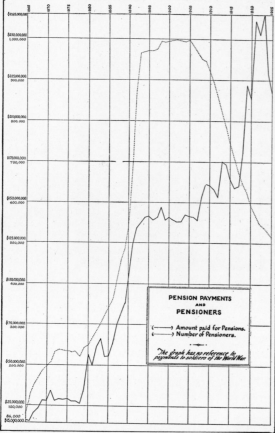

281   Drawn expressly for *The Pageant of America* from data compiled by David M. Matteson

LATER PENSION LEGISLATION

MEMBERS of each party were unwilling to offend the soldier vote, led by the voracious pension agents, and it was left to the President to save the Treasury from the despoilers. In 1887 a bill passed Congress to pension all old soldiers and widows of old soldiers who were dependent upon other people, regardless of the source of their disability. Cleveland vetoed the bill and it failed to pass over his veto. In the same year the President accepted an invitation to address the G.A.R. at its national encampment in St. Louis. Learning that the feeling against him was so intense that he was likely to be insulted Cleveland cancelled the engagement. His motive was not to avoid personal humiliation but to protect the dignity of the office of President of the United States. No man more courageous than Cleveland ever held that high office. When the Republicans returned to power in 1889, one of their first acts was to pass the Dependent Pension Law of 1889, which in twelve years raised the expenditures for pensions from fifty million dollars to one hundred and sixty million dollars and the number of pensioners from two hundred thousand to more than six hundred thousand. The war with Spain increased the pension roll, and under Roosevelt it was provided that all old soldiers should be considered disabled when they reached a specified age and thus entitled to pensions, varying with the age attained.

DEMOCRATIC NOMINATION, 1888

As the time for the Presidential election of 1888 approached, a split appeared in the Democratic party. Those who had opposed Cleveland's liberal policies gathered around Governor David B. Hill of New York, whom they announced as a supporter of "Jacksonian principles," meaning, in fact, that he was a consistent believer in the spoils system. At this time Tammany Hall had become dissatisfied with the reform policy of the administration, and Hill hoped that its influence would be strong enough to turn the state's delegation against the President in the nominating convention. He had the support of Senator Arthur P. Gorman of Maryland, and a number of other "practical" leaders to whom reform meant only the vaporings of men who had no real party loyalty. He summed up his position in the words, "I am a Democrat."

Simple David went a-fishing.   And all the water he had got
For to catch a whale;   Was in a leaky pail.

282   From a cartoon by F. Opper in *Puck*, Mar. 9, 1887

283   Renomination of Cleveland at the St. Louis Convention, 1888, from sketches by Charles Graham
and Paul E. Harney in *Harper's Weekly*, June 16, 1888

NOMINATION OF CLEVELAND

THE Hill faction did not appreciate the strength of Cleveland with the rank and file of the party. The only Democratic President since the beginning of the Civil War, he was also a man of sincerity and honesty. A supreme illustration of these traits was given by his action in making the tariff the only subject of his annual message of 1887. That message fixed the main issue of the coming election, and on that issue it was folly to nominate anyone but the man who had raised the tariff flag. The convention met at St. Louis and re-nominated Cleveland without opposition. The Hill-Gorman faction accepted their defeat and bided their time. They were one day to embarrass profoundly the man whom they so thoroughly disliked.

284   From a cartoon *The Persistent Suitor*, by F. Opper in *Puck*, Oct. 26, 1887

BLAINE AND THE REPUBLICANS

WHILE the Republicans had several candidates for the nomination not one of them showed enough strength to make it probable that he could carry off the prize. With the party at large Blaine was undoubtedly the most popular man. His narrow defeat in 1884 seemed to indicate that he could win in 1888 when the protected interests would be strongly united in support of the Republicans. But his own attitude seemed to make it impossible to nominate him. His health was bad and his spirit had been worn down in resistance to the charges of corruption, which were sure to spring up again if he appeared once more as a candidate for the Presidency. He said nothing to indicate his position and the party was left in a state of uncertainty, which was a source of annoyance to the other candidates, who thought that if he were out of the way they could make headway with their own schemes. His hold on the party arose from his popularity with a large portion of the Republicans and from the fact that to reject him would seem to sanction the charges against his moral character.

285 Benjamin Harrison, 1833-1901, from a photograph
by Clark, Indianapolis

NOMINATION OF BENJAMIN HARRISON

WHEN the Republican convention met Blaine was in Europe. In spite of two early assertions that he would not allow his name to be used his friends were still enthusiastic for his nomination by a unanimous vote and did not give up hope until, a month before the convention met, he declared explicitly that his decision was final. When the convention met nine candidates were placed in nomination, but in several ballots the convention failed to make a choice and there was prospect of a deadlock. Thinking that the presentation of his name would sweep the convention unanimously, his friends again appealed to be allowed to bring him forward. Again he refused but suggested that Benjamin Harrison of Indiana should be the nominee. His popularity was shown in the prompt nomination of Harrison, who was a good lawyer but without large political experience.

ELECTION OF HARRISON

THE campaign was fought on the issue of the tariff. Up to that time the Republicans had talked chiefly about matters connected with sectionalism or about the currency. Cleveland's steady support of sound money left no opportunity for attack on that score, and the public was tired of "waving the bloody shirt." Harrison had the advantage of being unconnected with the older politics, and he was not touched by any of the scandals attributed to several of the older leaders. At the same time he gained strength from the party through having been suggested by Blaine. Cleveland suffered from the coolness of the Hill faction and through the dissatisfaction of some extreme reformers due to his trying to take a moderate position between the spoilsmen in his own party and the reform extremists, he lost votes on each hand. Harrison won the election by two hundred and thirty-three electoral votes to Cleveland's one hundred and sixty-eight, although he had a slightly smaller popular vote.

286 Levi P. Morton, 1824-1920, Vice-President of the United
States, 1889-93, from a photograph by Bogardus, New York

Hill said: "I am a Democrat still — very still."

287 Democratic office seekers haunting the White House during the first year of President
Cleveland's term, from an illustration in *Frank Leslie's Illustrated Newspaper*, Mar. 9, 1889

CHAPTER VI

NEW POLITICS UNDER HARRISON

THE passing of the old type political leader and the arrival of new men on the stage coincided with the Presidency of a quiet, cool, unaggressive and lawyerlike man from the Middle West. Harrison was a Senator before he was President and had the confidence of his Senatorial colleagues as a safe man who had no theories. It was not expected that he would try to shape the policies of the Government, as Cleveland had done, but only that he would maintain the position of Chief Executive strictly, leaving Congress to decide what laws should be passed without Presidential suggestion or incitement. This conviction had something to do with his nomination, giving him a respectable following before the receipt of Blaine's deciding cablegram. During his administration he gave Congress no trouble at all. He was also a strictly party man, not too good to reward his supporters, if he could do it within the law, and yet not so bad as to violate the civil service law in a case that was plain. A popular witticism of the day represented him as preserving his equanimity by reading no newspaper but the *New York Daily Tribune*.

In general, political issues shift gradually, one passing into another, and a new phase growing up as an old one disappears. But the policies of our reconstruction days were so rigidly defined and roused the people to such degrees of feeling that they persisted longer than most issues do. They dominated the scene long after the more liberal-minded element of the Republican party was willing to abandon them. The prolongation of these issues tended to keep in office men who believed in them. Thus it happened that the party continued to struggle for its sectional issues until 1884. The success of Cleveland in that year was notice that the country wanted a change, and in the following four years a great deal of party reorganization took place. Although several leaders of the old type offered themselves for the nomination in 1888, such as John Sherman, Joseph B. Foraker, and William B. Allison, they were set aside and a man chosen who had been in national politics but a short time. New problems came with a new man.

The new issues were economic. From its organization in 1856, the Republican party had for the most part contended for ends political in nature, such as the exclusion of slavery from new territories, the preservation of the Union, the reconstruction of the South, and the enforcement of negro suffrage. The chief issue of 1888 was the protection of manufacturers, and along with it went a flock of smaller pleas for public aid to industries. This turn of affairs brought business men into active participation in politics. Now and then a great millionaire got himself elected to the Senate, with the result that the scoffers began to speak of that body as a "millionaires' club." For the most part, business men were content to send to Congress men who could be trusted to protect business. Henceforth "the business interest" became a strong influence in nominating conventions of all ranks and took effective control over newspapers. A new kind of sectionalism then appeared, the opposition between the industrial areas and the agricultural areas. With these changes went a wide extension of the use of money in political campaigns. When business went into politics it was called upon to support the work of those who followed the policies it thought wise. What one party did the other must do so far as it could. The result was that campaign expenses became enormous. There was danger that money would be the deciding factor in political life.

288   President Harrison and his Cabinet, from a drawing by Bernard Gillam in *Judge*, March 9, 1889
LEFT TO RIGHT, *Seated:* William H. H. Miller, Attorney-General; President Harrison; John Wanamaker, Postmaster-General; James G. Blaine, Secretary of State. *Standing:* John W. Noble, Secretary of
the Interior; William Windom, Secretary of the Treasury; Jeremiah M. Rusk, Secretary of Agriculture;
Redfield Proctor, Secretary of War; Benjamin F. Tracy, Secretary of the Navy

HARRISON'S INAUGURATION

HARRISON'S inaugural address gave pleasure to most people. He promised to enforce the civil service law but added that honorable party service did not disqualify one for office. He announced a firm friendship for protection and said that some way could be found for reducing the surplus without lowering the tariff. The cabinet, with one exception, was made up of men of only moderate ability. Among them was John Wanamaker, a rich merchant of Philadelphia, who had never before appeared in public life and of whom rumor said that he had given four hundred thousand dollars to the Republican campaign fund during the canvass of 1888. The appointment was much criticized.

290   From a cartoon *He Has Arrived In Washington*, by Joseph Keppler in *Puck*,
Jan. 16, 1889

289   John Wanamaker, 1838–1922, from a
photograph by Gutekunst, Philadelphia

HARRISON AND BLAINE

THE one exception was Blaine, who became Secretary of State. His eminence in the party and his share in the nomination of Harrison warranted his appointment. His natural tendency to dominate and the conceded weakness of the other Cabinet members led to the belief that he would control the President; and as Blaine was considered a "jingo" in his foreign policy a general feeling existed that the diplomatic attitude of the nation during the new administration was likely to be aggressive and blustering. In general, these predictions were not fulfilled. Blaine did not dominate the administration, and in his own department "jingoism" was not notably apparent.

291   From a cartoon "*The Minority Be D——d!*," by Louis Dalrymple in *Puck*, Feb. 4, 1890

292   Thomas B. Reed, 1839–1902, from a photograph by Parker, Washington

"CZAR" REED

FOR the first time in eight years, the Republicans controlled the House, though their majority was small. It was in the power of the Democrats to hamper legislation by refusing to vote on roll calls and thus prevent a quorum. The practice had long been a recognized method of obstruction and had been used again and again by the Republicans when they were in the minority in the House. The Democrats were, therefore, quite unprepared when the new Republican speaker, Thomas B. Reed, ordered the clerk to count as present those whom he could see with his own eyes even though they had refused to respond to the roll call. A fiery altercation ensued as to whether the recalcitrant Democratic members were or were not "present." But Reed remained firm and parried the Democratic assaults upon him with humorous sallies. The public, usually hostile to obstructive tactics in Congress, applauded the speaker. But the positive action won for its author the title of "Czar" Reed.

ATTACK OF THE SPOILSMEN

ALTHOUGH Harrison had promised to enforce civil service reform, he was no sooner in power than he was beset by troops of office seekers. They surrounded the Capitol, sought out their particular Representatives and Senators, and demanded rewards for services in the preceding campaign. Congressmen neither dared nor wished to oppose them. Harrison's promise to respect the law of 1883 was construed as not applying to offices outside the classified service.

293   Office seekers at the Capitol, Washington, from a drawing by W. T. Smedley in *Harper's Weekly*, March 14, 1891

294　From a cartoon *Unconditional Surrender*, by Louis Dalrymple in *Puck*, April 17, 1889

PLATT AND THE NEW YORK PATRONAGE

THOMAS C. PLATT had succeeded Conkling as head of the New York machine, wielding the authority it gave him with despotic thoroughness. No local leader dared resist his will on pain of losing standing in the party. Platt insisted that he should dictate the appointments in his state, and Harrison was afraid to refuse him. Garfield had appointed Pearson, a sincere Republican, postmaster in New York city. Cleveland had reappointed him. But Platt wanted the position for one of his henchmen. The President gave way and Pearson was dropped at the expiration of his term. Harrison's action brought down upon him the criticism of the civil service reformers, but it gratified the men who believed in preserving party organization.

ROOSEVELT AS CIVIL SERVICE COMMISSIONER

HARRISON appointed to the Civil Service Commission Theodore Roosevelt of New York, a vigorous young reformer who believed in sticking by the party organization. Roosevelt's friends, realizing the opposition of the politicians to reform, urged him to decline the offer, but he replied that he would take the place and make it worth holding. In watching the efforts of Congressmen to undermine the law and in attempting to thwart them, he performed useful service to the public. At the same time he attracted a certain amount of attention as a frank opponent of bad government, and in doing so he laid the foundation of that popularity which later made him one of the most conspicuous leaders in our history. Harrison supported the Commission, and, while he made a very large number of partisan appointments, he tried to select honest men, often doing it against the protest and craft of bad advisers. Before he went out of office he placed a large number of his appointees within the classified service, most of them after he had been defeated in 1892. This course, imitated by many of his successors, had the solid advantage of extending the area of operation of reform.

295　　From a cartoon *The Brave Little Giant-Killer*, by Louis Dalrymple in *Puck*, July 10, 1889

MATTHEW S. QUAY, 1833–1904

WHAT Platt was in New York, Matthew S. Quay was in Pennsylvania. For many years before Harrison's inauguration he
was the ruler of the Republican party in his state. He was
resourceful, vigilant and loyal to his party, but his political
standards were low. He headed the machine and sustained it
in its cynical indifference to good government. Under him
state politics became as bad as in any part of the Union. Quay
had been chairman of the Republican national committee in
1888, and Harrison's election was largely due to his skillful
management. He did not sympathize with the President's
efforts to carry out reforms and was opposed to his renomination
in 1892. Quay was popularly considered a typical boss, and an
exponent of machine government.

HARRISON AND HIS RELATIVES

PRESIDENT HARRISON, following the example of Grant, appointed to office a large number of his kindred and also relatives
by marriage, which caused his opponents to accuse him of
"nepotism." The fact that he did this and thought it proper
shows to what extent men of the day had come to think that

296   Matthew S. Quay, from a drawing after a photograph

appointments constituted a means by which a politician had the right to discharge debts of gratitude or grant
favors, provided that in doing so the public was not actually defrauded of money. Harrison doubtless thought
his relatives would serve the public no less faithfully for being connected with him by family ties. The same
principle cropped out in the custom of Congressmen and other officials who obtained offices for many of their
kindred. The public condemned the practice and it served to increase Harrison's unpopularity. In spite of
the work of the Civil Service Commission Harrison's administration is marked by an extensive application
of the spoils system. J. S. Clarkson of Iowa, First Assistant Postmaster-General, removed some thirty
thousand officials in a single year before he himself fell from power. He won the title of "headsman." His
activities are typical of the attitude of the professional politician of this period.

297   From a cartoon "*Public Office is a 'Family Snap'*," by C. J. Taylor in *Puck*, June 5, 1889

298   James Tanner, 1844–1927, from a photograph

"CORPORAL TANNER"

HARRISON appointed James Tanner a Commissioner of Pensions, thus giving him authority in the granting and increasing of pensions. "Corporal Tanner," as he was called, was an old soldier who had lost both legs in battle. Possessed of a witty and jovial disposition, he was popular at Grand Army meetings where he was usually in attendance, and always busy in behalf of Government aid to Union veterans. He seems to have been sincere in the belief that "nothing was too good for an old soldier." His appointment as Pension Commissioner was the result of pressure on the President from the Grand Army of the Republic which looked forward with pleasure to a more liberal pension policy on the part of the Government.

That was a curious ceremony at which Secretary of the Navy TRACY assisted in Brooklyn on Saturday evening in honor of "Corp." TANNER. TANNER's official place is not one of such intrinsic importance that a member of the Cabinet should feel called upon to pay tribute to him, but it was in his political capacity that he received the honor of the Secretary's recognition, and that is considerable. The "Corporal" is just now the representative of Republican policy in two directions—that of increasing the soldier vote and that of decreasing the amount of money in the Treasury. His means are very simple, and are embodied in the President's advice to "treat the boys liberally." But surely this is a policy of which Judge TRACY, who is a lawyer of eminence and man of essential good sense, when he chooses to indulge it, can hardly approve, tempting as it is politically. He must know that "liberality" in construing the pension laws merely opens the doors of the Treasury to men who have not a sound claim, for the laws are very generous in themselves, and it is not honoring real veterans, but the reverse, to class unfounded claims with theirs. And he must know, also, that every dollar paid from the Treasury comes from the taxpayers' pockets, and that the Government is under the strictest obligation to spend the taxpayers' money not only honestly but carefully. Secretary TRACY seems to be easily the leader of the present Cabinet in ability and character, but he cannot retain his reputation for pre-eminence by consorting with the Tanners of his party.

299   Editorial from the *New York Times*, April 5, 1889, criticizing Secretary Tracy for honoring Tanner by his presence at a Tanner meeting

TANNER'S GENEROSITY

AT this time the General Disability Pension Act of 1890 had not been passed, and the Commissioner had to content himself with action under the old law. He was prodigal in granting pensions and in giving higher rates to those already on the roll. He began with his own office, awarding higher rates to all the old soldiers in it. This example brought many applications, and his office became a center of activity. In public speeches he exhibited the joy he felt in doing something for the old soldiers. His procedure attracted public attention, and the comment in the newspapers was not for the good of the administration. After several months of this conduct he was dismissed because he fell into a quarrel with his immediate superior, the Secretary of the Interior. His removal was a decided relief to President Harrison's administration.

300   From a cartoon *The Horn of Plenty*, by C. J. Taylor in *Puck*, May 29, 1889

VARIATIONS IN POLITICAL POWER

THROUGH the longer term of Senators as compared with the terms of Representatives, the Senate changes its political character less frequently than the House. It is therefore a more stable indicator of the political intention of the country. During the period extending from Cleveland's first inauguration to his second withdrawal from public life the Republicans held the major power most of the time, but there were times when the margin was very close; and through the rise of a third party the Democrats were in a position to menace the position of their opponents. In this same period the Democrats held the Presidency for eight years, and in turn were for a part of the time balked by the dominance of the Republicans in the Senate.

THE McKINLEY TARIFF, 1890

THE first Congress under Harrison met in December, 1889, determined on passing a tariff bill in which the principle of protection was embodied fully and thoroughly. The prepara-

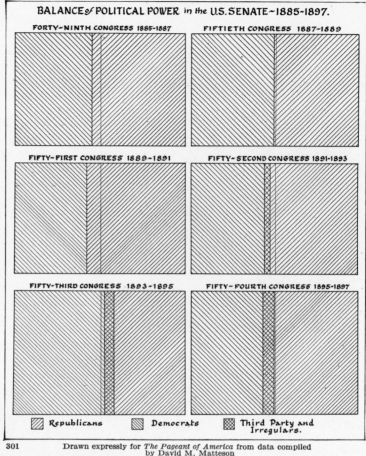

BALANCE of POLITICAL POWER in the U.S. SENATE ~ 1885-1897.

FORTY~NINTH CONGRESS 1885-1887   FIFTIETH CONGRESS 1887-1889

FIFTY~FIRST CONGRESS 1889-1891   FIFTY~SECOND CONGRESS 1891-1893

FIFTY~THIRD CONGRESS 1893-1895   FIFTY~FOURTH CONGRESS 1895-1897

Republicans   Democrats   Third Party and Irregulars.

301   Drawn expressly for *The Pageant of America* from data compiled by David M. Matteson

tion of such a bill devolved on the Ways and Means Committee of the House, of which William McKinley, Jr., was chairman, hence the name of the bill. The general purpose of the committee was to produce a bill that would give more systematic protection to the manufacturers and at the same time avoid piling up a surplus in the Treasury. The first of these ends was accomplished by raising the duties; the second was obtained in

302   The Ways and Means Committee of the House of Representatives, 1889, from a drawing by Hamilton in *Frank Leslie's Illustrated Newspaper*, July 12, 1890

LEFT TO RIGHT. *Seated:* Roswell P. Flower; J. G. Carlisle; C. R. Breckinridge; J. H. Gear; Robert M. La Follette; J. Barrows; Nelson Dingley, Jr.; B. McMillin; William McKinley. *Standing:* S. G. Payne; J. McKenna; T. M. Bayne; Roger Q. Mills

two ways: some articles not produced in the country and hitherto taxed were placed on the free list, thus diminishing the revenue. Other articles were taxed at such high rates that they were no longer imported, which also diminished the revenues. In defending this tariff bill nothing was said about paying the debts incurred during the Civil War. It was presented as a protectionist measure purely and simply, and no other problems were introduced.

303 Claus Spreckels, "The Sugar King," from a drawing by T. V. Chominski, after a photograph by Gutekunst, Philadelphia, in *Harper's Weekly*, Jan. 31, 1891

FREE RAW SUGAR

THE McKinley Tariff Act placed raw sugar on the free list. This action was, in itself, a blow at the sugar growers of Louisiana, who produced only a small part of the sugar used in the country. To save them, and to avoid the charge of sacrificing an American industry, McKinley gave these sugar growers a bounty, equal to what they would lose by reason of free sugar. He and his party hoped that Louisiana would thus be led to support the Republican ticket, but the memories of reconstruction were too strong to turn her away from the Democratic following. Placing raw sugar on the free list proved of great advantage to the sugar refiners, then organized in a small number of companies. The sugar trust especially was supposed to be benefited, and much was said about the effect of the tariff in building up this monopoly.

CREATING THE TIN PLATE INDUSTRY

THE McKinley Act also placed a high tariff on imported tin plate, which up to that time had not been manufactured to any considerable extent in the United States. This step was taken in order to create an American tin plate industry, and after a few years of experimentation, the desired result was obtained. Great advantage also accrued to the iron manufacturers, who in making the sheets for tin plating found a large new demand for their products. But the prices of tinware and tin roofing went up, and the opponents of protection seized the opportunity to create in the popular mind a strong aversion to the act. The duty on tin gives an excellent idea of the character of the act. This feature of the Act of 1890 laid a burden on the consumer and benefited no previously existing tin plate mills. It was exceedingly unpopular at the time it was passed. The McKinley Act was the first tariff act up to that time to be advocated primarily because it was a protective measure. Several previous tariffs had been protective in effect and had been supported because of their protective features; but the raising of revenue was the avowed reason for their passage. In 1890 the Republicans believed that a majority of the American people favored the principle of protection and supported the McKinley Act mainly on this ground. The measure serves as a milestone in the tariff history of the United States. Since 1890 protection has been a clear cut issue in American politics. Only once since the passage of the McKinley Act has the principle of protection been abandoned.

304   From a cartoon *Piling It On*, by C. J. Taylor in *Puck*, Jan. 30, 1889

305   From a cartoon *The Political Poor Relation.* — *An Unwelcome Guest*, by C. J. Taylor in *Puck*, June 4, 1888

PROTECTION AND THE FARMERS

THE farmers of the West and Northwest were largely Republicans, and looked with disfavor on their exclusion from the benefits of protection. It is true that small duties had been laid previously on some agricultural products, and raw wool had long been taxed to a considerable extent. But the wool-growing section was mostly limited to Ohio and the other duties amounted to little; the farmers felt that they got nothing worth while out of protection. To keep their good will higher duties were now laid on barley, bacon, hams and butter, and eggs were taken from the free list. These and other features of the law were used in defending it before the farmers, and with good effect. The McKinley Act was the first tariff that made a bold gesture toward giving the farmer protection. The gesture, however, proved deceptive; for with the exception of wool the agricultural produce was in excess of what the country could consume, and the prices were fixed under conditions of oversupply. A country producing more food than it needed for its own use at a lower rate than most other countries was not likely to feel the need of a tariff to raise the price of its own farm products.

BLAINE AND RECIPROCITY

BLAINE saw with deep concern the proposition to put non-competitive articles on the free list. Most of these articles were imported from Latin America, and he wished to retain the duties at least temporarily, on the understanding that they would be repealed when the Latin-American countries were willing to admit our agricultural products free of duty. They were thus to be a club to force our southern neighbors to accept reciprocity with us for the benefit of our farmers. At first McKinley refused to accept the idea, but after a time a compromise was made by which it was agreed that the duties in point should not be laid for the present, but that if concessions were not made by the countries in question within a certain time the duties should be imposed. Under this arrangement several reciprocity treaties were actually made, but they were overthrown in the tariff legislation of Cleveland's second term before there was an opportunity to see what effect they would have.

306   James G. Blaine, 1830–93, from a photograph

307   John D. Rockefeller, 1839–, from a portrait by John
   Singer Sargent, photograph by Brown Brothers, New
   York

DEVELOPMENT OF THE TRUSTS

HARRISON'S Presidency saw the trusts attain control in many kinds of industrial activity. They had risen to power by waging stern war with their competitors, forcing some of them to join the combinations and driving others to the wall. They were hated because they were monopolies and because along their pathways lay the dead enterprises of a vast number of men whose prosperity they had destroyed. The first effort against them was to pass state laws forbidding their existence. These laws were set at defiance by the trusts, which took refuge in the clause of the Constitution giving Congress sole authority over interstate commerce. Then the attack was taken into Congress. John D. Rockefeller, founder of the Standard Oil Company, was looked upon as the embodiment of the trust spirit.

THE ANTI–TRUST ACT OF 1890

THE appeal to Congress took formidable shape in the first Congress under Harrison. Many bills against trusts were introduced, but all set aside for a simple measure, of which Senator Edmunds of Vermont was the chief author, although it was popularly accredited to Senator Sherman. It passed Congress and became law in 1890. It forbade in general terms the formation of any combination doing interstate business in restraint of trade with the purpose of establishing a monopoly. It was a direct interference with the long accepted principle that a man might do as he willed with his own, for it assumed that he could not unconditionally sell his business to another. A long time passed before the courts were willing to enforce the law as it was intended. They were inclined to hold that it sought to accomplish the impossible. In the political field opinion was strongly against trusts, but it was hard to say how they could be destroyed.

308   From a cartoon *Farmer Jonathan: "I guess this New Breed of Cattle has got to Go Next,"* by W. A. Rogers
                                 in *Harper's Weekly*, Dec. 3, 1887

POPULAR VIEW OF THE SENATE

THE growth of trusts and the attacks upon them made it natural for the owners to form designs for influencing politics. Often they were content to support for office persons in whom they had implicit confidence; but now and again the prominent master of a trust went into politics for himself. In such a case the goal was usually the Senate of the United States; the result was

309   From a cartoon *The Bosses of the Senate*, by Joseph Keppler in *Puck*, Jan. 23, 1889

that in a few years several very rich men were members of that body. It was easy to get an election, if a man only gave largely to the party campaign fund. This connection between great wealth and legislation stimulated popular dissatisfaction and led to the belief that the tariff and the trusts were intimately related.

310   Richard P. Bland declares opponents of the free silver resolution guilty of bad faith, from a drawing by B. West Clinedinst in *Frank Leslie's Illustrated Weekly*, March 24, 1892

A NEW FIGHT FOR SILVER

WHILE the trust flourished agriculture languished. Grain and cotton sold unusually low, farmers were unable to pay or to reduce their debts, and a cry arose for governmental help equal to that which was given to the manufacturers and capitalists. The silver advocates took up the cry and another outburst of monetary agitation was the result. The few silver men in the Senate, aided by the Senators from the new states created in 1889, were strong enough to prevent the passage of the new tariff bill until the House agreed to "do something for silver." The result was a compromise and the enactment of the Sherman Silver Purchase Act of 1890, by which the Government was to buy four million five hundred thousand ounces of silver bullion a month, paying for it in Treasury notes which were made legal tender. The Republicans, who, for the most part, opposed free silver, supported this compromise because they thought that the alternative was out-and-out free coinage. Richard P. Bland was the leader of those who supported the more drastic measure. They were not satisfied and declared that the fight for free and unlimited silver coinage would go on until victory was won. They were earnestly convinced that a great wrong had been done them and spoke of their cause as a "crusade."

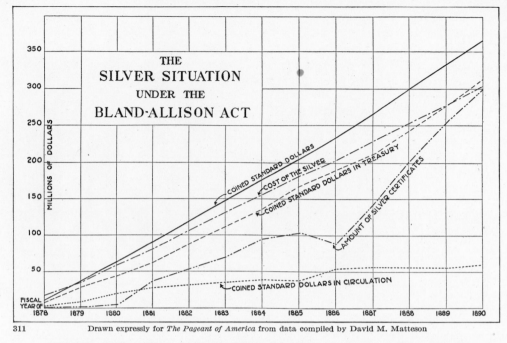

THE
SILVER SITUATION
UNDER THE
BLAND-ALLISON ACT

311   Drawn expressly for *The Pageant of America* from data compiled by David M. Matteson

SILVER SITUATION UNDER THE BLAND–ALLISON ACT, 1878–90

DURING the twelve years from the passage of the Bland-Allison Act of 1878 to the time of its replacement by the Sherman Silver Act of 1890, the total amount of standard dollars coined increased enormously — more than three hundred million — while the standard dollars in circulation remained relatively constant.

THE LODGE ELECTION BILL

THE legislation of the Congress of 1890 was a complex tissue of bargaining. Southern votes for silver were secured by giving western votes against the so-called Force Bill. The southern white had found a way to "suppress" the negro vote, sometimes through intimidation, sometimes by fraudulent counting and sometimes by other means. By enfranchising the negro the southern states had gained in representation; and since the negro vote was largely "neutralized," the net result was a gain for the South. In the North this situation was resented. Consequently, a bill was introduced in the House in 1890 by Henry Cabot Lodge of

Massachusetts, to allow the appointment of bi-partisan supervisors of elections. The bill passed the House with little difficulty. It aroused a storm of protest from southerners. There could be no doubt that if passed it would undo all the reconciliation that had grown up since reconstruction times. Public opinion slowly arose against it and it hung fire in the Senate for some time, while the deal over the tariff was being engineered. Finally, it was defeated there, when eight free silver Republicans voted against it in return for southern support in the silver compromise. This resulted in the South having its fears allayed.

312   From a cartoon *Base and Unpatriotic*, by C. J. Taylor in *Puck*, Aug. 20, 1890

SOUTHERN SUFFRAGE AMENDMENTS

THE narrow defeat of the Lodge bill set the South to thinking, with the result that it adopted amendments to most of its state constitutions for ridding itself of the ignorant negro vote. The Fifteenth Amendment of the Federal Constitution forbade the denial of the suffrage on the grounds of "race, color, or previous condition of servitude." The southerners thought that to deny it on the ground

313 Negroes voting in Richmond, from a drawing by W. L. Sheppard in *Harper's Weekly*, June 4, 1870

of a lack of education or the ownership of a specific amount of property was not against this Amendment and proceeded to adopt state amendments to that end. The result was that the majority of the negroes were not able to qualify. In the execution of these state amendments the ruling race made it very difficult for any negro to pass the ordeal laid down in the amendments. To get them adopted in the face of the large number of ignorant white voters they were made to include, in some states, a clause permitting any person to vote whose ancestor could vote under the old régime in the South. This feature was called the "grandfather clause." Without it the state amendments could not have been adopted in some states. One result was the elimination of a large amount of badly disguised deception in holding elections.

CONGRESSIONAL ELECTIONS OF 1890

THE high rates provided for in the McKinley tariff of 1890 caused much discussion. The bill was not passed until October 1, 1890, less than five weeks before the elections, and was followed at once by a rise in prices which was most vividly apparent at the precise moment when the people were called upon to express their opinion of the new law. The Democrats forced the fighting on this issue, and their opponents were not able to meet their arguments to the satisfaction of the electorate. The result was that the Democrats won the House by a majority of two hundred and thirty-five to eighty-five Republicans, a veritable political revolution. The victory, however, was not so much on account of the party as on account of Cleveland, its leader. The action of his opponents in wasting the surplus in the Treasury on pensions, and in laying unheard of duties to benefit a few, created a feeling of revulsion in the minds of the important independent group to which the result was due.

314   From a cartoon *Getting His Eyes Open*, by Louis Dalrymple in *Puck*, April 2, 1890

315 Senator William A. Peffer of Kansas, from
a drawing by B. West Clinedinst, after a
sketch by C. Upham, in *Frank Leslie's Illustrated Weekly*, May 12, 1892

THE PEOPLE'S PARTY

THE drift of the Republican party toward the coöperation with the
large business interests in the strongly industrial sections of the country
produced much discontent in the rural sections. At the same time the
farming portions of the South became dissatisfied with the Democratic
custom of taking the leaders from the lawyer class and other representatives of conservatism. In each section a vigorous Farmer's Alliance had
grown up and in 1890 these two movements, acting in sympathy with
one another, made a strong impression on the election results. They
captured many local offices in the South where they seemed about to
split the Democracy in two. In Kansas they elected William A. Peffer
to the United States Senate, in the place of John J. Ingalls, a noted exponent of conservative Republicanism. In 1891, the supporters of the
farmers' movement held a convention in Cincinnati and organized the
People's party, appealing especially to farmers and workingmen. This
party strongly favored free silver, for which neither of the old parties
was as yet willing to make an out-and-out declaration. The People's
party was the final phase of an agrarian movement which began with
the Grange and which was the result of the economic distress to be found
in the rural sections.

PACIFIC OCEAN DIPLOMACY

FOR three centuries after its discovery the Pacific ocean aroused little
interest in western Europe. Early in the nineteenth century Great
Britain established herself on its northeastern limits, in British Columbia,
and on its southwestern limits in Australia. She also got an important
commercial foothold at Shanghai when that place was made an open port.
From these vantage points, she built up a considerable trade and influence in the islands of the Pacific. After
the German Empire was formed in 1871, the Germans decided to extend their influence far and wide. They
found that Great Britain
had acquired the best
places in the Pacific and
they were forced to select
from what was left. As
the states of our Pacific
coast grew in population
and wealth, they also be-
gan to look at the Pacific
as a region in which the
power of the United
States was to be extended.
It happened that all these
tendencies drew to a head
in Harrison's administra-
tion. The effect was a
clash of interests and the
threat of a conflict which
seemed for a time to have
far-reaching results.
When the nations took
time to think they com-
promised the dispute
without difficulty.

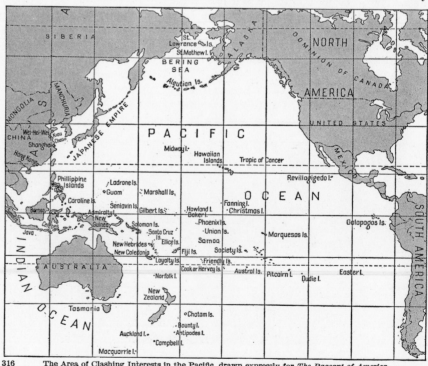

316   The Area of Clashing Interests in the Pacific, drawn expressly for *The Pageant of America*

THE SAMOAN CONTROVERSY

THE Samoan Islands, though commercially unimportant, form an important station on the route from San Francisco to Australia by way of Hawaii. In 1886 there was sharp quarrelling among representatives in Samoa of British, German and United States interests, chiefly due to the aggressive attitude of the Germans. The home Governments of the disputants took the matter up in a conference in Washington. Here the United States tried to get Germany to agree to joint supervision by the three powers, but without success, and the conference broke up with each side in a state of irritation.

317   From a cartoon *More Bluster than Blood*, by Joseph Keppler in
Puck, Feb. 6, 1889

318   From a cartoon *United in Grief*, by Ehrhart in *Puck*, April 10, 1889

A SAMOAN HURRICANE

WHEN Harrison was inaugurated in 1889, this feeling was at its height. One British, three German and three United States men-of-war were anchored in the harbor at Apia, ready to begin destroying one another at a word. On March 16 a great hurricane descended on the islands, and when it was gone all but one of the bristling warships were hopeless wrecks. The angry Governments were shocked into listening to reason. Six weeks later a joint commission met in Berlin and settled the whole dispute amicably, agreeing to a joint protectorate by the three powers over the islands. But the arrangement did not work well. In 1899 Great Britain definitely withdrew; the United States took the island of Tutuila, with the excellent harbor of Pago-Pago and Germany took the rest. In the World War, Germany lost her portion which is now governed by New Zealand under a mandate from the League of Nations.

319   Harbor of Apia, Samoa, from a drawing after a photograph by Assistant Surgeon H. W. Whitaker, U. S. N., in
Harper's Weekly, July 31, 1886

320 Liliuokalani, Queen of Hawaii, 1892–93, from a photograph by Rau Studios, Inc., Philadelphia

HAWAIIAN REVOLUTION

ANOTHER field of American influence was Hawaii. As far back as 1820 it was visited by missionaries from the United States through whose efforts the reigning dynasty and most of their subjects were speedily brought to accept the Christian religion. Over the rulers the missionaries established a strong influence, which enabled them in course of time to work many changes in the government. In 1875 the United States entered into a treaty with the king of the islands as a result of which sugar and other Hawaiian products were admitted free to the American market in return for a guarantee that the Hawaiian Government would not lease or alienate any territory to another country. In 1882 the reigning king was induced to proclaim a constitution granting the suffrage to the resident whites as well as the natives. This produced a native reaction, and in 1891 Queen Liliuokalani declared the constitution repealed. In 1893 the whites, of all nationalities, combined to effect a revolution. They seized the government, deposed the queen, declared Hawaii a republic and invited the United States to annex it.

HAWAIIAN ANNEXATION

PRESIDENT HARRISON willingly received the Hawaiian overtures of annexation and a treaty was quickly prepared and sent to the Senate. By this time it was rumored that the revolution had been carried through with the coöperation of the United States, and that otherwise it could not have succeeded. This report checked the action of the Senate and it was decided to leave the matter unsettled until Cleveland took office. His first act was to recall the treaty from the Senate, and his second was to send an agent to Hawaii to investigate the revolution. The agent reported that its success was due to the American minister who by landing troops had overawed the natives opposing the movement. Cleveland took no further steps for annexation and made an apology to the dispossessed queen, though he was powerless to restore her to her throne. The republic continued to exist, and in 1898, when Dewey's victory at Manila altered radically the American position in the Pacific, Hawaii was annexed by a joint resolution. Dewey's position in the western Pacific during the Spanish-American War brought home forcibly to the American people the desirability of having a mid-Pacific naval base. The annexation of Hawaii was the logical and immediate outcome.

321 Gathering at the Executive Building, Honolulu, upon the announcement of annexation; from a drawing by T. de Thulstrup after a photograph, in *Harper's Weekly*, Aug. 13, 1898

A DEBTOR NATION

THROUGHOUT the early part of our national history we were largely dependent on foreign nations for the money with which we built railroads, bridges and many other improvements. From Great Britain we got the largest amount of such funds, but as Germany developed into a strong industrial and financial nation we began to use money advanced by her bankers. This intricate process of selling bonds abroad and utilizing the proceeds at home was not understood by the majority of the people. To them it was humiliating that Britons owned so many of our bonds, thus holding us in "economic vasalage." The feeling accentuated a long-held hostility to all that was British and had its effect in political matters. It was not until the World War that we were able to pay off these foreign obligations and ceased to be a debtor nation. Since the World War we have become a creditor nation.

322 From a cartoon *John Bull after us again*, by F. Opper in *Puck*, July 24, 1889

SAVING THE SEALS IN BERING SEA

BY Harrison's time the country had begun to take notice of the imminent danger of the extinction through reckless hunting of the fur-bearing seal of the northern Pacific. These animals spent the autumn and winter in deep water, but came back in the spring to the Pribiloff Islands in Bering Sea for the rearing of their young. Here they encountered the hunters who slew them in large numbers for their skins, making no distinction between the breeding and the non-breeding seals. It was easy to see that if the seals were to be saved from extinction their slaughter must be regulated. The Pribiloff Islands belong to the United States, which therefore had the right to make and execute protective regulations. But the Government went further: it took the position that its rules applied not only to the islands and the territorial waters, but to the whole of Bering Sea; and it proceeded to arrest persons taking seals contrary to the regulations more than three miles from shore. It held that the sea was *mare clausum*.

323 The Seal Fisheries on Bering Sea, from a sketch in *Frank Leslie's Illustrated Weekly*, April 7, 1892

324   From a cartoon *The Revival of Blaine's Celebrated " Vigorous Foreign Policy*," by Ehrhart in *Puck*, Aug. 14, 1889

SECRETARY BLAINE'S POSITION

OUR claim that we controlled Bering Sea was derived from a similar claim by Russia, who preceded the United States in the ownership of Alaska and the Aleutian Islands. It rested on the assumption that the Aleutians, although much more than six miles apart, made an effective land-rim to the sea on the south.   The claim was resisted by Great Britain, who contended that the passages between the islands entering the sea, more than three miles from land on either side, were open sea. Blaine conducted a long and earnest correspondence with Lord Salisbury, the British Prime Minister. At first neither side showed any inclination to make an adjustment.   Blaine's zeal in the matter gave rise to the belief that he was engaged in what was called "the popular sport of twisting the British lion's tail," but the "jingoism" attributed to him was largely a reflection of American public opinion at the time.

THE FUR SEAL ARBITRATION

THE Bering Sea controversy soon reached such a state that arbitration was the only way to settle it short of force, and through the pressure of public opinion in each country arbitration was finally agreed upon. A tribunal of arbitrators in session in Paris, 1893, decided that Bering Sea was not *mare clausum*, that the United States had no exclusive right to protect the seals outside the three-mile limit, and that the seals were *ferae naturae* and not the property of any particular nation. It also prepared a set of rules under which the United States and Great Britain would regulate seal-fishing in the future, and assessed damages against the United States for the ships that had been seized by our officers. A large portion of these ships were owned in Canada.

ARBITRATION.

THE SEAL. "BELAY, YOU TWO JOHNNIES!—AVAST QUARRELLING! GIVE ME A 'CLOSE-TIME,' AND
LEAVE THE 'SEA' AN OPEN QUESTION."

325   From a cartoon *Arbitration*, by John Tenniel in *Punch*,
                          Jan. 17, 1891

THE MAFIA INCIDENT
IN NEW ORLEANS

IN 1891 New Orleans had witnessed a series of assassinations for which it was believed the secret Mafia band composed of Italian immigrants was responsible. When the popular chief of police, who was seeking to break up the Mafia, was himself slain, the city burst into wrath. The general opinion of the aroused populace was that the murder had been committed in revenge for police activity in arresting Italian criminals. A number of Italians were arrested and tried, but obtained verdicts of "not guilty." The public was convinced that the acquittals had been achieved through bribery or terrorization. At the instigation of leading citizens, an orderly mob, in broad day, without disguises, marched to the jail, where the acquitted were still kept, drew them from their cells into a courtyard and shot them to death. All but three of the eleven victims were naturalized American citizens. It was an appeal to barbarism, defended on the ground that justice could be obtained in no other way. The people of New Orleans did not, it seems, take into consideration the fact that a miscarriage of justice, as alleged, could not have taken place without the assistance of the jury or the court officials; for no effort was made to make such persons responsible for the acquittal.

326   The killing of six of the Italians in the yard of the Parish Prison in New Orleans, from a drawing by Charles Graham in *Harper's Weekly*, March 28, 1891

A FAIR EXCHANGE.

UNCLE SAM. "SEE HERE, UMBERTO!—GIVE US BACK YOUR *'MINISTER,'* AND TAKE AWAY THAT DARN'D *'MAFIA,'* AND WE'LL CALL IT A SQUARE DEAL!"

327   From a cartoon *A Fair Exchange*, by John Tenniel in *Punch*, April 11, 1891

A BREAK WITH ITALY

THE New Orleans affair naturally gave offense to the Italian Government, which demanded that the leaders of the mob be punished. To this demand Blaine could only reply that the incident was within the jurisdiction of the state of Louisiana, which would no doubt do what was right. As that state did nothing effective, Italy withdrew her minister from Washington and the United States recalled its minister from Italy. For nearly a year intercourse between the two Governments was suspended. It was resumed when Italy came to realize the peculiarities of the American system of dual jurisdiction in the administration of law. The United States made reconciliation easier by causing twenty-five thousand dollars to be distributed among the families of the slain Italians. In this incident was illustrated an inconvenience inherent in our system of federated government. A foreign state has no power to negotiate with one of the states in the Union, and at the same time the National Government has not the power to interfere with a state's administration of law in the ordinary criminal courts. Fortunately, but few incidents have occurred in our history in which such a conflict of principles has come into play.

328   From a cartoon *The Debut of the Younger Sisters*, by C. J. Taylor in *Puck*, March 13, 1889

THE ADMISSION OF NEW STATES

FOR some time before Harrison was President the people living in the southern part of Dakota Territory had been trying to induce Congress to create the state of South Dakota. As the region was Republican in sympathy, the movement had the support of the Republican Senate and the opposition of the Democratic House. The South Dakotans in disgust held a convention, December, 1886, and resolved that if Congress did not admit them to statehood in a year they would set up a state without its consent. Though this rash threat was not carried out it introduced a new chapter in the discussion. At last, in 1889 Congress admitted four new states, North and South Dakota, Washington and Montana. In 1890, Idaho and Wyoming were admitted. Utah, long kept out by Mormonism, was admitted in 1896, after the Mormon Church had taken action to prohibit plural marriages in the future.

CLEVELAND AND FREE SILVER

A LARGE majority of the Democrats favored free and unlimited coinage of silver, and they gave support to a continued agitation in its behalf in and out of Congress. The movement was especially strong in the West, where Democratic leaders thought a large portion of the Republicans voters could be captured by stressing free silver. At the same time it was evident that the party could not carry the East on that issue, and without the aid of some large eastern state such as New York it could not hope to elect a President. In this critical situation, Cleveland undertook to restore the dominance in the party of Eastern influence. He made several outspoken utterances against the silver doctrine. At the moment he seemed to have accomplished little. Apparently, he had merely made himself unpopular with his friends; members of the Hill-Gorman wing of the Democracy freely predicted that he had killed his chance for nomination in 1892.

329   From a cartoon *The Romance of a Weather-Cock*, by
        T. F. Powers in *America*, Chicago, July 16, 1891

POPULAR VIEW OF HARRISON

As Harrison's administration drew near its close, the country began to cast up its estimate of him as President. Undoubtedly its conclusion was that he was a man of small stature, his policies determined by others. Blaine was still supposed to dominate him. Reed, symbolizing the power of the House in an era of new policies, was supposed to stand for another strong force which the President could not resist. The Senate, which in later days has become the overtopping part of the Congress, seems at that time to have had less place in the popular mind than its sister branch.

330   From a cartoon *The Happy Triumvirate*, by Syd B. Griffin
in *Puck*, Oct. 1, 1890

HARRISON RENOMINATED IN 1892

As the election of 1892 approached, it became evident that Harrison would not make a good run, partly because he was too cool-tempered to win the applause of his own party, and partly because he had not the leadership to command the situation facing him. The only man, however, who could displace him was Blaine, still Secretary of State. The newspapers frequently spoke of him as a candidate, but he disclaimed any intention of running. Finally, three days before the national convention met, he resigned from the Cabinet, and it became known that he would take the nomination if it were offered to him. He had waited too long. Harrison had already received the indorsement of the major portion of the party, and he was nominated on the first ballot with Blaine a poor second. Blaine's hesitation in this matter seems to have proceeded from an incipient nervous illness destined to prove very serious later.

331   The National Republican Convention at Minneapolis, from a drawing by T. de Thulstrup and
Graham in *Harper's Weekly*, June 11, 1892

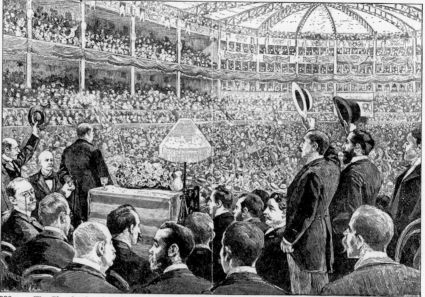

332   The Cleveland and Stevenson Notification Meeting at Madison Square Garden, New York,
              from a drawing by T. de Thulstrup in *Harper's Weekly*, July 30, 1892

NOMINATION OF CLEVELAND

CLEVELAND's opposition to silver did not do his political career the damage that his opponents had predicted. The Republicans were too much divided over silver to bring it forward in the Presidential campaign, and the Democrats were forced to admit that Cleveland was their only hope. Hill, who had carried New York twice in the contest for Governor, aspired to displace him; but when the convention met, his following was so slight that he could not get on the first ballot the one-third vote that was necessary to prevent Cleveland's nomination. The convention placed silver in the background and took the tariff as the issue of the day; Cleveland resumed the fight where he had left off in the last months of his first term.

THE CAMPAIGN OF 1892

To refute the charge that his policies would disturb industry, Cleveland in his letter of acceptance declared that, "We believe that the advantages of freer raw materials should be accorded to our manufacturers, and we contemplate a fair and careful distribution of necessary tariff burdens rather than the precipitation of free trade." This declaration, taken with his opposition to free silver, gave him a good position in New York, and in other centers of business in the East. The People's party had its own candidate in the field, and he drew votes from the Republicans in the farming West. Everywhere, the Democrats forced the fight on the effects of the tariff and the development of trusts. The result was the success of Cleveland by a majority of two hundred and seventy-seven electoral votes to one hundred and forty-five for Harrison and twenty-two for Weaver, the Populist candidate. Cleveland's success was occasioned by the vote of the independents.

333   From a cartoon *The Republican Galley*, by Joseph Keppler in *Puck*, Sept. 28, 1892

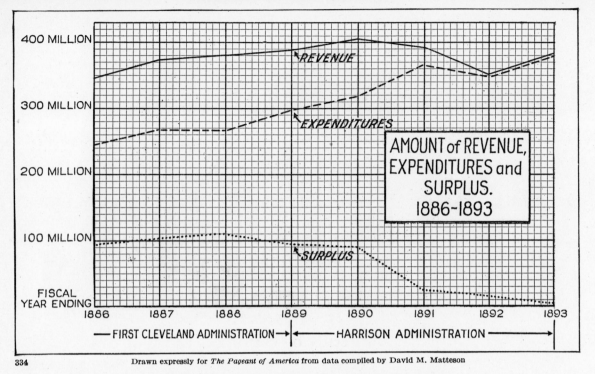

400 MILLION

REVENUE

300 MILLION

EXPENDITURES

AMOUNT of REVENUE,
EXPENDITURES and
SURPLUS.
1886-1893

200 MILLION

100 MILLION

SURPLUS

FISCAL
YEAR ENDING

1886   1887   1888   1889   1890   1891   1892   1893

— FIRST CLEVELAND ADMINISTRATION → ← HARRISON ADMINISTRATION —

334   Drawn expressly for *The Pageant of America* from data compiled by David M. Matteson

HARRISON AND NATIONAL EXPENDITURES

HARRISON's administration is usually looked upon as the time at which our National Government launched
into a career of liberal, not to say, loose expenditures. In some ways the reputation is well deserved; but it
must not be forgotten that the tendency to extravagance was established before Harrison became President.
The accompanying graph shows that expenditures were going up nearly as rapidly under Cleveland as they
went up under Harrison. But Cleveland was ever fighting against extravagance, while Harrison made no
such struggle. The graph also shows how the revenues fell under the McKinley tariff, carrying with the
fall a sharp reduction of the surplus revenue and its eventual disappearance.

335   The crowd acclaiming President Harrison at his inauguration, Mar. 4, 1889, from
an illustration in *Frank Leslie's Illustrated Newspaper*, Mar. 9, 1889

CHAPTER VII

DEMOCRATIC REVOLT UNDER CLEVELAND, 1893–97

PROBABLY ninety-five per cent of the voters who elected Cleveland in 1892 were Democrats. They voted for him because he was the nominee of the party. The other five per cent were independents, who voted for him because they thought he would make a better President than Harrison. After election it was natural for the regular Democrats to wish to control the policies of the administration. At any rate they did not think it proper in their President to go contrary to the general desires of the majority of the party. When this situation was presented to Cleveland he found that he had to decide between doing what he believed was for the interest of the country and preserving party harmony by following the views of the major part of his followers. In such a dilemma he acted, as he believed, for his country, fully realizing what it meant for his party.

The occasion of this crisis was the rise of free silver as a party issue. Cleveland deceived nobody as to his views on that subject. Repeatedly and distinctly he had said he was opposed to free silver. Believing that they could not win under any other candidate the Democrats took him in spite of this warning, but when he was elected they harried him day and night because he acted on the principles he had avowed before the election. When he proposed to repeal the Silver Purchase Act of 1890, many Democrats opposed him. When he turned to the Republicans and carried the repeal, they pronounced him a traitor to his party. His victory only made his hostile party colleagues hate him the more. While the financial condition of the country, as a result of their opposition, remained in the most doubtful plight they did what they could to embarrass him, denounced his motives, and at last refused in the party convention of 1896 to give him the formal indorsement that political parties under such circumstances are accustomed to give to outgoing Presidents.

While this state of affairs existed the Hill-Gorman group of Democrats, opposed to Cleveland because he favored reforms, found themselves in an awkward position. Their own constituencies were opposed to free silver and they had the unpleasant duty of supporting Cleveland in his currency policies. Secretly they were pleased to see the silver men tear him to pieces. Then came their day of punishment. The great silver movement that had been built up in the agricultural South and West had no use for men associated with the capitalists of the East. Up to 1896 the Democratic party had been led for many a year by New Yorkers. A western-southern combination now took charge, and was destined to rule the party for many years under the leadership of William J. Bryan. To this group New York interests were anathema.

336   Stephen Grover Cleveland, 1837–1908, from a photograph by Sarony, New York

CLEVELAND VINDICATED

On March 4, 1889, President Cleveland drove up Pennsylvania Avenue by the side of his successful rival, Benjamin Harrison, to hand over to him the reins of authority.   Four years later, in a storm of mingled sleet and rain, he drove up the same classic street to take them back again.   For four years he had watched the efforts of the Republicans to govern the country, and had seen the nation turn to him again for leadership. Never before nor since has a man once defeated in the race for the Presidency been able to enjoy such a triumph.   His inaugural address laid special emphasis on the danger lying in unsound financial legislation and the need for a sound revision of the tariff.   Referring to the tariff he said: "The lessons of paternalism ought to be unlearned and the better lesson taught that while the people should patriotically and cheerfully support their government its functions do not include the support of the people."   The Democratic sweep in 1892 had been complete as a result of the election.   The party controlled the Senate and House of Representatives as well as the Presidency.   This was the first time since the Civil War that the Democrats had been in complete control of the National Government.   Events were soon to demonstrate, however, that their party harmony was only nominal.   Their power was paralyzed as a result of internal dissension.   The responsibility for this state of dissension is disputed.   The friends of Cleveland held that it lay on the Hill-Gorman group, who did many things contrary to Cleveland's announced views, and who meanwhile did not conceal their opposition to him.   Their reply to their critics was that Cleveland was not the whole party and that he arrogantly tried to impose his will on those whose efforts and sacrifices had placed him in office.   As he stood steadily by his views and refused to act with them they pronounced him a stubborn autocrat who thought himself better than others.   Perhaps the answer to the dispute is that a party with a forceful leader should give him the reins or take the consequences.

IX—12

337   Richard Croker, 1843–1923, from a photograph
by Pach Bros., New York

CLEVELAND AND TAMMANY

In the long column of victorious Democrats marching in the sleet before Cleveland's reviewing stand on March 4, 1893, was a large Tammany delegation, with black coats and high hats, and on each man a diminutive tiger hanging from a buttonhole. At the head marched Richard Croker, leader of the organization, for nine years one of Cleveland's sternest enemies. In theory and practice Croker was a typical spoilsman, and he did not comprehend the meaning of a civil service that existed for the good of the country. Marching in this parade he wished to show that he was a good Democrat; but he had in no way given up his desire to control the patronage in his own state. The fight between him and Cleveland was not yet ended.

CLEVELAND'S CABINET

The new Secretary of State was Walter Q. Gresham, of Indiana, lately a Federal judge. Until a few months before Cleveland's second election he was a stanch Republican, and in 1888 he had been a prominent candidate for the Presidential nomination in the Republican convention. Refusing to endorse high protection, he left his party and came out for Cleveland in the campaign of 1892. He was a man after Cleveland's own heart. While Gresham's appointment pleased the independent vote, the typical old-line Democrats were angered at seeing a recent convert at the head of the Cabinet. Gresham died in office in 1895 and was succeeded as Secretary of State by Richard Olney, who since the beginning of the administration had held the office of Attorney-General. Probably the ablest man in the Cabinet was John G. Carlisle, of Kentucky, Secretary of the Treasury. He played a strong part in the silver and tariff history of the time, and gave Cleveland strong support in all his troubles with the free and unrestricted coinage of silver by the National Government.

338   Cleveland's Cabinet, from a drawing by Louis Loeb in *Harper's Weekly*, Mar. 4, 1893
LEFT TO RIGHT: President Cleveland; John G. Carlisle, Secretary of the Treasury; Richard Olney, Attorney-General; Hilary A. Herbert, Secretary of the Navy; J. Sterling Morton, Secretary of Agriculture; Walter Q. Gresham, Secretary of State; Hoke Smith, Secretary of the Interior; Wilson Bissell, Postmaster-General; Daniel S. Lamont, Secretary of War

339   The United States warship *Colorado*, built of wood in 1855, in service until 1885, courtesy of the Office of Naval Records and Library, Navy Department, Washington

A NEW NAVY

CLEVELAND'S Secretary of the Navy was Hilary A. Herbert, of Alabama, a former Confederate colonel. With a long record of service in Congress he had for three terms been chairman of the Naval Committee of the House, during the period of the transformation of the navy from wooden to iron ships. It was not until 1883, during Arthur's administration, that this process began. In Cleveland's first administration it was carried on successfully and also under Harrison, Democrats and Republicans uniting to carry it out. In 1893, the navy had twenty-two modern steel ships and was rated as fifth in strength among the navies of the world. The "Great White Fleet," as the new navy was called, gave strength and confidence to the national spirit, and Congress willingly voted thirty million dollars a year for its development. For many years we had been satisfied with a small fleet. The decline of our merchant marine because of the tariff had led us to think that a strong navy was not needed.

340   The Great White Fleet, courtesy of the Office of Naval Records and Library, Navy Department, Washington

341   Inside a Treasury Vault in Washington, from a sketch by
T. de Thulstrup after a photograph by Bell, in *Harper's Weekly*,
July 15, 1893

THE DWINDLING GOLD RESERVE

THE Resumption Act of 1875 had brought about the accumulation in the National Treasury of a gold reserve of one hundred millions by January 1, 1879, at which date redemption of legal tender money in gold began. Until the last year of Harrison's administration no question arose about maintaining this reserve or continuing redemption. But about this time Europe began to call for gold, offering a premium which made it profitable for speculators to buy up free gold in other countries and ship it to Europe. The abundance of paper money circulating in this country made it peculiarly easy for them to draw gold from the Treasury. This paper was being printed and paid out for silver bullion under the Silver Purchase Act at a rate larger than the business needs of the country necessitated. It passed into the hands of the speculators who demanded gold for it. The Secretary of the Treasury dared not refuse, knowing well that the public would begin to hoard gold and sell it at a premium the moment the Treasury refused to pay it out freely on demand. All this time great quantities of silver lay in the Treasury and could not be made to circulate. If some of it got out into the channels of trade, it was thrown back by the people who got it into banks, who in turn presented it to the Treasury and asked for notes in its place.

THE PANIC OF 1893

BEFORE 1890 about eighty-five per cent of the receipts from customs duties at the ports was in gold, but after that year the percentage declined, and after February, 1892, it did not reach more than nineteen per cent in any month, until the return of happier times. This situation was the result of the European demand for gold. It increased the sense of uneasiness in the business world already started by the refusal of Europe to buy our bonds, and even by a tendency to sell back to us those she had already bought. All these signs pointed to depression. They came upon the heels of a year of reckless borrowing for speculation and the borrowers were now caught in a storm. Their notes went to protest, the creditors went bankrupt, and by the end of February, 1893, the country experienced a severe panic. All the time the outflow of gold went on steadily. The year 1892 witnessed general prosperity in the United States. Abroad the reverse was true. A collapse of credit in Argentina, in 1890, had already caused great trouble for some of the best British banks, so that the constant buying of our railroad and other bonds in Great Britain was seriously checked. About this time Austria-Hungary began to collect a gold reserve for redemption of her Treasury notes, and other countries began to strengthen their supplies of gold. The situation had in it two elements of danger to us. When Europe bought our bonds she paid for them either in goods or gold, or in both, and when she ceased to buy them this inflow of gold was checked and it interfered with the balance of trade. It also made our bankers cautious about lending money for railroad development, which, in turn, had the effect of slackening business in many ways. It produced, moreover, in Europe a demand for gold, and in exchange this metal went to a premium, so that it began to be drawn to Europe from outlying countries, including the United States, thereby endangering the reserve held for specie payment.

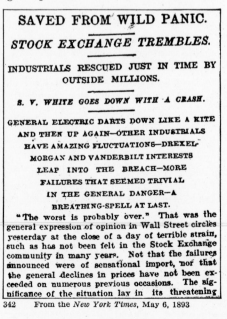

SAVED FROM WILD PANIC.

STOCK EXCHANGE TREMBLES.

INDUSTRIALS RESCUED JUST IN TIME BY OUTSIDE MILLIONS.

S. V. WHITE GOES DOWN WITH A CRASH.

GENERAL ELECTRIC DARTS DOWN LIKE A KITE
AND THEN UP AGAIN—OTHER INDUSTRIALS
HAVE AMAZING FLUCTUATIONS—DREXEL
MORGAN AND VANDERBILT INTERESTS
LEAP INTO THE BREACH—MORE
FAILURES THAT SEEMED TRIVIAL
IN THE GENERAL DANGER—A
BREATHING-SPELL AT LAST.

"The worst is probably over." That was the general expression of opinion in Wall Street circles yesterday at the close of a day of terrible strain, such as has not been felt in the Stock Exchange community in many years. Not that the failures announced were of sensational import, nor that the general declines in prices have not been exceeded on numerous previous occasions. The significance of the situation lay in its threatening

342   From the *New York Times*, May 6, 1893

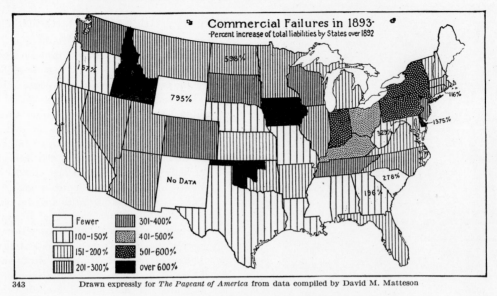

Commercial Failures in 1893·
·Percent increase of total liabilities by States over 1892

795%

157%

598%

116%

1375%

329%

No Data

278%

196%

Fewer	301-400%
100-150%	401-500%
151-200%	501-600%
201-300%	over 600%

343   Drawn expressly for *The Pageant of America* from data compiled by David M. Matteson

EFFECTS OF THE PANIC ON BUSINESS

THE accompanying graph shows the increase of business failures as a result of the panic of 1893 as compared with those of the preceding year, the amount of the liabilities being the basis of estimate. In some states the results of the panic came slowly, so that more failures occurred in 1894 than in 1893. In such cases the percentage over 1892 has been shown by numerals over the face of the map, as in Georgia where the failures in 1894 were one hundred and ninety-six per cent of those in 1892. The graph shows that this panic, while severest in certain western farming states, had, nevertheless, a notable effect in the great industrial states of New York and Pennsylvania.

ANGER OF THE SILVER MEN

THE Treasury continued to redeem in gold all paper money presented to it in spite of the fact that some of the outstanding paper bills were redeemable in silver. The motive was to keep the currency sound by holding it on a gold basis. The silver men in Congress, with Richard P. Bland at their head, resented this discrimination by the Secretary of the Treasury. Let him, said they, only meet the speculators with bags of silver and offer it for their proffered Treasury notes, and if they see that gold will not be paid they will cease to demand it. Cleveland took the side of Secretary Carlisle, and in consequence the ire of the silver men was turned upon him. Grimly, the silver men forced Congress to oppose all executive plans for financial safety. To the great agricultural and industrial classes they announced that the President had become a worshiper of the plutocrats. There was truth in each contention. The agriculturists were suffering from a prolonged period of falling prices. Year after year their debts accumulated. At the same time eastern manufacturers, bankers, railroad men, merchants, and factory operatives were in a much better condition. There was no doubt that inflation would lead to higher prices nominally and higher prices would enable the farmers to pay their debts. On the other hand inflation would undermine Government credit, lessen the volume of all kinds of permanent investments and its disturbing results would be transferred to all parts of the country. To resist free silver was to forward the interests of the East. "Why should the East prosper at the expense of the West?" said the other. Experience shows that when inflation by legislative action begins, it soon runs into disastrous extremes through lack of popular self-control. Such was the danger in 1893.

344   Richard Parks Bland, 1835–99, after a drawing from life by G. W. Breck in *Harper's Weekly*, March 24, 1894

345 From a cartoon *Out of the Silver Flood*, by Louis Dalrymple in *Puck*, Sept. 13, 1893

REPEAL OF THE SILVER PURCHASE ACT

THE Sherman Silver Purchase Act compelled the Government to issue each month paper money to buy silver. After the panic broke, this law seriously embarrassed the Government and threatened the stability of the currency. Cleveland decided in this emergency that the first thing to do was to repeal the act by which the currency was being inflated. To that end he called Congress in extra session for August 7, 1893, and when it met strongly advised the repeal of the obnoxious law. The silver men included a majority of the Democrats, and they felt that they could defeat the President's recommendation. But the gold Republicans came to his help and thus the repeal bill passed the House. In the Senate it encountered stiff resistance. Again the Republicans helped the President, and to their aid he added a discreet use of the patronage by which several Senators voted for the bill, who might otherwise have voted against it. But the repeal did not fully relieve the situation. The reason for the lateness of the calling of Congress into extraordinary session to deal with the crisis caused by the panic was a physical infirmity which the President was discovered to be suffering under. Such was the state of mind of the public that its very existence had to be kept secret. An operation by a skilful surgeon removed the difficulty quickly, and the President recovered his normal health before the public was aware of his illness.

THE WILSON TARIFF BILL

WITH the Silver Act of 1890 repealed, Cleveland turned to the tariff reform, the leading issue of the preceding election. William L. Wilson, of West Virginia, a scholarly type of Congressman, was chairman of the Ways and Means Committee and by hard work quickly introduced into the House a bill expressing the President's ideas of tariff revision. These included an enlargement of the free list by the addition of several of the most important raw materials, the lowering of the prohibitive duties imposed in the McKinley Act, and the substitution of *ad valorem* duties for specific duties wherever possible. It was believed that the loss in revenue under the proposed law would be fifty million dollars, and to make this sum good an income tax was to be laid. After a short debate, the bill passed the House by a vote of two hundred and four to one hundred and ten. The tariff reformers considered it a very good bill from their point of view, and it provided for only moderate rates to raise a necessary revenue.

346 William L. Wilson, 1843–1900, from a drawing from life by G. W. Breck in *Harper's Weekly*, Feb. 17, 1894

THE TARIFF BILL IN THE SENATE

IN the Senate two Democrats, Gorman and Brice, who were frank protectionists, induced the bulk of the Senators of their party to combine with Republicans in imposing such radical changes on Wilson's bill as to give it an entirely new character. Claiming that it would reduce the revenue more than was estimated, they began to put up the rates one after another, yielding to the persuasion of an active lobby. In this way coal, iron ore, lumber and raw sugar were taken off the free list. Cleveland saw this procedure with disgust and declared that it meant "party perfidy and party dishonor." The total number of changes made in the bill by the Senate was six hundred and thirty-four.

THE NADIR OF SENATORIAL HONOR

MANY things have happened to diminish the popular respect for the United States Senate, but nothing else was quite so effective as the vote on the sugar schedule. Debate on that item went on day by day and the stock of the Sugar Trust rose or fell as debate seemed favorable or hostile. It soon became known that certain Senators were buying and selling the stock, while by their votes they were doing the things that made it go up and down. Outraged public opinion forced the Senate to make an investigation, but it was not conducted

347 Arthur P. Gorman, 1839–1906, from a photograph by Bell, Washington

with vigor. Quay of Pennsylvania cynically avowed that he was speculating in sugar stock but added that it did not affect his vote. The dishonor of the Senate did not lie so much in the fact that some of its members used their votes to support their speculation, but in the fact that under the grave suspicion aroused, the Senate did not make an effective investigation. The impression prevailed that the Senate of the United States had become a body careless of its honor and afraid to open a drastic investigation of its members.

348 From a cartoon *Senator Quay's Position on the Sugar Question as Defined by Himself*, by W. A. Rogers in *Harper's Weekly*, June 30, 1894

349   From a cartoon *Gorman's Triumph — A Humiliating Spectacle*,
by W. A. Rogers in *Harper's Weekly*, Sept. 8, 1894

HOW IT WAS DONE

THE McKinley tariff had placed raw sugar on the free list and laid a duty on refined sugar. This action was largely engineered by the Sugar Trust, and gave it a great advantage, enabling it to get raw material free and to keep out competing refined sugar. To satisfy the Louisiana sugar growers a bounty was given to domestic raw sugar. The Wilson Bill placed both raw and refined sugar on the free list and did away with the bounty. When the bill reached the Senate the Louisiana Senator attacked it, and with Gorman's aid they got a duty of forty per cent placed on raw sugar. Then the Sugar Trust brought its influence to bear, also supported by Gorman, and by Brice, his colleague, with the result that a duty of one eighth of a cent a pound was placed at last on refined sugar. It was estimated that this was worth to the Trust twenty million dollars a year. Cleveland expressed his disgust at the proceedings by refusing to sign the bill; but it became law without his signature.

FAILURE OF THE INCOME TAX

ABOUT the only surviving features of the original Wilson Bill were free wool and the income tax. The legality of the income tax was disputed and a test case was soon brought before the Supreme Court. The justices were so divided that the opinion of the court was not satisfactory to itself and the case was re-argued. In its final opinion the court held that the income tax is a direct tax and that the statute was unconstitutional because it did not conform to the requirement that direct taxes must be apportioned among the states, according to the population. The final decision was made possible because a member of the court, Judge Shiras, changed his opinion upon the second hearing of the case. If he had remained constant the tax would have been upheld. While not doubting his integrity, the country felt some disgust for a high justice who had so much trouble in making up his mind.

350   From a cartoon *After the Hold-Up*, by Louis Dalrymple in *Puck*, June 6, 1894

COXEY'S PLAN FOR INFLATION

ONE of the effects of the panic of 1893 was a period of unemployment and social distress. The public mind was abnormally sensitive to suggestions for improvement and many silly ideas were afloat. Of all these the most conspicuous was the plan announced by Jacob S. Coxey, of Ohio. He proposed that the Federal Government should issue five hundred million dollars in legal-tender notes and with it pay for the construction of better roads. The advantages of the scheme, he said, were that it would relieve unemployment, give the country good roads, and provide an increased supply of money with which the people could pay their debts. The idea was not new, but it received wide publicity from the author's novel way of placing it before the country.

"COXEY'S ARMY" ON THE MARCH

CALLING himself "General Coxey," he gathered a body of unemployed men and set out on a foot journey to Washington, where he proposed to present a petition to Congress. The newspapers saw in the affair most interesting "copy" and daily gave their

351   Jacob S. Coxey, 1854–, from a drawing after a photograph, in *Harper's Weekly*, May 12, 1894

readers minute accounts of the progress of the "army," which was an orderly party of something more than a hundred men. It was easy for the papers to turn the event into ridicule, and the public soon lost sight of the purpose that lay behind the march. Coxey and his band reached Washington on May 1, 1894, but the leaders were arrested for "trespassing on the grass." They were in prison for twenty days and their followers dispersed. Coxey's was not the only "army" on the march during this troubled year. "The United States Industrial Army," headed by one Frye, started from Los Angeles. Another group under a man by the name of Kelley headed eastward from San Francisco. By traveling in freight trains and by tramping these two miscellaneous aggregations made their way east of the Mississippi River. They did not, however, reach the national capital.

352   "General Coxey" escorted from the Capitol, from a drawing by T. Dart Walker in *Harper's Weekly*, May 12, 1894

THE PULLMAN STRIKE OF 1894

Business depression led to the reduction of wages, and consequently of widespread discontent. Frequent strikes occurred; the most notable was at the works of the Pullman Car Company at Chicago. It began on May 11, 1894, in resistance to a reduction of wages. The strikers belonged for the most part to the American Railway Union, which demanded arbitration. This the employers refused. Members of the Union were ordered not to handle the cars of the Pullman Company. The strike was

353   National Guardsmen firing into the mob during the Pullman strike, from a drawing by
C. W. Peters after a sketch by G. A. Coffin, in *Harper's Weekly*, July 21, 1894

initiated by the discharge of a switchman who refused to couple a Pullman car to a train in Chicago. The disturbance spread rapidly, and throughout a wide area, with Chicago as the center, the trains ceased to move. This halting of traffic resulted in seriously impeding business. To a city the size of Chicago, dependent on a steady inflow of food from the agricultural districts, it was essential to have uninterrupted railroad service.

354   United States troops encamped in front of the Post Office and the Sub-Treasury,
from a drawing by Charles Mente after a sketch by G. A. Coffin, in *Harper's Weekly*,
July 21, 1894

355   John P. Altgeld, 1847–1902, from a drawing after a photograph

CLEVELAND AND THE STRIKE

The Governor of Illinois, John P. Altgeld, sympathized with the strikers and would not call out the state militia to keep the peace until much property had been destroyed, some of it by hoodlums who mixed with the strikers in order to plunder railroad cars. On the ground that the mails were interrupted, Cleveland, ignoring the protests of the Governor, ordered Federal troops to Chicago. As the rioting still went on, he made arrangements to fill the city with soldiers and compel obedience to law. He was said to have declared that if it took the whole regular army to deliver one postal card in Chicago he would call the army there. Under this prospect the elements of disorder yielded and the strike failed.

BLANKET INJUNCTIONS

WHILE the Pullman strike continued the Federal courts issued what were called "blanket injunctions" directed to the officials and members of the railroad union, and all other persons whomsoever, ordering them to refrain from interfering with the business of twenty-three specified railroads. Notices embodying the orders of the court were printed on large broadsides and pasted on the sides of freight cars, so that they might be well observed.

356   From a cartoon *The Vanguard of Anarchy*, by W. A. Rogers in *Harper's Weekly*, July 21, 1894

357   Eugene V. Debs, 1855–1926, from a drawing after a photograph

DEBS PROSECUTED

FOR defying this notice Eugene V. Debs, president of the union, was arrested. After trial in a Federal court he was convicted and sent to prison for six months. Labor in general raised strong protests against using "blanket injunctions." Injunctions are issued for the purpose of preventing something which if allowed to take place will inflict a damage not easily made good through the slow process of a civil suit for damages. It was contended this legal decree ought not to be used as a means of preventing an orderly strike. The readiness with which judges granted it to the railroads created the impression that their sympathies were with the roads and raised harsh criticisms against the courts. But the judges followed the doctrine, old as the courts, that law exists to protect property.

BONDS SOLD TO SUSTAIN THE GOLD RESERVE

DESPITE all the efforts of Secretary Carlisle to draw gold from American banks into the Treasury, the continued exportation of gold caused the reserve to shrink alarmingly. Presently, it had fallen below the hundred million mark; though this did not precipitate more panic than already existed, the continued shrinkage added to the general sense of insecurity. Late in 1893 it was evident that the reserve was in danger of exhaustion if some means of replenishment was not found. Carlisle suggested that Congress give him authority to sell bonds for gold in order to stem the tide, to which Congress replied that danger would pass if he paid out silver as well as gold. He then turned to the law of 1875, which he had formerly said was doubtful as to its meaning, and under it offered, in January, 1894, fifty million dollars in bonds for gold, allowing the subscribers to pay for it in instalments.

358   John G. Carlisle, 1835–1910, from a sketch by Renouard in *Harper's Weekly*, June 2, 1888

359   From a cartoon *Will it Rise?*, by Victor in *Judge*, March 7, 1896

"THE ENDLESS CHAIN"

THE buyers of the bonds paid their first instalment out of the gold in the banks, but as it went out the banks sent notes to the Treasury for gold to fill the vacancy in their own supplies. Out of what they got they paid, at least in part, the second instalment, and again withdrew Treasury gold. When they had paid the Treasury the fifty-eight million, six hundred and sixty-one thousand dollars they had agreed to give for the bonds, twenty-four million dollars of it had been taken back into the vaults of the banks. This putting in and drawing out was named an "endless chain." It gave temporary relief, but in November the reserve was so low the Government had to sell a second fifty million dollars. This action also gave only temporary relief, forty-five million dollars of the amount received being drawn out of the Treasury in order that it might be paid back to the Government for the bonds now being sold. By such a process the Government was rapidly enlarging its debts and getting only temporary relief.

PLACING THE RESPONSIBILITY

IN one sense the gold speculators were responsible, for they saw an opportunity to make money and did not hesitate to do it even at the expense of the Treasury. But it was the business of good administrators to circumvent them. Cleveland tried to do this by selling bonds with the guarantee of Congress, and when its consent was refused, by selling bonds on his own responsibility. The Republicans said the trouble was due to Democratic blundering, and pointed to the new tariff which did not provide sufficient revenue. The Democrats pointed to the large permanent increase in expenditures fixed on the Government by the Republicans under Harrison, especially the pensions. It is certain that the expenditures played a strong part in Cleveland's embarrassment, and also the failure of the new tariff to provide adequate revenue; for when the gold received from bond sales was exchanged for notes, the notes had to be paid out again to meet the expense of government. Thus they were available for squeezing more gold out of the Government. In effect, Cleveland's bond sales signified borrowing money to meet the high expenses saddled on him by his predecessor. All the time the silver dollars coined by the Government remained in the Treasury with the bullion bought under the Act of 1890.

360   From a cartoon *Their Troubles Begin*, in the *Review of Reviews*, June 1893, reprinted from the
Wasp, San Francisco, May 6, 1893

INTERNATIONAL BIMETALLISM

THE silver men demanded that the two metals, gold and silver, should be taken as money and made the joint basis of currency. Their opponents believed that such action would draw to America all the free silver of the world, and lead to its coinage with consequent inflation of prices, depreciation of our money in exchange for the money of other nations, and such an outflow of gold as would leave no gold coin in the country. They urged that the only way to sustain bimetallism was for all the important nations to agree to maintain it. In 1892, an International Monetary Conference in Brussels had tried to make a plan for such an agreement but had not succeeded. In 1894, much was said about the renewal of efforts of this nature. There was little prospect that Europe would take up bimetallism to please the United States, but most of the Republicans and the anti-silver Democrats dwelt upon the idea as a means of satisfying the silver sentiment in their ranks. The silver leaders derided these attempts to befog the issue and declared for free coinage without waiting for the assent of any other nation. In time, President McKinley approached Britain on this point but received a firm refusal.

"LET WELL ALONE."

John Bull. "No, thank ye, Jonathan. I've done very well with my Gold, and I don't want any Change!"

361   From a cartoon *Let Well Alone* in *Punch*, Oct. 30, 1897

THE CLEVELAND–MORGAN AGREEMENT

ON February 5, 1895, J. Pierpont Morgan, 1837–1913, the leading figure in the New York banking group, had a conference with Cleveland at the White House. At that time the gold reserve stood at less than forty million dollars, and it was believed that it would be speedily exhausted unless something was done. So critical was the situation that Cleveland felt justified in making an agreement with Morgan and other bankers, who formed a syndicate to buy three million, five hundred thousand ounces of gold at a little more than seventeen dollars an ounce, payable in bonds to run for thirty years. The syndicate agreed to get half of the gold abroad and to use its influence with the bankers to break up the "endless chain." This step saved the Treasury from embarrassment for nearly a year, but in January, 1896, it was necessary to sell more bonds. This time one hundred million dollars were sold by popular subscription and at prices seven points higher than in preceding sales. This loan afforded the Treasury enough gold to tide it over to the days of safety. Probably no act of Cleveland's caused more bitter criticism than the Morgan agreement. He turned to Wall Street for aid in keeping the national currency from going automatically to a depreciated silver basis which was exactly what a majority of his party followers desired. Cleveland's action required rare courage. The episode demonstrated his willingness to take abuse when he knew that his action was necessary and right. When it was known that the Government would not hesitate to go to extreme limits to protect the credit of the Treasury, all fears of depreciation passed, and that in itself went far to meet the emergency.

MORGAN TALKS WITH CLEVELAND.

The New York Banker Calls Upon the President to Discuss the Financial Outlook.

MEETING OF THE CABINET.

Its Session Lasts Several Hours and Gives Rise to a Lot of Disquieting Rumors.

REED'S SCHEME PRESENTED.

He Disappoints His Friends by Not Coming Out Squarely for a Sound Money Measure.

[BY TELEGRAPH TO THE HERALD.]
HERALD BUREAU,
CORNER FIFTEENTH AND G STREETS, N. W.,
WASHINGTON, Feb. 5, 1895.

Secretary Carlisle and J. Pierpont Morgan were among the first visitors at the White House this morning, and from the time of their arrival until late this evening the President devoted himself exclusively to the consideration of the financial situation.

Secretary Carlisle remained after Mr. Morgan left, and the other members of the Cabinet arrived at eleven o'clock and remained until nearly four o'clock—one of the longest Cabinet meetings since the beginning of the administration. This unusually long session of the Cabinet, and the fact that Secretary Carlisle remained until nearly dinner-time, set in motion several rather sensational rumors. It was reported that the administration had struck a snag in its effort to place an issue of coin bonds at anything like a low rate of interest. It was said there was a great deal of friction in the syndicate that was expected to buy the bonds for foreign account, and that Mr. Belmont, who was in the city to-day, had informed Secretary Carlisle that he could not purchase anything for the foreign establishment he represents except gold bonds.

It was also said there had been a great deal of difference of opinion manifested in the Cabinet meeting, and that the President had lost hope of placing the bonds at anything like a reasonable rate of interest. The difference of opinion in the Cabinet was declared to be of such a grave character that the resignation of Secretary Carlisle was to be looked for at almost any moment.

These reports caused considerable apprehension, and it was feared the bond issue would collapse, and a panic follow, which would wipe out the gold reserve and place the Treasury upon a silver basis.

NO CHANGE OF PLANS.

There was little or no foundation for any of these disquieting rumors. While there has been some difference of opinion in the Cabinet as to all the details of the course which ought to be pursued in the present emergency, there has been nothing of such a serious character as to make it necessary for Secretary Carlisle or any one else to resign, and I have the best authority for the statement that there is no more truth in the present report of the coming resignation of the Secretary of the Treasury than there has been in any other reports that were about to leave the Cabinet which have been circulated from time to time.

362   From the *New York Herald*, Feb. 6, 1895

363   President Cleveland at his desk, from a photograph, courtesy of Mrs. Thomas J. Preston, Jr.

CLEVELAND DENOUNCED

THE silver leaders were waiting with grim satisfaction to see the finances of the administration break down through sticking to a gold policy. When they saw the President escape from what seemed certain destruction by agreeing with Morgan they broke into cries of rage. As the syndicate had taken the bonds at one hundred and four and offered them at once at one hundred and twelve and a quarter, they denounced Cleveland for "selling out to Wall Street." In their rage some of them went to the extreme of charging that he received a portion of the syndicate's profits, a charge that sensible and cool-headed people dismissed immediately. Cleveland had acted in full realization of what would be said, but he did not think his personal interests should count when, as he thought, the safety of the country's business demanded action. He was a man possessed of old-time honesty and moral courage. To him the duty of self-elimination was a real thing. He rose in politics by reason of these homely virtues which made other people trust him. The charge that he profited personally by the Morgan contract was forgotten by fair-minded people.

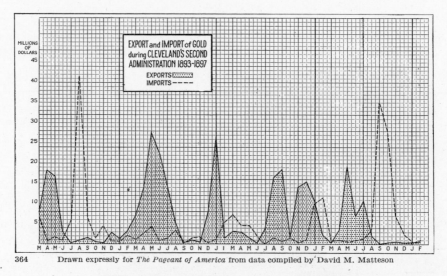

364   Drawn expressly for *The Pageant of America* from data compiled by David M. Matteson

THE GOLD IMPORTS AND EXPORTS

THE exportation of gold took place with marked irregularity. Some months almost no gold was sent out of the country, while in others the amount was large. This varying action was due to the peculiar conditions of demand in Europe and to the special plans of the men engaged in the business. The graph shows this process. It also shows that between the large importations in the panic days of 1893 and the latter half of 1897 there was a large and continuous outgo of gold. One of its interesting points is that it indicates with what a comparatively small importation of gold the country was enabled to escape from the feeling of impending disaster after it was known that the Morgan agreement was in operation.

THE VENEZUELAN BOUNDARY DISPUTE

THE United States now became involved in a South American controversy of long standing. It can be traced back to 1815 when Great Britain acquired present British Guiana from Holland. This territory lay vaguely eastward of Venezuela. Each country was largely wilderness and no definite boundary had been laid out between them. Several times Venezuela asked that a joint commission should be created to run such a line, but Great Britain did not assent. In 1841–42, she sent out Schomburgk, a Dutch surveyor, who ran a line on the basis of Dutch maps. This line made a wide sweep westward and ended on the coast near the mouth of the Orinoco, which Venezuela considered perilous, since her domain was the valley of that river and the presence of another power on one side of the mouth was a menace. She protested the line, but without effect. After Schomburgk ran his line, gold was discovered west of it,

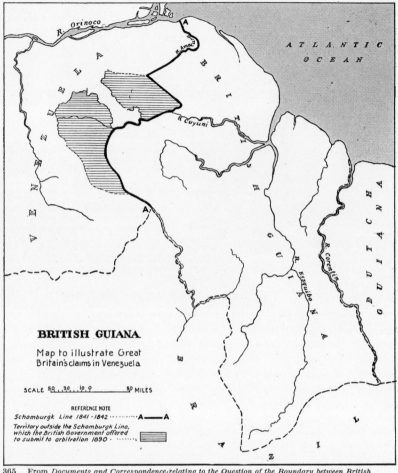

BRITISH GUIANA

Map to illustrate Great Britain's claims in Venezuela.

SCALE 50 30 10 0   50 MILES

REFERENCE NOTE

Schomburgk Line 1841-1842 .... A——A

Territory outside the Schomburgk Line, which the British Government offered to submit to arbitration 1890 ....

365   From *Documents and Correspondence relating to the Question of the Boundary between British Guiana and Venezuela Presented to the Houses of Parliament, March 1896*, London, 1896

whereupon the British found an excuse for extending their line still further westward. For fifty years Venezuela tried in vain to induce the British to come to terms she could accept. Finally, she asked the United States to use her good offices to get Britain to consent to arbitration. Her powerful adversary took the position that the line was settled and there was nothing to arbitrate.

366   Richard Olney, 1835–1917, from a photograph by James Notman, Boston

CLEVELAND'S SYMPATHY WITH VENEZUELA

CLEVELAND felt that Great Britain was bullying a weak neighbor, and that the gradual extension of her boundary was contrary to the spirit of the Monroe Doctrine. He supported the Venezuelan request for arbitration; but the British Government would concede nothing. Then Cleveland, early in 1895, got Congress to pass a resolution endorsing arbitration. Thus armed, he acted vigorously. On July 20, the Secretary of State, Olney, wrote a dispatch to the Prime Minister, who was also Foreign Secretary, pointing out the connection of the situation with the Monroe Doctrine, urging the recourse to arbitration and explicitly requiring information as to what Great Britain would do about it. The tone of the dispatch showed that Cleveland's patience was exhausted.

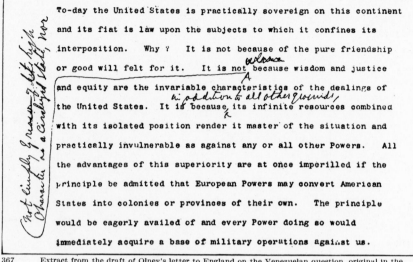

To-day the United States is practically sovereign on this continent and its fiat is law upon the subjects to which it confines its interposition.   Why ?   It is not because of the pure friendship or good will felt for it.   It is not because wisdom and justice and equity are the invariable characteristics of the dealings of the United States.   It is because its infinite resources combined with its isolated position render it master of the situation and practically invulnerable as against any or all other Powers.   All the advantages of this superiority are at once imperilled if the principle be admitted that European Powers may convert American States into colonies or provinces of their own.   The principle would be eagerly availed of and every Power doing so would immediately acquire a base of military operations against us.

367   Extract from the draft of Olney's letter to England on the Venezuelan question, original in the Department of State, Washington

OLNEY'S MISTAKE

OLNEY's dispatch of July 20, 1895, was much too outspoken for good diplomacy.   He was an excellent lawyer and had just been promoted from Attorney-General to Secretary of State.   Perhaps he had not yet cast off the manner of the prosecutor, and certainly he had not acquired the tact of the negotiator.   He evidently felt that a strong statement was necessary to make the Prime Minister treat the situation as serious.   In claiming that the United States was supreme in the Western Hemisphere and that its fiat was law, he issued a challenge that could not be ignored.   But the language he used was so violent that it weakened his case needlessly.

LORD SALISBURY'S BUNGLING

As early as the late 'seventies Lord Salisbury, then a young assistant in the Foreign Office, had become acquainted with the Venezuelan situation and hence he was thoroughly cognizant in 1895 of the whole nature of the dispute.   It is hard to avoid the conclusion that his conduct toward Venezuela was sheer bullying.   When suddenly he awoke to find that the cause of this little state was taken up by a big state, his first impulse was to scold and defy.   The reply he sent to Olney's bristling letter was in the nature of the reproof an elderly man administers to an uninformed little boy.   He declined to arbitrate the Schomburgk line and he read Olney a lecture on the meaning of the Monroe Doctrine which, he said, had ceased to be an active principle in international relations, since the occasion for which it was created was past.   His lordship was undoubtedly irritated; it is probable also that he thought Olney's temper would improve if it encountered a similar display of vigor on the other side.   It seems certain that if Cleveland had acquiesced in his idea of the Monroe Doctrine that famous instrument would have passed into the lumber room of historical curiosities.

"THE COMPLIMENTS OF THE SEASON!!"

President Cleveland. "Waal, Salisbury, Sir, whether you like it or not, We propose to arbitrate on this matter Ourselves, and, in that event, We shall abide by Our Own decision."

368   From a cartoon The Compliments of the Season, by Linley Sambourne in Punch, Dec. 28, 1895

CLEVELAND EXPLODES A BOMB

THIS quarrel of diplomats reached its most critical state without the knowledge of the people of either country. Great was their astonishment when, on December 17, 1895, Cleveland sent to Congress a special message reciting the whole story and pointing out the bearing it had on the Monroe Doctrine. He asked Congress to create a commission to ascertain the true dividing line between Venezuela and British Guiana and declared that, the line once ascertained, the United States should see that it was enforced. Congress did all he asked promptly and without misgivings. This sudden raising of a war cloud shocked public opinion, business men became alarmed, and all minds turned to some way of adjustment.

THE DISPUTE ADJUSTED

GREAT BRITAIN did not protest against our commission but even put her papers at its disposal. On March 3, 1896, Salisbury announced that he would accept a suggestion

369 From a cartoon *Getting the Old Gun Ready*, by Homer C. Davenport in the collection of the American Antiquarian Society

made by Olney on November 12 for referring the dispute to an international tribunal, one feature of which was that British subjects should not be turned out of lands held for fifty years. The tribunal received the finding of facts by the commission in an amicable spirit and produced a treaty which was accepted by each contestant as a settlement of the long dispute. As might have been expected in light of the fifty-year rule, it defined a line corresponding to a large extent to the Schomburgk Line.

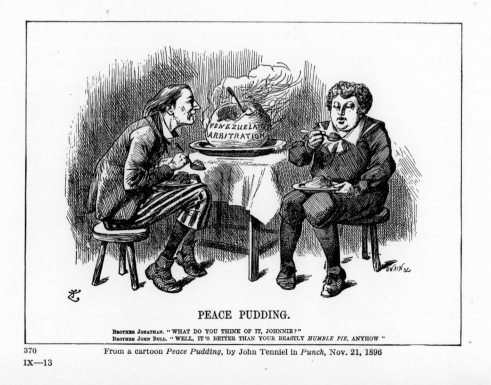

PEACE PUDDING.

BROTHER JONATHAN. "WHAT DO YOU THINK OF IT, JOHNNIE?"
BROTHER JOHN BULL. "WELL, IT'S BETTER THAN YOUR BEASTLY *HUMBLE PIE*, ANYHOW"

370   From a cartoon *Peace Pudding*, by John Tenniel in *Punch*, Nov. 21, 1896

A SIMPLE DEFINITION.

Master Johnny Bull. "Monroe Doctrine! What *is* the 'Monroe Doctrine'?"
Master Jonathan. "Wa-al—guess it's that everything everywhere belongs to *us*!"

371   From a cartoon *A Simple Definition*, by John Tenniel in
       Punch, Nov. 2, 1895

A NEW MONROE DOCTRINE

The Monroe Doctrine of 1823 applied chiefly to colonization, and had been called forth by a specific emergency. It was invoked when France entered Mexico in 1861, and it was frequently alluded to in the discussions over the construction of the Isthmian Canal. It was bound to be mentioned in the correspondence over Venezuela, and for Cleveland to accept Salisbury's view of the Monroe Doctrine was to abandon it. His strong insistence that the right to prevent colonization carried the right to protect a state from encroachment by a European nation gave the Doctrine a very real significance for the future. Europe did not agree with the new view, but having asserted it so strongly in 1895 the United States could not take a weak position on it thereafter. Many very excellent people in the country regretted Cleveland's interpretation, but his position was popular with the majority.

MARK HANNA IN CONTROL OF THE REPUBLICAN PARTY

As the thoughts of the nation swung back from foreign affairs to domestic politics the figure of Mark Hanna of Ohio arrested general attention. He was a great manufacturer who saw public life from the business man's point of view. In 1891 he took an important part in the Ohio campaign and had come to love the struggle for political success. He had a warm affection for McKinley and made up his mind he would make him President in 1896. In the winter before the convention Hanna traveled far and wide, interviewing business men and presenting McKinley to them as the business man's friend. When the Republican convention met he had promises from enough delegates to nominate his candidate. Old-time politicians were surprised at the sudden power of this new man who had never before taken a conspicuous place in party councils. The majority of the delegates came and went to and from his headquarters, describing the situation, reporting promises, and in various ways building up his support. Wise and strong management was necessary, for there were forces working under the surface which might, unless watched, cause an explosion at any moment.

372   Mark Hanna receiving Delegates at Republican Headquarters, from a sketch by M. de Lipman in the
       New York Journal, June 13, 1896

373   Senator Teller receiving visitors in the Colorado Headquarters, from a sketch by M. de Lipman in the
New York Journal, June 17, 1896

A GOLD PLANK ADOPTED

WHILE the Democrats had been drifting toward silver, the Republicans had become more and more a gold party. In 1896, a majority of the Republican convention were ready to declare for gold, but Hanna did not wish them to make the declaration until the last possible moment, fearing that if it was made early in the meeting it would give the silver Republicans an opportunity to get up some kind of a movement against the nomination of McKinley. The silver delegates sensed the situation but were powerless to affect it. When the platform was reported, with a plank declaring for the gold standard, thirty-four delegates with Senator Teller, of Colorado, at their head withdrew from the convention. To soften its blow the convention indicated its approval of the free coinage of silver with international coöperation. The first ballot gave McKinley the nomination by a large majority.

MEETING OF THE DEMOCRATIC CONVENTION

FOR two years before the Democratic convention met in Chicago, the silver men had been working hard to organize silver sentiment in the party. They succeeded in capturing most of the delegates from the western and southern states, which gave them control of the convention. For the gold Democrats they had no consideration. Though the executive committee had decided upon Hill for temporary chairman the majority voted him down. None but silver men were to receive recognition in this convention. The platform had a plank declaring for "the free and unlimited coinage of both gold and silver at the present legal ratio of sixteen to one, without waiting for aid and consent of any other nations." A substitute offered by the gold supporters failed by a vote of three hundred and three to six hundred and twenty-six, and a motion to endorse Cleveland's administration was lost by a vote of three hundred and fifty-seven to five hundred and sixty-four.

374   William Jennings Bryan, 1860–1925, from a photograph taken in 1896 by Pach Bros., New York

375   Bryan accepting the nomination at Madison Square Garden, New York, from a drawing by
                C. S. Reinhart in *Harper's Weekly*, Aug. 22, 1896

THE WEST AND THE SOUTH

In an interval, while waiting for the report of the committee on the platform, various persons made speeches. David B. Hill, of New York, tried to defend sound money, but his cold manner and his staccato voice displeased the audience as much as his ideas. The Cleveland men then put up Governor William E. Russell of Massachusetts, a fine speaker and popular, but the delegates would not listen to him.

The silver men first put up Senator Benjamin Tillman, of South Carolina, whose theme was the union of the West and the South in resistance to New York domination. He spoke with force but with so much bitterness that his friends felt he was not convincing his hearers. At this juncture William Jennings Bryan, until then little known nationally, came to the platform. Opening with a clear, unimpassioned voice that reached all parts of the hall he spoke the words of a prophet for silver. The turbulent scenes that his speech produced have led us to think that the speech was itself passionate. The reverse is true. It was a wonderfully plain presentation of the free silver idea. But it was more than that; it was a strong plea for the desires of the middle and lower class man against the policies that minister to the comforts of the rich and fortunate. Perhaps its greatest appeal was in the latter sense. The South and the West, Tillman and Bryan, had spoken and the West had taken the leadership of the new movement. Bryan's speech won him the nomination.

BRYAN GOES TO THE PEOPLE

The campaign soon resolved itself into a contest between Hanna and Bryan. The Republicans had counted on a quiet appeal to the people, with the tariff as the main talking point. Bryan forced the issue on silver, which the Republicans wished to keep in the background. He thus took the initiative in the fighting and the campaign assumed a vigorous character. He made four long speaking tours, drawing immense crowds. No candidate before this had made such an appeal in his own canvass. The size and eagerness of the crowds which listened to him showed that he was making a strong impression. In fact, political campaigning in the United States was entering a new stage of development. Previously a nominee for a high office had kept himself in a cloud of dignity and the mass of the people had been content to read what the newspapers said of him. Bryan's innovation was to allow the candidate to show himself to the people in all the realism of everyday humanity.

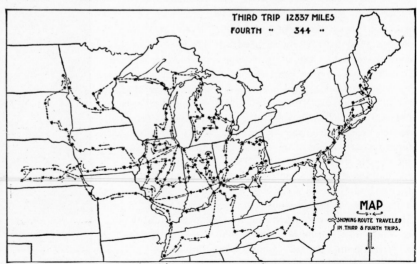

376   Part of Bryan's tour as candidate in 1896, from W. J. Bryan, *The First Battle*, Chicago, 1897

377   McKinley addressing survivors of his old regiment at Canton, from a drawing by Lucius Hitchcock in *Harper's Weekly*, Aug. 29, 1896

McKINLEY'S FRONT-PORCH SPEECHES

HANNA thought that the people would tire of Bryan's spectacular method of campaigning and planned that McKinley should do just the reverse, remaining at home in Canton and receiving delegations brought to him from various places. The speeches he made on these occasions were given to the country through the press, and read in every corner of the land. McKinley's front-porch campaign, as it was called, lasted through the summer, in spite of some doubts whether it was an effective offset to the methods of Bryan. It was an expensive form of campaign.

HANNA'S USE OF MONEY

IN former times the expenses of a Presidential campaign were comparatively moderate. Fighting for political ideals was likely to elicit more unpaid service than fighting for the economic advantage of some particular class or individuals. Furthermore, under the old régime many of the campaign workers were paid with offices. Hanna, as a practical business man, realized that much money would be needed to carry a nation-wide campaign of economic propaganda. The issues were such as enabled him to draw large contributions from wealthy men. To give money for establishing protection was wise in the minds of many manufacturers, and to spend money to ward off the evil of free silver was looked upon as virtuous by many capitalists in the highest stations. Hanna had a large sum to spend, estimated at from four and a half to eight million dollars, or even more. It is commonly thought that he needed all he had to compass the defeat of Bryan.

378   From a cartoon *Honest Money*, by Homer C. Davenport in the *New York Journal*, Sept. 12, 1896

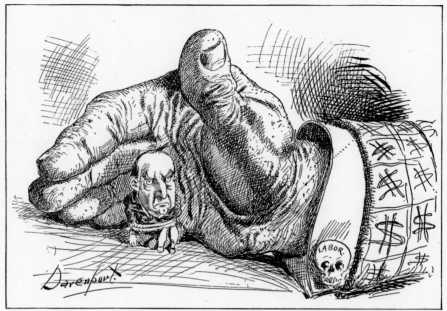

379   From a cartoon *A Man of Mark*, by Homer C. Davenport in the *New York Journal*, Oct. 13, 1896

McKINLEY ELECTED

THE strong part taken by Hanna in conducting the campaign of 1896 led to the popular opinion that he dominated McKinley, but the relation between the two men was otherwise. McKinley was a man of kind and firm character, quite able to take care of himself, but he trusted Hanna as a manager of things political. It seems that Hanna did not try after the election to influence McKinley's policies, being content to elect him to office and to live closely at his side.   Hanna's campaign management was brilliantly successful; for McKinley carried the election of 1896 by a vote of two hundred and seventy-one to one hundred and seventy-six. His strength lay in the manufacturing states and in the large cities; Bryan had most of the South and two of the agricultural states in the West, Kansas and Nebraska, with Washington and all of the mining states except California. He was not cast down and wrote an account of the campaign with the title, *The First Battle*. He was destined to have a remarkable career but strategically he had made a bad beginning. He never fully recovered from the effect of having championed what most Americans held to be false economic views in his first appearance in national politics.

380   Grover Cleveland at the polls, from a sketch by V. Gribayedoff
in *Frank Leslie's Illustrated Weekly*, Nov. 17, 1892

CHAPTER VIII

McKINLEY AND THE WAR WITH SPAIN

AFTER the turbulent administration of the Democrats under Cleveland when his party was divided against itself, the country turned with relief to quiet times under a sure conservative. It was opened with a brief period of tariff legislation, but soon came the war with Spain, a short struggle, victory, and then the solution of a number of problems which that conflict had created. The war set into active play many kinds of business. Contractors prospered by furnishing supplies to the quickly raised armies, and the stimulus thus given to industry, together with the general sense of gratification on account of the victory achieved, produced a feeling of confidence in the public mind. McKinley's Presidency became a period of national and business content.

A protective tariff and the gold standard were the two chief promises of the Republicans in the campaign of 1896. Soon after his inauguration, McKinley called Congress in extra session to consider the tariff. During the preceding campaign the gold Democrats had been urged to vote for the Republican candidate, and to that end they had been assured that no violent policy of protection would follow the election of McKinley. When the matter came before Congress, however, these assurances were forgotten. The President did, in fact, try to keep the promises made; but the manufacturers were too strong for him, and the Dingley tariff of 1897 embodied the desires of the extreme protectionists in the country.

As to the other campaign promise, the gold standard, McKinley was able to get Congress to proceed in a leisurely manner. To its impatient advocates he replied that the platform of 1896 promised that gold should be adopted as the standard if it was not possible to obtain international bimetalism. Holding back their demands for immediate action, he went through the form of suggesting to European powers that steps be taken to set up a double money standard by joint action. To his overtures no favorable reply was received. But almost immediately the country was thrown into war, and nothing was done in the matter until peace returned. It was not until 1900 that he felt at liberty to take it up. In that year Congress passed a law adopting the gold standard and providing for the creation of a separate gold reserve fund for the redemption of the notes issued by the Government.

During the war, party feeling was abated. All sorts of people united to help win a victory. It was of special interest that the South showed itself as loyal to the cause as the North. The President's kindly spirit was particularly manifested in this connection. He appointed to high military rank men who had served in the Confederate armies and made speeches in the South which were marked efforts at conciliation. At Memphis, Tennessee, he went so far as to suggest that the time might come when the national Government would do something to make comfortable the old age of indigent former Confederates. These efforts produced a very deep feeling of gratitude in the South. McKinley's popularity and the sense of national oneness reacted strongly on the election of 1900, in which he was victorious by a large majority over William J. Bryan, who still mastered the national Democratic organization. In the process of adjusting the country to the results of the war, McKinley was already launched when he was slain by a crazed anarchist, September 14, 1901.

381　　William McKinley, 1843–1901, from a photograph by L. C. Handy, Washington

THE RETURN OF THE REPUBLICANS

McKinley was inaugurated, March 4, 1897, with every indication of relief on the part of the public. The prospect of free and unlimited coinage of silver had struck the average business man as a nightmare of unsound finance. It would have meant the inflation of prices, the suspension of the redemption of Treasury notes in the only money that was accepted as standard in the markets of the world, and the upsetting of business obligations of all kinds. To such persons McKinley meant safety. They hailed his advent to office as an indication that business would go on as before and a guaranty that prosperity would revive and continue. The return to prosperity was aided by the unexpected discovery of gold in the Yukon valley. A rush followed. The result was an increase in the amount of gold available for currency which, of itself, was a species of inflation.

McKINLEY'S CABINET

McKinley's Cabinet was headed by John Sherman, as Secretary of State. His appointment, made when it was already evident that our relations with Spain over Cuba demanded the greatest care, was intended to satisfy Hanna, who wished to be near McKinley. Hanna had been offered the Secretaryship of the Treasury. Unwilling to bind himself to an office of routine, he declined, announcing that he would accept no office from the administration. Then he got McKinley to appoint Sherman, who in order to become Secretary gave up the office of Senator. Hanna, with McKinley's approval, then secured the vacant senatorship. Sherman was nearly seventy-four years old and his intellectual powers were weakened; it was soon evident that he could not discharge in a proper way the duties of his office. William R. Day succeeded Sherman in April, 1898, and was followed in turn by John Hay in September.

382　　　　McKinley's Cabinet, from a drawing in *Harper's Weekly*, Mar. 13, 1897

LEFT TO RIGHT: Lyman J. Gage, Secretary of the Treasury; President McKinley; John Sherman, Secretary of State; Joseph McKenna, Attorney-General; John D. Long, Secretary of the Navy; James A. Gary, Postmaster-General; Cornelius N. Bliss, Secretary of the Interior; James Wilson, Secretary of Agriculture; Russell A. Alger, Secretary of War.

THE POSITION OF HANNA

In Washington, Hanna's real position was that of unofficial advisor of the President in matters political. He was also the powerful friend of "big business." He was very honest and in general he was frank. He had a firm grip on the organization of his party and his word was as good as his bond. He was the author of the term "stand pat," coined to express political conservatism. His mastery of the machine, which made him so much respected by politicians, was a source of weakness; for it aroused popular suspicion and made many people think of him both as a tyrant and as a tool of the trusts. He was, in fact, an early manifestation of the business man in politics with business methods and a long purse.

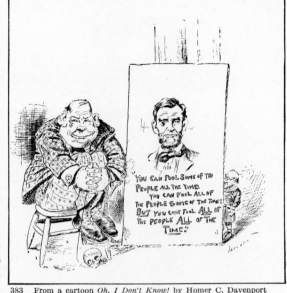

383 From a cartoon *Oh, I Don't Know!* by Homer C. Davenport in the *New York Journal*, 1897

384 Marcus A. Hanna, 1837–1904, from a photograph by Underwood & Underwood, New York

HANNA AND McKINLEY

The general talk about the large part played by Hanna created an impression that he overshadowed the President and reduced him to a nullity. The idea was erroneous. While not so aggressive as Hanna, McKinley was by no means a nullity. He was a man of political theories, which cannot be said of Hanna, and he was conscientious in living up to them. In such matters he played his own hand, and Hanna looked on admiringly. There was implicit confidence between the two men and no small degree of personal affection. Hanna does not seem to have influenced his friend's great decisions, such as the war against Spain and the retention of the Philippines. It was his task to keep solid the basis of party power which kept his friend in office. His influence at McKinley's side gave confidence to the business world.

FUTILE ATTEMPTS TO ESTABLISH ARBITRATION

The diplomatic flurry caused by the Venezuelan incident caused many people to turn to arbitration as a means of settling disputes between nations. This conviction led to the formulation of a general arbitration treaty between the United States and Great Britain, which was drafted in Washington, approved by the British Government, and sent to the Senate for ratification in the last days of Cleveland's administration. McKinley took it up with zeal and urged the Senate to accept it; but that body rejected it by a majority of two votes. The Senators based their objection on the ground that it reduced the constitutional power of the Senate, to which was entrusted the authority to make treaties in settlement of diplomatic disputes as they arose. The principle was taken up in the Hague Conference, which met for the first time in 1899,

385 Signing of the Arbitration Treaty with Great Britain, from *Harper's Weekly*, Jan. 30, 1897

386   From a caricature *Nelson Dingley, Jr., the Gentleman from Maine,*
by Homer C. Davenport in *Cartoons,* New York, 1898

THE DINGLEY TARIFF, 1897

McKINLEY called Congress in extra session on March 15, 1897, to consider the tariff. He attributed a business depression to the recent Democratic tinkering with the tariff and said that the "distress among the people" made it necessary to have an immediate change. The result was the Dingley Act. As passed by the House, it was a more moderate bill than the McKinley Act of 1890; but the Senate amended it to such an extent that the rates, when the bill finally became law, were higher than those of 1890. It was estimated that the rates under the McKinley Act averaged $49\frac{1}{2}\%$, under the Wilson-Gorman Act from 40% to $41\frac{3}{4}\%$, and under the Dingley Act from $49\frac{7}{8}\%$ to 52%. This action greatly disappointed the gold Democrats who had voted for McKinley with the assurance that his election would not be followed by extreme tariff legislation. (See page 193.) The Democratic tariff, moreover, had been predicated upon an income tax which the Supreme Court had declared unconstitutional. This decision had brought about a serious derangement of Government finances. A revision of the revenue measures was, therefore, necessary.

In passing the Dingley tariff the Republican leaders were merely carrying forward a protectionist policy which they had openly espoused in the passage of the McKinley tariff in 1890. They interpreted the election of McKinley as a popular endorsement of their stand.

HOW THE TRUSTS USED THEIR POWER

REFLECTION showed that the trusts were the results of the application of intelligence to the processes of productive industry. A great business was able to dominate its smaller competitors, who soon came to see that it was wiser to follow its example than to provoke it to war. In an investigation by a Senate committee in February, 1897, John Arbuckle, head of the largest coffee firm in America, admitted that the prices which he set were of necessity adopted by other dealers in the same article. Such a practice had the practical effect of placing him at the head of the trade; and it showed that by acting in unison the coffee men had thrown over the laws of competition, on which economists had previously relied to insure fair prices to the consumers. The integration of business was an inevitable result of the industrialism that followed the Civil War but the modification of the law of competition presented many new and difficult problems to the Government, problems unsolved to this day.

387   John Arbuckle, from a sketch by M. de Lipman in the *New York Journal,* Feb. 8, 1897

SPAIN'S CUBAN POLICY

ABOUT this time the country became deeply interested in Cuba. Spain had used Cuba for her own advantage. In 1895, the Cuban revenues amounted to twenty-six million dollars, half of which went to pay the Spanish debts, one fourth to support Spain's army and navy, and much of the remainder to maintain offices created in the island for the benefit of Spaniards. Only one million dollars went to the support of schools and pub-

388   The Prado, Havana, from a drawing by Childe Hassam in Harper's *Pictorial History of the War with Spain*, New York, 1899

lic improvements. Against this kind of exploitation the native Cubans revolted. From 1868 to 1878, they waged a Ten Years' War against Spain and were at last persuaded to lay down their arms upon the promise of reforms, the most important of which was autonomous government. On one pretext after another, autonomy was postponed until finally in 1895 an edict of so-called autonomy was issued from Madrid. It placed the government of the island under a Council, half of which were to be appointed by the Crown and half elected in Cuba on the basis of a suffrage which left the large majority of the natives without votes. The result was that the liberals in Cuba again took up arms and vowed not to submit until *Cuba Libre* was an accomplished fact.

389   "The Ditches," Havana, for the shelter of *Reconcentrados*, by W. A. Rogers, from a drawing after a photograph, in *Harper's Weekly*, April 2, 1898

THE UNITED STATES AND CUBA

THE war in Cuba made complications for the United States. Many Cubans came to the United States, took out papers of naturalization, and then escaped to the scene of conflict. When captured, they claimed the protection of this Government. Spain's policy toward the insurgents was very severe. Although she sent a large army to the island, no progress was made in restoring peace. She issued orders of *reconcentration*, forcing the inhabitants of villages to live in fortified towns where no provision was made for their support, shelter and health, so that many of them died from exposure and starvation. The policy itself was not bad, and was used by the American army later on in the Philippines: its harshness in Cuba arose from the poor sustenance given by the Government to its victims. General Weyler, the Spanish commander, carried out this policy with sternness. He let it be seen that he despised the sympathy manifested in the United States for the victims of his cruelty, with the result that American opinion ran strongly for the Cubans.

390 From a cartoon *She Is Getting Too Feeble To Hold Them*, by J. S. Pughe
in *Puck*, Nov. 18, 1896

CLEVELAND'S ATTITUDE

FROM the beginning of their struggle of 1895, the Cubans endeavored to get the United States to intervene on their behalf. They organized an active propaganda, which had such success that public opinion was strongly aroused. Popular sympathy for Cuba naturally found its echo in Congress. In February, 1896, Congress passed a concurrent resolution recognizing the insurgents as belligerents and offering the good offices of the United States for the recognition of Cuban independence. Cleveland was not willing to go that far and ignored the resolutions. But he took occasion to offer his services to Spain to mediate between her and Cuba with the view of establishing autonomy in the island. Spain declined his offer with scant courtesy. In his last message to Congress Cleveland said that if Spain did not restore order in her colony and if Cuba reached the point of becoming merely a scene of desolation and human distress, it might become the duty of the United States to intervene at the behest of "higher obligations" than the recognition of Spain's sovereignty.

McKINLEY'S ATTITUDE

McKINLEY was supposed to be still more in sympathy with the insurgents than Cleveland had been, but for a year he followed the same policy as his predecessor, trying to get Spain to give Cuba effective self-government, which at that time would have been accepted as a basis of peace. He was much handicapped by the inability of Sherman, his Secretary of State, to deal with the situation efficiently; therefore he placed William R. Day, a good lawyer, at Sherman's side as Assistant Secretary of State, giving him so much authority in Cuban affairs that Sherman eventually resigned, but not until April 25, 1898, when the tense diplomatic situation had given place to actual war. Day then became head of the department. He proved to be sensible and industrious. He managed the Cuban situation in a manner that suited McKinley, who was confronted by a strong public demand that the United States should do something that would help the Cubans gain autonomy if not complete independence. McKinley did not feel like opposing the demand and so the country drifted toward war.

391 William R. Day, 1849–1923, Assistant Secretary of State, from a drawing made at
Washington, in the *New York Herald*, March 27, 1898

FITZHUGH LEE CONSUL IN HAVANA

DURING this time, Fitzhugh Lee, nephew of the commander of the Confederate armies in the Civil War, was our consul-general in Cuba. He had been appointed by Cleveland, but the state of affairs was so critical when McKinley became President that it was thought proper not to remove him. Lee found his position extremely difficult. The leading business men of Cuba, for the most part Spaniards, were against the insurgents; and they looked upon the offers of a United States President to promote a settlement as nothing less than presumptuous meddling. This feeling was particularly strong in Havana, where the consul-general was obliged to witness many expressions of popular hostility to his country's flag, attempts which the Spanish authorities did little to restrain.

DESTRUCTION OF THE *MAINE*

So violent were the demonstrations against the United States that Lee asked that a man-of-war be sent to Havana harbor as a warning to the furious populace. The suggestion was accepted at once by the government in Washington, and on January 25 the United States battleship *Maine*

392   Fitzhugh Lee, 1835–1905, from a photograph by Keystone View Company, New York

dropped anchor in Havana harbor ostensibly on a friendly visit. During the night of February 15, she was destroyed by a great explosion, which subsequent investigation showed came from some force, probably a mine, outside her hull. The incident caused much indignation in the United States and increased the tension of the hour.

393   From a cartoon *The Nation's Grief*, by Charles Nelan in the *New York Herald*, Feb. 18, 1898

394   Praxedes Mateo Sagasta, 1827–1903, from
Harper's *Pictorial History of the War with
Spain*, New York, 1899

RECALL OF WEYLER AND THE POLICY OF SAGASTA

ALTHOUGH Spain held her head so high, the course of events had begun to modify her unwillingness to treat with the Cubans. A liberal party had arisen in Madrid insisting that something be done to satisfy the demands of the United States. At the head was Sagasta, who became Prime Minister in September, 1897. His first act was to recall General Weyler and to place Cuba under General Blanco, known in the island for his mild views. The policy of re-concentration was modified, and on November 27 an order for Cuban autonomy was issued in Madrid. McKinley decided to wait and see in what manner it would be en-

395   General Valeriano Weyler, 1839–, from
a photograph

forced. Sagasta was sincere in the offer, but Spanish opinion was very stiff; time and tact would be needed to bring it around. Woodford, our minister in Madrid, urged McKinley to be patient, saying that in the end Spain would grant all that we desired.

McKINLEY'S TRUST IN DIPLOMACY

SAGASTA'S efforts to bring Spanish opinion around to a point of conceding our demands for Cuba slowly bore fruit. On March 31, 1898, he felt strong enough to agree that a Cuban parliament should assemble by

May 4 and take up the question of the pacification of the island; that an armistice would be granted if the insurgents asked for it; and that matters connected with the destruction of the *Maine* were to be settled by arbitration. Woodford sent these proposals to McKinley with the assurance that Sagasta would be driven from office if he consented to grant an armistice unasked, which McKinley had insisted that he should do. Congress was greatly agitated, and only the President's persistent hope of settling the affair by diplomacy kept it from rushing into war to coerce Spain. Thus it happened that McKinley found two tasks on his hands. He had to hold back the hot heads at home and in Spain

396   From a cartoon *Another Old Woman Tries To Sweep Back The Sea*, by Homer C.
Davenport in the *New York Journal*, March 30, 1898

McKINLEY'S SUDDEN CHANGE OF FRONT

In demanding an armistice McKinley had said that he would lay the situation before Congress if the demand was not granted by April 6. On that day nothing had come from Madrid, but he received a visit from the representatives in Washington of six of the leading European powers who united in an appeal for peace. At the same time came word from the consul-general in Havana asking for more time to get United States citizens out of Cuba before war began. The message to Congress was held back. In

PRESIDENT M'KINLEY RECEIVING THE NOTE OF THE SIX EUROPEAN POWERS.

397 President McKinley receiving the note of the six European powers, from a drawing in the *New York Herald*, April 8, 1898

Europe efforts were made by the Pope to induce Spain to yield, and finally, on April 10, the conservatives gave way. McKinley was informed officially that Blanco, commanding in Cuba, had been ordered to suspend hostilities. It seemed that diplomacy had won; yet the following day McKinley sent to Congress the war message he had prepared, merely adding: "Yesterday, and since the preparation of the foregoing message, official information was received by me that the latest decree of the Queen Regent of Spain directs General Blanco, in order to prepare and facilitate peace, to proclaim a cessation of hostilities, the duration and details of which have not yet been communicated to me." After winning a long diplomatic fight he threw the question to Congress to be settled as popular passions dictated.

398   From the *New York Journal*, March 29, 1898

THE HYSTERICAL PRESS

McKinley's change of front was due to the pressure brought to bear by what was known as "the Yellow Press." Some powerful newspapers had taken his restraint as evidence that he was subservient to "Wall Street." They challenged his honesty, declared that he did not dare call his soul his own, and created such an impression in the average mind that some of the leaders of his party became alarmed. They protested against his course. To satisfy them and preserve party harmony he gave up his efforts for a peaceful adjustment. Says James Ford Rhodes: "McKinley feared a rupture in his own party, and on account of that fear had not the nerve and power to resist the pressure for war." Had he persisted in his negotiations, it is likely that he would have obtained the independence of Cuba within half a year. At any rate, that was the opinion of Woodford in Madrid, where he had the best opportunity to gauge the pressure of public opinion. He was a man of good judgment and was earnestly striving to reach a pacific settlement of the dispute. It was a part of the irony of fate that all his efforts were destined to fail before the home feeling.

DOCTRINE AND PRACTICE.

Dame Europa (coldly). "TO WHOM DO I OWE THE PLEASURE OF THIS INTRUSION?"
Uncle S. "MA'AM—MY NAME IS UNCLE SAM!"
Dame Europa. "ANY RELATION OF THE LATE COLONEL MONROE?"

399 From a cartoon *Doctrine and Practice*, by John Tenniel in *Punch*,
Aug. 6, 1898

EUROPEAN SUSPICIONS

Neither Spain nor the rest of Continental Europe believed that the United States could offer effective force in the coming struggle. Europe, in the main, believed that we had been made soft and flabby by trade and prosperity, that we had no organized army and no officer class, that our appeal to arms was rash, and was sure to lead to defeat. In the Spanish comic press American statesmen, from McKinley down, were depicted as pigs. In Germany, and to a less degree in France, the press and the upper classes were for Spain and against her antagonist. Through the Monroe Doctrine we had long insisted that Europe keep out of American affairs. By briskly stepping between Spain and her colony we were charged with interfering in European affairs, in contradiction to the spirit of the Monroe Doctrine. French people naturally sympathized with their Latin neighbors and looked with some disfavor upon the increase in power of the United States. The Germans probably foresaw that an American victory would remove valuable Spanish colonial territory from possible future German control. Of course our attitude in regard to Cuba was not against the Monroe Doctrine; for Cuba as an American area was within the protection of the Doctrine.

WAR DECLARED BY CONGRESS

Congress deliberated eight days over McKinley's message, and then, on April 19, passed resolutions declaring: (1) that the Cubans were and ought to be free and independent; (2) that the United States demanded the relinquishment of Spanish authority over the island; (3) that the President was directed to use force to carry these resolutions into effect; and (4) that the United States would not take Cuba permanently but would withdraw after the war and leave Cuba to be governed by her own people. It was with their tongues in their cheeks that European statesmen read this last declaration. Their scepticism was shared by the peoples of Hispanic America who looked upon the American declaration of war as an attempt to secure Cuba.

400 Scene in the House after the reading of the war message, from a drawing by W. A. Rogers
in Harper's *Pictorial History of the War with Spain*, New York, 1899

401 Recruiting the Army for War with Spain, courtesy of the United
      States Signal Corps, War Department, Washington

THE SOUTH IN THE WAR

A CALL for an army of volunteers gave an opportunity to show how much the spirit of reunion had grown in the thirty-three years that had elapsed since the end of the Civil War. Sons of Confederate soldiers volunteered as freely as the sons of Union men. In the same uniform and under the same flag they went forth to war in solemn loyalty to their country. In recognition of this

402 General Joseph Wheeler, 1836–
      1906, from a photograph

spirit McKinley nominated Joseph Wheeler and Fitzhugh Lee, who had been major-generals under the Confederacy, to the same military rank in the armies of the United States, and they served effectively in the war now beginning. The manifestation of this feeling of sectional reunion did not surprise men who knew the South; but it gave the North confidence in its former foes and went far to lay the old suspicions, while it gave the southerners a feeling of oneness in the national future.

McKINLEY'S APPEAL TO THE SOUTH

McKINLEY was deeply impressed by the evidences of reconciliation in the South, and he sought to strengthen them with an eye to future conditions. In 1898, he made a tour through that region, speaking with good effect in many cities. For the time political feeling was in abeyance, and the people there met in the frankest spirit this northern President who came to them bearing good will and benevolence. He was particularly impressive in a speech at Atlanta, where he said that the time had come when the North and the South should unite in caring for the graves of Confederate soldiers. The effects in the South of this expression of good feeling were excellent. For many years the South had been made to feel its isolation. Its solid political situation had meant that most of the political advantages, such as offices and Government appropriations, had gone to other parts of the country. It had come to feel that it was not fully a part of the Union; but McKinley's speech was taken as evidence of a changed relation and it forgot its aloofness.

403 McKinley speaking at Memphis. © Underwood & Underwood, New York

404 The common crier reads the proclamation of Great Britain's neutrality,
     from a drawing by Begg in the *Illustrated London News*, May 7, 1898

ATTITUDE OF GREAT BRITAIN

WHILE the Continental nations leaned toward Spain, Great Britain showed sympathy with the United States. When the Continental nations formed plans for a joint move to restrain the United States, the British Government, by refusing to support the protest, blocked its execution. In 1898, while Dewey commanding an American fleet in Manila Bay was awaiting reinforcements; he was seriously threatened by a large German squadron that disregarded his rights. It seemed probable that a clash would occur, but the commander of the British naval forces there gave clear evidence that he was on Dewey's side, with the result that the German commander assumed a more civil attitude. The feeling of the British was expressed in the phrase, "Blood is thicker than water."

SPAIN IN DEFEAT

DESPITE many evidences that the United States began the war without sufficient preparation, her armies and navies proved to be vastly more efficient than Spain's. In a brief period Dewey destroyed Spain's power in the Philippines, Sampson and Schley broke her naval force in the West Indies, and Shafter took Santiago and held her large Cuban army at his mercy. Sea power was the controlling factor in the war, and the American navy gained the ascendancy in both the Pacific and the Western Atlantic. When Spain started a fleet eastward through the Mediterranean to win back the Philippines, the United States countered with a threat to send a naval force against the Spanish coast. This not only brought about the hasty recall of the eastbound Spanish ships but aroused the neighbors of Spain, who did not desire to see an American fighting force undertake hostile activities in European waters. To resist further was madness, and by the advice of her friends on the Continent Spain sued for peace. On July 18, less by one day than three months after the war began, she asked the French Government to arrange with the United States the preliminary terms of peace. She had gone to war in a fine fit of indignation, thereby showing her sense of honor, and having satisfied that claim she had nothing more to gain. Her defeat in Cuba and in the Philippines ended her long-sustained empire beyond the seas. She had never tried to develop it on a self-supporting basis but had used it as a means of extracting a revenue for her own use. The result of her policy was that the provinces, outside of a small upper class, were not attached to her rule and would not defend it.

"PINNED!"

405   From a cartoon "*Pinned!*" by John Tenniel in *Punch*, July 16, 1898

THE PROTOCOL OF PEACE

CARRYING out the Spanish request for terms of peace, the President on August 10 submitted in a protocol the demands of the United States. It required the cessation of hostilities, the evacuation of Cuba by Spain with the relinquishment of sovereignty, the cession of Porto Rico and one of the Ladrone Islands to the United States as indemnity, and the occupation by the United States of Manila and Manila Bay.

406   M. Jules Cambon, the French Ambassador, signing The Peace Protocol on behalf of Spain, from a painting by T. de Thulstrup in Harper's *Pictorial History of the War with Spain*, New York, 1899

The final disposition of the Philippines was left for settlement in the formal treaty, which was to be drafted at a later date. Spain considered these terms severe and tried to obtain their modification, but the victor was unyielding and on August 12 she signed the protocol in humiliation. It was a confession of her weakness in the world and a severe blow to her pride.

TO RETAIN OR NOT TO RETAIN THE PHILIPPINES

COMMISSIONERS from the two nations met in Paris on October 1, 1898. McKinley was in cable communication with his own commissioners who did nothing without his approval. The main question, left unsettled in the protocol because at that time his mind was not made up, was what to do about the Philippines. Public opinion was divided with reference to it and McKinley hesitated day after day, even after the commission had assembled. His doubts weighed heavily upon him. As he said himself, he consulted the politicians, Republicans and Democrats, and got little help from them. Then he turned to the Deity. "I went down on my knees and prayed Almighty God for light and guidance more than one night. And one night late it came to me this way — I don't know how it was, but it came: (1) that we could not give them back to Spain — that would be cowardly and dishonorable; (2) that we could not turn them over to France or Germany — our commercial rivals in the Orient — that would be bad business and discreditable; (3) that we could not leave them to themselves — they were unfit for self-government — and they would soon have

407   John Hay, Secretary of State, signing the Memorandum of Ratification for the United States, from Harper's *Pictorial History of the War with Spain*, New York, 1899

anarchy and misrule over there worse than Spain's was; and (4) that there was nothing left for us to do but to take them all, and to educate the Filipinos, and uplift and civilize and Christianize them, and by God's grace do the very best we could by them as our fellowmen for whom Christ also died. And then I went to bed and went to sleep and slept soundly." In this manner it was decided that the Philippines should be demanded, but as a salve for her feelings we offered to give Spain twenty million dollars without actually saying that it was in payment for the islands. She could do nothing but accept our demands. The treaty was signed December 10, and ratified by the United States Senate February 6, 1899.

408   Major-General Leonard Wood, 1860–1927, in Cuba, from a
         photograph by Underwood & Underwood, New York

CLEANING UP CUBA

OUR sudden victory left us with two unexpected problems: what should we do with Cuba, and what should we do with the Philippines? Some people wanted us to keep Cuba, with the purpose of introducing our own civilization there. But McKinley, mindful of the promise made in the declaration of war, insisted that it should be given over to the Cubans as an independent state. The island was in a wretched state of sanitation and the schools were sadly neglected. Before withdrawing our forces we gave it a thorough cleaning. Under the direction of Americans the schools were reorganized, teachers were trained, towns were made healthy, roads were built, local government was established, banditry was put down, and the worst effects of misrule were wiped out. It should be remembered that the United States had a vital interest in cleaning up Cuba. The island is close to our shores and there is much intercourse between it and the mainland. A logical way of keeping yellow fever out of the United States was to stamp it out in Cuba. The work of cleaning up Cuba was entrusted to the able military Governor, Major-General Leonard Wood. During Wood's administration Major William C. Gorgas eliminated yellow fever from Havana.

PROTECTORATE OVER CUBA

LATE in 1900 a constitutional convention was elected to make a permanent form of government. As it was completing its labors, our Congress passed the "Platt Amendment to the Army Appropriation Bill." This authorized the withdrawal of the army from Cuba when the Cubans had agreed in their constitution to do seven things, chief among which were to contract no debt which the ordinary revenues would not provide for; to allow the United States to intervene to preserve life, property and liberty; and to sell or lease to the United States coaling and naval stations in Cuba. The Cubans were loath to accept these terms but finally complied, whereupon our troops were withdrawn. A President of Cuba, elected by the people, was installed in office on May 20, 1902. The Island of Cuba is independent, but the United States has a protectorate over it with the power to step in when we think that it is necessary to preserve good government. Thus control has been maintained over these people while they have learned the rules of self-government with the habit of fair elections and submission to the will of the majority.

409   The Cuban Cabinet in 1902, from a photograph by Underwood
         & Underwood, New York

PUTTING THE PHILIPPINES IN ORDER

THE Philippine problem was more difficult. The population consisted of various tribes, some of them in a low state of civilization. To leave the islands in the hands of the natives would lead to chaos and ultimately invite their conquest by some powerful foreign state. McKinley's idea of doing our best by them was entertained by the majority of his fellow-citizens. The situation was complicated by a revolt that broke out just as we acquired treaty rights over the archipelago. The leader of the revolt, Aguinaldo, had coöperated with the Americans against Spain in the hope of setting up a Philippine Republic. It was not until 1902 that Aguinaldo was captured and the revolt put down. That same year Congress passed the "Organic Act" for the Philippines creating a permanent civil government. Under the first Governor, William Howard Taft, the work of educating the natives, training them

410   From a cartoon *What Will He Do With It?*, by Charles Nelan in the *New York Herald*, June 3, 1898

in citizenship, and giving them local and central government was pushed forward steadily. While the United States Government has always talked of ultimate Philippine independence, it has never been willing to say at what time complete independence can be expected.

OUR DEPENDENCIES

FOR our new possessions, acquired from Spain, we used the word "dependencies." It was generally agreed that the dependencies whose inhabitants were racially so different from the people living in continental United States, could not expect to be organized as states and admitted into the Union. They were encouraged to hope for the greatest amount of local self-government, but not for equality with the American states. The form actually adopted did not differ materially from that fixed upon us by Great Britain when we ourselves were colonies. There was to be a Governor and council, appointed from Washington, a legislature elected by the people, and a system of courts, the judges appointed either by the executive at Washington or at the capital of the dependency. Porto Rico was given this kind of government, and the Filipinos were encouraged to expect a wider participation in their government as they showed that they could make it work. As the years have passed this promise has been kept, at least formally, but the amount of self-government granted has not been large enough to satisfy the people.

411   The Escolta, principal thoroughfare of Manila, from a photograph reproduced in *Harper's Weekly*, Aug. 6, 1898

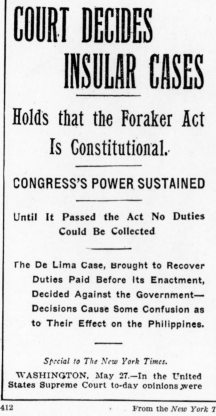

COURT DECIDES INSULAR CASES

Holds that the Foraker Act Is Constitutional.

CONGRESS'S POWER SUSTAINED

Until It Passed the Act No Duties Could Be Collected

The De Lima Case, Brought to Recover Duties Paid Before Its Enactment, Decided Against the Government— Decisions Cause Some Confusion as to Their Effect on the Philippines.

Special to The New York Times.

WASHINGTON, May 27.—In the United States Supreme Court to-day opinions were handed down in all but two of the cases before that court involving the relation of the United States to its insular possessions. The two cases in which no conclusion was announced were those known as the fourteen-diamond-rings case and the second of the Dooley cases. The undecided Dooley case deals with a phase of the Porto Rican question, and the diamond-ring case involves the right to the free importation of merchandise from the Philippines to the United States.

The original intention of the court had been to adjourn for the term after to-day's sitting, but discussion of the cases passed on to-day took about five hours, so the court adjourned until to-morrow, when it is presumed the remaining cases will be passed on.

Of the several cases decided to-day, the two which attracted the greatest share of attention from the court were what is known as the De Lima case and that known as the Downes case, and of these two, the opinion in the Downes case is considered the most far-reaching, as it affects our future relations, whereas the De Lima case dealt with a transitional phase of our insular relations. The De Lima case was the first to receive the attention of the court, and as it appeared to be quite sweepingly opposed to the Government's contentions, many persons precipitately arrived at the conclusion that the Government had been worsted all along the line. This view suffered a decided change when the conclusion was announced in the Downes case. The court was very evenly divided on both cases, but political lines were not at all controlling.

412   From the *New York Times*, May 28, 1900

THE INSULAR CASES

IN connection with the organization of "dependencies" there arose a constitutional debate. Did the Constitution "follow the flag"; that is, should the inhabitants of a dependency have all the privileges granted to American citizens by the Constitution? The issue was brought to a head by the Foraker Act, April 12, 1900, which among other things levied duties on products of Porto Rico imported into continental United States. Under the Constitution Congress cannot thus embarrass the produce of a state in the Union. What are known as the "Insular Cases" brought the question of its right to do so in a dependency before the Supreme Court. In 1901 the court decided in substance that Congress has a free hand legislating for a dependency. So the Government of the United States sought to solve problems of empire not much different from those which had confronted Great Britain in the eighteenth century.

THE "OPEN DOOR" IN CHINA

THE acquisition of the Philippines gave the United States a vital interest in the Orient. Americans were much concerned to see that Great Britain, Germany, Russia and France had established footholds on the Chinese coast and, by creating "spheres of influence" for purposes of trade, were steadily making ready for a division of China. In 1899 John Hay, Secretary of State, sent notes to the European powers concerned asking them to give assurances that they would not, in their respective "spheres of influence," discriminate against the interests of foreigners in port duties and railroad rates or in vested interests, and that they would respect China's right to levy and collect tariffs. This policy was called keeping an "open door." Britain expressed willingness to agree, but the other powers gave polite but inconclusive answers. Hay blandly wrote that he was pleased to see that all agreed as to the wisdom of his suggestion and his Government would consider that the "open door" was to be maintained. His action had, indeed, given wide publicity to what was going on and it constituted a rallying-point in international opinion for opposition to the dismemberment of China by powerful and rapacious nations.

413   John Hay, 1838–1905, from a photograph by Pach Bros., New York

THE GOLD STANDARD ESTABLISHED

THE war with Spain brought about a business revival, due to the stimulus it gave to production of various kinds of supplies and the general feeling of satisfaction that followed the quick and sharp victory. At the same time the world's supply of gold increased largely through the discovery of that metal in the Yukon valley. There was no longer doubt that there was enough gold to support the currency of the world and, in 1900, Congress passed an act to make gold the standard of value. It also decreed that one hundred and fifty million dollars in gold should be set aside as a

414   From a cartoon *Nailing It To The Mast*, by Charles Nelan in the *New York Herald*, Feb. 26, 1900

reserve fund for the redemption of currency, that such notes when redeemed should not be re-issued, and that if the fund fell below one hundred and fifty million dollars the Secretary of the Treasury should sell bonds for gold to raise it again to that mark. Thus the gold standard was legally adopted and the free silver specter was definitely laid in politics.

BRYAN'S CONTINUED DEMOCRATIC LEADERSHIP

BRYAN's defeat in 1896 did not break his hold on his following; this was because his position fundamentally was antagonistic to the standpat conservatives. He was the leader of the small business men and farmers. Although free silver was dead, Bryan with his challenge to the New York business men was alive and very powerful. When the Democrats met in convention in 1900, it was quickly seen that he held the convention in his hand. The mention of his name brought forth enthusiastic demonstrations. The fact that he was the butt of ridicule by the conservatives made his followers only the more determined to retain him as their hero. The convention placed him at the head of the Democratic ticket and pledged him the loyal support of all true Democrats. They could not forget those campaigning tours of four years before when Bryan had appealed to the people with powerful effect. In 1900 he was still a political evangelist with his glamor undimmed.

415   William Jennings Bryan, from a drawing by William Nicholson in *Harper's Weekly*, Oct. 27, 1900

416   From a cartoon *Trying to Paint Out the Old Sign*, in *Harper's Weekly*, Aug. 4, 1900

417   From a cartoon *Ring Master Jones: "That old Imperialism hoop is much safer, William,"* in *Harper's Weekly*, Aug. 4, 1900

BRYAN'S "PARAMOUNT ISSUE"

THE Democrats had not abandoned their theory of free silver though willing to set it aside as a practical issue. Bryan's opponent tried to force him back upon the issues of the previous election with the intention of painting him as the advocate of exploded theories. He met them by saying that the increase of the world's supply of gold made free silver unnecessary at that time, and that other issues were to be met. Among them, he declared, the "paramount issue" was the question of "imperialism," by which he meant the expansion of the United States as a result of war, the possession of the Philippines and Porto Rico, and the consequent need of a large navy and army to defend these remote possessions. He professed to see in America the development of a desire for imperial power, similar to that of ancient Rome, and he predicted that it would lead to national decay. It was on this issue that he staked the chances of his party in the Presidential campaign of 1900. The result showed that the voters were not as much frightened as Bryan thought.

418   The announcement of McKinley's renomination at the 1900 Republican Convention, from a drawing by A. Hencke in *Leslie's Illustrated Weekly*, June 23, 1900

McKINLEY RENOMINATED

McKINLEY was at the height of his popularity and his party turned to him for another term with unanimity. His nomination came as a matter of course. He was praised truly for having brought prosperity to his own people and for having maintained the honor of the country in the eyes of foreign nations. On fundamental points the platform was similar to that of 1896, but with a notable change on the currency plank. It was full of "point-with-pride" spirit and exuded national contentment. McKinley bore himself with his usual natural modesty amid all these outbursts of praise.

MARK HANNA AT THE HELM

MARK HANNA was again chairman of the Republican campaign committee, but his task was far different from that of 1896. Then he had to fight tooth and nail for the victory he obtained; now his road was easy and pleasant. He was no longer a newcomer in party leadership. His direction was accepted by men who hitherto had been the most powerful and the most feared among the leaders of the party. On all domestic matters they were Standpatters. They believed in letting business have its way. Most of these leaders were at the head of powerful state machines and wielded their local power relentlessly. They did not represent the will of the people, and some of them were generally believed to represent almost altogether what Roosevelt later denominated "big business." Rightly or wrongly, there was much popular distrust of Hanna's position; but he had made himself so firm in it that few people thought he could be unseated. In 1900 Hanna reached the acme of his career. But in this year appeared on the national stage in the person of the nominee for Vice-President, a man who was destined to curb the power of the Senator from Ohio. Theodore Roosevelt was Hanna's political rival, taking the opposite tack in matters of principle, but preserving with him the outward forms of friendship.

419   Mark Hanna conferring with party leaders, from a drawing by T. Dart Walker, in *Leslie's Illustrated Weekly*, Oct. 20, 1900

420   From a cartoon *The Most Popular Poster Issued by the Republicans*, in the *American Monthly Review of Reviews*, Nov. 1900

McKINLEY REËLECTED

McKINLEY made few speeches during the campaign. Hanna, who suddenly manifested much talent as an effective public speaker, went into the Far West on a speaking tour. His good nature, courage and capacity for convincing argument went far to counteract the impression that he was the embodiment of a brutal money power. The burden of the argument everywhere was that McKinley had given the country prosperity and a safe issue from the war and that it would be folly to turn him out and put in Bryan with his wild theories. The result was never in doubt, although for a brief period in the midst of the campaign some excitable souls showed signs of nervousness. On the final count, McKinley had two hundred and ninety-two and Bryan one hundred and fifty-five electoral votes. The Democrats carried only four northern states, Colorado, Nevada, Idaho and Montana. This second defeat shook but did not break the hold of the "peerless leader" upon his party. Bryan's power rested on a solid conviction in the West and South that the policies supported in the East were designed to favor the business men of that section at the expense of the rest of the country.

421   From a cartoon *Is He Setting the Switch For the Roosevelt Flyer?*, by Leon Barritt in the
                New York Daily Tribune, June 13, 1900

THEODORE ROOSEVELT

THE most interesting incident in this campaign was the nomination of Roosevelt for Vice-President. This powerful young man had been before the country for several years as a political reformer and especially as champion of reform in the civil service. In 1898, he resigned his position as Assistant Secretary of the Navy to organize and lead a volunteer regiment of "Rough Riders" in the war with Spain. His dashing military career gave him so much popularity that he was nominated by the Republicans for Governor of

New York and elected by a large majority. His election was due in part to the alarm of the party machine, Senator Platt at its head, who felt that because of the bad sort of men they had recently put in office, that now they must put up a popular hero or the party would be defeated. Platt did not want a real reformer, and he thought he could manage Roosevelt. In this hope he was disappointed. Platt then formed the plan to get Roosevelt elected Vice-President, which would rid New York of a Governor over whom the machine was not able to exercise effective control.

ROOSEVELT'S UNSUCCESSFUL PROTEST

ROOSEVELT well understood Platt's purpose. He did not want to give up the New York Governorship, and he believed that he would be sidetracked as Vice-President. He declared he would not accept the proposed nomination and he urged his friends to do all they could against it. Mark Hanna was equally opposed to the scheme. He spoke of Roosevelt as "that madman" and said it was folly to have him in line for the succession if McKinley should die. But Platt persisted. He enlisted the powerful aid of Senator Quay, of Pennsylvania, who had a grudge of his own against Hanna, and together they secured the nomination of Roosevelt against the wishes of Hanna and Roosevelt himself. The reluctant nominee did not dare make good his threat to refuse the offer. Such a course would have aroused bitter enmity on the part of party leaders and perhaps imperiled his political future.

422   Governor Roosevelt calls a halt to his boom, from a sketch in *The World*, New York,
                June 19, 1900

ROOSEVELT IN THE CAMPAIGN

Once in the campaign, Roosevelt let himself go. He was most unlike his running mate. McKinley was gentle, tactful, mild, cautious and conservative. Roosevelt was brusque, outspoken, bold, indiscreet, and a reformer by instinct and long habit. McKinley and Hanna were intimately tied up with the business interests and had stood by them in their general policy of getting aid from the Government in the conduct of large and profitable enterprises. They were also at one with the Federal and state organizations in the party. Roosevelt was known for his belief that the business interests should not have special protection in the conduct of their affairs, and for his continued and sometimes successful antagonism to party machines. Platt's whim to link two such dissimilar men together in the campaign cannot be defended on any

423   From a cartoon *His Running Mate*, by C. G. Bush in *The World*, New York, June 25, 1900

ground of reason or expediency. Roosevelt spoke many times, and always with good effect. He was determined that he should not seem to be a mere cipher candidate.

A MORE NATIONAL McKINLEY

The last months of McKinley's life were a period of triumph. Relieved of anxiety as to his position with the country, largely replaced by Hanna of attention to party management, he seems to have come to view the Presidency in its purely national aspect. He became less of the party man and more of the impersonation of the Federal headship. Recalling the tributes paid him in the South, he said to his secretary: "I can no longer be called the President of a party: I am now the President of the whole country." In the last speech he made, at Buffalo on the day before his assassination, he again shook off party bonds and declared for the modification of the tariff so as to encourage international trade. "The period of exclusiveness is past," he said. "The expansion of our trade and commerce is the pressing problem. Commercial wars are unprofitable. A policy of good will and friendly trade relations will prevent reprisals. Reciprocity treaties are in harmony with the spirit of the times, measures of retaliation are not." Thus he spoke in a spirit of national harmony and in that spirit his utterance was received by the people of the country.

424   McKinley's second inaugural, March 4, 1901, from a photograph by Underwood & Underwood, New York

425 McKinley's Funeral Procession, from a photograph by
Underwood & Underwood, New York

DEATH OF McKINLEY

ON September 6, 1901, at the Pan-American Exposition at Buffalo, the President was shot and mortally wounded by a crazed anarchist, Leon Czolgosz, who wished to kill all rulers. On the 14th McKinley died. The patience and courage with which he bore the suffering of these eight days, and the pious faith with which he faced the end in full consciousness of its approach made a deep impression on the country. He went down into the grave with the blessings of all classes of men and women. With him passed the hope of that conservative business man's régime in the national political arena which Hanna had so ably built up.

PRESIDENT McKINLEY AND THE JINGO BIRD.

426 From a cartoon by Linley Sambourne in *Punch*, Apr. 16, 1898

CHAPTER IX

ROOSEVELT AND POLITICAL REFORM

WHEN Roosevelt came to the Presidency through the death of McKinley, the conservatives were in consternation. Despite his assurance that he would follow the policies of his predecessor, they looked for trouble. Roosevelt was too individualistic to make another man's policies his own. He soon veered away from McKinley's ideas and gradually dropped one after another of McKinley's Cabinet. At the same time, he built up a following of his own in the party, steadily gaining in popularity in the country at large; and when the election of 1904 came around he was the accepted leader of his party.

Roosevelt's triumphant election now gave him the feeling of assured support by the people. Up to that time he was serving only as President through the act of an anarchist: now he was President through the choice of the people. Moreover, he had given them due notice of his principles and he felt that he had a right to take their approval as their authority to proceed in the execution of those principles. He was a leader among those who wished to break up the spoils system and to place the civil service on the basis of merit appointments. In doing so, he endeared himself to the reform element in the nation at large and won the opposition of the spoilsmen. As Police Commissioner of New York he learned, as he said, to know and fight against the power of wealth in politics. As Governor of New York he continued the fight and made life unpleasant for Thomas C. Platt and his state machine. He came to the Presidency at a time when the trusts were continually being organized, despite the law of 1890 which forbade their existence, and when the common man looking on had come to the conclusion that Hanna and his friends could not be successfully opposed.

It was in his second administration that Roosevelt accomplished most. To his credit, among other things, must be placed the passage in 1906 of the Hepburn Railroad Rate Act, strengthening the power of the Interstate Commerce Commission, the passage of the Pure Food and Drug Act, making it unlawful to label food and drugs so as to make it appear that they contained what they did not contain, and the passage of several smaller acts that stood for the same general restraint of unruly capital. He also introduced the policy of the conservation of natural resources by the National Government and gave a powerful impulse to the adoption of nominating primaries as a means of lessening the power of party machines. He fought his battles in a spectacular way, which was his nature, and he sometimes gave his enemies handles to use in flailing him by his rash and inconsistent actions. But he was accepted by the people as a sound patriot, a courageous and honest public servant, and a man who loved democratic equality, with the purpose of giving every man an opportunity to live untrammeled by privilege. When he retired from office in 1909, he had not accomplished all the reforms that he had in view. He wished to correct and systematize the Anti-Trust Act of 1890, to make it impossible for railroads to sell new bonds without permission of the Government, and to forbid the consolidation of business in the hands of a few by means of interlocking directorates. He went out of office with the Senate ranged strongly against him. Woodrow Wilson, whom he later attacked most bitterly, took the lead in putting into actual statutes many of the reforms that were first advocated by Theodore Roosevelt.

427   Theodore Roosevelt, 1858–1919, as a young man,
                    from a photograph

ROOSEVELT ENTERS POLITICS

A YEAR after graduating from Harvard, Roosevelt entered politics by winning a seat in the assembly at Albany, where, at once, he became the leader of a group of liberal Republicans. He opposed the nomination of Blaine in 1884 but did not vote against him when he could not have his own candidate. After several years of ranching, he came back to the East when Harrison ran for office. For his campaign services he was made a member of the Civil Service Commission. His friends had urged him to refuse the office because of its obscurity, but he had replied that he would take it and make it known as an important position. His striking record as Civil Service Commissioner made him a national figure. Retiring from Washington when Cleveland became President again, he came back with the election of McKinley, who appointed him Assistant Secretary of the Navy. Although he made his best reputation in enforcing the civil service law in a non-partisan way, he was always a party man. This political philosophy often brought him into situations in which his familiar association with party bosses seemed inconsistent with his reform stand and led his enemies to call him a hypocrite. But, in spite of such attacks, he stuck to his position until 1912.

ROOSEVELT AS A ROUGH RIDER

ROOSEVELT used his position as Assistant Secretary to prepare the navy for the war that he thought he saw approaching. He was very active in fitting out Dewey's fleet in anticipation of its brilliant campaign at Manila. Nevertheless, as soon as war began he retired from the department and became Lieutenant-Colonel of the "Rough Riders," a regiment of volunteer cavalry which he was chiefly instrumental in recruiting. In the brief campaign around Santiago, he played a creditable part, and returned as a military hero to enter upon the political adventures recounted in the previous chapter. But the basis of his popularity was the belief among the people that he was a reformer.

428   Theodore Roosevelt as Lieutenant-Colonel of the "Rough Riders," from a photograph
              taken at Montauk Point in 1898 by Pach Bros., New York

ROOSEVELT'S POLICIES

WHEN he took office in September, 1901, Roosevelt said that he would follow the policies of McKinley. He also said to a friend that he was not going out of office as Cleveland went out with his party divided. In each case he was sadly mistaken. It was impossible for him to follow McKinley's ideas; for he was an entirely different kind of man. Roosevelt was impulsive, outspoken, quick to form resolves and eager to express them in his own way. McKinley's idea of government was to follow such a course as would give business the opportunity to proceed in prosperity; Roosevelt's was to cut down the privileges business had been able to secure from the Government, regardless of the probability that in cutting them down he would produce confusion in the business world. Roosevelt was also unfortunate in regard to party harmony. He left office in 1909 with his party split as hopelessly as Cleveland's party had been divided in 1897.

429   From a cartoon *A New Uniform And New Responsibilities*, by Louis Dalrymple in *Puck*, Oct. 2, 1901

One of Roosevelt's most striking characteristics as a public man was his ability to compress certain of his ideas in catch phrases which became current among the people. He popularized the "strenuous life" and the "square deal." He denominated certain naturalists as "nature fakirs." He frequently admitted some of his opponents to the "Ananias club." Perhaps his most striking phrase is one which he applied to certain reformers who became active during his own administration. The term "muck raker" became a part of the language of the people. Roosevelt had a rare ability to judge public opinion and to know what course of action would be popular. Rarely did the issues which he supported fail to meet with general approval. His most conspicuous failure in this respect was his later advocacy of the recall of judicial decisions.

ROOSEVELT A MAN OF LETTERS

ROOSEVELT was a lover of books and read much in serious literature. Early in life he wrote history, his most important books at that time being *The Winning of the West*, the *Life of Thomas H. Benton* and the *Life of Gouverneur Morris*. After he came before the public as a leader of men, he wrote much of a hortatory nature, mostly in the form of books that were made up of speeches and magazine articles. His style was clear but not distinguished. Nevertheless, it became the custom, while he was President, to rate him high for literary ability, which was praise rather too strong for his actual attainments. He had a ready pen and knew how to use it for the promotion of his own purposes; but it is not likely that he will be remembered as a distinguished writer. It would be better to describe him as a political preacher writing his sermons as books.

430   From a photograph by Harris & Ewing, Washington

431   President Roosevelt in Yosemite National Park, 1904, courtesy of the National Park Service, Washington

ROOSEVELT THE HUNTER AND TRAVELER

ROOSEVELT was keenly devoted to the outdoor life. He was a constant rider, hunter and tennis player. He loved the woods and the wild things that inhabited them. He never forgot his experience as a young man on a ranch, living the life of a cowboy. In mature life he was something of an explorer. His *African Game Trails* and *Through the Brazilian Wilderness*, describing two famous journeys, are his best books of this kind. His outspoken love of truth led him to denounce some of those persons who wrote about nature without having actually seen it in the phases treated. The authors he criticized replied and the result was one of his many public controversies.

ROOSEVELT THE POLITICIAN

ROOSEVELT was one of the few reformers in our history who was able to overcome the abuse of their enemies and maintain to the end the confidence of a considerable portion of the people. He was charged with many forms of bad conduct and he was beset with many political snares; but he was never convicted in the public mind of serious wrongdoing. His political life was a battle from the beginning to its end, in which he fought with great vigor and shrewdness and generally came out with success. His personality was so powerful that men who did not approve his views usually disliked him intensely, while those who approved the objects for which he strove and gave themselves up to his influence were likely to find no evil in his ways or words. It was also observed that among those who opposed him were the leaders of party machines and the crowd of political jobbers who fatten on political favors.

432   From a photograph by Underwood & Underwood, New York

433   From a photograph by L. C. Handy, Washington

434   Roosevelt and his "Tennis Cabinet," from a photograph. © Clinedinst, Washington

THE "TENNIS CABINET"

ALTHOUGH Roosevelt, after he became President, continued in friendly relations with Hanna and his supporters, he soon began to show his leaning toward reforms. In that respect he got little encouragement from the regular Cabinet. Then it was observed that he was gathering around him a group of unofficial advisers and friends with whose aid he made plans and whose services he used in executing them. This group was the basis of those whom he later organized into the Progressive party. Since he frequently played tennis with them, the group was dubbed the "Tennis Cabinet." Many men of liberal and athletic taste were asked to join the circle, and not all of them were politicians. He loved the society of cultured people with varied tastes.

ROOSEVELT AS A PUBLIC SPEAKER

ROOSEVELT was not a smooth and eloquent speaker, like Woodrow Wilson, nor a fluent and popular orator, like Bryan. But he had a remarkably clear and direct way of stating plain ideas in simple words. He drove home his arguments with emphatic gestures. His hearers had no difficulty in getting his points. He was generally aggressive and spoke with so much sincerity that few people who heard him doubted his honesty. He traveled a great deal on speaking tours, carrying to the whole country the consciousness of being in actual touch with the Chief Executive of the Government.

435   Theodore Roosevelt on the stump, 1904. © Underwood & Underwood, New York

IX—15

436   From a cartoon "*Will You Please Hush*," by W. A. Rogers in the *New York Herald*,
Feb. 23, 1908

THE "BIG STICK"

THE keynote of Roosevelt's methods was to make his appeals directly to the people. If politicians opposed him he sought to go over their heads to their constituents. His disposition to drive his adversaries before him was expressed in the term "Big Stick," taken from one of his utterances, "Speak softly and carry a big stick." In the eyes of his enemies this kind of agitation was only noise and much ridicule was poured upon him. He was constantly accused of talking in a way that was bad for business. It was true that his attempts to reduce the privileges of trusts, to regulate the conduct of railroads and to break up the habit of adulterating food and drugs were bad for the businesses concerned. Roosevelt reiterated that he did not propose to interfere with business that was conducted properly, but his opponents did not believe this. They painted him as a wild man, digging up the flowers with the weeds and dangerous to all kinds of growing things. The agitation by his adversaries tended to increase the confusion they complained of and promoted a sense of distrust in the business world.

ROOSEVELT AND SPELLING REFORM

ROOSEVELT'S innate feeling for reform led him to take up the cause of simplified spelling. On August 27, 1906, he ordered the Public Printer to use the system in public documents. So great was the protest which resulted that he became discouraged, and when the House of Representatives passed a resolution against the measure he recalled the order. He gave as his reason the impossibility of the task he had undertaken and said that he intended to use simple spelling in his own correspondence, but the printed letters in his official biography do not sustain the announcement.

TWISTING THE LION'S TONGUE.

FATHER TIME (*closely examining small incision in tree-trunk*). "WHO'S BEEN TRYING TO CUT THIS TREE DOWN?"
"TEDDY" ROOSEVELT (*in manner of young George Washington*). "FATHER! I KANNOT TEL A LI. I DID IT WITH MY LITL AX."
FATHER TIME. "AH WELL! BOYS WILL BE BOYS!"

437   From a cartoon by Linley Sambourne in *Punch*, Sept. 5, 1906

McKINLEY'S CABINET CONTINUED BY ROOSEVELT

ROOSEVELT realized fully that his sudden elevation to the Presidency placed him in a doubtful position. Standing for ideas to which his predecessor was indifferent, if not opposed, he now took over that predecessor's Government, with his majority in Congress and all his incomplete plans. What would he do with them? His first care was to give the country the assurance that no sudden change was to be expected, and to do this he announced that he would keep McKinley's Cabinet and be guided by their advice. This assurance had a favorable immediate effect and was followed for a time by carefully considered moderation in most of his measures. The country applauded and he gained confidence in his own position, which led him to begin to formulate policies of his own. Not many months passed after his elevation to the Presidency before he had drifted far from the course of McKinley, but the drift was so gradual and moderate that it produced no actual shock in the public mind.

438   McKinley's Cabinet, continued under Roosevelt, from a photograph.
© Underwood & Underwood, New York
LEFT TO RIGHT *Around table:* President McKinley; Lyman Gage, Secretary of the Treasury; John W. Griggs, Attorney-General; John D. Long, Secretary of the Navy; James Wilson, Secretary of Agriculture; Ethan A. Hitchcock, Secretary of the Interior; Charles E. Smith, Postmaster-General; Elihu Root, Secretary of War; John Hay, Secretary of State

439   From a cartoon *The American Samson,* by J. S. Pughe in *Puck,*
Dec. 13, 1905

A PERIOD OF HESITATION IN DOMESTIC AFFAIRS

DURING his first administration, Roosevelt did little to carry out his ideas in domestic Government. He was evidently in doubt about his relations with Congress; and there was enough to do in straightening out the problems left over by the war with Spain. The construction of an Isthmian canal, the regulation of affairs in recently acquired territories, the assertion of the Monroe Doctrine in the Caribbean region, and the maintenance of our national interests in Asiatic countries formed his chief concerns until the election of 1904. In all these matters of foreign policy Roosevelt played the game of diplomacy vigorously. His methods won him applause but also called forth sharp criticisms. In particular his treatment of the United States of Colombia at the time of the Panama revolution created problems which were not settled for practically two decades, if they can be said to be settled at all.

440   Philander C. Knox, 1853-1921, from a photo-
      graph by Harris & Ewing, Washington

ROOSEVELT'S ABLE ASSISTANTS

In the Cabinet, Roosevelt found Elihu Root, who was remarkable for his administrative genius and for general political insight. He had been called to the war department in 1899, to
straighten out confusion due to the incompetency of his predecessor, Alger. That done, he took up the state of the army and
made several reforms, chief of which was the creation of a
general staff. In politics he was a conservative, but he recognized Roosevelt's sincerity and served him faithfully. Another
member of the Cabinet to whom Roosevelt owed much was
Attorney-General Knox, also a conservative. He had long been
a corporation lawyer, and he now placed all his knowledge of
corporation law at the disposal of the Government in dealing
with "Big Business." These two conservatives gave Roosevelt
invaluable aid in carrying out his most important reforms.

A NEW VENEZUELAN INCIDENT

Cleveland had reasserted the Monroe Doctrine in a vigorous
form in the Venezuelan incident of 1895. Roosevelt gave it a
still further extension in 1902. German and British citizens
held unpaid claims against Venezuela and their Governments,
undertaking collection, first suggested arbitration. When
Venezuela refused to arbitrate a joint naval force established a blockade, bombarded and destroyed the forts
defending Caracas. Venezuela now declared a willingness to arbitrate, but her offer was refused. Roosevelt,
watching these proceedings with much interest, ordered Admiral Dewey to Porto Rico with the best ships in
the navy. When he learned that the Germans were going to land forces he protested to the German minister,
who replied that the occupation would be "temporary." Roosevelt said that the German occupation of
Kiaochow, in China, on a ninety-nine year lease was also "temporary," but that he did not intend to see any
foreign power establish "another Kiaochow" in a position to threaten the approaches to the Panama Canal.
He added that if he did not in ten days have assurance that Germany would arbitrate he would order Dewey
to resist the proposed German attempts to occupy Venezuelan territory. A few days later the German minister called at the White House on other business. Roosevelt asked him whether a reply to his demand had come
from Berlin. The minister had had no instructions. Thereupon Roosevelt shortened the term of his ultima-

tum by one day. The min-
ister, now alarmed, made
such representations to his
Government that in twelve
hours he was able to reply
that the Kaiser would arbitrate and wished Roosevelt
to act as arbiter. Roosevelt
did not accept the request but
managed to have the legal
points in dispute referred to
the Hague Court. The re-
sult showed that Venezuela
was justified in resisting the
payment of the claims as
made; for the commission
reduced the British and German claims from about four
million five hundred thousand dollars to two million
three hundred thousand.

441   From a cartoon *Uncle Sam — That's A Live Wire, Gentlemen!*, by W. A. Rogers
                    in the *New York Herald*, Dec. 16, 1902

ROOSEVELT'S MONROE DOCTRINE

In the Venezuelan affair Roosevelt had rested his right to oppose Germany's scheme on the Monroe Doctrine. He was careful to let the British and the Germans know that he did not object if they took steps to collect debts justly owed by Venezuela, but he was unwilling to have the affair become the pretext for territorial occupation. In assuming to say what steps for collection were proper and what were improper he set up a claim which foreign states found it hard to recognize. Roosevelt realized that he could not maintain such a position unless he was willing to see that those American states benefited by it observed their obligations scrupulously. Out of this conviction he developed the principle that the United States had the right to supervise certain phases of the domestic policies of their southern neighbors. This doctrine had immediate repercussions in the relations between the United States and South American countries. As a result of it our neighbors on the south charged the United States with using the Monroe Doctrine as an excuse for imperialistic control of weak nations. The reply to this point is that the United States cannot protect South America without some way of checking the cause of offense.

442   "We stand firmly on the Monroe Doctrine," from
Leslie's Illustrated Weekly, Sept. 18, 1902

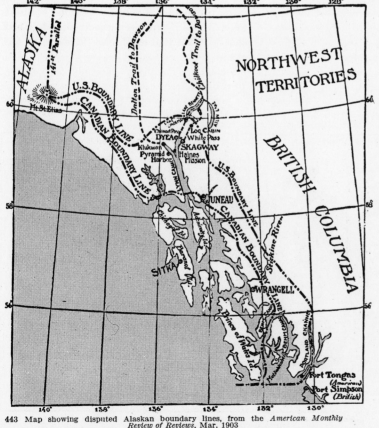

443 Map showing disputed Alaskan boundary lines, from the *American Monthly Review of Reviews*, Mar. 1903

THE ALASKAN BOUNDARY

The boundary between Alaska and Canada depended upon a treaty between Great Britain and Russia, made in 1825, wherein it was provided that for the part immediately north of latitude fifty-four degrees and forty minutes it should follow a chain of mountains supposed to be in the main ten marine leagues from the sea — taking due account of the "sinuosities" of the coast, which in this region are deep. After the discovery of gold in the Klondike in 1897, this coast country became important as the means of approaching the gold-bearing region. Canada now advanced the claim that her boundary ran so near the ocean as to give her the harbors at the heads of the source of the Pacific estuaries. The United States resisted the claim, and after much discussion Roosevelt reluctantly agreed to refer the dispute to a tribunal of three persons appointed by each side. This was in 1903.

JOHN BULL: "Yes, 'e's makin' a lot of noise, Sam, but 'e'll get over it."—From the *North American* (Philadelphia).

444   From a cartoon by Charles Nelan in the *American Monthly Review of Reviews*, Dec. 1903

THE DISPUTE SETTLED

THE tribunal met in London. The three representatives of the United States were politicians, and it was not believed that they would budge an inch from the position held by their Government. Two of the British representatives were Canadians equally likely to stand out on their own side; the third was Lord Alverstone, Chief Justice of England. If he supported Canada the final vote would be three to three. If he took the side of the United States they would triumph. Thus the United States might win and could not lose. As the tribunal was about to meet, Roosevelt took steps unofficially to inform the British Government that if no decision was reached he would ask Congress to authorize him to run the line himself, which was in fact a threat to do something that could hardly have led to anything but war. This dire prospect was avoided by Lord Alverstone's voting with the United States on the main contentions. Canada resented the decision and was inclined to think that she had been deserted by her mother country.

SELECTING A CANAL SITE

SHORTLY after Roosevelt came into power, the Hay-Pauncefote Treaty, which cleared the way for the construction of an interoceanic canal under United States authority, was completed. A discussion at once arose whether the proposed canal should be across Panama or across Nicaragua. Colombia, controlling Panama, made difficulties. An old charter for a Panama Canal was owned by a group of French speculators and would expire in 1904. Colombia wished to delay action until then, when she and not the French Company would make a sale. The Company wished to act at once, and after considerable dickering it was made possible for the United States to buy it out for forty million dollars, which was considered cheap. To such proceedings Colombia interposed her veto. Roosevelt, who preferred the Panama site, announced that he would turn to the route through Nicaragua and ordered negotiations to be opened to that end. Such, in brief, were the events that preceded a sudden change in political authority in Panama in 1903, an event which more than any other has brought criticism on Roosevelt's public conduct.

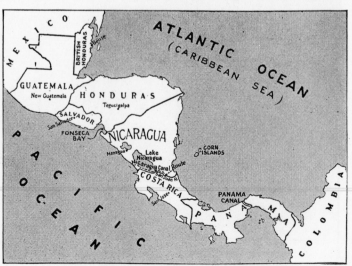

445   Map Showing Proposed Canal Routes Across Nicaragua and Panama, from the *American Monthly Review of Reviews*, Feb. 1916

THE PANAMA REVOLUTION

THE people of Panama were dismayed when they thought the canal project would be transferred to Nicaragua. A junta was formed to revolt from Colombia and set up an independent state, which could act without waiting for Colombian consent. Philippe Bunau-Varilla, one of the French speculators who had control of the company, advanced a large sum of money with which a small army was raised in Panama and a revolution began on November 3, 1903. Roosevelt, who seems to have

446 From a cartoon *The News Reaches Bogota*, by W. A. Rogers in the *New York Herald*, Nov. 15, 1903

known about these proceedings but refused to take part in them beforehand, now gave support with naval ships, forbidding any further hostile forces to land in the Isthmus, or the Colombian troops at Colon to proceed to Panama City, under the pretext that the United States was bound by treaty to keep transit open on the Isthmian railroad. Since Colombia was unable to send troops to suppress the revolt, the Republic of Panama came into existence.

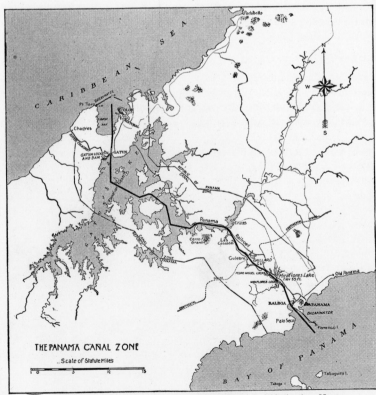

THE PANAMA CANAL ZONE

Scale of Statute Miles

447   The Panama Canal Zone, from a map by the Bureau of Navigation, Navy Department, Washington

A TREATY WITH PANAMA

WHEN Bunau-Varilla advanced the money for the support of the Panama revolution, he stipulated that he should be the first minister from Panama to the United States. The bargain was carried out speedily. He was in Washington when he received a cablegram announcing his appointment on November 6. Twelve days later he and Secretary of State John Hay signed a convention by which the United States guaranteed the integrity of Panama and received full control over a ten-mile strip from sea to sea within which the canal was to be constructed. It also stipulated that Panama should receive from the United States ten million dollars in cash and an annual sum of two hundred and fifty thousand dollars for the future. Under this agreement, steps were promptly taken for building the canal.

448   From a cartoon *The New Governor of Panama*, by McCutcheon in the *American Monthly Review of Reviews*, Dec. 1903, reproduced from the *Daily Tribune*, Chicago

ROOSEVELT'S RESPONSIBILITY

ROOSEVELT later declared that he took Panama and justified his action by comparing the Government at Bogota to a group of highwaymen who were holding up a great work that was to confer vast benefits on the world. His interpretation of our treaty with Colombia guaranteeing to keep transit open on the Isthmus was bad; for he did not keep it open, but in reality closed it to the nation that had the most right by law to use it, Colombia herself. Moreover, it is inconceivable that any nation would have signed a treaty giving away her right to preserve her own authority in her own territory. On Colombia and on the rest of the world his action made a very bad impression. It convinced South and Central Americans that all our assertions of benevolent intentions toward them under the Monroe Doctrine were hypocrisy. Public opinion in the United States slowly came to realize that Roosevelt's impetuosity had led him into an unfortunate error, and eventually, when Roosevelt was in his grave, Congress made amends by paying Colombia the sum of twenty-five million dollars.

CONSTRUCTING THE CANAL

BUILDING the Canal was one of the world's greatest engineering achievements. Important changes in the machinery expedited the actual work of construction; great steam shovels and dredges made the task of digging less formidable; but even more important was the discovery of the part taken by the mosquito in spreading the germs of yellow fever. Under the French about one third of the employees had died from this disease. By draining the nearby marshes and strictly isolating the sick the fever was controlled, with the result that it was not a factor in the work to be done. For some time there was discussion between those who wished to have a sea-level and those who desired a lock canal: it was finally decided to use the lock type on the ground that it could be built more quickly and for less money. It was estimated that the canal as projected would cost two hundred millions and take ten years in the building. It was found eventually that while Congress gave the final word to go ahead with a lock canal in June, 1906, the first self-driven boat to pass through made the trip on January 4, 1914. The cost of construction, not including the fortifications erected to defend it, was a little more than three hundred and eighty millions. It was opened to commercial traffic August 15, 1914. The work was directed by army engineers with Lieutenant-Colonel George W. Goethals at their head, and the sanitation was under the direction of Colonel William C. Gorgas, an army surgeon.

The Canal is placed at the spot where the mountains that form the backbone of the Isthmus are lowest. It is fifty miles long from deep water to deep water. Steaming seven miles from the Caribbean, ships reach the Gatun locks, where they are lifted eighty-five feet. A twenty-four mile trip across the artificial Gatun Lake, and nine miles through the Gaillard (Culebra) cut, brings vessels to the Pedro Miguel locks, where they are lowered to the two-miles-long Miraflores Lake, fifty-five feet above sea level. After traversing Miraflores Lake ships enter the Miraflores locks and descend to the sea-level channel which extends eight miles to deep water in the Pacific.

449   Major-General George W. Goethals, 1858–1928, Chief Engineer of the Panama Canal, 1907–14, and first Civil Governor of the Canal Zone, 1914–16, courtesy of Charles Scribner's Sons, New York

ACQUIRING AUTHORITY IN SANTO DOMINGO

THE finances of the Republic of Santo Domingo were in a chaotic state and the European creditors appealed to Roosevelt to know if they would be allowed, through their respective Governments, to take steps to collect what was due. Here was the possibility of much trouble. Roosevelt met it by getting from the Dominican Government in 1904 a request that the United States take charge of its revenues for the purpose of putting them in order — much as a receiver takes over and restores to credit the finances of a private concern. On the basis of this request a protocol was drawn up by which the United States was to administer Santo Domingo's revenues, settle its debts, and do what financial house cleaning was necessary. At the same time

450 From a cartoon *Is This What We Want*, in *The World*, New York, Aug. 1, 1904

we were to guarantee the integrity of the Santo Dominican Republic. The Senate refused to accept the protocol, but Roosevelt proceeded to carry out the spirit of it under a *modus vivendi* by which the Dominican Government appointed a receiver of the customs nominated by President Roosevelt. The Senate scowled for a time, but in 1907 it concluded to recognize the *modus vivendi*. It saw that under this form of agreement the United States had been pledged and felt that if pledges were to be given they ought to be under Congressional authority. Under the arrangement thus described, Santo Domingo was able to refund her debt and to improve the administration of her revenues to such a degree that her financial troubles cleared up.

451 America's New Navy, from a drawing by F. C. Schell in *Leslie's Weekly*, Apr. 11, 1903

ROOSEVELT'S POLICY OF NATIONAL DEFENSE

ROOSEVELT believed in maintaining a strong army and navy, and he often expressed such views to Congress or to the public at large. He could not induce Congress to increase the army materially, but he did much to improve the navy. His program comprised an increase of four new battleships a year. Congress cut the increase in two. Nevertheless, he soon had, completed or provided for, a fleet of forty armor-clad ships. In 1907 he sent out a fleet of sixteen new battleships, on a journey around the world. European naval experts were inclined to believe that the thing could not be done successfully, but the event proved that they were entirely mistaken. The American fleet excited much comment in all the ports it visited.

452 John Mitchell, 1870–1919, President of the United Mine Workers of America, from a photograph by Pach Bros., New York

THE ANTHRACITE STRIKE OF 1902

ALTHOUGH Roosevelt's most conspicuous achievements in domestic policy belong to his second administration a very notable one occurred shortly after he succeeded to the Presidency. This was his adjustment of the anthracite coal strike of 1902. During fifty years before that labor had developed a great deal of strength as an influential factor in industry. Its earlier fights were for shorter hours, better conditions of employment and higher wages. While these objects have not ceased to concern it, recent controversies have taken on, also, the ideas of establishing labor as one of the controlling factors in industry, allowing to it a voice in determining how business shall be run and how the proceeds shall be distributed. When Roosevelt became President, this second process had not gone very far and most of the strikes that occurred were for the betterment of actual conditions. Such was the character of the strike of the anthracite miners of Pennsylvania under their able leader, John Mitchell, which began in May, 1902, and continued until autumn. It was a strike that affected the comfort of a large number of people; for anthracite coal was used as fuel in most of the homes in the eastern part of the United States.

ROOSEVELT'S SETTLEMENT

WHEN the country realized that it faced a winter without fuel it began to be panicky. Then Roosevelt took notice of the situation. Owners and miners were evidently waiting for the distressed public to force one side or the other to come to a settlement. Convinced that neither side would back down completely, Roosevelt attempted to get them to make a compromise through the services of a committee of arbitration, but the owners objected. He then formed plans for taking over the mines by the Government, placing troops on guard, and getting out the coal for the relief of the public. Pending this extreme course he induced powerful financial interests to fend it off by bringing all their influence to bear on the mine owners who were at length convinced that their true interests demanded that a compromise be made. At this point arbitration was agreed upon. Cardinal Gibbons, John Mitchell and many others gave Roosevelt strong support in his efforts to get the miners to accept this compromise.

END OF STRIKE

The President Names Six Arbitrators.

MITCHELL HAS ACCEPTED

And Now the Mines Will Turn Out Coal, Full Force.

WASHINGTON, Oct. 16., 1:15 A M —At 1 o'clock this morning Secretary Cortelyou announced that a conference consisting of President Roosevelt, Secretary of War Root, Labor Commissioner Carroll D. Wright, Frank P. Sargent, and George W. Perkins and Robert Bacon of J. P. Morgan & Co., which had been in session since 10:30 o'clock in the President's room at the temporary White House was about to adjourn and would issue a statement.

The conference adjourned at 1:05 with the announcement that the President had appointed a commission of six arbitrators to pass upon the points in dispute between the coal operators and the miners.

It was realized at once that this official announcement that the commission had been appointed meant that an agreement had been reached and the strike was practically at an end

The news was received with the utmost enthusiasm

An official statement about the make-up of the arbitration commission was promised for about 1:30 o'clock this morning.

In the meantime it was quickly seen that the plan originally proposed by the coal operators had undergone some modifications. They suggested a commission of five members. The announcement gave the number of members of the commission as six.

At 2:15 A M., Mr Cortelyou handed out the following:

THE ARBITRATORS.

After a conference with Mr. Mitchell and some further conference with representatives of the coal operators, the President has appointed the members of the commission to inquire into, consider and pass upon all questions at issue between the operators and miners in the anthracite coal fields as follows:

Brig.-Gen. John M Wilson, U S A., retired (late Chief of Engineers, U. S. A.) Washington, as an officer of the engineer corps of either the military or naval service of the United States.

Mr. E. W Parker, Washington, D. C., is an expert mining engineer. Mr. Parker is chief statistician of the coal division of the United States Geological Survey and the editor of the Engineering and Mining Journal of New York.

The Hon. George Gray, Wilmington, Del., as a Judge of a United States Court.

E. E. Clark, Cedar Rapids, Ia., Grand Chief of railway conductors, as a sociologist, the President assuming that for the purpose of such a commission the term sociologist means a man who has thought and studied on social questions and has practically applied his knowledge.

Mr. Thomas H. Watkins, Scranton, Pa., as a man practically acquainted with the mining and selling of coal.

Bishop John L. Spalding of Peoria, Ill. The President has added Bishop Spalding's name to the commission.

The Hon. Carroll D. Wright has been appointed recorder of the commission.

THE LEGAL COMMISSIONER.

George Gray has been Judge of the Circuit Court, Third United States Circuit, since 1899. He was born at New Castle, Del., May 4, 1840, the son of Andrew C. and Elizabeth M. Gray. He graduated from Princeton in 1859, received the degree of A. M. in 1853 and LL. D., 1859. He studied law at Harvard and was admitted to the bar in 1863, practised at New Castle from 1863 to 1869 and afterward at Wilmington He married Margaret J. Black.

He was Attorney-General of Delaware from 1879 to 1885; United States Senator from 1885 to 1889 and is a Democrat. While in the Senate he was a member of the Foreign Relations and Judiciary committees.

In 1896 he was affiliated with the National Gold Standard Democrats in the Presidential election. In 1898 he was a member of the Peace Commission at Paris, and was appointed by the President member of the Joint High Commission at Quebec, 1898, and member of the International Commission of Arbitration under The Hague Convention, November, 1900. His home is in Wilmington, Del.

THE GEOLOGICAL MEMBER.

Edward Wheeler Parker is a statistician, is attached to the United States Geological

453

From *The Sun*, New York, October 16, 1902

THE ANTHRACITE COAL COMMISSION

THE dispute was finally settled by an arbitration commission composed of seven eminent men appointed by the President. They met at Washington, also in the coal-producing area, and took the testimony of many witnesses. Their finding came at the end of five months. The strikers who had asked for an increase of twenty per cent in their wages were given ten per cent; a sliding scale was agreed upon by which wages should increase in the future as the price of coal went up. A Board of Conciliation was created for the adjustment of future

454   The President's attempt to end the coal strike, from *Harper's Weekly*, Oct. 18, 1902

disputes. This agreement was to be in force for three years. One effect of the settlement was the increase of the price of coal to the consumer. In his course with reference to this strike Roosevelt set an example, followed by his successors more than once, for Government interference in strike settlements in such a way that the net benefit went to the laborers.

ROOSEVELT AND THE TRUSTS

ROOSEVELT'S attitude toward the trusts was that they were the result of economic development, that some were good and should be allowed to exist under Government regulation, while others were bad and should be destroyed. His position was assailed by the capitalists in general, who, having taken a stand against Roosevelt, were in no frame of mind to give him credit for honest motives. As he came to believe himself strong with the country he made preparations for carrying out a program for regulating these great enterprises. As a step toward that result he got Congress in 1903 to create the Department of Labor and Commerce; within it was a bureau of corporations which set out at once to gather evidence about the organization and the conduct of several of the greatest trusts. He relied on the Anti-Trust Act of 1890 which forbade combinations in restraint of trade. This act had been steadily violated by the trusts, which relied upon a decision of the Supreme Court in the Knight Case, 1895, when the Court held that the interstate commerce clause of the Constitution applied to trade strictly and not to manufactures. Roosevelt proposed to turn the Sherman Anti-Trust Law which had become almost a dead letter into an effective weapon for fighting combinations whose activities were against the public interest. He believed this course incident to his sworn duty to provide for the general welfare of the Union and to see that its laws were duly executed.

455   From a cartoon "*You Dirty Boy*," by Joseph Keppler, Jr., in *Puck*, Sept. 7, 1907

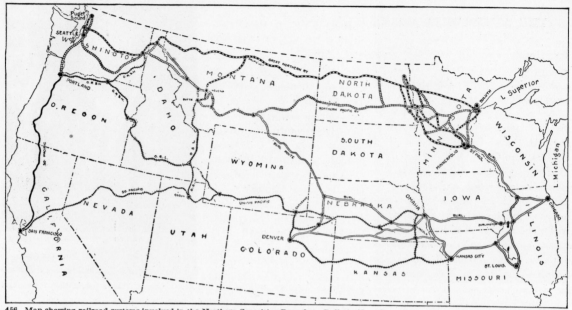

456 Map showing railroad systems involved in the Northern Securities Case, from Bulletin No. 142 — University of Wisconsin — Economics and Political Sources Series I (1904–06), after a map which appeared in one of the government documents in the suit

THE NORTHERN SECURITIES CASE

AN important step in the history of the relation of the Government to the trusts was the Northern Securities Case decided in 1904. James J. Hill and a group of his friends owned the Northern Pacific and the Great Northern Railroads, competing lines, which ran from Lake Superior to Puget Sound. In order to get a connection into Chicago and thus build up a great system, they then bought the Burlington Road. To assure permanence for his plans, Hill created the Northern Securities Company, a holding company, to take over the shares in the three companies, and to receive and pay out the earnings to the stockholders. He and his lawyers thought themselves secure because of the decision in the Knight Case. On the advice of Knox that the Securities Company was against the Anti-Trust Act of 1890, Roosevelt brought suit and the courts sustained him completely. The Securities Company was ordered to dissolve. To Hill, and to many others, this seemed an unjust decision. He had been trying to build up a great railroad for the most efficient service of the region through which it ran, and the Government had stepped in with its veto. The Government, however, was acting on the basis that railroad competition was essential to the public welfare and that combinations were bad.

THE VIEWS OF "BIG BUSINESS"

JAMES J. HILL was much chagrined by the decision in the Northern Securities Case. He was a great railroad builder and as such had carried civilization into vast spaces that were waste before he touched them. His merger of the three railroads did nobody harm, so far as could be seen, and he looked upon any law that made it impossible as foolish and unjust. To him the apprehension that monopoly might, if established, inflict a great damage on the industrial life of the people meant nothing. His view was shared in general by persons associated with great financial concerns. Subsequent to the Northern Securities incident Roosevelt received, at last, only grudging support from the masters of "big business."

457   James J. Hill, 1838–1916, from a photograph by Pach Bros., New York

458 Frank B. Kellogg, 1856–, Government Lawyer in the Standard Oil Case, from a photograph by Harris & Ewing, Washington

ROOSEVELT BRINGS SUITS AGAINST TRUSTS

THROUGH the activity of the bureau of corporations in collecting evidence, and of the Department of Justice in prosecuting, suits for dissolution were eventually brought against some of the trusts, notably against the Standard Oil Company and the American Tobacco Company. In the lower courts the decisions were against the companies, and it was not until 1911, when Roosevelt was no longer President, that they came to a hearing in the Supreme Court of the United States. The Chief Justice was then

459 George W. Wickersham, 1858–, Government Lawyer in the Standard Oil Case, from a photograph by Underwood & Underwood, New York

Edward D. White, who in previous cases had laid down the principle that the court ought to "follow the rule of reason" in interpreting the act of 1890. By that rule, he held, it was the intent of Congress merely to break up such combinations as produced monopolies. He had previously been outvoted by the older members of the bench who had held that Congress aimed to destroy all combinations in restraint of trade; but these older members were now gone and younger men held their places. In 1911 they took the point of view of the new Chief Justice, and the "rule of reason" was followed. Nevertheless the Standard Oil and the American Tobacco Companies were ordered to dissolve on the ground that they were held to be monopolies in violation of the act of 1890. It was hard to carry out the decision, but plans were made satisfactory to the court and each company resolved itself into several other companies. The importance of the decision lay in the fact that it was a warning to other trusts and checked the tendency toward industrial combinations.

ROOSEVELT SPARRING FOR THE NOMINATION OF 1904

THE capitalistic wing of the Republican party, as 1904 drew near, turned toward Hanna, who in a famous tariff speech at Akron, Ohio, in 1902 had declared that the true course was to "stand pat" in the face of the demand for reform. He thus became known as the leader of the "Standpatters." In 1903, Hanna was re-elected to the Senate, thus clinching his position as favorite son of the great state of Ohio. At once he became the rallying point of the Standpatters, and was mentioned far and wide as a candidate for the nomination in the year 1904. This was noted carefully by Roosevelt, who was traveling through the country, making

speeches and building up a strong following with the great mass of farmers and small business men. It was evident that he was tremendously popular, but Hanna had the backing of a great deal of money. Then death intervened, taking off the Ohio Senator. Roosevelt was left with a clear field and received the nomination without serious opposition. His trust policy and his courage in attack had made him popular with a large part of the people.

460 Roosevelt Notification Committee, from a photograph by Underwood & Underwood, New York

461   Alton B. Parker, 1852–, from a photograph by Albany Art Co., courtesy of the *New York Herald Tribune*

THE DEMOCRATS AND BRYAN

THE Democrats took courage from the hostility of the large business men to Roosevelt and conceived the hope that by nominating a man of sound business ideas they might draw from the Republican party the discontented element. With this end in view a movement was started to nominate Judge Alton B. Parker, of New York. With much difficulty the Bryan following was induced to support him and he was named by the convention.

EFFECT OF PARKER'S TELEGRAM

PARKER telegraphed the convention that he considered the gold standard as fixed and if elected would act accordingly. This rash announcement angered the Bryan men, who took it as a thrust at their leader. They also took it to indicate that the men supporting Parker were currying favor with the big business men of Wall Street. Since the underlying fact in the Bryan movement was distrust of Wall Street, Judge Parker, therefore, by a most ill-conceived stroke had succeeded in setting against him in the beginning of his campaign a very large portion of his own party. From this handicap he did not recover during the whole course of the race. He also lost the expected support of the business men; for on consideration they concluded they would rather have Roosevelt at the head of a Republican party, much as they disliked him, than "a safe and sound" Democrat with radicals at his back. Roosevelt carried the election by an electoral vote of three hundred and thirty-six to one hundred and forty, with both houses of Congress strongly Republican.

462   From a cartoon "*Where Every God Did Seem to Set His Seal to Give the World Assurance of a Man*" — *Hamlet*, by Maybell in the *Brooklyn Daily Eagle*, July 11, 1904

CAMPAIGN CONTRIBUTIONS

ROOSEVELT had some difficulty in obtaining a campaign manager. Finally the task was accepted by George B. Cortelyou, who gave up the Secretaryship of Commerce and Labor. At the same time it was reported that Cortelyou would be Postmaster-General if Roosevelt was elected. As Secretary he had had an opportunity to learn much about the business of the wealthy people, and it was charged that he used his knowledge to obtain large campaign contributions. The prospect of having Cortelyou at the head of the post offices was likely to make the many postmasters in the country active Roosevelt men. Parker alluded to this situation in one of his speeches, which brought from Roosevelt a stinging repudiation of the idea that Cortelyou was getting money on the ground of promises made to the donors, which, in fact, was an ardent denial of something that had not been charged.

463   From a cartoon *Putting the Screws on Him*, by Joseph Keppler, Jr., in *Puck*, Nov. 2, 1904

ROOSEVELT TRIUMPHANT

THE magnitude of his victory astonished even Roosevelt himself, and showed how warmly the country desired to see adopted a progressive policy administered by an aggressive leader. It was evident that he had carried the mass of Republicans and drawn to a considerable extent from the Democrats. It seemed evident, also, that he could have things his own way in the coming Congress. Full of confidence, he believed he foresaw the enactment of many reform measures. On the night of the election he gave a statement to the newspapers in which he said that he shared the feeling against a third term, would take the election of 1904 as his second, and refuse to stand again for the Presidency. He probably thought that he would accomplish all his reforms in his coming term and be ready to retire at its end. In this respect he was disappointed. He went out of office with many of his objectives unattained, and the day came when he tried hard to recover office in order to carry his projects forward. Roosevelt was imbued with the courageous spirit of the born fighter and enjoyed his attempts to dominate opponents. He would never retire from a struggle in which he had become engaged until it had been brought to a definite conclusion. It must be added that Roosevelt loved power for its own sake and fancied the glamour of office holding.

464   From a cartoon *All His Own*, by J. S. Pughe in *Puck*, Mar. 1, 1903

465   Roosevelt's inauguration, March 4, 1905, from a photograph by Underwood & Underwood, New York

ROOSEVELT'S INAUGURAL ADDRESS

IN his inaugural address Roosevelt had an opportunity to express his ideas of the task before him. While he was conscious of its gravity he was too politic to offend by threatening those from whom he anticipated opposition. The inaugural dealt chiefly with two things: the preparation of adequate national defense and the establishment of social and industrial justice. The second of these objects embraced the field of action that made him the "trust buster" of the day, loved and trusted by the people at large because of his bold attacks and his honesty. Drawing a distinction between good and bad capitalists, he called the nation to face calmly and seriously the task of reform.

466 Roosevelt with the Russian and Japanese Peace Delegates on
board the *Mayflower*, 1905, from a photograph by Underwood &
Underwood, New York

THE TREATY OF PORTSMOUTH

IN 1905, Roosevelt played a leading part in bringing Japan and Russia to make peace at Portsmouth after a severe war in which Japan had won a signal victory over her antagonist. In this negotiation he had the support of the German Kaiser, who was interested in seeing Russia remain a strong power in the East. The war had been very expensive to Japan and although she was the victor her treasury was in a bad state. Roosevelt used this fact to induce her to make peace on terms that her people thought inadequate. They wanted all the Island of Sakhalin, north of Japan and commanding the mouth of the Amur. By controlling that great river which drains a large part of Manchuria they hoped to find in northern Asia a field for future expansion. In the settlement they got the southern half of the island, full control of Korea, and concessions on the Port Arthur Peninsula. Roosevelt's insistence that Japan should moderate her demands on Russia was taken by the Japanese to reflect American jealousy of rising Japanese influence in Asia; it resulted in a swift change of Japanese feeling from trust in the United States to suspicion.

ROOSEVELT AND THE ALGECIRAS CONFERENCE

IN 1905, France and Spain were apparently about to divide a large portion of Morocco between them into "spheres of influence," and Germany was disappointed because she was left out. The Kaiser appealed to Roosevelt to use his influence to get the matter referred to an international conference for settlement. This seemed possible because not only France but Great Britain who was supporting France passively had confidence in the honest neutrality of the United States. With some reluctance he agreed to take part and was at last able to get France and Britain to comply. When the conference met he used his good offices to get the Kaiser to modify his demands, with the result that what had seemed to be a menacing cause of war was smoothed out. Roosevelt sent two representatives to the conference, but it was stipulated that the United States was not to be held responsible for the execution of the terms agreed upon. Apparently, Roosevelt acted solely in the interest of humanity; but it was not clear that Germany had a right to object to the action of France in Morocco.

467   From a cartoon *Kindred Spirits of the Strenuous Life*, in *Punch*, Nov. 16, 1904

THE "ELKINS AMENDMENT"

Two of the things that Roosevelt wished to get changed were the practices of the railroads in connection with rebates and passes. All the roads felt constrained to give rebates to big shippers. Passes were given also, to public officials as well as to many favored shippers. Thus the revenues of the roads were diminished. In 1903, Paul Morton, president of the Santa Fé Railroad, suggested to Roosevelt that the roads would help him get through Congress a bill to forbid rebates and passes. With the approval of the President an act was passed to that effect as an amendment of the act of 1887. It took its name from Senator Elkins, a consistent friend of the railroads. As time passed it was observed that one of its effects was to turn away from the railroads many Congressmen who were displeased because they no longer received passes.

468 ⋅ Paul Morton, from a photograph by Underwood & Underwood, New York

GOVERNMENT REGULATION OF RAILROADS

A PRIME feature of Roosevelt's program was the establishment of an effective control over the railroads. In the preceding twenty years the railroads through a long struggle of rate-cutting and other forms of expensive competition had gradually grouped themselves in a small number of great systems, and these systems were now anxious to do away with some of the very practices that had brought about their consolidation. Roosevelt wished to reduce the power of the roads by strengthening the hands of the Interstate Commerce Commission, which in 1905 was practically moribund. Its decisions were overruled by the courts and ignored. Roosevelt desired to get Congress to strengthen the Commission. The railroads through a powerful lobby opposed increasing the power of the Commission. On the other hand the public depending on railroads for supplies were insistent on the reduction of their power to affect business by means of freight rates. This feeling was especially strong in the great interior states which depended on the main trunk lines.

469 From a cartoon *Elisha Roosevelt Sicketh the Bears on the Bad Boys of Wall Street*, by Joseph Keppler, Jr., in *Puck*, May 8, 1907

470   From a cartoon *Belshazzerfellers Feast*, by J. S. Pughe
in *Puck*, May 31, 1905

THE HEPBURN RAILROAD–
RATE LAW

THE Elkins Amendment pleased the railroads, but it did not go far enough for Roosevelt; and soon after his inauguration in 1905 he took steps to get Congress to pass a law strengthening the powers of the Interstate Commerce Commission and giving it authority to fix maximum rates. A bill introduced by Chairman Hepburn of the House Committee on Interstate Commerce passed the House by a vote of three hundred and forty-six to seven. In the Senate it encountered powerful opposition and there was a long and bitter debate, at the end of which the bill in amended form passed with only three dissenting votes. It was characteristic of these battles of Roosevelt's that although Senators fought hard to amend the bills under discussion, on the final vote they did not dare go on record in the negative. The act increased the Commission from five to seven members, extended its jurisdiction to include pipe-lines, express companies and sleeping-car companies, and forbade a railroad to carry any commodities it produced, except timber and articles needed for its own use. It also gave the Commission the right to fix a maximum rate on complaint that existing rates were too high. The act applied only to interstate transportation, and rested on the clause in the Constitution giving Congress authority over trade between the states that make up the Union.

PURE FOOD AND DRUGS

A SERIOUS situation had developed with the growth of the manufacture of food products. Without adequate Governmental regulation fraud and injurious practices of many kinds were common. Upton Sinclair's novel, *The Jungle*, did much to arouse the public to an attempt to put an end to the evil practices. Roosevelt lent the movement his support and aided in bringing about the passage of an act requiring food and drugs to be labeled with respect to their contents. Adulteration was common in food stuffs, especially in preserved fruits and cereals. The proposal to make the labels true statements of the contents was only a plan to promote truth, but it was fought by powerful interests; there was much difficulty in getting the bill passed. The execution of this salutary law was given into the hands of Dr. Harvey W. Wiley, who had been a strong advocate of its passage. A later attempt to curb the patent medicine industry was doomed to failure through the effects of a power ful lobby in Washington. Its fate was a great disappointment to the reformers.

471   Dr. Harvey W. Wiley, 1844–, from a photograph
by Clinedinst Studio, Washington

472   The Roosevelt Dam in Flood Time, Tonto National Forest, Arizona, from a photograph by M. W. Talbot,
courtesy of the United States Forest Service, Washington

ROOSEVELT AND CONSERVATION

BEFORE Roosevelt's time many people had remarked the reckless manner in which our forests and other natural resources had been wasted; but no President had taken effective steps to bring the waste to an end. Roosevelt developed a conservation policy, embracing efforts to save the forests so as to conserve the timber supply and preserve the watersheds; also to promote irrigation and thus extend the area of arable land, as well as to drain swamp lands, and to develop and utilize in a better way water power and inland waterways. He did much for some of these projects, but here again his chief service was to call the attention of the people to the things that ought to be done and to suggest ways in which his ideas could be carried out.

GIFFORD PINCHOT, 1865–

IN the effort to save the forests, Roosevelt's right-hand man was Gifford Pinchot, a professional forester, trained in the best schools of Europe. In 1898, Pinchot had been placed at the head of the newly created forestry bureau in the Department of Agriculture where his work was merely theoretical. When Roosevelt became President and established a genuine forestry service with actual supervision over the public lands, he put Pinchot in charge. Up to that time about forty-five million acres of public lands had been set aside as permanent reservations, mostly because they were desired as recreation areas. Pinchot in his new position adopted a policy of setting aside much larger areas for economic reasons. During Roosevelt's administration, one hundred and forty-eight million acres were thus withdrawn from public sale, most of it in the Far West. During these years conservation became a much advertised Governmental policy. In particular vast areas of forest lands were saved. The profession of the forester became popular and schools of forestry made their appearance in many parts of the country. The results of the movement were of great national benefit.

473   Gifford Pinchot, from a photograph

474 Governors' Conservation Conference, 1908, from a photograph by Underwood & Underwood, New York

THE CONSERVATION COMMISSION

ROOSEVELT'S interest in conservation extended from forestry to irrigation. Late in his Presidency it led him to espouse all kinds of conservation. It was in this connection that he called in 1908 a conference of the Governors of the states. In an impressive meeting at the White House, with the President of the United States in the chair, various means of promoting conservation in general were taken up and explained, and a broad system of efforts was recommended to Congress and to the state legislatures. A second Governors' congress met in 1909. The President also created a Conservation Commission, which in 1909 made a comprehensive report about the nation's resources in water, forests, mines and soils. Roosevelt's activities gave a considerable stimulus to the reclamation of arid lands by irrigation. Roosevelt Lake remains a monument to his services to the nation in this regard.

CUBAN INTERVENTION

ROOSEVELT could not escape in his second term the oft recurring problem of Cuba. In 1905, the Cubans held an election for president and other officers. The defeated party was greatly disappointed and following an old Latin-American custom took up arms. So threatening seemed the prospect of internal confusion that the existing Government in the island appealed to the United States for aid in maintaining order. Roosevelt sent Secretary Taft to see if he could bring about harmony between the rival factions, but the effort proved unsuccessful. The president in office sought to better the situation by resigning. The Cuban congress could not find a satisfactory successor, and for a time the Government threatened to fall into chaos. Parties were forming in a spirit of bitterness; business was becoming alarmed for the safety of its property; and plantation owners faced the prospect of raids, with the choice between paying for protection and having their cane mills burned. Such a state of affairs would undo most of the recent work of Cuban restoration.

475 William Howard Taft, 1906, in the Palace at Havana, Cuba, in charge of Cuban administration, from a photograph by Underwood & Underwood, New York

AN ARMY IN CUBA

THEN Roosevelt thought it time to act under the Platt Amendment of 1902, which recognized that the United States might reënter Cuba to preserve order. He appointed a provisional Governor for the island and gave him an armed force to support his authority. Under this régime quiet was restored, rules were made for the better regulation of the franchise, and many improvements were accomplished in the sanitary conditions. At the end of two years Roosevelt announced that the objects for which occupation had been ordered were achieved; control of the island was handed back to its own rulers. The expedition cost the United States six million dollars, but it was worth much more than that in showing the Cubans that they must control their impulses and not try to settle political differences by resorting to arms.

ROOSEVELT'S SUCCESSOR

As the end of Roosevelt's administration approached he was forced to admit that many of the reforms he had planned were not yet realized. There was danger also that some of those which he had wrung by force out of Congress would not be fully enforced if his successor should not believe in them. These considerations caused anxiety to his supporters, and they

"A POLICEMAN'S LOT...."

POLICEMAN ROOSEVELT. "NOW THEN, YOU TWO, STOP THAT GAME!"
CUBAN COMBATANTS. "WHAT 'LL YOU DO IF WE DON'T?"
POLICEMAN R. "GUESS I'LL MAKE IT MIGHTY UNPLEASANT FOR YOU—(aside)—AND FOR MYSELF!"

476 From a cartoon by Linley Sambourne in *Punch*, Sept. 26, 1906

began to say that he ought to consent to be reëlected. But Roosevelt returned a steady "No." He stood by his announcement of election night, 1904, that he would consider his election of that day as the second and would respect the tradition that a President should not have a third term. He was sincere in his declaration that the third term tradition served a good purpose in our political life and ought to be respected, even by our most popular Presidents.

477   From a cartoon *The Courtship of Bill Taft*. *Priscilla — Why don't you speak for yourself, Theodore?*,
by Joseph Keppler, Jr., in *Puck*, Apr. 24, 1908

478   William Howard Taft, 1857–, from a photograph
by L. C. Handy, Washington

ROOSEVELT SELECTS THE CANDIDATE

In this emergency the Standpat element of his party were at Roosevelt's mercy. The wave of popularity caused by his battles for reform had completely overwhelmed them. From one end of the country to the other the mass of Republicans recognized him as their leader, and the politicians, however much they disliked him, were ready to take the man he indicated. That man was William H. Taft, Secretary of War. In making the selection he turned aside the friends of Governor Hughes of New York, very popular in the state for his opposition to the Platt machine, but not having as Roosevelt thought a sufficiently widespread personal following. Having decided for Taft, Roosevelt left no stone unturned to get Taft delegates chosen to the national nominating convention, with the result that Taft was named on the first ballot by seven hundred and two votes out of nine hundred and eighty, the remainder going to favorite sons.

THE REPUBLICAN PLATFORM

Roosevelt dictated the platform adopted by his party in 1908. Many of the things he had tried to do remained unaccomplished, and he was greatly concerned for their completion. Most notably, he had tried to get Congress to amend the Anti-Trust Act of 1890, so that it would be possible to distinguish between trusts that were merely an expression of the economic advantages of combination and trusts that were organized to drive their competitors to the wall and to put money into the pockets of promoters through dealing in watered stocks. The latter he wanted to prohibit; the former he wanted to tolerate, but under a moderate form of Government control. One of his ideas was that railroads should not be allowed to issue securities without the consent of the Government. Roosevelt sought to ensure the continuance of his policies by writing them into the platform of his party. He was conscious of the rift developed in the Republican ranks between the conservatives and the liberals but he does not seem to have foreseen the possibility of an open split in the party. In supporting Taft, Roosevelt thought he was advancing the cause of party harmony for if anyone could reconcile the divergent factions among the Republicans, that person, it seemed, was the genial and judicious Secretary of War.

479   From a cartoon The Standard-Bearer, in The World, New York, July 29, 1906

THE TARIFF AS AN ISSUE

THE Republican platform also took notice of the tariff. Eleven years had passed since the last tariff was adopted and there was some demand that it should be revised so as to bring it into keeping with the needs of the time. It was said that the tariff ought to be revised by its friends. There was also much talk about "revision downward." The argument advanced for downward revision was the fact that many American industries were no longer

480   Taft in the 1908 campaign, from a photograph in the possession of the *New York Herald-Tribune*

to be classed as "infant industries" and, therefore, did not need protection. In his speeches Taft gave color to this expectation. It was taken to mean that the high protection wall was crumbling. The Democrats could

481   From a cartoon *My Fish*, in the *New York Herald*, Aug. 31, 1908

not object to a turn of policies that was so much in line with what they had demanded for many years; but they spoke sarcastically about what they declared was the purloining of their own doctrine by their opponents. They also expressed their doubts of getting the genuine tariff reduction by a party that had so long believed in high protection.

BRYAN'S THIRD CANVASS

THE Democratic nominating convention met in Denver. The small figure cut by the "safe and sane" policies of Parker in 1904 had discredited those who thought that all would be well if the party were only turned back on the old track. The Bryan men had yielded to the easterners in 1904: they were now in no frame of mind to yield an inch. Determined to run this campaign on Bryan principles, they believed rightly that to defend such principles Bryan himself was the strongest candidate. From the beginning it was Bryan's convention. He was nominated on the first ballot by a vote of eight hundred and ninety-two and one half out of a total of one thousand and eight. For the third time he was a Presidential candidate.

WILLIAM JENNINGS BRYAN SPEAKING AT CARNEGIE HALL

482   William Jennings Bryan speaking at Carnegie Hall, from the *New York Herald*, Sept. 19, 1908

483   From a cartoon *First Bonfire of the Campaign*, by W. A. Rogers in the *New York Herald*,
Aug. 15, 1908

THE DEMOCRATIC PLATFORM

THE platform adopted at Denver was notable for its omissions. Nothing was said about the free coinage of silver nor about several other policies which the candidate had espoused at one time or another in his impassioned career. The ease with which they were put aside seemed to indicate a lack of serious conviction. It was observed that the platform itself was somewhat in the same vein; for its chief characteristic was to rake up a number of issues which seemed to the makers to have in them the power to attract votes. It demanded that trust-made articles should be placed on the free list, that the rates on other articles should be reduced gradually until they reached a basis necessary to produce the revenues of the Government, that private monopolies should be driven out of existence and their officials punished under the criminal law, that interlocking directorates should be forbidden, and that Federal licenses should be required of corporations. It was a composite platform not unified by a single broad principle.

THE DEMOCRATIC BID FOR THE LABOR VOTE

ANOTHER feature of the Democratic platform was its position on labor. Both parties were anxious to get labor support, but the Democrats went further than their opponents in that direction. They declared that injunctions should not be issued "in any cases in which the injunctions would not issue if no industrial dispute were involved." They also advocated an eight-hour day on Government work, a general employers' liability act, and the creation of a Department of Labor whose Secretary was to sit in the President's Cabinet. The event showed that these concessions were futile; in most states labor seems to have voted as it had voted in the preceding election, showing that laboring men, like most others, are guided chiefly by attachment to a party when they go to the polls.

"HERE, PUSS, PUSS!"

I love little pussy,   So I'll not pull his tail,
His coat is so warm,   Or drive him away;
And if I don't hurt him,   But pussy and I
He'll do me no harm.   Very gently will play.

484   From a cartoon by L. M. Glackens in *Puck*, Aug. 5, 1908

CAMPAIGN CONTRIBUTIONS

FOR many years public opinion had been growing against the increasing use of money in elections. This feeling had led several states to enact laws limiting the amount that could be used in this way. On January 26, 1907, Congress passed a law forbidding corporations to contribute to campaign funds in Federal elections. The Democratic platform in 1908 contained a plank which stated that contributions should be limited to "a reasonable minimum." During the campaign the Democratic National Committee announced that no money would be received from corporations, that no one person should give more than ten thousand dollars, and that all contributions above one hundred dollars would be published before election day. As the Democrats rarely received large sums for election purposes the announcement did not affect them

HARD TO RAISE THE WIND.

485   From a cartoon *Hard To Raise The Wind*, by W. A. Rogers in the *New York Herald*, Aug. 26, 1908

materially. Their opponents were supposed to have more reason for not wishing to make known their list of contributions. As to the laws on the subject so many ways were found of evading them that their restrictions were nearly inoperative. The increasing size of the campaign chests has produced a like growth in the total expenditures for campaigns. These funds tend to give wealth great powers.

THE ELECTION OF TAFT

As the campaign neared its close two things became evident. Taft was drawing a large number of independently-minded men to his side. Conservative business men still shared the old fear of Bryan, who during his long career was never able to escape the charge of radicalism, due to his early espousal of the cause of free silver. To the country at large it seemed that the choice lay between a policy of mild and steady progress carried forward by Taft on a Roosevelt basis and a program of radicalism carried forward by one who had several times changed his "paramount issue." The choice of the country was seen in the return — Taft, three hundred and twenty-one electoral votes and Bryan one hundred and seventy-two. It was a great victory for the Roosevelt policies; but it did not mean as much of a Democratic defeat as the vote on the Presidency might seem to show. The Democrats carried local elections in five states in which Taft ran ahead of Bryan, and in some other states the previous Republican majority was materially reduced.

486   Taft and Roosevelt at Taft's inauguration, March 4, 1909, from a photograph. © Underwood & Underwood, New York

487   From a cartoon *"When the tumult and the shouting dies,"* by Berryman in *Outing*, March 1908

THE RETIREMENT OF ROOSEVELT

THERE was much speculation as to what would be Roosevelt's course after retiring.   Some persons suggested that he should run for the Senate, others had him in mind for a university presidency: nobody thought he was likely to subside into the routine of a simple private citizen.   He soon answered their queries by announcing that he intended to spend a year hunting big game in Africa.   When a witty politician heard the news he exclaimed, "Health to the Lions!"   By going on this journey Roosevelt satisfied a longing for hunting, made an exit from public life in keeping with his sense of the spectacular, and gave Taft a fair opportunity to lay the course of his administration as he wished and without suggestions from his predecessor.   He and Taft parted good friends.

THE WORLDS CONSTABLE.

488   From a cartoon *The World's Constable*, by Louis Dalrymple in *Judge*, Jan. 7, 1905

CHAPTER X

TAFT'S EFFORTS TO OBTAIN HARMONY

MOST people hailed the accession of Taft to the Presidency as a beginning of party harmony. Roosevelt's methods had displeased many quiet souls. Slashing about with a "big stick," meeting his opponents more than half way, assuming the aggressive in anticipation of their attacks upon him, all these things had produced a deep division in the Republican party though this was not fully apparent when he left office. At first it seemed that the new President would be able to preserve harmony. He had been a good judge in early political life, a successful administrator in the Philippines, and a popular as well as efficient member of the cabinet of his predecessor. He was a distinguished graduate of Yale and his intellectual strength was conceded by all who knew him. Few Presidents came to authority with so much native ability, good humor and experience in their favor. Nevertheless, Taft's administration was destined to end in disappointment.

This result was partly due to Taft's personal character. Kind he was ever, but he lacked the power to compel the acceptance of his ideas. He did not give orders successfully. Roosevelt had always been the captain of a host and gave it its tone as well as its fighting principles. Taft, who entered office for the assumed purpose of carrying on the policies of his predecessor, was a kind friend and a lover of peace, but never a captain of a host. Roosevelt had never tried to heal the breach in his party but was content to endeavor to make his views the accepted views of the whole organization. He had cajoled the Standpat wing when he felt it necessary, but neither they nor the country ever felt that he yielded any of his principles in order to obtain their coöperation. He was a militant man and the policy he left to his successor was a militant policy. Taft, however, was in no sense a militant leader. His impulses were at bottom conservative and his method of procedure was to get the two sides of a controversy to come together. It was thus that fate ordained that the radical policies of the fighting captain came for continuation into the hands of a man who was not a captain and whose nature was averse to waging battle. Taft, however, was a man of too much individuality to play to Roosevelt the part that Martin Van Buren played to Jackson. He looked upon his administration as his own and undertook to set its course in his own way. The result was the unhappy quarrel whose fury brought the Taft Presidency to a tragic and painful end.

This contest had the unfortunate effect of diverting public attention from much of the excellent work accomplished by Taft while in office. He was a man of great industry, and had a high appreciation of his responsibilities to the nation. He also did a great deal to carry out Roosevelt's ideas of conservation and to place its measures on a sound constitutional basis, a thing which the impetuous nature of his predecessor had not taken care to do. While he did this he was the butt of bitter attacks by the Roosevelt men.

489   Sereno Payne, 1843–1914, from a photograph by
Harris & Ewing, Washington

THE TARIFF PLEDGE OF THE REPUBLICANS

A GREAT development of business and industry in the United States had taken place since the passage of the Dingley Act. That measure was out of adjustment with the conditions at the opening of the Taft administration. A new tariff was needed and the President promptly set the legislative machinery at work to carry out the campaign pledges of the party. Taft turned his attention immediately to the tariff, calling Congress in extra session March 15, 1909. The House of Representatives prepared the Payne Bill, making a general reduction of rates and passed it quickly, less than a month after the extra session began. The principle on which it was believed to rest was that the tariff should be only so high as to equalize the difference between the cost of production abroad and in the United States. Many men, among them Andrew Carnegie, the great iron manufacturer, had said that the Dingley Act of 1897 was too high for that purpose. There were, of course, many men who took a view quite opposed to that of Mr. Carnegie. The actual application of the principle of protection to concrete cases has ever called forth wide differences of opinion, and such was the case in 1909. Many protectionists felt that if a beginning of tariff reduction were now made more drastic steps would follow.

SENATOR NELSON W. ALDRICH

THE Payne Bill went from the House to the Senate where it fell into the hands of Senator Nelson W. Aldrich, chairman of the Finance Committee. Here it experienced the severe overhauling which most important bills undergo in the Senate, and because of which the upper house is often the chief factor in lawmaking, displacing to a large extent the House of Representatives chosen on a more popular basis. Senator Aldrich, representing a New England state in which the dominant interest was manufacturing, played a leading part in the revamping of the Payne Bill. He was a Republican of the Mark Hanna school who by his ability and length of service had risen to an influential position in party councils. He now set to work with his accustomed energy to make the new tariff law conform more accurately to what he conceived to be the needs of the nation. When the gigantic task was completed and the differences between the House and the Senate had been smoothed out in conference, the Payne-Aldrich tariff required a volume for its printing. Because of its complexity only a highly trained expert can make very much out of the rates. And different experts who have studied it have reached somewhat different conclusions as to whether or not it increased the protection afforded by the old Dingley tariff. At any rate it did not revise the tariff downward.

490   Senator Nelson W. Aldrich, 1841–1915, from a drawing by
Robert Carter in *The World*, New York, June 13, 1909

THE WORK OF THE "INTERESTS"

THE Payne Bill was no low tariff measure, and actually raised the rates on certain articles, such as tropical fruits, many of which had come into the hands of a large importing company that demanded protection. But several of the important raw materials were put on the free list and reductions were made on iron and steel manufactures and lumber, refined sugar and many other articles. It met the requirements of the campaign pledge and the expectations of the voters. When the bill came back from Aldrich's committee its character was completely altered. To satisfy a combination of interests he had restored many of the rates lowered in the House and actually increased some under the form of new classifications. The Senate Finance Committee estimated

491   From a cartoon *Tangled*, by C. R. Macauley in *The World*, New York, Apr. 5, 1909

that instead of reduction the tariff as finally passed made an actual increase of the average rate by one and one-tenth per cent. It provided for a permanent Tariff Board of experts to supply information regarding the economic needs of the country and also created a Court of Customs Appeals. The bill was passed as the Payne-Aldrich Act of 1909, and it was signed by the President. The Customs Court and the Tariff Board were new features and were looked upon as greatly strengthening the Government in its handling of the difficult tariff problem. The court was later abolished but the principle of the tariff board to make a constant and expert study of the tariff needs of the nation has been retained. The idea that a board of scientific economists shall modify the tariff so as to keep it adjusted to the needs of the country is attractive; but it is difficult to operate; for laying a tariff is laying a tax, a power Congress will, in all probability, insist on keeping in its own hands.

492   Albert J. Beveridge, 1862–1927, from a photograph by Harris & Ewing, Washington

THE REPUBLICAN PROTEST

ALDRICH's forcing upon the country the protection of the "interests" in violation of party pledges was resented in the West. Ten Republican Senators, led by Beveridge and Dolliver, refused to vote for the bill, thus breaking away from the authority of party leadership. It was not a coincidence that they were men who had supported Roosevelt's program of reform. They had built under Roosevelt's leadership a solid opposition to Standpatism. Aldrich's course in forcing on the country his own philosophy of the tariff was resented by these men as personal wrongs. Herein lay the seed of much later history.

493   From E. W. Kemble's caricature of Senators Dolliver and
        Cummins, in *Leslie's Illustrated Weekly*, Jan. 15, 1910

EAST AND WEST

INTO the controversy went also the long-continued feeling of separateness between the East and the West. Aldrich's New England hand had controlled party action through party loyalty. The beneficiary of the Payne-Aldrich Act was the East, and the burden of it fell with slight compensation on the West and the South. The opposition of the latter section went without saying. The South had been fighting the tariff for nearly a century, but it was Democratic and nothing was to be conceded to it. But the West had been faithful to the Republican party and felt that to be ignored in the present instance was a grievous indignity. The Payne-Aldrich tariff helped to bring to a climax the growing popular opposition to the trusts. Men either ranged themselves for or against the measure. In the language of the day they became either "Standpatters" or "Insurgents." The tariff was a dividing force bringing into the open the schism which had taken place in the Republican party. There were many comments on the adroitness of Roosevelt in avoiding this thorny problem. Taft did not try to dodge the issue but faced it squarely. He took the question of the tariff to the voters.

TAFT'S SPEECH AT WINONA

SHORTLY after the tariff of 1909 was enacted President Taft made a tour in the West, speaking at many places. His first speech was at Winona, Minnesota. James A. Tawney, a Member of Congress, lived there.

An insurgent a few years earlier, he had recently been turning to the conservatives, in consequence of which he was losing popularity in his district. In this place Taft undertook to justify the tariff. Discussing it at length, he said it was "the best tariff law the Republican party ever made." Proceeding westward, he continued to praise the law, although everyone knew that it had not met his views in all respects. To the West at large the Winona speech seemed disingenuous. To the Roosevelt men it seemed bad faith for Taft to go out of his way to serve politically a man whose opposition to Roosevelt had been so pronounced. The President, disappointed at the schedules, was influenced by the great advance which the bill had brought about through the creation of the Tariff Board and the Customs Court. Vast numbers of voters were not able to accept his judgment and the speeches injured his prestige. Tawney had been noted for his opposition to Roosevelt, and Taft's efforts to help him were offensive to the Roosevelt men, who looked on Tawney as a renegade. They also resented his attempt to convince them that the Payne-Aldrich Act provided for tariff reduction. They considered that Taft, made President by Roosevelt, had deserted his cause and joined the Standpat camp. The Winona speech was a very unfortunate affair and was the beginning of much trouble for Taft.

494   William Howard Taft speaking at Winona, from a photograph
        by Underwood & Underwood, New York

CONSERVATION ON TRIAL

CONSERVATION became another cause for the diminution of the President's popularity. The people of the Far West were not altogether in sympathy with it, and they protested that they were being made to bear a burden for the benefit of future generations at the expense of their own development. R. A. Ballinger, Taft's Secretary of the Interior and a Pacific Coast man, shared this feeling. Nevertheless, in some respects he supported conservation, and through his efforts nine conservation measures were adopted providing for a new classification of the public lands with the recognition of the principle that the sale of the surface did not carry with it the transfer of the timber upon it nor the minerals below it. The minerals were to remain Government property and be leased to individuals. These laws were excellent, but they had little effect, since they were not passed until most of the land concerned had gone into private hands. However, they put conservation on a sound legal basis. Taft, who did not have Roosevelt's gift for the spectacular, derived no personal advantage as a result of this important legislative achievement. The public took little notice of it, realizing how ineffective it was; but it is only fair to Taft

495   Richard A. Ballinger, 1858–, from a photograph by Harris & Ewing, Washington

and Ballinger to call attention to the nature of the legislation which they sponsored. Although these laws were enacted too late to prove effective, Taft and Ballinger strove to protect the natural resources of the nation.

THE BALLINGER CONTROVERSY

SECRETARY BALLINGER became involved in a controversy with Gifford Pinchot, in charge of the forestry service. The occasion of the difference was the effort of a rich syndicate to get possession of a large area of mineral lands in Alaska; it attempted to have its employees obtain land grants from the Government and then transfer them to the syndicate, a measure contrary to the law. Ballinger had been legal counsel for the same syndicate in an unimportant matter. An investigation of the Alaska claims was being conducted when he became Secretary. He quashed it and ordered the land warrants to be issued to the syndicate against the protest of Pinchot, who appealed to the public and was dismissed from office for insubordination.

496   Map showing comparative sizes of Alaska and the United States, from the *American Monthly Review of Reviews*, Nov. 1910

497   From a cartoon *Some Census Questions*, in the *American Monthly Review of Reviews*, May 1910, reproduced from the *North American*, Philadelphia

THE BALLINGER INVESTIGATION

OUT of office Pinchot kept up the attack, and so dark were the charges made that Congress created a committee to investigate. The imputation was that the Secretary was biased by his former relation to the syndicate. The idea got abroad that he was violating Roosevelt's conservation policy, which had a tendency to unite against him the Roosevelt wing of the party. The investigating committee proceeded in a partisan way, making two reports, one by the majority exonerating Ballinger and one by the minority condemning him. Though Taft defended the Secretary the hostility of his critics became so violent that on March 11, 1911, the President accepted his resignation. The "Roosevelt policies," particularly conservation, had become a popular fetish in which were to be found all that was good and wise. Ardent Roosevelt supporters turned the Ballinger-Pinchot controversy into an indirect attack upon the President. The charges were never proved.

THE "INSURGENTS"

THE fights over the tariff and the Ballinger-Pinchot affair brought into prominence a more or less radical group who were dubbed "Insurgents." The Standpatters decided that they should feel the weight of party discipline. Joseph Cannon, Speaker of the House, undertook to apply the discipline, so far as the members of that body were concerned. It was done by cutting them off from places on the good committees, thus endangering their legislative careers. "Uncle Joe," as he was called, was personally popular in the House, but he had a heavy hand when he struck, and his blows at the Insurgents were meant to tell. The recipients were equally in earnest, and his corrections served in no sense to bring them into a state of humility. Far from being cowed they began actively to plan to break the power of the Standpat group in the House of Representatives and to force consideration of legislation which they deemed of the greatest public importance. The event showed that the attempt of the party to impose discipline on this group of men was to end in failure. They did not control a large following in Congress but they were very active and capable of doing many things to retaliate on their opponents.

498   Joseph Cannon, 1836–1926, Speaker of the House, from a photograph by Underwood & Underwood, New York

CANNON UNHORSED

INTERWOVEN with the attack upon Ballinger was a movement in the house to break the hold upon it of the Speaker, Cannon, who was a supporter of Taft. The Speaker's control over the House rested on his power to appoint the members of committees and on his dominating position in the Committee on Rules. By calling this committee and changing a rule he could give direction to House action and kill or sustain any member's bill. He also had the habit of refusing to recognize a member rising to speak unless previous arrangements had been made to that end. By using these powers he made life dismal for the "Insurgent" Republicans opposed to the administration and they grew desperate. At last, on March 19, 1911, they combined with the Democrats to reform the Speakership. They introduced a motion to enlarge the Rules Committee, to make the Speaker ineligible for membership on it, and to permit the House to appoint its committees. Cannon ruled it out of order, but they appealed to the floor and outvoted his ruling. Then they passed the motion under consideration, whereupon Cannon said he would entertain a motion to declare the chair vacant, and a Democrat offered such a motion. But the Insurgents would not go that far, and "Uncle Joe" remained in the chair, though with his authority greatly reduced. The Insurgents in the Senate were supposed to be prepared to move against Aldrich, but his announcement that he would not stand for election cooled their ardor. These suc-

ONCE CLOTHED WITH POWER, NOW ALMOST BARE,
HE'S LOST HIS PULL, BUT SAVED HIS CHAIR.

499 From a cartoon by E. W. Kemble in *Harper's Weekly*, April 2, 1910

cesses reassured the members of the Insurgent group and tended to strengthen their sense of group solidarity.

500 From a cartoon *They Never Tire, but Uncle Sam Does*, by W. A. Rogers in the *New York Herald*, June 3, 1909

SIGNIFICANCE OF INSURGENCY

INSURGENCY was an outgrowth of the agitation set on foot in Roosevelt's time. It sincerely aimed at reforms. It was inclined to be vituperative and to paint its opponents blacker than truth warranted. On the other hand, its foes showed it no mercy. They gave curse for curse and jibe for jibe. The result was that in some sections of the country there grew up an impulse to believe that people living in some other sections were essentially dangerous to society. But such is the way in which political contention is usually conducted. It seems certain that out of the protests of men like Senators Dolliver, Beveridge and La Follette came an impulse that put new life into our politics and reduced in a healthy way the authority of the small group of men who had been able to establish themselves at the center of the Government. This group had acquired more power than they could use with safety.

501   From a cartoon *The Opening of the Parcels Post Tunnel*, by Joseph Keppler, Jr., in *Puck*, Jan. 1, 1913

POSTAL SAVING BANKS AND PARCEL POST

THE theoretical basis of most of the measures demanded by the insurgents was the belief that certain economic functions could be exercised by the Government better than by private enterprise. One of the demands was for the establishment of postal saving banks. It had been started long before, but the existing banks opposed it as setting up competition with their own business. Under the pressure of the new conditions this opposition was overridden in 1910, but the postal banks thus created were handicapped by fixing the rate of interest at such a low point that they have not become very prosperous institutions. To create a parcel post was a similar task but more difficult because of the strong influence of the important private express companies. It was accomplished in 1912 through the efforts of Insurgents and Democrats. (For postal savings banks and parcel post see Vol. IV.)

ADDRESSING CROWNED HEADS IN EUROPE

IN March, 1910, Roosevelt emerged from the African forest. While still in Egypt he began to receive requests to visit the leading capitals and the invitation usually comprehended a request to take part in some function which made it proper for him to deliver an address. A speech which he made in Egypt on the relation of that country to the British Empire aroused biting comment from the national party among the natives. In Berlin he was treated with high honor by the Kaiser and gave a lecture at the University. His various visits and addresses were made the subject of much good-natured sarcasm by European newspapers. On a photograph of the Kaiser and Roosevelt at army maneuvers the Kaiser wrote, "The Colonel of the Rough Riders lecturing the Chief of the German Army." Roosevelt, on the other hand, formed shrewd opinions of the attitude of the Germans toward the United States. The upper classes, military, bureaucratic and well-organized, he said, "regarded America with a dislike which was all the greater because they could not make it merely contempt." They looked down upon our loose organization, our strong individualism and our firm position among industrial nations, and they felt that we stood in the way of the vindication of their militaristic theories. The lower classes in Germany were socialists and equally at variance with the great individualistic republic of the West. Even the middle class did not like us, for they saw in us a formidable business rival. This fundamental antagonism played a significant part when Germany had to decide whether or not she should take steps which would bring the United States into the World War. Her decision in that matter rested on the conviction that the people of the United States would not fight effectively. They did not think that a war with us had any possible danger to them.

502   Roosevelt and the Kaiser, from a photograph by Underwood & Underwood, New York

HIS SUBJECT MATTER

Roosevelt's habit of making many speeches left him little time for preparation, with the result that much that he said was platitude. In the United States such speech-making goes quite well with a popular audience, and public men who speak much get the habit of pointless improvisation. To this tendency Roosevelt added the faculty of telling people to be good. Speeches of this kind amused the more keen-witted of the newspaper men in Europe, and they made many sly digs at him on account of them. The French humorous paper, *Le Rire*, represented him as saying before the Sorbonne in effect: "Educated folk know more than ignoramuses; peace is less bloody than war; rich men are not poor; race suicide is one of the causes of decline in population," etc. It was true that many of his ideas were obvious, but there were few men who dared champion them so frankly as he, and because of the fearless expression of his views the people liked him.

503 From a cartoon *Emphasizing the Obvious*, in *The American Monthly Review of Reviews*, June 1910, reproduced from *Le Rire*, Paris

TO. A FAUNAL NATURALIST

Uncle Sam: "Hello, Teddy; what we need is a live elephant, not dead ones."

504 From a cartoon *To a Faunal Naturalist*, by Marcus in the *New York Times*, April 17, 1910

ROOSEVELT'S RETURN

Roosevelt arrived in New York on June 18, 1910, amid the frantic shouts of joy of a vast assemblage of friends. In a speech at the Battery he repeated an announcement formerly made that he did not intend to give up his habit of discussing public questions but that he would not again run for office. He soon demonstrated his meaning by coming out in support of Governor Hughes' fight in New York for the adoption of direct primaries.

UNCLE SAM: "NOW THAT THE BATTLE IS OVER, YOUR HUMBLE SERVANT BEGS TO SUGGEST THAT YOU GO INTO RETIREMENT AND GIVE BUSINESS A CHANCE TO BOOM"

505 From a cartoon by E. W. Kemble in *Harper's Weekly*, Nov. 12, 1910

"NEW NATIONALISM"

On August 31, 1910, Roosevelt made a notable speech at Ossawatomie, Kansas, at the dedication of John Brown's battlefield. There he announced under the heading of "The New Nationalism" a program of reform. It consisted of many of the principles for which he had fought while President. Issued as the rallying cry of an approaching contest, it was assailed in strong terms by the conservatives, especially his assertion that the true friend of property "is he who insists that the creature of man's making shall be the servant and not the master of the man who made it. The citizens of the United States must effectively control the mighty commercial forces which they have themselves called into being." On that platform he was about to commit himself to the leadership of the extreme group of Republicans The views expressed at Ossawatomie were later published in a volume entitled "The New Nationalism."

THE DONKEY: "AND DON'T FORGET THERE'S ANOTHER ONE COMING TO YOU TWO YEARS FROM NOW"

506   From a cartoon *The Donkey: "And Don't Forget There's Another One Coming to You Two Years From Now,"* by E. W. Kemble in *Harper's Weekly,* Nov. 12, 1910

CONGRESSIONAL ELECTIONS OF 1910

THE rising tide of opposition to Taft in the western states produced grave fears in the minds of the Republican leaders. It soon became evident that the East was also seriously disaffected, as was shown early in 1910 in special elections for Congressmen in New York and Massachusetts. The underlying cause was the conviction that the President was acting with the Standpatters. In the autumn elections the Republican fears were fully realized. The official count showed that the Democrats had elected two hundred and twenty-seven members of the House, the Republicans one hundred and seventy-three, and the Socialists one, while the Republican majority in the Senate was cut from twenty-eight to ten. The Democrats elected Governors in several regular Republican states, one of them being Woodrow Wilson in New Jersey, put forward as a reform candidate.

CANADIAN RECIPROCITY

IN the election of 1910 the Democrats had talked much about the tariff, and Taft concluded from the result that there was still much popular interest in revision. He thought he would be supported, therefore, if he could establish reciprocity with Canada. Accordingly he negotiated an agreement to that effect, providing for lower duties on lumber, some kinds of food, wood pulp and other articles with lower Canadian duties on agricultural implements and other manufactured products. In Congress the agreement was opposed by the lumber states and the agricultural interest and Taft called Congress in extra session on April 4. With the aid of the Democrats the President carried reciprocity against strong opposition in his own party.

507   President Taft signing the Reciprocity Bill, June 26, 1910, from a photograph by G. V. Buck, Washington

REJECTED BY CANADA

In Canada reciprocity, championed by Sir Wilfrid Laurier, encountered strong opposition from the manufacturers, who were most numerous in the cities situated in the older parts of the Dominion. It was popular in the newer West because it would make agricultural implements cheaper. As the Canadian general elections drew near it became the chief subject of discussion. While the campaign was at its warmest stage the Democratic Speaker of the United States House of Representatives, Champ Clark, made a speech in which he said that reciprocity was a step toward Canadian annexation. This remark was used in Canada by the opponents of reciprocity with telling effect, especially in the Maritime Provinces, whose people were largely descendants of Loyalists who had fled from the United States in the Revolution. The opponents of reciprocity made the most of the bugaboo of annexation, raised the cry of Patriotism, and carried the election in triumph. This demonstration of the feeling in Canada brought to an end the belief which still lingered in certain quarters in the United States that Canada and the United States would be united.

508   Sir Wilfrid Laurier speaking for Reciprocity, from *Harper's Weekly*, Sept. 30, 1911

DEMOCRATIC TARIFF BILLS OF 1912

The Democrats had helped Taft to pass the Reciprocity Bill. Following the election of 1910 they formed with the Insurgents a tacit alliance to put the President "in a hole" just as the campaign of 1912 was approaching. They passed bills reducing the tariff step by step. The first was known as a Farmer's List Bill, placing on the free list agricultural implements and many other things used by farmers, such as boots, shoes, lumber and meat. It passed through each House with the support of the Democrats and the insurgent Republicans but was vetoed by the President. Another was a Woolen Bill, reducing the rates on wool and woolen goods from an average of ninety per cent to an average of forty-eight per cent. This also was vetoed, as was another, known as the Cotton Schedule Bill, reducing the rates on a number of articles, one of which was cotton. The President gave as reasons for his course the hasty preparation of the bills and the lack of exact information on the part of their advocates. They had been brought forward to embarrass the Republicans, but the public took the action of the President as mere partisanship and as a result opposition to high protection was increased. The protected interests have long feared that high tariffs would come down sometime, since they were laid to benefit infant industries, and they were now fearful that the time for reduction had arrived.

509   From a cartoon *Letting "I Dare Not" Wait Upon "I Would,"* in the *American Monthly Review of Reviews*, June 1911, reproduced from *Inter-Ocean*

510   Joseph Bailey, 1863–, from a photograph
          by Harris & Ewing, Washington

THE INCOME TAX AMENDMENT

WHILE the tariff of 1909 was being debated in the Senate, Cummings, an Insurgent, and Bailey, a Democrat, introduced bills providing for the levying of an income tax. In view of previous experience, the bills were dropped, but the sentiment of the Senate, acting on a suggestion by President Taft, was indicated by adopting resolutions unanimously for a Federal amendment authorizing an income tax. The amendment was prepared, ratified by two-thirds of each House, and submitted to the states. It was approved by the states and became effective in 1913. The way for an income tax was then clear.

TROUBLE ON THE MEXICAN BORDER

IN the midst of a very trying domestic situation President Taft found himself confronted with a puzzling foreign problem. From 1877 to 1911 with the exception of four years, Mexico was ruled by the strong-handed dictator-president, Porfirio Diaz. His overthrow in 1911 by Francisco Madero was partly due to the weakening of his hand in old age and partly to the protest of the Mexicans against a régime in which the wealth of Mexico was controlled by a few very rich men and the great mass of people were left without land or hope of getting it. Madero was an idealist and something of a visionary. He declared himself a crusader for the landless masses. But he failed to overcome the inevitable counter revolution, was driven from power by Huerta, imprisoned and assassinated. In this state of confusion United States citizens in Mexico were afraid that their interests and even their lives were not safe. On their account Taft called out, in March, 1911, a body of twenty thousand troops whom he held on the Texas border in readiness for use and as a manifestation of United States power. In Europe his action was taken as untoward activity under the Monroe Doctrine, and it aroused much unfavorable comment, for every move of this kind was looked on as a step toward United States control.

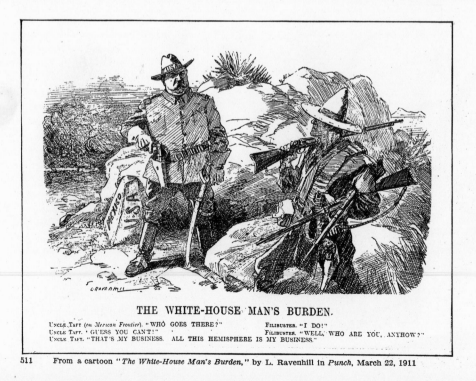

THE WHITE-HOUSE MAN'S BURDEN.

UNCLE TAFT (on Mexican Frontier). "WHO GOES THERE?"   FILIBUSTER. "I DO!"
UNCLE TAFT. "GUESS YOU CAN'T!"   FILIBUSTER. "WELL, WHO ARE YOU, ANYHOW?"
UNCLE TAFT. "THAT'S MY BUSINESS. ALL THIS HEMISPHERE IS MY BUSINESS."

511   From a cartoon "The White-House Man's Burden," by L. Ravenhill in Punch, March 22, 1911

PANAMA CANAL TOLLS

In 1912 the Panama Canal was nearing completion and Congress passed an act to regulate its operation. The act dealt with tolls, and one of the toll regulations permitted free passage to ships engaged in coastwise trade. The purpose of the exemption was to make the canal a competitor of the inter-coastal railroads and thus force freight rates down on traffic from coast to coast. The regulation brought forth a protest from Great Britain on the ground that it violated the Hay-Pauncefote Treaty of 1901 which provided that no discrimination in tolls should be made as between the nations accepting the rules provided in 1888 for the Suez Canal. The United States replied that foreign powers were by law excluded from coastwise transportation, so that Great Britain was in nowise affected.

AMERICAN OPINION ON TOLLS

The British claim caused an outburst of public sentiment, at the bottom of which was the conviction that the United States had built the canal and had a right to control it. This feeling was the reply to the British charge of bad faith. It figured in the campaign of 1912, Democrats and Republicans alike putting it into their platforms. Exemption on coastwise trade, though not technically a violation of the treaty, did affect materially the British ships taking freight from Vancouver, British Columbia, to Atlantic ports, and thus it violated the spirit of the treaty. In 1914, President Wilson obtained the repeal of the objectionable clause.

512 From a cartoon *The Deadhead*, by Nelson Harding in *Cartoons*, May 1914, reproduced from the *Brooklyn Daily Eagle*

513 From a cartoon *Uncle Sam's Canal*, in the *American Monthly Review of Reviews*, Sept. 1912, reproduced from the *Irish World*

514   Elbert H. Gary, 1846-1927, from a photograph by
Underwood & Underwood, New York

INVESTIGATING THE STEEL TRUST

In the days when public sentiment was running strong against the trusts, Congress had created a committee to investigate the origin and the operations of the United States Steel Corporation. The report, made in 1912, was favorable to the company. A Federal suit for its dissolution was unsuccessful, the court holding that the corporation was not a monopoly in restraint of trade. This incident may be regarded as a turning point in the relation between the Government and the great corporations. It marked the end of the demand that trusts should be destroyed. Andrew Carnegie, who was a diverting witness before the committee, voiced what was perhaps the opinion of the average man when he said that trusts should not be destroyed but brought under the control of the Government. At first the trusts produced many bankrupt and bitter victims, but a softer policy prevailed as time healed the breach and the victims died.

LA FOLLETTE AND THE INSURGENTS

Robert M. La Follette, of Wisconsin, was the most conspicuous of the Insurgents in Congress. In his early career he had made a great record in opposition to the rule of railroads and other corporations in his own state, and he had been the means of passing a series of reforms there which had created a new régime of popular government. Fresh from these triumphs at home he went to the United States Senate eager to win new victories checking the power of great corporations. He was an idealist, earnest, sincere and a powerful fighter, but lacking in the reserve strength that appeals to the best kind of public opinion. All fire and mettle, he did not impress the country as Presidential timber. His many devoted followers bestowed on him in admiration the name of "Battling Bob La Follette."

515   Robert M. La Follette, 1855-1925, from a photograph
in the possession of *La Follette's Magazine*, Madison, Wis.

516   From a cartoon *Mr. La Follette's Strongest Card*, in the *American Monthly Review of Reviews*, Feb. 1912, reproduced from the *Chicago Tribune*

THE PROBLEM OF LA FOLLETTE

La Follette had a following in the western agricultural states, but no hold on the eastern states. While political observers did not believe that Taft could be elected in 1912, they also thought that La Follette could not take the nomination from him or be elected if by chance he got it. It seemed to be a Democratic year. Many Republicans agreed that the best to be expected was to let the Standpatters have their way in the convention and learn their lesson in the defeat that would surely come at the polls. The result, they said, would be a clearing of the air in 1916.

WILL ROOSEVELT RUN?

THERE can be little doubt that in 1910 and most of 1911 Roosevelt was sincerely unwilling to run for the Presidency. Many times he said so, but his opponents persisted in asserting that he was trying to get the nomination. His name was kept before the public, and in his own mind the effect was to develop the conviction, urged upon him by many friends, that he was necessary to the success of his cause. His letters of the time to his close friends are full of this idea. He was placed in a quandary, having to choose between a fight to the

LIONIZATION—SPECULATION—PERTURBATION

THE LION: "I wish I knew what you are going to do with me."
T. R. (thoughtfully): "So do I."
CHORUS FROM WINDOW (with great fervor): "So do we."

517   From a cartoon *Lionization — Speculation — Perturbation*, in *Harper's Weekly*, July 16, 1910

finish against the Standpat wing of the party in which victory would be nearly as bad as defeat, and a quiet submission, which he feared would mean the dissolution of all he had fought for up to 1909. During the winter and spring of the campaign year he made a number of speeches reiterating his principles; conservation, an income tax, direct primaries, labor legislation, the popular recall of judges and popular review of certain types of judicial decisions.

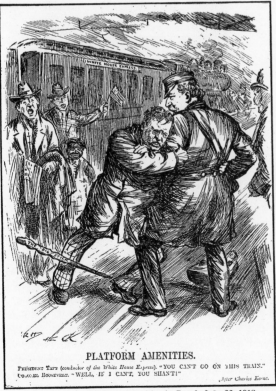

PLATFORM AMENITIES.

PRESIDENT TAFT (conductor of the White House Express). "YOU CAN'T GO ON THIS TRAIN."
COLONEL ROOSEVELT. "WELL, IF I CAN'T, YOU SHAN'T!"

After Charles Keene

518   From a cartoon *Platform Amenities*, in *Punch*, June 26, 1912

THE EASTERN INSURGENTS

THE Insurgents in the East centered their hopes on Roosevelt. They first got him to agree to be a candidate if there was a sufficiently strong popular demand for him. They did not believe that they could win with La Follette, who up to the early weeks of 1912 was the accepted leader of the Insurgent faction in the Presidential race. Speaking on February 2 in Philadelphia, while under a severe nervous strain, La Follette fell into a rambling and incoherent state and was removed to a hospital by his friends. Eight days after this unfortunate episode the Governors of seven states sent out a joint appeal urging all who desired prosperity and progress to join in a demand for Roosevelt. On February 24, Roosevelt replied to a specific request from the seven Governors: "I will accept the nomination for President if it is tendered to me, and I will adhere to this decision until the convention has expressed its preference." This action of Roosevelt was severely resented by La Follette who thought that he had been shelved in unseemly haste. It was also criticized by the Standpat supporters of Taft with the object of showing that in general Roosevelt was not true to his friends. But it is not to be denied that La Follette could not have united the Roosevelt following under any circumstances.

519   Roosevelt speaking in June 1912, from a photograph reproduced by the courtesy
                     of the Roosevelt Memorial Association, New York

THE BATTLE FOR DELEGATES

ALL through the spring months the two sides fought for delegates to the National Nominating Convention. It was soon seen that for the most part the fight was by the organization men to keep Roosevelt out. Where they were in control Taft generally got the delegates. Where the delegates were chosen by primaries Roosevelt was usually the winner. Of the three hundred and eighty-two delegates allotted to the thirteen states that had primaries, Roosevelt got two hundred and seventy-eight, Taft sixty-eight (twenty-eight of them in Georgia, a southern state whose delegates were selected under the influence of Federal office-holders), and La Follette thirty-six. Taft got the southern delegates, always at the disposal of a President since they consisted chiefly of Federal appointees and negroes. In the final result, the validity of the election of two hundred and thirty-nine delegates was contested, each party challenging freely.

520   The National Republican Committee, 1912, from a photograph by Moffett Studios, Chicago

THE NATIONAL COMMITTEE

THE Republican National Committee consisted of one person from each state and five from territories and dependencies, in all fifty-three. By custom it had the right to make up the temporary roll of the nominating convention. Meeting several days before the convention, it gave preliminary consideration to the contests and decided to put on the temporary roll two hundred and thirty-three of the contestants who were for Taft and six who were for Roosevelt. In the convention itself these delegates took up again the question of passing on contests. A Committee on Credentials was appointed and made a report in favor of the Taft delegates. The Roosevelt men protested seventy-four of the delegates thus placed on the roll. In the election of a temporary chairman they cast five hundred and one votes to five hundred and fifty-eight by their opponents, with nineteen that were scattering.

ROOSEVELT AT CHICAGO

WHEN the result of the deliberations seemed to hang in the balance Roosevelt went to Chicago to keep his eye on the situation. Asked how he felt, he replied "Like a Bull Moose," and from that time the term "Bull Moose" was associated with his followers. He watched with strenuous fidelity the progress of events. When the "steam roller" methods of the Taft faction flattened out all his hopes, he advised his followers to sit silent and take no part in the convention. The evident deter-

521 California delegates pledged for Roosevelt, from a photograph by Underwood & Underwood, New York

mination of the Standpat majority in the National Committee to put Roosevelt under, whatever means it was necessary to employ in doing it, discouraged the Roosevelt men on the committee and they ceased to fight against the seating of some of the delegates whose legal right to sit in the convention they denied. This course was not approved by Roosevelt, but it was consummated before he reached Chicago. Defenders of the Standpatters have taken it to mean that the Roosevelt group recognized that they had no ground of contest for enough seats to give them a majority if they won them. The conclusion is erroneous; for there was no time when the men of this group did not protest that they were treated unfairly. Some of the more moderate minds among them, going over the matter after the convention adjourned, estimated that Roosevelt lost by unfair dealing about fifty delegates. On the election of temporary chairman they lost by five hundred and one votes against five hundred and fifty-eight, with nineteen scattering. They had made a mistake in opening many flimsy contests, whose loss obscured the merits of their sound claims.

522 From a cartoon *A Perfectly Corking Time*, by C. R. Macauley in *The World*, New York, June 21, 1912

VICTORY DEARLY PURCHASED

THE Taft victory cost the Republican party much more than it was worth. Under the belief that it was necessary to put an end to Roosevelt's domination, the conservatives split the party to its foundation. They expected that Roosevelt beaten would submit and that his followers would soon accept the situation and resume their places in the party fold. But neither Roosevelt nor his associates were of that opinion. To them it seemed their duty to make such a protest as would show practical men that a wrong may prove too costly. Their decision to set up a third party was not merely an angry retort: it was also a deliberate effort to show party manipulators that there was a limit beyond which the game ought not to be played. To this decision, however, we must add Roosevelt's strong self-assertion. He was thoroughly aroused and he assured his followers he would not "take it lying down," but would fight to a finish.

523   Republican Convention of 1912, from a photograph by Moffett Studios, Chicago

NEW POLITICAL METHODS

In none of his political battles did Roosevelt give more telling blows than in the campaign of 1912. Old-line politics were discredited in the minds of the people. The political bosses who controlled party conventions had become unpopular. Roosevelt's success in smashing their system in the election results of 1912 made it impossible for them to exercise in the future as much power as they had formerly enjoyed. He did not break them utterly, but he made them take a less dominant position. It was Roosevelt's habit to put into a fight

his utmost endeavor. He did not spare himself, nor his adversary. His attacks on Taft were filled with bitter criticisms. Possessed of the idea that he was dealing with dishonest men, he used language about them which might have been applied to criminals. He was ever a hard opponent, and his foes were very certain that he did not fight fairly.

DEMOCRATIC PARTY SITUATION

In 1912, Bryan still controlled the western and southern sections of his party. A small group of conservative Democrats were disposed to rally around Harmon, of Ohio, and later took up Underwood, of Alabama, in the hope of drawing the southern delegates to the help of the northern conservatives. But the South continued true to Bryan ideals in the main, and by the time the delegates had been selected it was evident that the fight was to be between those who stood for the active restraint of "Big Business" and those who were mere organization men, and not likely to endeavor, if successful, to carry out any vigorous constructive policy. On the conservative side were ranged most of the northwestern states, an area in which the Democratic party could hardly hope to carry any electoral contests.

524   The Democratic Convention of 1912, from a photograph by
Underwood & Underwood, New York

CHAMP CLARK AND WOODROW WILSON

Of the two leading Democratic candidates Wilson had a record as a positive reformer while president of Princeton and Governor of New Jersey. He had shown himself in the latter position a strong opponent of the party bosses; he had carried out several measures designed to curb the actions of the trusts and had a still larger program in prospect. It was this proved devotion to reform that won for him the support of Bryan. Clark was an able man and a popular Speaker of the House of Representatives, but he had not been prominently identified with Bryan's reform ideas. The conservatives, disappointed in their hopes of getting an out-and-out conservative, turned to Clark as less objectionable to them than Wilson, who had displayed a spirit of independence while Governor that indicated he would not be easily led.

525   Champ Clark and Woodrow Wilson in 1912, from a photograph by Underwood & Underwood, New York

THE EASTERN LEADERSHIP

In the days of Cleveland the leaders of the Democrats in the East were men of reform impulse, but after Cleveland's time the New York Democracy fell strongly under the influence of Tammany Hall, by no means a reform organization. In 1912, its leaders were in close association with kindred organizations in Illinois and other Mid-Western states; they organized a strong *bloc* which threw its influence to Champ Clark as against Wilson. This New York – Mid-Western combination gave out that "its chief aim was to break the hold of Bryan." Eventually most of the conservative Democrats came to its support. From 1912 on, it was a strong factor in shaping the decisions of the Democratic party.

526   Charles F. Murphy, 1858–1924, Tammany leader, from a photograph by Underwood & Underwood, New York

THE INFLUENCE OF BRYAN

In the election of delegates to the National Nominating Convention, Bryan's state, Nebraska, chose him as a delegate, with other Bryan men; while the state convention adopted resolutions supporting Clark, probably on the ground that he was a western man, from the state of Missouri. This did not keep Bryan from using his own judgment in the general strategy of the convention, although he voted consistently for Clark as long as success seemed possible. But as the conservatives veered over to the Missourian, Bryan exerted his influence for Wilson. Among the delegates were two very rich capitalists ranged with the conservatives. Bryan shocked the convention by offering resolutions against their appearance. Both men were regular Democrats and very liberal in their financial support of the party. His attack on them as representatives of Wall Street angered their friends, but it called the attention of the country to their presence and they thought it proper to retire. The net result of the incident was in favor of Wilson. Bryan was able to capitalize his strong influence with a large portion of the people in favor of the man he wanted to see nominated.

527   From a cartoon *Weighing Them In*, by E. W. Kemble in *Harper's Weekly*, Mar. 9, 1912

528 Woodrow Wilson and Thomas Marshall, from a photograph by Underwood & Underwood, New York

WILSON NOMINATED

THE Democrats held their national convention in Baltimore, where they had nominated many successful candidates in the *ante-bellum* period. On the first ballot Clark received the largest vote, four hundred and forty and one half, with Wilson second with three hundred and twenty-four. Seven hundred and twenty-eight, two thirds of the entire number, were necessary for a choice. Harmon had one hundred and forty-eight and Underwood had one hundred and seventeen and one half. On the succeeding ballots these two *blocs* of votes drifted to Clark, and when Bryan saw it he turned against him. On the completion of the fourteenth ballot, he announced that he could no longer vote for Clark and transferred his support to Wilson. The Clark men flouted him, but his influence gradually broke down Clark's following. On the twenty-eighth ballot Wilson took the lead and on the forty-sixth he was nominated, the tide running strongly at the end. Laboring here in behalf of another man, Bryan did better work than he ever did for himself: he won the victory for Wilson by calling the attention of the country to the conservatism of the men who opposed him. As that fact was impressed on the public mind, the leaders of the party did not dare oppose the nomination of the more progressive candidate. For Vice-President the convention put up Thomas R. Marshall, who had been a popular Governor of Indiana.

A NEW PARTY LAUNCHED

WHEN the Republican convention of 1912 adjourned after putting Taft at the head of the ticket, the Roosevelt men took council over their future course. Their indignation was so great that few of them were willing to submit. It was decided to call a new convention and by way of protest to launch a third party. Resolutions were adopted declaring that fraud had been committed in the nomination of Taft and appealing for support to all who believed in maintaining the foundations of political morality. An executive committee was named, which, on August 5, brought together the national convention of the "Progressive Party." Roosevelt was the central figure in this movement. His speeches called into action, far and wide, a vast amount of energy, and the deep response of the country showed how formidable a movement was set in motion.

ROOSEVELT GIVES UP HOPE OF REPUBLICAN NOMINATION; SAYS HE'LL BE A CANDIDATE ON PROGRESSIVE PLATFORM

Roosevelt Delegates Meet and Ratify Surrender of Leaders.

DARK HORSE THE TALK

Hadley Badges Appear and Many Taft Men Give Him Favor.

HUGHES STILL LEADS

Cummins and La Follette Supporters Talk Hopefully.

CHICAGO, June 20.—Those who have talked with Col. Roosevelt to-night say, guardedly, that they interpret his words to mean that he has abandoned all hope that he will be nominated by the Republican party.

As further proof that he realizes that this is the situation they point to the refusal of many of his most ardent supporters to follow him in a bolt of the convention or to take part in a rump convention after the regular convention has adjourned.

They also draw attention to the paragraph in his latest statement that reads:

"If there is to be a progressive party I will be in it, but we will have to see first if the people want such a party."

Men close to Col. Roosevelt say that in his formal statement he is careful of his language. They say that this quo-

I'LL RUN ANYWAY, SAYS ROOSEVELT

Will Accept Any Progressive Nomination That's Offered.

APPEAL TO THE PEOPLE

Promises to Fight the Campaign Through, Win or Lose.

AGAIN SHOUTS "THIEF!"

Says Taft Encouraged Plan to Win by Means Fair or Foul.

"A FIGHT FOR HONESTY"

Warns Supporters That Battle Is for Principles, With No Rewards.

CHICAGO, June 20.—Theodore Roosevelt this afternoon declared that he would be a candidate for President.

In a long statement he said that he would accept a nomination from the "honestly elected" majority of the Republican convention or a nomination made

Expected to Wait to Learn What Democrats Do in Baltimore.

FRIENDS REJECT BOLT

Illinois, Missouri and Other States Refuse to Leave Party.

WILL SIT TIGHT TO-DAY

Colonel Asks Followers to Take No Part in the Convention.

personal advisers. He got off to bed a little after 11 o'clock.

Resting on Their Arms.

The Taft and the Roosevelt leaders are resting on their arms to-night pending the report of the committee on credentials and the verdict in to-morrow's session of the convention on that report.

There is every indication that the committee's report will take up the time of the convention all of to-morrow and perhaps far into the night. A roll call of each individual delegate, 1,078 in all, is to be had on all Congress district contests, while the verdict in contests for delegates at large is to be rendered by the States voting en bloc.

The hearing on the Alabama contests before the credentials committee to-day was so protracted that the Roosevelt representatives on the committee decided to hear only the contests in Arizona, California, Washington and Texas, thus practically withdrawing all other contests.

529　　　　　　　From *The Sun*, New York, June 21, 1912

530   The Progressive Convention, 1912, from a photograph by Moffett Studios, Chicago

THE CONVENTION OF THE PROGRESSIVES

THE delegates to the Progressive convention were filled with a spirit of earnestness and devotion that gave the assemblage the character of a religious meeting, recalling to some observers the early days of the Republi-

can party. There were many speeches of the inspirational kind, patriotic songs were sung, and the fervor of the delegates burst forth in the lifting notes of *Onward, Christian Soldiers*, sung by the convention standing. Among the group, however, were many professional politicians who for one reason or another thought that their best interests would be served by climbing onto the Roosevelt bandwagon. The nation watched the developments with deep interest. There was some hasty talk about the passing of the Republican party.

ROOSEVELT AND JOHNSON

THE selection of candidates caused little trouble. Everyone expected Roosevelt to head the ticket and he was selected by acclamation. For Vice-President, Senator Hiram Johnson was named with little less enthusiasm. The platform swung a long way toward out-and-out radicalism. It advocated the initiative, the referendum, the recall of officials and the recall of judicial decisions. It also demanded the election of Federal Senators by the people, the grant of the suffrage to women, a direct primary with nation-wide preferential choice of delegates to the Presidential nominating convention, the registration of lobbyists, and easier ways of amending the Federal Constitution. It contained many demands for social improvement, such as social insurance, regulation of child labor, industrial education and a legal minimum wage.

531   Roosevelt and Johnson, from a photograph by
Moffett Studios, Chicago

532   Wilson campaigning, from a photograph by Underwood & Underwood, New York

A STRENUOUS CAMPAIGN

PRESIDENT TAFT did not take a vigorous part in the campaign after nomination, but contented himself with making a few speeches at important places. Wilson, however, was an excellent speaker and traveled extensively, addressing large audiences in cities and towns and from the platform of his special train. Roosevelt, long used to this kind of campaigning, now outdid himself. Through two months he was on tour nearly all the time. The one halt was due to the bullet of a crazy man in Milwaukee, who attempted to assassinate him. The wound inflicted proved to be slight and Roosevelt was able to resume speech-making the last week of the campaign. Wilson refused to continue his canvass while his rival was incapacitated.

THE ELECTION OF WILSON

ELECTION day showed the triumph of Wilson by a great majority of the electoral college. Returns gave him four hundred and thirty-five votes, with eighty-eight for Roosevelt and eight for Taft. Only two states, Utah and Vermont, had stood by the Republican party, and five — Pennsylvania, Michigan, Minnesota, South Dakota and Washington — with a part of California, had gone for the Progressive party. The popular vote was not so decisive. Six million two hundred and eighty-six thousand two hundred and fourteen people voted for Wilson; for Roosevelt, four million one hundred and twenty-six thousand and twenty, and for Taft, three million four hundred and eighty-three thousand nine hundred and twenty-two. Wilson, therefore, did not receive a majority of the entire vote. It seems certain that his vote would have been larger had there been no split in the party of his opponents; for had Roosevelt not appeared in the field many of his followers would have gone for the Democratic candidate, and had he been the Republican nominee with a Roosevelt platform many conservative Republicans would have deserted the party or refused to vote. It is, therefore, not possible to say under these circumstances that Wilson's election was not approved by a majority of the nation.

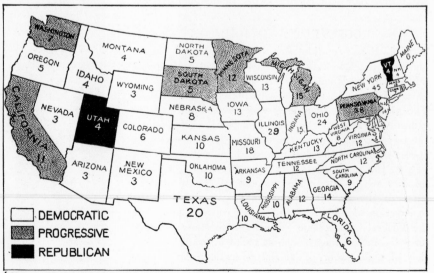

DEMOCRATIC
PROGRESSIVE
REPUBLICAN

533   *The Presidential Election of 1912*, from the *American Monthly Review of Reviews*, Dec. 1912

THE SOCIALIST PARTY

IN the election of 1912 the Socialist party nominated Eugene V. Debs for President. This able leader had been the founder of the party, and his strong personal appeals in 1912 enabled it to cast eight hundred ninety-seven thousand and eleven votes. Many people were alarmed by this large showing of a party which they considered dangerous to the existing order. The future was to show that they were needlessly concerned. In 1916, the party, led by a man less magnetic than Debs, could muster only five hundred eighty-five thousand one hundred and thirteen votes. In 1920, it again nominated Debs, then in a Federal prison on charges which his followers thought persecution. His vote under these circumstances ran up to nine hundred nineteen thousand seven hundred and ninety-nine, again a personal tribute to the leader. In 1924, the Socialists indorsed the candidacy of La Follette.

534 Eugene V. Debs, 1855–1926, from a photograph by Underwood & Underwood, New York

THE ACTIVITIES OF WOMEN IN 1912

THE election campaign of 1912 marks a rapid advance of the cause of woman's suffrage. A number of women sat as delegates in the Progressive National Convention. By the beginning of the twentieth century, four states, Wyoming, Utah, Colorado, and Idaho, had given the ballot to women. Under the influence of the Progressive movement, which indorsed the reform, five other states adopted it from the beginning of 1910 to the end of 1912. Other advances were made, so that in 1916 women had full suffrage in eleven states, with partial suffrage in several others. It was no longer possible for either of the large parties to oppose their demand for the ballot and Congress gave way. In 1919, a suffrage amendment was submitted to the states, and in 1920 it was ratified by three fourths of them and duly proclaimed as a part of the National Constitution. This adoption of universal suffrage marks the climax of that wave of democracy which made its appearance in the opening years of the twentieth century, and in promoting which Roosevelt, Bryan, and many others had worked most assiduously. Direct primaries, the initiative, referendum, and recall had all been strongly advocated but in the matter of the suffrage the forward-looking leaders won their greatest victory.

535 Miss Jane Addams, 1860–, from a photograph by Harris & Ewing, Washington

536 Mrs. Carrie Chapman Catt, 1859–, from a photograph by Harris & Ewing, Washington

IX—18

CHAPTER XI

WILSON AND DOMESTIC ISSUES

WILSON became President when the country was aflame with the desire for reform. Roosevelt had raised a great popular cry for the submission of the trusts to the control of the Government and the reduction of the power of the political machine, but time was not left him to get his ideas enacted into laws. Then came the insurgents of the Taft régime and at last the Progressives. With a well-defined purpose of capturing the party control they prepared a platform; and in their desire to make it so distinct from the pronouncement of the regular Republican party, they went further in the course of radicalism than Roosevelt had gone when President. The country witnessed the unusual spectacle of a great party in which existed side by side the most radical and the most conservative political groups, both of considerable size. And when these two groups could not live together harmoniously they became two parties, neither of which was strong enough to carry the election.

It was Wilson's fortune to be at the head of a party that occupied a middle position between the other two. It was the custom to say that the Democrats stood for "liberal" rather than conservative or radical policies. Wilson was thus able to take over all the moderate demands of the Progressives without approving their most extreme ideas. For a full century the Democrats had stood for the interests of the common people as against the privileged class; they had been opposed to trusts from the day that trusts had begun to exist, and they felt it no theft to take all Roosevelt's thunder of that nature. Wilson, therefore, entered office ready to take up at once all that Roosevelt had been doing in 1908 to restrain "big business" and several other things in addition. The first sixteen months of his administration were given to an energetic effort to meet the demands of this situation. He not only carried through a tariff bill in this period, but he also got Congress to pass laws creating the Federal Reserve Bank, establishing the Federal Trade Commission and amending and enlarging the Anti-Trust Act of 1890. He was about to get a law passed requiring Government approval of the issue of railroad securities, but withdrew the measure when it was evident that the unsettled condition of the money market due to the war in Europe made it unwise to pass the law at that time. With the exception of the tariff, all these measures were such as might have had the support of Roosevelt in their main features. Wilson got them through Congress with increasing ease.

The changed conditions resulting from the World War brought up many new problems for the head of our Government. The foreign situation overshadowed all else and diverted attention from the policies on which the election of 1912 had turned. Matters connected with the position of a neutral nation and policies looking toward the preparation for war now became all-important. Over these new issues public opinion formed a new alignment. Dominating his own party by his strong will and his clear-cut idea of the way he wished to go, Wilson kept a steady hand on the situation; but at the same time a strong attack was developed on his foreign policy, based on the belief that he was careless of the national honor. The irritating Mexican incident served to strengthen that idea. In this way was laid the foundation of a strong popular dislike that was to burst into vigorous activity when it came to the solution of post-war problems.

537 Thomas Woodrow Wilson, 1856–1924, from a photograph by Pirie MacDonald, New York

THE "SCHOLAR IN POLITICS"

AMONG early American Presidents several were men of bookish habits, such as Jefferson, Madison and the two Adamses. Then for a long middle period no such person occupied the President's chair. At last we had Roosevelt, writer of books, and representative of the higher culture of the country. His intellectual achievements set off in a pleasant manner his political activities, and the public mind became accustomed to the idea that a statesman might also be a noted author. All this helped to clear the way for Wilson, intellectually as eminent as Roosevelt, and more scholarly. Wilson had taken the doctor's degree at the Johns Hopkins University, taught in college positions, and risen to be president of Princeton University. His special field of study was politics and government and he had written excellent things on the American system of government. He was strongly attracted to the parliamentary form of government practiced in England and thought that it had some features which could be applied with profit to American political problems. In addition to his work in political science he occasionally wrote American history, producing one general account that was widely read. His administrative work as president of Princeton checked of necessity his scholarly output during that part of his career; but his interest in reading and lecturing on intellectual subjects remained fresh and vigorous. He had, also, a warm appreciation of good literary style and the ability to use it. His published literary and political essays rank high among similar work produced in the United States. They were smooth and elegant and filled with a warmth of feeling which, perhaps, was due to his southern heritage.

538   Woodrow Wilson, from a photograph

WILSON AS AN ORATOR

In spirit Wilson was formed after the manner of the liberal English statesmen of the classical period of the English reform struggle. Burke, Chatham, and Brougham were his models. Possessed of a ready power of speaking, he turned to them for the standards of good political oratory. No man in his own party, perhaps no man in his opponents' party, could present ideas to the average American audience in so convincing a manner. His remarkable career was due in no small degree to his superiority as a speaker. In that respect few of his contemporaries could equal him and none excel him.

WILSON'S INFLEXI- BILITY

The result was that while he was very success-

540 From a cartoon in *Cartoons*, Aug. 1912

ful in party leadership he was not always on terms of understanding and sympathy with the rank and file of his party. In the early years of his Presidency he showed a willingness to compromise when it was necessary to reach a practical result. When he became interested in his great idea, the creation of a league of peace, he put aside compromise, so that his opponents came to think of him as stubborn. His firmness grew of the conviction that he was dealing with what he considered a measure of

539   Wilson in 1919, from a photograph by
         Harris & Ewing, Washington

vast world significance to which he had committed himself; therefore he was unable to compromise. It is probable that Wilson would not have taken up the ideal of a league if he had been of the more usual political type. Wilson knew political science well; but he had not grown up in politics and while he had recently acquired a good working knowledge of how political affairs are run, he had not had an opportunity to enter deeply into the mind of the practical politician and to understand his motives.

WILSON'S "SCHOOLMASTERLY WAYS"

Wilson's opponents sometimes referred to his firmness as "schoolmasterly." He was never a schoolmaster in the sense here intended. His teaching experience was confined to positions in which he was a mere lecturer, in which dialectic rather than dictatorial qualities were brought out. Moreover, in modern education the schoolmaster is not the dictatorial personage the term assumes. Wilson undoubtedly dominated the stage when he was upon it and did it consciously, but it was by reason of inherent traits and not through having followed a calling that in itself is anything but despotic. The modern schoolmasters succeed by appealing to the imagination of the pupil and by being able to stimulate his interest in the subject that is being taught.

WILSON AND THE PARTY

THE long absence of the Democrats from office left them with few experienced men from among whom Wilson could take high officials, and his own previous career had given him few personal associates who were in touch with the political world. A party whose strength lay in the rural parts of the country found itself under the necessity of installing officials who would have to direct under severe criticism the policies of a highly urbanized nation. By habits which can be accounted for, it has been our custom to take for Presidents men who are rarely trained in public business. Wilson had the double embarrass-

541   From a cartoon *Now Mind Your Step!* in the *American Monthly Review of Reviews*, Dec. 1912, reproduced from the *Jersey City Journal*

ment of being an amateur in public office and of having to select as his advisers for the most part other amateurs. There were, moreover, some divergent factions in the party whose claims and interests had to be carefully taken into consideration. Taking these conditions into consideration it is, perhaps, remarkable that he succeeded as well as he did in his political measures. The early months of his administration saw the enactment of a very important program of reform, all carried through under his masterly leadership.

542   Wilson and Colonel House, from a photograph by Underwood & Underwood, New York

WILSON AND COLONEL HOUSE

WHEN Wilson appeared as a commanding figure in national politics many men who felt as he felt, or who wished to attach themselves to a rising star, joined the group of his supporters. Such a man was Edward M. House, of Texas, quiet, tactful, energetic and practical, who had a talent for party management, and whose ambition was to make the fortunes of other people than himself. While keeping himself in the background, House gave Wilson material aid in the selection of the Cabinet and diplomatic officials. He had unusual ability for meeting emergencies.

543   Wilson and his secretary, Joseph P. Tumulty, 1879–, from a photograph by G. V. Buck, in the possession of Underwood & Underwood, New York

A PARTISAN PRESIDENT

To many persons it seemed that Wilson, who had won public esteem as a reformer, should administer his office in a thoroughly non-partisan manner. He was too practical to agree with them. He did not forget that he was elected by a party and that only through party support could he hope to carry out his ideas. His supporters had long been out of office and had seen their opponents in the enjoyment of high honors for many years. Fate had brought them to victory and they did not think self-abnegation a virtue under existing circumstances. Consequently the distribution of patronage, as far as it could be done under civil service rules, was one of the earliest cares of the administration. Wilson yielded as little to mere partisanship as he could, but it would have been fatal to party harmony to have resisted altogether. Any President depends upon party harmony to accomplish the results he has in view. Wilson believed strongly in the party system of government and was convinced that the President should be the head and active leader of the successful party. Through his personality he had the instinct of a commander of a host and by combining it with the capacity of convincing argumentation he welded his party into a powerful organization.

POSITION OF THE SOUTH

THE return of the Democrats to power brought the South into prominent national influence for the first time since 1861. Wilson himself was southern by birth and by temperament. Through the habit prevalent in that section of reëlecting Senators and Representatives who satisfied their constituencies, it had come about that the ranking minority members of most of the committees were from the South. By the ordinary custom these ranking members now became chairmen, so that it happened that southerners headed most of the important committees in each House of Congress. The effect on the South was important; for it tended to break down the old sense of separateness that had grown up during the half century in which that section had been almost completely excluded from a share in the direction of national business. The part taken by southerners in the administration now beginning was creditable to their ability and tended to lessen the fear, long haunting the northern mind, that some dire calamity would occur if southerners again got a foothold in the Government. Nevertheless, there were some people who expressed regret that the direction of the Government had come so largely into the hands of men from one section of the country. They forgot that for nearly two generations it had been in the hands of men of one section — that is, in the hands of northern men. Perhaps the net result was an advantage.

544   Henry Clayton, 1857–, Alabama, chairman House Judiciary Committee, from a photograph by G. V. Buck, Washington

WILSON AS PRIME MINISTER

DURING the first sixteen months of his administration, the President took a leading part in the initiation of legislation. Each important measure was submitted to him before it was introduced into Congress, and to a considerable extent each was altered to suit his views. In the passage of all of them he used pressure, personal and official, to get the measures adopted. Men like Roosevelt, Cleveland and Jefferson had followed the same practice. Some observers pointed out that the practice was at variance with the intent of the framers of the Constitution, who wished to keep the executive and legislative organs of Government distinct and separate. On the other hand, the general public saw in the President the only man elected by all the people and looked to him for the carrying out of the

545   From a cartoon *Is It Coming to This?*, by Césare in *The Sun*, New York, Oct. 9, 1913

policies indorsed in the elections. They thus made of him a kind of Prime Minister, leader of his party, and responsible head of public opinion for the time being. Wilson's strong personality brought into unusual notice this tendency in our public life. In the first sixteen months of the new administration, a number of original measures were carried through Congress. The President took a leading part in the initiating of this legislation as well as in guiding it on its way through Congress.

BRYAN AND WILSON

THE prominent part taken by Bryan in behalf of Wilson's nomination and the support he gave him in the campaign placed the President under obligations to the Nebraskan, and it was conceded that Bryan should have the choice of the high offices to be filled. He became Secretary of State, a post for which previous experience did not fit him; but it was a time of profound peace and no one could foresee that his department was about to assume vast importance through the outbreak of the World War. In a political sense Bryan was of great service to Wilson. He had a strong influence over many Democrats by whom Wilson's ideas were poorly comprehended; by means of this influence he secured Congressional support which otherwise the administration might not have had. The unanimity with which his party supported Wilson was due to an important extent to the hearty support he received from Bryan.

546   William Jennings Bryan, from a photograph by Underwood & Underwood, New York

547   William G. McAdoo, 1863–, from a photograph
by Underwood & Underwood, New York

WILLIAM G. McADOO

It was expected that the tariff and the currency would be prominent subjects for consideration by the new administration, and on this account much pressure was exerted on the President in connection with the office of Secretary of the Treasury. He decided upon William G. McAdoo, who was reputed to have withstood in private enterprise a powerful banking group of New York city. In the settlement of the currency question the great banks of the country were much concerned, and it was feared that they would try to influence in their own interest the enactment and enforcement of laws on the subject. McAdoo probably owed his appointment to the belief that he would not be unduly swayed by the bankers. His appointment was opposed by them very earnestly.

WILSON BEFORE CONGRESS

On April 7, 1913, Congress met in an extra session, called by Wilson to take up the matters he had brought forward in the preceding campaign. It was the first Democratic Congress since the party went over to free silver in 1895. Wilson caused mild surprise when he appeared before Congress to read his own message, thus breaking a custom which had been followed since Jefferson instituted it in 1801. The innovation checked a tendency toward longer and longer messages. In Wilson's hands the Presidential message became a

548   Wilson reads his message to Congress, Apr. 7, 1913, from a photograph by G. V. Buck, in the possession of Underwood & Underwood, New York

brief and pointed statement of policy with arguments in its support. The change was received by the public as a wholesome reform. The old long-winded messages were so dull that people rarely read them. The short summaries of political conditions with pointed recommendations of things to be done, which Wilson stated in attractive language, were better and more effective when read.

THE UNDERWOOD TARIFF BILL

The first subject taken up by the extra session of 1913 was the tariff, upon which the Democrats had laid much stress during the campaign. For two years Oscar Underwood, of Alabama, had been chairman of the Ways and Means Committee, and he was now promptly reappointed to the same position. When Congress met he introduced a tariff bill which had been prepared by his committee in close conference with Wilson, carrying out the ideas advanced in the late campaign. The bill was promptly accepted by the House and by the Senate after a more deliberate debate, becoming law with the signature of the President on October 5, 1913. It passed with the support of nearly all the Democrats and despite the opposition of most of the Progressives and Republicans.

549   Oscar Underwood, 1862–, from a photograph
by Harris & Ewing, Washington

NATURE OF THE TARIFF BILL

It was a favorite idea of the Democrats that the trusts were fostered by the high tariff and that the reduction of the rates would be a blow at special privilege. "Give up," said Wilson, "even the semblance of privilege or of any kind of artificial advantage and put our business men and producers under the stimulation of a constant necessity to be efficient, economical and enterprising." Herein lay his idea of "the New Freedom," freedom of the mind of the producer from what he regarded as a coddling of protection from the attractive prospect of "the whet-

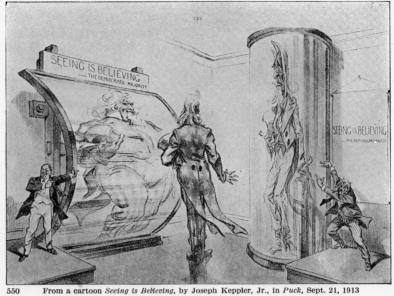

550   From a cartoon *Seeing is Believing*, by Joseph Keppler, Jr., in *Puck*, Sept. 21, 1913

ting of American arts by contest with the arts of the rest of the world." Underwood, more practical by nature, said that his bill was intended to produce revenue without injury to legitimate industry.

REVISION DOWNWARD

The country had no difficulty in determining whether this tariff was revision upward or downward: its only debate was over the effect it would have on business. The Democrats predicted immediate benefits and the Republicans foresaw nothing but immediate distress. It was admitted that the bill would produce a deficit through the reduction of the rates, but it was proposed to make up the loss through the imposition of an income tax, lawful by the Sixteenth Amendment, which had been proclaimed law by the Secretary of State on February 25, 1913. This tax was laid upon the unexempted net income of all citizens and corporations at a normal rate of one per cent, but on incomes of twenty thousand dollars or more a surtax was laid running from one per cent to six per cent on incomes of five hundred thousand dollars or more. The outbreak of the World War followed the imposition of the Underwood tariff so closely that it was not possible to observe the economic effects of the law.

The industries affected by the proposed legislation lost no opportunity, as in the past, to modify the bill while it was before Congress and supported an expensive lobby at Washington. So greatly did their efforts embarrass the administration that Wilson, in order to attract the attention of the public and thus disarm the lobbyist, issued a public statement charging them with "insidious" activities. The assault did violence to the feelings of the persons attacked, but it brought out a full investigation by the House of Representatives, covering a period of thirty years, in which abundant information was obtained to show that the practices alleged by Wilson had been used by the protected industries in the past. The Senate had appointed a committee to investigate this subject, but its report, less critical than that of the House, was not generally approved.

551   Income Tax Form for Corporations, 1913, from the Internal Revenue Bureau, Washington

552 The Tariff Commission, 1916, from a photograph by Clinedinst, in the possession of Keystone View Company, Inc., New York
LEFT TO RIGHT, *Seated:* D. J. Lewis; F. W. Taussig, chairman; E. P. Costigan. *Standing:* William Kent; W. S. Culbertson;
D. C. Roper.

A TARIFF COMMISSION

IT has long been contended that there should be a tariff commission armed with power to examine the relation one to another of the rates in a tariff law and to readjust those rates as changing conditions make it necessary. Several times Congress has created such a commission, but it had never given it authority to do more than investigate and advise. The idea had been a favorite feature of the protectionist doctrine. The Democrats rejected it in 1913, deliberately refusing to maintain the commission that the Republicans had set up under Taft. In time they changed their minds, and in 1916 they created a bi-partisan Tariff Commission authorized to study the operation of the tariff and observe its effects upon industry. It was organized early. In 1917 the Commission was made permanent. By an act of 1922 its powers were somewhat enlarged and the President was given the right to modify the rates on suggestion by the commission. The upshot of this last action is that such alterations as have been made under this provision seem to have been on a partisan basis.

REFORM IDEALS POPULAR

THE American people have at times displayed a profound belief in the badness of their own Government. Wilson's efforts at reform were warmly received by the majority. His many speeches on the subject expressed the desire for reform in the most alluring terms. A popular cartoonist hit off the state of public feeling on the subject by showing Diogenes hastily offering his lantern to the President with the assertion, "You need it more than I do." At this time there was unmistakable evidence that political reform was popular in the country at large. So complete had been the rule of party organizations that there was a too common opinion that all the Government machinery was inefficient and most leaders were selfish. The public was in a mood to relish a good shaking up in political circles.

553   From a cartoon *Take My Lantern, You Need It More Than I Do*, by L. M. Glackens in *Puck*, Jan. 22, 1913

CURRENCY REFORM

THE periodic recurrence of financial panics had long been a characteristic of American economic life. One of the causes was the inelastic condition of our currency which helped to bring about periods of uncontrolled inflation followed by inevitable deflation. When speculation had run high some speculators were sure to be caught in dire need of money and would be willing to sell valuable securities to avoid bankruptcy. There were always also a number of capitalists who drew in their money in such times of danger in order to take advantage of the necessities of the imperiled speculators. The crisis resulting would have been less severe had it been possible, as in Europe, to issue more currency as needed with provision for destroying it when the emergency passed. The capacity to expand and contract the currency to meet the needs of business is known to financiers as "elasticity." In European states it is obtained by permitting great banks to issue their own notes in times of crisis and lend them on approved security but at interest so high that the borrower will pay them back when the crisis is past, whereupon the excess of issue is destroyed and permanent inflation is prevented. By this means the volume of money tends to be stabilized, with only enough money to adapt itself to the rise and fall of demand for it by the business community. At that time we had not yet mastered the lesson offered us by this situation.

554   From a cartoon *Move On*, by Césare in *The Sun*, New York, Nov. 17, 1914

555   Nelson W. Aldrich, 1841–1915, from a photograph by Harris & Ewing, Washington

THE ALDRICH PLAN

SPURRED on by the experience of the Panic of 1907, Congress created in 1908 a National Monetary Commission, with Senator Aldrich as chairman, to report on a complete revision of the monetary system. The result was the "Aldrich Plan," submitted to Congress in January, 1911, recommending the creation of a National Reserve Association composed of banks in all parts of the country grouped in fifteen district reserve associations and having the power to issue notes to obtain elasticity. The entire management of the Association was to be in its own hands, which meant that the issue and contraction of the money supply would be directed by a small group of private financiers who controlled the great banks of the country. The Aldrich Plan was a bankers' plan and had the approval of the American Bankers Association. Congress did not approve it because of the power it gave to the banks, and the general problem had been left over for solution in the administration of Woodrow Wilson. It was evident that there was a demand for a plan operating under Governmental supervision.

THE GLASS–OWEN BILL

WHEN the House passed the tariff bill a month after it was introduced, some of the members thought that enough had been done for an extra session and proposed to take a rest; but Wilson urged them to take up the currency problem and he had his way. Chairman Glass of the committee on banking and currency introduced a bill that he had made ready on conference with the President, Secretary McAdoo, and Senator Owen. After a strenuous fight it passed the House with some amendments and went to the Senate where it advanced in the wake of the tariff bill. It became law when signed by the President on December 23, 1913, the second legislative triumph of the administration.

FEDERAL OR PRIVATE CONTROL?

THE main difference between the Aldrich Plan and the scheme in the bill introduced into the House by Chairman Glass was in the control of the proposed institution. Aldrich would have bound together in a powerful association all the important banks of the country and given them the power of a great corporation. It was to be under the control of the bankers themselves. The House Bill proposed to give the supreme control to a board appointed by the Government. The banks opposed this suggestion on the ground that it would take the banking function into politics. They fought as hard as they could to defeat this feature of the bill; for they had an honest fear of political interference with business. The President and Secretary of the Treasury remained unmoved and insisted that the reserve bank should not become a great monopoly in the hands of any group, however well-meaning. Since the Federal Reserve system has gone into effect the judgment of its authors has been vindicated not only by its success in operation but by the unanimity with which it has been approved by the American people. No effort to modify its structure in any important particular has been made. At the same time it is unanimously agreed that the plan adopted has been a great advantage to business and not seriously impaired by politics.

557   From a cartoon *Hands Across the Land*, by Joseph Keppler, Jr., in *Puck*, Aug. 20, 1913

THE FEDERAL RESERVE SYSTEM

As passed, the law provided that the national banks of the country must, and the state banks and trust companies might, be organized as members of not more than twelve regional banks, each to have a stated reserve fund and to lend money on approved security. Over them all was to be a Federal Reserve Board of seven members, two of them to be the Secretary of the Treasury and the Comptroller of the Currency, and the other

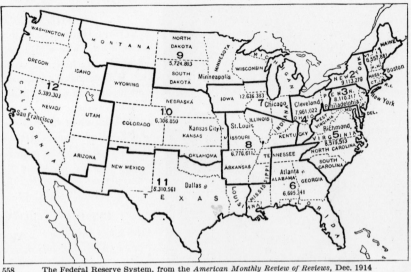

558   The Federal Reserve System, from the *American Monthly Review of Reviews*, Dec. 1914

five (two of whom must be bankers) to be nominated by the President and confirmed by the Senate. The board was to issue "federal reserve notes" and lend them to the regional banks on approved security and to pass on the rate of interest. The Federal Reserve Bank went into operation November 16, 1914. On July 1, 1922, the number of members of the Federal Reserve Board was increased to eight.

THE FEDERAL RESERVE BOARD

THE appointment of the members of the Federal Reserve Board put the system itself to a severe test. Wilson nominated to the board Paul Warburg, member of a prominent banking firm in New York, and immediately there arose a wide protest from that portion of the public which believed that "Wall Street" had designs on all possible parts of the Government. Wilson insisted on confirmation against the apparent hostility of the Senate, and at last the matter was carried through as he wished. It was important because it showed that the administration realized the necessity of getting the banks to coöperate in launching the new system and making it work afterward. (For the Federal Reserve System see Vol. IV.)

559   The Federal Reserve Board, 1914, from a photograph by Harris & Ewing, Washington
LEFT TO RIGHT, *Seated:* Charles S. Hamlin; William G. McAdoo; Frederic A. Delano. *Standing:* Paul M. Warburg; J. S. Williams; W. P. Harding; Adolph C. Miller.

560   From a cartoon *Reading the Death Warrant*, by C. R. Macauley
in *The World*, New York, June 24, 1913

REDUCING THE "MONEY TRUST"

In these days much was said about the "money trust." The expression was used to refer to centralized groups of great banks in leading cities and interrelated groups connecting cities. Each of these groups, known as a "chain" was dominated by some powerful financial interest and was held together by interlocking directorates. In 1912, Congress authorized an investigation to determine whether they were organized in a joint control over the country's money. The committee taking charge of the matter could not find any such organization as was popularly supposed to exist; but their report did not convince the public, and the passage of the Federal Reserve Act was hailed as the death warrant of the "money trust." They were supposed to be combined in a consolidated control over the country's money.

THE FEDERAL TRADE COMMISSION

It had been a part of Roosevelt's program that the Government should exercise a fair and wholesome control over the trusts and other forms of "big business," and Wilson held the same opinion. To carry out this purpose, Congress in 1914 passed a law creating the Federal Trade Commission. The step was pronounced radical by the conservatives, and Wilson, realizing that great reforms come slowly, was satisfied at first to have the Commission exercise powers of investigation and publication only, thus letting it feel its way until the country should give it more authority. It was supposed that he would have its development parallel that of the Interstate Commerce Commission, which from a weak condition had grown into strong authority because the public became convinced that it was necessary to the prosperity of the country.

561   The Federal Trade Commission, from a photograph by Clinedinst, Washington
LEFT TO RIGHT, *Seated:* William B. Colver; William H. Parry; William J. Harris, chairman; Joseph E. Davies;
John F. Fort. *Standing:* Leonidas Bracken, secretary.

THE CLAYTON ANTI–TRUST ACT

THE Anti-Trust Act of 1890 was expressed in terms of general significance, and there was a prevalent desire that it should be amended so as to be more precise and definitely to forbid several kinds of action that had come to be common on the part of trusts. One demand was the prohibition of interlocking directorates, which led to nearly the same results as actual mergers or combinations. As soon as Congress passed the Federal Trade Commission Bill it took up this project of amending the Anti-Trust Act. The fight was led by Chairman Clayton of the House Judiciary Committee, supported by the earnest efforts of the President. A new law forbade interlocking directorates, forbade the purchase by one corporation of stock in another in restraint of competition, and defined more precisely discrimination tending to monopolies. It was a broader and more effective shackle for the trusts than the act of 1890. The law, moreover, gave a privileged position to labor organizations. But these labor provisions were later profoundly modified by the interpretation of the Supreme Court, which held that the act was not to be construed as sanctioning the boycott of persons or firms that maintained relations with boycotted individuals or organizations.

562   From a cartoon *Vindicated*, by Fitzpatrick in *Cartoons*, Mar. 1914, reproduced from the St. Louis *Post Dispatch*

THE CONTROL OF RAILROAD SECURITIES

THE next main feature of Wilson's anti-trust legislation was a plan to make it necessary for the roads to get the consent of the Interstate Commerce Commission before issuing new bonds or stock. This measure was believed to be necessary in order that the Commission might decide intelligently upon the rates that should be charged by the roads. There was a dispute of long standing upon the actual value of the property of the roads. It was generally believed that their stock was largely "water" upon which it was not fair to expect the public to pay its dividends. Chairman Rayburn, of the House Committee On Railroads, introduced the bill in the House and got it passed by a large majority. It then went to the Senate where it was reported favorably by the Committee On Railroads and was in a fair way to pass when the President agreed to withdraw it because of the outbreak of the World War. The difficulties in the way of selling securities had suddenly become very great and it was generally felt that no restriction ought to be imposed at that time. But this restriction became a part of the Transportation Act of 1920.

563   Samuel Rayburn, 1882–, from a photograph by Harris & Ewing, Washington

564   La Follette and Gompers, from a photograph by Underwood & Underwood, New York

LABOR'S GAIN

PRESIDENT GOMPERS of the American Federation of Labor had long been in Washington watching over the interests of the unions. During Roosevelt's administration it had been held that a union engaged in a strike was a combination against trade. Gompers now used his influence with the Democrats to get clauses inserted in the Clayton Act providing that injunctions should not be issued in labor disputes except when necessary to prevent property damages of a sort for which there was no remedy at law. It also announced that labor associations and others not conducted for profit were not combinations in restraint of trade, and it declared that strikes, boycotts and picketing were not violations of any Federal law. In 1920, the Supreme Court declared that the exemption of labor from the operation of the Clayton law was unconstitutional in so far as exemption involved the commission of an otherwise unlawful act.

THE ADAMSON LAW

FOR many years before 1916 the four railroad brotherhoods had been demanding an eight-hour day with a rate for work overtime half again as large as the regular rate, which, in effect, was a demand for increased wages. The immense business of the railroads during the World War, due to the transportation of products purchased by the belligerents, gave the brotherhoods the opportunity to insist upon their demand with a dire threat of what might happen in case they were refused. From March to August, 1916, there were proposals and counter-proposals. At last the men announced that they would call a general railroad strike on September 4 if their demands were not granted. Thereupon, Wilson went before Congress with a large program for adjusting the railroad situation, one feature of which was an eight-hour day. After a brief debate, Congress passed the Adamson Act, providing for an eight-hour day with *pro rata* pay for overtime. It also

provided for a commission to study the wage problem. Later on, the Supreme Court upheld the law. Its passage brought Wilson great criticism from the conservative portion of the public, who thought he had yielded to the dictation of labor for political reasons. There was truth in the charge thus made. But it must be admitted that the moment was critical. To tie up transportation at that time when a vast supply of food, supplies and munitions were being manufactured and shipped to Europe would have aroused a strong protest. It is doubtful if any party in control of the Government would at that time have resisted the demand.

565   Wilson addressing the House in an effort to avert the threatened railroad strike, from a photograph by Underwood & Underwood, New York

566   Bryan signs the announcement of the Seventeenth Amendment, from a photograph by G. V. Buck, in
the possession of Underwood & Underwood, New York

THE ELECTION OF SENATORS

DURING the period of the Standpatters there was a great deal of complaint against the United States Senate. A number of the members were extremely rich and it was believed that they were chosen through the lavish use of money. It was also observed that certain Senators were protectors of specific industrial interests. The upshot was the formation of a well-defined opinion that this situation would be changed if the Senators were elected by the people instead of by the state legislatures, as the Constitution provided. Several times the House had showed a willingness to change the Constitution so as to allow popular elections, but the Senate had blocked the move. Under the impulse of the Roosevelt upheaval it was possible in 1912 to get through the Senate a Constitutional amendment providing for popular election of Senators. The rest was easy. The necessary three fourths of the states ratified and the result was the proclamation of the Seventeenth Amendment in 1913. Although this measure was completed during Wilson's Administration, the main part of the struggle for it came under Taft.

THE PROTECTION OF THE CHILDREN

THE outbreak of the World War forced the administration to withdraw its attention from social and political reform; but several such matters were acted upon, despite the prevalence of problems arising from the foreign situation. One of these was the regulation of child labor. After the failure of Senator Beveridge's bill in 1906, friends of the movement turned their attention chiefly to state legislatures, where they were able to get many laws passed of varying degrees of efficiency. They built up a strong public opinion on the subject, and in 1916 each of the political parties made it a plank in its platform.

567   From a cartoon *Government Care* vs. *Government Neglect*, by Joseph Keppler, Jr., in *Puck*, Feb. 5, 1913

IX—19

568   Wilson signing the Child Labor Bill, from a photograph by Harris & Ewing, Washington

THE CHILD LABOR ACT OF 1916

WHEN Senator Beveridge's bill was before Congress, Wilson had called it "absurd," but by 1916 he had changed his views; it was through his earnest efforts that Congress took up the subject again and enacted a law that had large majorities in both Houses. Like the Beveridge proposal, this act made it unlawful to ship by interstate carriers articles made in any factory, shop or cannery employing children under fourteen years of age. Competent Constitutional lawyers gave warning that the act would not stand judicial interpretation, and there was little surprise when the Supreme Court later decided that it was unconstitutional on the ground that the Interstate Commerce clause could not be stretched to the point of determining who should work in factories.

THE JAPANESE LABOR PROBLEM

THE people of the Pacific coast have long feared the influx of a mass of Asiatics. First it was the Chinese, whose exclusion they obtained by the acts of 1881, 1891 and 1901. About the beginning of the present century the Japanese began to arrive in large numbers. They bought land and seemed on the way to absorb a large part of the fruit-growing industry of California. They also proved strong competitors of the native shopkeepers. By reason of their willingness to work for cheap wages they encountered the hostility of the labor unions. Race prejudice also flared up. The net result was a strong anti-Japanese feeling.

A crisis occurred in 1906 when San Francisco decided that Japanese children must attend an Oriental school, giving as the reason the attendance of mature Japanese boys in the same grades as the small native girls and boys. Japan protested this action, on the ground that it violated her treaty with the United States, in which her citizens were granted the privileges of the citizens of the most favored nation. Much feeling was aroused against California in other parts of the country, but her only concession was to admit to her ordinary schools Japanese children under sixteen years. At the same time, Japan, by a "gentleman's agreement," undertook to withhold passports from her laborers for the United States. In 1911, she made a new treaty with us, and in a separate note continued the "gentleman's agreement." Japan justified her position on the ground that no discrimination should be made in the United States against her citizens that was not made against citizens of other nations.

569   From a cartoon *Up To His Old Tricks*, by C. R. Macauley in *The World*, New York, April 21, 1918

THE WEBB ALIEN LAND–HOLDING BILL

IN 1913, the Japanese question came up again when a bill was introduced in the California legislature prohibiting the purchase or lease of land by aliens ineligible to citizenship, which would include the Japanese. A protest came at once from Japan, and for a time the situation seemed serious. President Wilson sent Secretary Bryan to California to try to adjust the matter. In the end, California substituted for the first bill the Webb Bill in which the language was a little less offensive to

570 Bryan addressing the California Senate, from a photograph by Underwood & Underwood, New York

Japan, but the meaning was not different. It provided that land might be held by aliens eligible to citizenship but that other aliens should have only such land-holding rights as were guaranteed them by treaty. As the treaty with Japan contained no such provision the Japanese were excluded from land-holding.

OUR CARIBBEAN POLICY

OUR Caribbean policy may be defined as a determination that the states on the rim of the Caribbean Sea shall not fall into such confusion as to invite intervention by European or other powers; with this attitude had grown up the assumption that we have the right to interfere whenever such states are in danger of falling into hopeless disorder. The policy has its roots in the past, but it came into definite form under

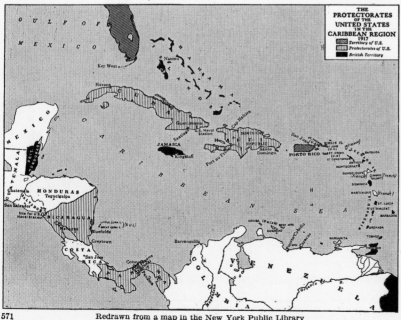

Roosevelt. When Wilson became President, the United States owned Porto Rico and the Canal Zone, exercised protectorates over Panama and Cuba and had fiscal control over Santo Domingo. Many people attributed the growth of the policy to Roosevelt's impetuosity and did not realize how much it was an outgrowth of the Monroe Doctrine, together with the peculiar conditions in the states concerned. Wilson did not reverse the policy; he even extended it further than it had been carried previously. But there were many people in the United States who declared that we were doing an injustice to our neighbors.

571 Redrawn from a map in the New York Public Library

572　President Menocal of Cuba, from a photograph
by Underwood & Underwood, New York

RELATIONS WITH CUBA

On the day Bryan became Secretary of State he sent a note to the Cuban President urging the veto of a law just carried in the island legislature, permitting the President to pardon without trial certain persons accused of public defalcation. The protest was effective. Wilson gave support to President Menocal, whose first term extending from 1912 to 1916, proved to be a period of good order. When, however, the time came for another election and Menocal had a victory on the face of the returns, his defeated rival took up arms. United States marines were landed at certain points to protect property, but Menocal was able to put down the revolt without the active support of our troops. From that time Cuban affairs have been more orderly.

A PROTECTORATE OVER NICARAGUA

During Taft's administration, the United States did much toward reorganizing the finances of Nicaragua, in somewhat the same way in which Roosevelt had aided Santo Domingo. Late in his Presidency, Taft sent the Senate a treaty establishing firm control in Nicaragua, but it was not ratified. Wilson renewed the attempt and was rebuffed. Not discouraged, he redrafted the treaty and sent it back to the Senate, where it was finally accepted in 1916. By this agreement Nicaragua ceded control of her fiscal administration, an exclusive right to construct a canal through her territory, a naval base in Fonesca Bay, on the Pacific coast, and a ninety-nine-year lease of the Corn Islands (see map No. 443), admirably suited for a naval base in the Gulf of Mexico. The terms of the treaty were conceived in the spirit of the Platt Amendment and granted the United States a protectorate over this important territory. This treaty enlarged our influence on the western edge of the Caribbean Sea.

573　Facsimile of the first and last pages of the Treaty between the United States and Nicaragua, from the original in the
Department of State, Washington

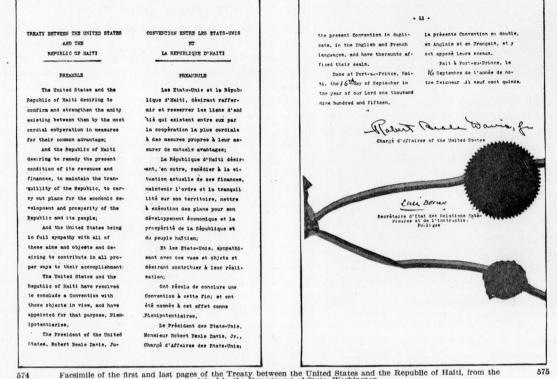

574   Facsimile of the first and last pages of the Treaty between the United States and the Republic of Haiti, from the   575
original in the Department of State, Washington

A PROTECTORATE OVER HAITI

THE negro republic of Haiti was in a state of great confusion, and early in 1914 Germany and France demanded that they should be allowed to take control of its customs. The United States now entered the Haitian situation, and the upshot was a treaty ratified in 1916 by which Haiti became an American protectorate. She placed her finances in the hands of the United States, agreed to the organization of a constabulary under United States officers, and was guaranteed independence and the maintenance of settled Government. This step, with the purchase of the Virgin Islands from Denmark in 1916, gave the United States effective control of the northern rim of the Caribbean.

PANAMA TOLLS

THE exemption of United States coastwise shipping from tolls when passing through the Panama Canal had been taken by Great Britain as a violation of her treaty rights. Though many of our people felt that the contention was unfounded, our action placed the Government in a bad light in the eyes of other nations. The Democratic platform of 1912 had indorsed exemption, but Wilson now asked Congress to rescind it in token of a desire to avoid any pretext for an accusation of bad faith. Congress took the suggestion unkindly; Wilson insisted and by strong pressure obtained a grudging consent. It was expressly stated that the action was taken on grounds of courtesy and not for legal reasons. The repeal had a favorable effect on foreign opinion.

576   From a cartoon *Nailing it to the Masthead*, by Rollin Kirby
in the New York *World*, March 6, 1914

Treaty between the United States of America and the Republic of Colombia for the settlement of their differences arising out of the events which took place on the Isthmus of Panama in November 1903.

The United States of America and the Republic of Colombia, being desirous to remove all the misunderstandings growing out of the political events in Panama in November

Tratado entre la República de Colombia y los Estados Unidos de América para el arreglo de sus diferencias provenientes de los acontecimientos realizados en el Istmo de Panamá en Noviembre de 1903.

La República de Colombia y los Estados Unidos de América, deseando remover todas las divergencias provenientes de los acontecimientos políticos ocurridos en Panamá en Noviembre de 1903;

present Treaty in duplicate and have hereunto affixed their respective seals.

Done at the city of Bogotá, the sixth day of April in the year of our Lord nineteen hundred and fourteen.

doble ejemplar el presente Tratado y le han puesto sus respectivos sellos.

Hecho en la ciudad de Bogotá, el día seis de Abril del año de Nuestro Señor de mil novecientos catorce.

577   Facsimile pages of the Treaty between Colombia and the United States, from the original in the possession of the   578
State Department, Washington

AN ADJUSTMENT WITH COLOMBIA

THE Republic of Colombia had protested against what she pronounced the bad faith of the Washington Government in supporting the Panama revolution of 1903 and refused to recognize the independence of the new Republic. She went further and asked that the dispute should be referred to the Hague Court; but

579   Francis Burton Harrison, 1873–, from a photograph by Harris & Ewing, Washington

Taft did not agree. When Wilson became President, he negotiated a treaty with Colombia offering her twenty-five million dollars as a gift, yielding certain privileges in the use of the canal and expressing "sincere regret" for the interruption of cordial feeling between the two nations. Friends of Roosevelt took the treaty as a reflection on him and it was rejected by the Senate. It was taken up again after Roosevelt's death by President Harding and was ratified by the Senate.

WILSON'S PHILIPPINE POLICY

FROM 1900 onward, the Democrats had opposed the permanent retention of the Philippines. Wilson's election was, therefore, received in the islands as the promise of early independence, and Governor Harrison, sent out by Wilson in 1913, gave encouragement to this expectation. Congress in 1916 passed the Jones Act substituting for the old Government by a Commission and a House of Representatives with a restricted suffrage a Government by a bicameral legislature. There were to be a Governor, a Chief Justice of the Supreme Court, and a few other officials appointed by the President, but in most respects self-government prevailed. The suffrage was so much enlarged that the voters increased from two hundred and twenty-five thousand to eight hundred thousand. The law encouraged the national aspirations of the Filipinos.

FOREIGN CAPITAL IN MEXICO

UNDER Porfirio Diaz foreign capital was encouraged to enter Mexico, and it came so rapidly that at length it seemed to many Mexicans that foreigners were about to master their country, so that a strong feeling was engendered against them.

MEXICO

A Weekly to Promote Intelligent Discussion of Mexican Affairs

VOL. I.—No. 3   NEW YORK, SATURDAY, SEPTEMBER 6, 1913   FIVE CENTS

THE SHAME OF FLIGHT

It is difficult for any red-blooded citizen to consider calmly the import of the Administration's "advice" that all Americans in Mexico leave that country, particularly when the motives that dictated that "advice" are fully understood.

Part of the press of this country may have deemed it proper to show its loyalty to the Government by approving its course in this respect, but it is hardly conceivable that it should fail to realize the loyalty which it owes also to the thousands of American citizens who live in Mexico.

And it is absolutely inconceivable that it should fail to realize the disastrous consequences which will be suffered by those heeding the advice of the Administration. These consequences can hardly be overestimated.

First, Americans leaving Mexico of their own volition will not have any right, according to international law, to claim damages for the losses which they will suffer by the simple fact of their absence.

A wage-earner, an employee or the owner of a business or of a ranch cannot claim from any Mexican Government, present or future, indemnity for the losses which he will suffer by abandoning his employment or his property for causes entirely foreign to the will of that Government.

Second, the Government of the United States has declared its determination to consider the Government of Mexico as a *faction* and to interpret the neutrality laws as applying equally to the Mexican Government and to the rebels. This is tantamount to extending a tacit recognition of belligerency to the rebels. In this case it cannot hold the Mexican Government responsible for any damage which the property of American citizens might suffer after their departure from Mexico. In fact, it is doubtful, according to international law, if after such a declaration it could *legally* enforce the payment of claims whether Americans remain in Mexico or not.

Yet this Mexican Government controls nine-tenths of Mexico and is extending rapidly its authority, bidding fair to obtain full control within a short time.

To this Washington Administration may retort that it is doing its utmost to prevent

Appoint John Lind Ambassador
Continue Friendly Negotiations
Enforce Neutrality Laws
Demand Protection for American Lives and Property

Here is a *positive* program, a *practical* policy, one that will commend itself to every fair-minded American. It is a policy that will get results. It will not signify any retreat from the Washington Administration's friendly efforts to bring about peace and better conditions in Mexico. It will mean simply that the Administration wants to place itself in a position where it can without unnecessary tension and misunderstanding further those efforts. In a position where it can demand the fullest protection for American lives and property in Mexico and press the just claims of American citizens for settlement. It will silence the cries of the jingoes for armed intervention by removing the slightest necessity for it. It will squelch the intrigues of self-seeking Mexican politicians and American financial interests who foment disorder in Mexico and supply across the border the weapons and ammunition for the bandits.

THIS IS A BIG MANLY AMERICAN POLICY. IS IT GOING TO BE THE PRESIDENT'S?

this obtaining of the full control by the Huerta Government and that its "advice" to American citizens to leave Mexico is the lever with which it expects to overturn the hated Huerta.

Thus the meaning of the mysterious words in the President's message:

The rejection of our friendship makes them new and will inevitably bring its own alterations in the whole aspect of affairs. The actual situation of the authorities at Mexico City will presently be revealed.

The steady pressure of moral force will before many days break the barriers of pride and prejudice down.

is now made clear.

The Washington Administration, baffled by a firm and logical rejection of its impossible

proposals, in order to carry its point and make the Mexican Government yield, decided upon forcing an exodus of Americans from Mexico.

As it is not to be supposed by any one conversant with Mexican conditions that President Wilson's proposals if accepted would have brought about peace and order in Mexico, it must be concluded that the proposals were merely intended to eliminate President Huerta from the political field.

Americans must fling to the winds the fruit of many years of labor. They must abandon their property. With their wives and children they must rush out of the country and become unwilling refugees.

"Why," they ask, "when we are contented here, why must we become paupers? Is there going to be a war, invasion, intervention?"

581   Facsimile of first page of *Mexico*, September 6, 1913

580   Porfirio Diaz, 1836–1915, from a photograph

MEXICAN UNREST

THE great mass of the Mexican people were landless peons, hopeless of improving their lot. Discontent manifested itself in the formation of great bands of irregular soldiers under guerilla leaders, ready to fight in defense of their interests. Diaz put down the weakest of these leaders: the stronger he made Governors of states. Mexico was on the verge of revolution in which the downtrodden masses were to rise against the privileged aristocrat.

582   Victoriano Huerta, 1854–1916, from a photograph by Underwood & Underwood, New York

AFFAIRS IN MEXICO

IN 1911, the long despotism of Porfirio Diaz in Mexico came to a sudden end, and the liberal Madero, who had taken arms against him, ruled as President. The promises he had made could not be kept and his old supporters turned against him. Victoriano Huerta, a military adventurer representing the old privileged classes, broke his power, seized the Government and threw Madero into prison. On February 18, 1913, Huerta proclaimed himself provisional President, and on the twenty-third Madero was shot while being shifted at midnight from one prison to another. Publicly it was said that he was trying to escape at the time; but this was a way, well-known in Mexico, of disposing of embarrassing prisoners. Huerta made no adequate effort to investigate the affair and punish the guilty. It was generally assumed that he had compassed the death of his captured rival, although he disclaimed in public any responsibility for the bloody deed.

583　From a cartoon *The Hand of Huerta*, by Weed in the
New York Daily Tribune, July 17, 1913

NO RECOGNITION FOR HUERTA

EUROPEAN countries were so accustomed to the irregularities of undeveloped nations that they took a cynical view of acts of violence like that attributed to Huerta. Holding that it was not their business to ask about Huerta's guilt, they recognized him as *de facto* ruler. Taft did nothing that would embarrass his successor and the problem was passed over to Wilson in the first days of his power. He soon let it be known that he would not permit the United States to take the bloody hand of Huerta. He would not send a new ambassador to Mexico, but allowed Henry L. Wilson, a Republican appointee and unsympathetic with Wilson's ideas, to stay in Mexico City, lest the country should have no one there to speak for the rights of our citizens. Huerta assumed an air of indifference and Mexican public opinion came to his support. It was thought an insult to the nation for a foreign Government to assume to say who should and who should not be President of Mexico. Such an attitude was looked upon as interference by a foreign Government in the domestic affairs of the nation. It offended the pride of the Mexicans, who to their racial sensitiveness added a long-established feeling of dislike for the United States. They were quick to take offense and violent in their expressions of contempt for what they considered an avaricious nation.

HOSTILE BUSINESS INTERESTS

UNITED STATES citizens owning property in Mexico were alarmed at Wilson's course. They feared for the safety of their holdings and declared that he ought either to recognize Huerta or be ready to fight. As he would do neither, they became very critical of his policy. Ridicule and denunciation were heaped upon him from this powerful source, which only encouraged Huerta to stand firm. Wilson, however, grimly held out. It was not the first time that the United States had refused recognition as a means of expressing its displeasure at the action of an irresponsible state, but not hitherto with so large a power. It became an endurance contest between Huerta and Wilson, described by the latter as "watchful waiting." The determination of President Wilson to extend no recognition finally settled into an attempt to oust Huerta from his usurped authority, and that wily leader used it as a means of exciting Mexican sympathy in his behalf. The American Ambassador to Mexico only faintly disguised his opposition to President Wilson.

584　From a cartoon *Helping It Along*, by Rollin Kirby in
The World, New York, Aug. 9, 1913

THE MISSION OF JOHN LIND

AFTER a few months, Ambassador Wilson resigned, through his opposition to the President's plan, and his place was not filled. Instead, John Lind, formerly a Governor of Minnesota, was sent to Mexico as the President's personal representative. He was a man of strong integrity and it was believed that he would be proof against the influence of the foreign capitalists in Mexico. He was empowered to come to an understanding with Huerta on the ground that Huerta would hold a fair election in which he would not be a candidate. The proposal was rejected promptly. Probably it was not expected that Huerta would accept and that the mission was chiefly to reach public opinion in Mexico. But Lind had none of the peculiar tact that was needed to reach the imagination of people of Spanish blood and the mission completely failed. The Mexicans naturally looked on his mission in Mexico as an arrogant and ill mannered attempt to sow the seeds of disaffection in the minds of the populace.

585 John Lind, 1854–, from a photograph by Underwood & Underwood, New York

THE RISE OF CARRANZA

HUERTA had never reduced to complete submission the Maderistas. Under Carranza they continued in the field in the north, and just when Wilson's plans took shape they were gaining notable successes. Carranza, however, did not dare become the defender of Wilson, for that would have been his undoing at home. Nevertheless, Wilson, in his desire to oust Huerta, gave encouragement to Carranza. He even allowed him to purchase arms in the United States. A new crisis was precipitated by the arrest of some bluejackets who landed at the wrong place in Tampico to purchase gasoline. They were released but the admiral commanding demanded that the Mexicans salute the flag. Huerta refused. Wilson felt that he ought to stand by the admiral. An awkward period ensued. A military force seized Vera Cruz and held it for months. Was this war? Wilson decided that it was not, much to the disappointment of those of his fellow citizens who thought that the time had come "to go in and clean up Mexico."

586 Venustiano Carranza, 1859–1920, from a photograph by Underwood & Underwood

EFFORTS OF THE A B C POWERS

PRESIDENT WILSON found relief when Argentina, Brazil and Chile — the "A B C Powers" — offered mediation which was accepted by him and Huerta. After deliberation at Niagara Falls, they proposed that Huerta and Carranza should agree to the creation of a provisional Government in Mexico, each stepping aside in the interest of peace. Carranza was then winning constantly and refused. Shortly afterward, Huerta resigned and sailed for Europe, July 15, 1914. His departure did not give peace to his country, for Pancho Villa, one of Carranza's generals, now took up arms against Carranza and soon Mexico was again in a sad state of chaos. By June, 1915, Carranza again seemed triumphant, and Wilson, acting with a conference of eight Latin-American republics, recognized him as *de facto* ruler and resumed formal diplomatic relations. It was not much of a Wilson victory, for the future soon showed that Carranza was as strong an opponent as Huerta.

587 Secretary of State Bryan with the Ambassadors of Chile and Argentina at the A B C Conference, from a photograph by Underwood & Underwood, New York

588   United States army camp at San Antonio, from a photograph in the possession of the
United States Signal Corps, War Department, Washington

VILLA'S REVENGE

THE recognition of Carranza infuriated Villa against Wilson, and he sought revenge by raids across the border into New Mexico and Texas. Taft had concentrated a large portion of the army on this border to protect United States property in Mexico and to overawe the Mexicans. Villa's raid of March 9, 1916, on Columbus, New Mexico, was followed by a punitive expedition led by Brigadier-General Pershing which penetrated four hundred miles into Mexico, marching at will but never finding the elusive Villa. While Pershing thus stabbed in the dark, Villa whipped around in his rear and made another quick dash across the border. The Government then ordered out all the National Guard and sent three fourths of them, about one hundred and ten thousand, to the Mexican border. Carranza gave an unwilling consent to our pursuit of Villa, and when it failed he became anxious for withdrawal, which was accomplished with little glory to the United States in January, 1917.

ELECTION OF 1916

THE renomination of Wilson by the Democrats in 1916 was a foregone conclusion. In the Republican party, defeat had had its usual disciplinary effect. The Progressive movement was receding, the Standpatters were holding out the olive branch, and Roosevelt was willing to come back into the party and participate in shaping its policy. In selecting a Presidential candidate the conservatives realized that the nominee should be one who could bring the Progressives back to the fold and partly with that end in view chose Charles E. Hughes, who had made a good reform Governor in New York and who resigned a justiceship on the Supreme Federal Bench to accept the nomination.

589   Charles Evans Hughes, 1862–, from a photograph
by Harris & Ewing, Washington

THE CAMPAIGN OF 1916

UNDER the circumstances, the Republicans could not denounce Wilson's domestic policies; for to do so would probably widen the split in their own party. In their necessity they attacked Wilson personally, assailed his Mexican policy, criticized his attitude toward Germany, and proclaimed him a pacifist.

590   Election Map, from the *American Monthly Review of Reviews*,
Dec. 1916

In defense the Democrats pointed out that his policy had kept the nation out of war — out of the war in Europe which was shattering the foundations of civilization, and out of a bitter and grueling war in Mexico. This reply had telling effects, especially where women had been admitted to the suffrage. In the end, Wilson was reëlected by two hundred and seventy-seven to two hundred and fifty-four votes for Hughes. Yet it was believed that Hughes would have been elected but for campaign blunders in California which offended the Progressives.

CHAPTER XII

WORLD WAR POLITICS AND RECONSTRUCTION

THE World War, which began in the summer of 1914, put a spell over all neutral nations, and made a vast difference in the domestic politics of most of them. In the United States it came as Wilson and the Democrats were about to complete their program of anti-trust legislation, when a breathing spell seemed about to come. But there arose at once the problem of preserving neutrality in a creditable way and the necessity for taking steps to defend the nation if it were drawn into the war. Matters connected with these two objects engaged the attention of the Government for the most part until 1917, when the United States became one of the belligerents. Thereupon outright political wrangling was discontinued, but there were differences of opinion on the war policies of Congress and they frequently followed party lines in a way more or less strict. With the return of peace came a restoration of party conflict which was then more severe than in the old days before 1912. It dealt with policies connected with our future international relations, and with domestic policies of readjustment.

During the period of neutrality Wilson thought that his duty made it imperative to keep the United States out of the war as long as it could be done without impairing the national honor. This task was peculiarly difficult on account of the many races that had furnished the people who had settled within our borders. The sympathy of each race element went out to that European state from which it was sprung. Our citizens of German descent leaned toward the Central Powers, and our Italians and Poles toward the Allies, who also had the sympathy of the people of British stock. As the struggle became fiercer in Europe, these different groups began to express their preferences, and Wilson was kept in a state of alarm lest the confusion should grow so great that his administration would become ineffective. His conduct under these conditions consisted in patient efforts to get Great Britain to restrict her interference with neutral trade and to get Germany to use her submarines in accordance with the accepted rules of international law. In neither case did he succeed. He made a difference between the wrongs inflicted on us. Those which we received from Great Britain were property damages, and redress was in the nature of restoration; those which we received from Germany were in the loss of human lives, and no restoration could be made. Protesting against the former, he allowed the settlement to remain for the future. For the wrongs received from Germany he found it necessary, after a long wait, to demand immediate cessation on pain of war.

After the war began, the points of debate at home turned to reliance upon voluntary or compulsory enlistment; on permitting the President to carry on the war of his own authority or under the guidance of a war ministry or a Congressional committee; on inquiring into the way the war was being conducted, and on devising means of supporting it by marshaling the economic and intellectual strength of the country. Into this series of events, politics did not interject itself, except probably into the inquiries on the conduct of the war. This phase of our political history is brief and easily described.

During the *post bellum* phase, discussion was violent and passion ran high. The strong attack made on Wilson's course in the peace negotiations at Paris, the attacks on the League of Nations, and the strenuous fight to hold or take the Presidency in 1920 all announced that politics again held sway.

PRESIDENT URGES PEOPLE TO BE IMPARTIAL IN THOUGHT AND ACTS.

Declaring that the Spirit of the Nation in European Crisis Will Be Determined Largely by What Individuals Do and Say, He Warns Them as Americans Against that "Deepest, Most Subtle, Most Essential Breach of Neutrality Which May Spring Out of Partisanship, Out of Passionately Taking Sides"—Resents Efforts to Embroil the United States in the War and Denies that the Kaiser Has Complained of Unfairness to Germany in This Country.

(Special to The World.)

WASHINGTON, Aug. 18.—With all official Washington wondering what effect Japan's warlike attitude toward Germany will have upon American interests in the Far East, President Wilson, following a long session of the Cabinet, to-day issued a solemn appeal, addressed to all citizens of the United States, calling upon them to use the utmost endeavor to refrain from any act or expression that might be construed into offensive partisanship of any nation engaged in conflict.

The extreme probability of war between Germany and Japan was displayed in the official information, coming from Ambassador Gerard, that the Japanese Ambassador in Berlin had already asked him to be prepared to take charge of Japanese interests in Germany.

Following the receipt of this and other intimations that the Japanese ultimatum, which has been formally delivered to the German Government via Copenhagen, might be followed by decisive action, which, it is universally conceded, means the seizure of Kiaochow, Baron Chinda, the Japanese Ambassador, held a long conference with Secretary of State Bryan.

Britain Reassures United States About Japan.

Colville Barclay, British Chargé d'Affaires, also called on Secretary Bryan and left a copy of a note from Great Britain announcing that Japanese action would be confined to German territory "in Eastern Asia."

There is a possibility that Germany may seek to arrange for the return of Kiaochow directly to China, rather than let it pass through Japanese hands; but it is not thought likely that Japan would accede to such a proposal. The German Chargé d'Affaires, Hamiel von Haimhausen, who also called on Secretary Bryan, said it was to be regretted that Japan had taken up the gage, as Germany had hoped to neutralize all the colonies on both sides in the Far East.

The President received to-day, through Ambassador Gerard, Emperor William's formal reply to his offer of mediation. The message expressed grateful appreciation of the tender of good offices on the part of the United States and at the same time took occasion to make a formal statement of the German position in the war.

The Cabinet meeting to-day spent considerable time on the question of neutrality and the wireless and cable censorship, but without, so far as could be learned, reaching any satisfactory conclusion. There is a general feeling, however, that the situation will remain about as it is, with the wireless censored and the cables free.

591   From *The World*, New York, Aug. 19, 1914

592   From a cartoon *America's Attitude*, by Carter in *Cartoons*, Feb. 1915, reproduced from the New York *Evening Sun*

AMERICAN NEUTRALITY IN THE WORLD WAR

On August 4, 1914, President Wilson issued a proclamation of neutrality warning all Americans to commit no act favorable to either side in the gigantic conflict that had begun in Europe. The immediate impulse of almost all groups in America was to support the President. Very soon, however, there appeared widespread disposition to take sides. In the East, where there was most intercourse with Europe, opinion supported the Entente Allies. The Middle West and western states were more neutral and the German-Americans were outspoken for strict neutrality.

593   From a cartoon *Tut, Tut, Theodore*, by Darling in *Cartoons*, July 1915, reproduced from the Des Moines *Register and Leader*

THE DEMAND FOR PREPAREDNESS

In a few months agitation began for a larger army and navy on the ground that we should be better prepared for war in case we were drawn into the European conflict. By a tradition long held to be American the country at large was deeply opposed to militarism, and on that account it did not accept the propaganda which Roosevelt was pressing with his usual earnestness. Wilson and Congress did not accept this demand for preparedness. To have done so would have raised such warm feeling as to have shelved the policy of neutrality.

IN THE INTEREST OF HUMANITY

THE Germans developed submarines rapidly during the war. They were soon able to send them with safety around the British Isles, and by 1917 they owned submarines large enough to cross the Atlantic and return. With these formidable weapons they expected to starve Britain into surrender. At first they sank only cargo boats; the great passenger ships were supposed to be protected by international law, which held that a merchant ship might not be sunk unless the non-combatants on board were placed in safety, something that the submarine was seldom able to do. Wilson protested against this use of submarines.

594   From a cartoon *Let Her be Heard*, by Césare in *The Evening Post*, New York, May 18, 1915

DESTRUCTION OF THE *LUSITANIA*

ON May 7, 1915, this matter came to a crisis. Near the coast of Ireland submarines destroyed the great passenger ship *Lusitania*, bound from New York to Liverpool. The dead numbered eleven hundred and fifty-three persons, one hundred and fourteen of whom were United States citizens. The act had been committed deliberately. Before the *Lusitania* sailed, the German Ambassador in Washington placed in some of the newspapers a notice warning persons crossing the Atlantic in British or French ships that they did so at their peril. The quick execution of this threat brought suddenly home to the American people the fact that it might be necessary to enter the war against Germany in order to protect the national honor. If we submitted to this violation of the right of neutrals to travel as non-combatants, we could not expect any nation to respect it in the future.

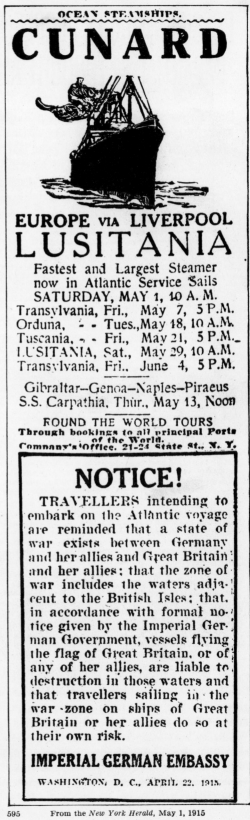

595   From the *New York Herald*, May 1, 1915

FULL TEXT OF NOTE SENT TO BERLIN AND TO BE DELIVERED TO THE GERMAN FOREIGN OFFICE TO-DAY

Herald Bureau,
No. 1,502 H Street, N. W.,
Washington, D. C., Friday.

FOLLOWING is the full text of the Note cabled to Berlin from Washington:—

"Department of State, Washington, May 13, 1915.

"The Secretary of State to the American Ambassador at Berlin:—

"Please call on the Minister of Foreign Affairs and after reading to him this communication leave with him a copy.

"In view of recent acts of the German authorities in violation of American rights on the high seas which culminated in the torpedoing and sinking of the British steamship Lusitania on May 7, 1915, by which over one hundred American citizens lost their lives, it is clearly wise and desirable that the government of the United States and the Imperial German government should come to a clear and full understanding as to the grave situation which has resulted.

"The sinking of the British passenger steamer Falaba by a German submarine on March 28, through which Leon C. Thrasher, an American citizen, was drowned; the attack on April 28 on the American vessel Cushing by a German aeroplane; the torpedoing on May 1 of the American vessel Gulflight by a German submarine, as a result of which two or more American citizens met their death; and, finally, the torpedoing and sinking of the steamship Lusitania, constitute a series of events which the government of the United States has observed with growing concern, distress and amazement.

"Recalling the humane and enlightened attitude hitherto assumed by the Imperial German government in matters of international right, and particularly with regard to the freedom of the seas: having learned to recognize the German views and the German influence in the field of international obligation as always engaged upon the side of justice and humanity: and having understood the instructions of the Imperial German government to its naval commanders to be upon the same plane of humane action prescribed by the naval codes of other nations, the government of the United States was loath to believe—it cannot now bring itself to believe—that these acts, so absolutely contrary to the rules, the practices and the spirit of modern warfare, could have the countenance or sanction of that great government. It feels it to be its duty, therefore, to address the Imperial German government concerning them with the utmost frankness and in the earnest hope that it is not mistaken in expecting action on the part of the Imperial German government which will correct the unfortunate impressions which have been created and vindicate once more the position of that government with regard to the sacred freedom of the seas.

"The government of the United States has been apprised that the Imperial German government considered themselves to be obliged by the extraordinary circumstances of the present war and the measures adopted by their adversaries in seeking to cut Germany off from all commerce, to adopt methods of retaliation which go much beyond the ordinary methods of warfare at sea, in the proclamation of a war zone from which they have warned neutral ships to keep away. This government has already taken occasion to inform the Imperial German government that it cannot admit the adoption of such measures or such a warning of danger to operate as in any degree an abbreviation of the rights of American ship masters or of American citizens bound on lawful errands as passengers on merchant ships of belligerent nationality; and that it must hold the Imperial German government to a strict accountability for any infringement of those rights, intentional or incidental. It does not understand the Imperial German government to question those rights. It assumes, on the contrary, that the Imperial government accept, as of course, the rule that the lives of non-combatants, whether they be of neutral citizenship or citizens of one of the nations at war, cannot lawfully or rightfully be put in jeopardy by the capture or destruction of an unarmed merchantman, and recognize also, as all other nations do, the obligation to take the usual precaution of visit and search to ascertain whether a suspected merchantman is in fact of belligerent nationality or is in fact carrying contraband of war under a neutral flag.

"The government of the United States, therefore, desires to call the attention of the Imperial German government with the utmost earnestness to the fact that the objection to their present method of attack against the trade of their enemies lies in the practical impossibility of employing submarines in the destruction of commerce without disregarding those rules of fairness, reason, justice and humanity which all modern opinion regards as imperative. It is practically impossible for the officers of a submarine to visit a merchantman at sea and examine her papers and cargo. It is practically impossible for them to make a prize of her, and if they cannot put a prize crew on board of her they cannot sink her without leaving her crew and all on board of her to the mercy of the sea in her small boats. These facts it is understood the Imperial German government frankly admit. We are informed that in the instances of which we have spoken time enough for even that poor measure of safety was not given, and in at least two of the cases cited not so much as a warning was received. Manifestly submarines cannot be used against merchantmen, as the last few weeks have shown, without an inevitable violation of many sacred principles of justice and humanity.

"American citizens act within their indisputable rights in taking their ships and in travelling wherever their legitimate business calls them upon the high seas, and exercise those rights in what should be the well justified confidence that their lives will not be endangered by acts done in clear violation of universally acknowledged international obligations, and certainly in the confidence that their own government will sustain them in the exercise of their rights.

"There was recently published in the newspapers of the United States, I regret to inform the Imperial German government, a formal warning, purporting to come from the Imperial German Embassy at Washington, addressed to the people of the United States, and stating, in effect, that any citizen of the United States who exercised his right of free travel upon the seas would do so at his peril if his journey should take him within the zone of waters within which the Imperial German navy was using submarines against the commerce of Great Britain and France, notwithstanding the respectful but very earnest protest of the government of the United States. I do not refer to this for the purpose of calling the attention of the Imperial German government at this time to the surprising irregularity of a communication from the Imperial German Embassy at Washington addressed to the people of the United States through the newspapers, but only for the purpose of pointing out that no warning that an unlawful and inhumane act will be committed can possibly be accepted as an excuse or palliation for that act or as an abatement of the responsibility for its commission.

"Long acquainted as this government has been with the character of the imperial government and with the high principles of equity by which they have in the past been actuated and guided, the government of the United States cannot believe that the commanders of the vessels which committed these acts of lawlessness did so except under a misapprehension of the orders issued by the Imperial German naval authorities. It takes it for granted that, at least within the practical possibilities of every such case, the commanders even of submarines were expected to do nothing that would involve the lives of non-combatants or the safety of neutral ships, even at the cost of failing of their object of capture or destruction. It confidently expects, therefore, that the Imperial German government will disavow the acts of which the government of the United States complains, that they will make reparation so far as reparation is possible for injuries which are without measure, and that they will take immediate steps to prevent the recurrence of anything so obviously subversive of the principles of warfare for which the Imperial German government have in the past so wisely and so firmly contended.

"The government and people of the United States look to the Imperial German government for just, prompt and enlightened action in this vital matter with the greater confidence because the United States and Germany are bound together not only by special ties of friendship, but also by the explicit stipulations of the treaty of 1828 between the United States and the Kingdom of Prussia.

"Expressions of regret and offers of reparation in case of the destruction of neutral ships sunk by mistake, while they may satisfy international obligations if no loss of life results, cannot justify or excuse a practice the natural and necessary effect of which is to subject neutral nations and neutral persons to new and immeasurable risks.

"The Imperial German government will not expect the government of the United States to omit any word or any act necessary to the performance of its sacred duty of maintaining the rights of the United States and its citizens and of safeguarding their free exercise and enjoyment. BRYAN."

596 The text of President Wilson's first *Lusitania* note, from the *New York Herald*, May 14, 1915

WILSON'S FIRST *LUSITANIA* NOTE

ON May 13, 1915, Wilson sent to the German Government a calm statement of the *Lusitania* incident, and of the legal contention of our Government; it closed with a polite declaration that a disavowal of the action of the submarine commander who sank the *Lusitania* was expected by the United States. The closing paragraph read: "The Imperial German government will not expect the government of the United States to omit any word or any act necessary to the performance of its sacred duty of maintaining the rights of the United States and its citizens and of safeguarding their free exercise and enjoyment." This note was signed by Bryan, but it was written by Wilson. It did not suit the extremists, and it was probably too soft-spoken to put respect for the President into the hearts of the men of Berlin.

GERMAN APPROVAL

THE mass of the German people were by this time very bitter toward the United States. Vast quantities of supplies of all kinds had been bought in our markets by the Entente Allies and carried to the scene of conflict. Germany had not been able to do the like because her opponents controlled the sea. The Germans desired the United States to refuse to sell munitions to any nation. We naturally refused; for a change of the rule after war had begun would have been an unneutral act. Disregarding this fact the German leaders through their fierce discussion of our course kindled a flame of hatred against us in the mind of the German nation. Therefore, when the news came that the good German submarines had sunk a huge British liner crowded with citizens of the United States, some of them millionaires, intemperate people in Germany raised a shout of joy which was ominous for future peaceful relations. Many of our citizens resented as mere mockery the action of the German Ambassador who sent a memorial wreath to be placed on the graves of those whom a German submarine had slain. The destruction of the *Lusitania* sent a thrill of horror through the American people. A vast majority of them could not comprehend how civilized men could deliberately commit such an act. German elation was so high that the German Government would have found it very difficult to have disavowed the destruction of the *Lusitania*.

597   From a cartoon by T. H. Heine in *Cartoons*, April 1915, reproduced from *Simplicissimus*, Munich, Germany

WILSON'S DELIBERATION

THE more impulsive portion of the people of the United States demanded that steps be taken to obtain an apology and disclaimer from Germany, or war be declared. Another large portion of the people were stunned and did not know what to do. A small pro-German group defended the incident. It is conceded that a large majority of the nation were not ready for war. Wilson understood this divided state of public opinion; doubtless it influenced his course. Furthermore, he had an inherent dislike for war, believing that a ruler in an emergency like this ought to try all other means before he opened the doors of battle. His idea was to check for the moment the tide of feeling that demanded war and in the meantime to bring Germany by a firm stand to agree to use her submarines in accordance with the rules of international law. If this end could be reached without war it would be a triumph of reason. His efforts to hold back the more impetuous people caused him to be denounced for timidity. On the other hand the pro-Germans pronounced him a British tool.

598   From a cartoon *What Will The Answer Be*, by Césare in the New York *Sun*, May 10, 1915

DEALING WITH GERMANY

THE German reply to Wilson's note of May 13 did not disavow the destruction of American lives on the *Lusitania*. Instead it restated the German position on the use of submarines and urged that the *Lusitania* was armed and had the status of a warship. To this reply Wilson sent a second note, June 9, declaring that the ship was not armed for offensive action and repeating firmly a demand for disavowal. The reply was a note full of evasion, and on July 21, 1915, Wilson sent his third *Lusitania* note. It declared that Germany's replies were "very unsatisfactory" and gave warning that a repetition of the recent incident would be regarded as "deliberately unfriendly." Shortly after this Germany ordered her submarine commanders to sink no liners without warning, which was taken as a sign of yielding and eased the situation somewhat. This impression seemed confirmed when Germany disavowed the sinking without warning of the *Arabic*, August 19. The outcome of the *Lusitania* correspondence was generally looked upon as a diplomatic victory for President Wilson although he was strongly criticized for the length of time which the episode was allowed to consume. He was also censured for an unconsidered phrase, "too proud to fight," used in trying to check the extremists.

599   From a cartoon *Each Line and Word*, by Pease in *Cartoons*, August 1915, reproduced from the Newark *Evening News*

RESIGNATION OF BRYAN

THE second *Lusitania* note should have been signed by Secretary Bryan, but he was strongly committed to peace at all costs and resigned rather than put his name to it. He was succeeded by Robert Lansing, who was willing to follow the President's policies. Bryan had nearly frustrated the President's plan of forcing a pledge from Germany by saying to the Austrian Ambassador, Dumba: "The United States desires no war. Her notes, however strongly worded, meant no harm, but had to be written in order to pacify the excited public opinion of America. The Berlin Government therefore need not feel itself injured, but need only make suitable concessions if it desires to put an end to the dispute." Naturally such sentiments promptly reached the German capital. As a consequence Zimmerman accused Gerard of bluffing when the American Ambassador said that Germany must yield. Bryan went out intending to rally the country to a demand that we keep out of the war, but when he realized the strength of the popular feeling against Germany he gave up the plan. Bryan was a sincere pacifist, but his presence at the head of the State Department in 1915 was most unfortunate. His attitude did much to make Germany think that Wilson would not fight.

600   Robert Lansing, 1864–, from a photograph by Harris & Ewing, Washington

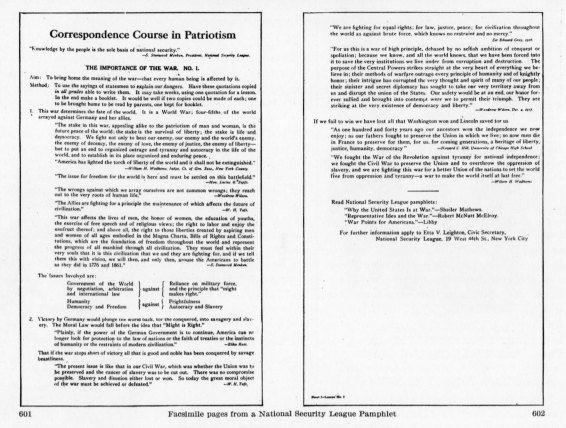

Correspondence Course in Patriotism

"Knowledge by the people is the sole basis of national security."
—S. Stanwood Menken, President, National Security League.

THE IMPORTANCE OF THE WAR. NO. I.

Aim: To bring home the meaning of the war—that every human being is affected by it.

Method: To use the sayings of statesmen to explain our dangers. Have these quotations copied *in all grades* able to write them. It may take weeks, using one quotation for a lesson. In the end make a booklet. It would be well if two copies could be made of each; one to be brought home to be read by parents, one kept for booklet.

1. This war determines the fate of the world. It is a World War; four-fifths of the world arrayed against Germany and her allies.

"The stake in this war, appealing alike to the patriotism of man and woman, is the future peace of the world; the stake is the survival of liberty; the stake is life and democracy. We fight not only to beat our enemy, our enemy and the world's enemy, the enemy of decency, the enemy of love, the enemy of justice, the enemy of liberty—but to put an end to organized outrage and tyranny and autocracy in the life of the world, and to establish in its place organized and enduring peace.
"America has lighted the torch of liberty of the world and it shall not be extinguished."
—William H. Wadhams, Judge, Ct. of Gen. Sess., New York County.

"The issue for freedom for the world is here and must be settled on this battlefield."
—Hon. Lucius B. Swift.

"The wrongs against which we array ourselves are not common wrongs; they reach out to the very roots of human life."
—Woodrow Wilson.

"The Allies are fighting for a principle the maintenance of which affects the future of civilization."
—W. H. Taft.

"This war affects the lives of men, the honor of women, the education of youths, the exercise of free speech and of religious views; the right to labor and enjoy the usufruct thereof; and above all, the right to those liberties created by aspiring men and women of all ages embodied in the Magna Charta, Bills of Rights and Constitutions, which are the foundation of freedom throughout the world and represent the progress of all mankind through all civilization. They must feel within their very souls that it is this civilization that we and they are fighting for, and if we tell them this with vision, we will then, and only then, arouse the Americans to battle as they did in 1776 and 1861."
—S. Stanwood Menken.

The Issues Involved are:

Government of the World by negotiation, arbitration and international law	} against {	Reliance on military force, and the principle that "might makes right."
Humanity Democracy and Freedom	} against {	Frightfulness Autocracy and Slavery

2. Victory by Germany would plunge the world back, for the conquered, into savagery and slavery. The Moral Law would fall before the idea that "Might is Right."

"Plainly, if the power of the German Government is to continue, America can no longer look for protection to the law of nations or the faith of treaties or the instincts of humanity or the restraints of modern civilization."
—Elihu Root.

That if the war stops short of victory all that is good and noble has been conquered by savage beastliness.

"The present issue is like that in our Civil War, which was whether the Union was to be preserved and the cancer of slavery was to be cut out. There was no compromise possible. Slavery and disunion either lost or won. So today the great moral object of the war must be achieved or defeated."
—W. H. Taft.

"We are fighting for equal rights; for law, justice, peace; for civilization throughout the world as against brute force, which knows no restraint and no mercy."
—Sir Edward Grey, 1916

"For us this is a war of high principle, debased by no selfish ambition of conquest or spoliation; because we know, and all the world knows, that we have been forced into it to save the very institutions we live under from corruption and destruction. The purpose of the Central Powers strikes straight at the very heart of everything we believe in; their methods of warfare outrage every principle of humanity and of knightly honor; their intrigue has corrupted the very thought and spirit of many of our people; their sinister and secret diplomacy has sought to take our very territory away from us and disrupt the union of the States. Our safety would be at an end, our honor forever sullied and brought into contempt were we to permit their triumph. They are striking at the very existence of democracy and liberty."
—Woodrow Wilson, Dec. 4, 1917.

If we fail to win we have lost all that Washington won and Lincoln saved for us.

"As one hundred and forty years ago our ancestors won the independence we now enjoy; as our fathers fought to preserve the Union in which we live; so now men die in France to preserve for them, for us, for coming generations, a heritage of liberty, justice, humanity, democracy."
—Howard C. Hill, University of Chicago High School.

"We fought the War of the Revolution against tyranny for national independence; we fought the Civil War to preserve the Union and to overthrow the oppression of slavery, and we are fighting this war for a better Union of the nations to set the world free from oppression and tyranny—a war to make the world itself at last free."
—William H. Wadhams.

Read National Security League pamphlets:
  "Why the United States Is at War."—Shailer Mathews.
  "Representative Idea and the War."—Robert McNutt McElroy.
  "War Points for Americans."—Libby.

For further information apply to Etta V. Leighton, Civic Secretary,
  National Security League, 19 West 44th St., New York City

Sheet 2—Lesson No. 1

601   Facsimile pages from a National Security League Pamphlet   602

THE PLATTSBURG MOVEMENT

A VIGOROUS popular campaign for preparedness was carried on by private organizations such as the National Security League and by a great number of centers and editors. Incidental to this campaign was the establishment of a summer camp at Plattsburg for training student and other volunteers in the duties of reserve officers who might be drawn into service on an emergency, but this did not occur until the summer of 1915.

STRONGER NATIONAL DEFENSE

THE day Wilson sent his third *Lusitania* note he asked the Navy Department for plans for a strong navy and a few days later he took similar steps with regard to the army. As a result, Congress was induced to adopt in the following year a program for constructing a large navy and to consider a plan for a "Continental Army" prepared by Secretary of War Garrison with Wilson's approval. Congress, however, refused this plan, largely through the political influence of the National Guard, and passed the Hay Act instead, by which the regular army was increased to one hundred and eighty-six thousand and the National Guard, enlarged to four hundred and twenty-four thousand, was taken under Federal authority. Secretary Garrison resigned his office when Wilson shifted his support from the "Continental" plan to the Hay plan. These two steps taken in 1916 to strengthen the national defense were all that could then be wrung out of a Congress sensitive to the charge that militarists were trying to stampede the country. The European war originated in conditions with which we had nothing to do and the country wished to keep out of it if possible.

603   Lindley M. Garrison, 1864–, from a photograph by Harris & Ewing, Washington

Dr. Dernburg: "How am I to get home?"
Uncle Sam: "You might try this."

604   From a cartoon *The Only Way*, by Césare in
The Sun, New York, May 18, 1915

DEPARTURE OF DR. DERNBURG

THE outbreak of the war in Europe had brought to the United States Dr. Bernhard Dernburg, formerly a member of the imperial cabinet, now dispatched, with a corps of able assistants, to conduct extensive propaganda in behalf of Germany. He found helpers in some of the more active of the Germans in the United States, and was able to enlist a few natives in his cause. By writing articles for periodicals, by combatting the views of the opposite side, by explaining in his own way the actions of Germany, and by other similar proceedings he put before the country the German side of the controversy. At the same time, he and his group became the target for a great deal of counter-agitation. The spectacle of a foreigner trying to convert the people to his views aroused much of the latent pro-Ally sentiment in this country. This feeling burst forth with great power after the *Lusitania* was sunk; and Dr. Dernburg, realizing that his usefulness had passed, took his departure from a land that daily became more and more enraged against Germany. It is not thought that his efforts converted many of the people to pro-German views, but they probably united and strengthened persons already on that side.

GERMAN RESENTMENT

AT this time Germany urged two complaints against the United States: first, that they sold munitions to the Entente, and second, that they ought to induce Germany's enemies to refrain from their practice of arming merchant ships. To the first demand America paid little heed, since it was covered by the rules of international law. While our Government did not agree with the principle involved in the second, it went so far as to submit the German demand to the British Government which refused to act, on the ground that it was out of the question to forego the right to arm merchantmen in a defensive way. The submarine was a new weapon of war and no generally accepted international usage governed its use. The arming of merchant ships was an adjustment to the German tactics in submarine warfare. As Americans disapproved strongly of German methods, they, naturally, did not look with disfavor upon the putting of guns on ordinary ships. The Germans professed to believe that our refusal to protest indicated that we acted at British dictation.

605   From a cartoon *The Dictator*, by W. Trier in *Cartoons*, Nov. 1915, from
Lustige Blaetter, Berlin

DR. DUMBA DISMISSED

It was a favorite idea of the pro-Germans that the German-born portion of the people could be united in a powerful political *bloc*. Holding up this idea as a club, certain leaders tried to coerce public men, and went so far as to try to get Congress to pass laws favorable to Germany. In these efforts a very large sum of money was expended; where it came from was a mystery never cleared up. It seems certain that the German Ambassador, von Bernstorff, was cognizant of these efforts, but he was too clever to use his official position in their execution. Dr. Dumba, Austrian Ambassador, was less subtle and when a letter from him fell into Government hands, showing that he favored spending Austrian money to support the agitation in Congress, his Government was asked to recall him on the ground that he was *persona non grata*. Dumba in order to escape humiliation asked to be allowed to depart on a leave of absence but the President did not consider such a mode of withdrawal sufficiently striking under the circumstances and denied the request.

606   Constantin Theodor Dumba, 1856–, from a photograph
by Harris & Ewing, Washington

AN APPARENT ADJUSTMENT

For some months matters went on smoothly, and then, on March 24, 1916, the *Sussex* was attacked by submarines and American lives were lost. An angry protest was made and again Germany seemed to retreat. She sent a note, May 4, promising not to sink merchantmen "without warning and without saving human lives, unless these ships attempt to escape or offer resistance." This statement was a fairly explicit compliance with Wilson's demands; but it was somewhat vitiated by a closing paragraph saying that, having agreed to our demands, Germany expected that we should get the Entente Allies to give up their restriction on neutral trade in violation of international law. To this last statement the American Government replied that our rights were absolute and we could not consent to hold them on conditions of any kind. For the remainder of 1916, however, German submarines respected the rules of cruiser warfare, and it seemed that Wilson's diplomacy had obviated the danger of war. Here the dispute rested for nearly nine months.

GERMANY AGREES TO MODIFY SUBMARINE WAR, BUT INSISTS WE OPPOSE BRITAIN'S BLOCKADE; WILSON MAY WAIT TO SEE IF PLEDGE IS KEPT

REPLY NOT OUT IN BERLIN

But the Lokal-Anzeiger, Apparently Inspired, Praises Its Tone.

AND HOPES FOR ACCEPTANCE

Thinks the Concessions to Us Are Such as the Dignity of the Empire Demands.

BRITISH COMMENT SEVERE

Document Is Denounced as a Humbug and Solely Designed to Gain Time.

Text of Germany's Reply to Our Note.

BERLIN, May 5, (by Wireless to Sayville.)—Following is the text of the note of the German Government in reply to the American note respecting submarine warfare, delivered yesterday by Gottlieb von Jagow, the Foreign Secretary, to Ambassador Gerard:

DIPLOMATIC BREAK AVERTED

Germany's Note "Irritating but Acceptable," First View at Capital.

NEW ORDER TO U-BOATS

Must Apply General Rules of Visit and Search with Safety of Lives.

CABINET VERDICT WITHHELD

President to Give No Decision Until He Has Studied the Official Text of the Reply.

608   From a cartoon *Let Us Have Peace*, by Winsor McCay in *Cartoons*, Nov. 1914, reproduced from the *New York American*

WILSON AS MEDIATOR

FROM the beginning of the World War Wilson was spoken of as the man who might act as friendly intermediary in persuading the warring nations to come together and make peace. A feeble attempt to do so was made in 1914, but it was premature. Wilson decided to wait for a more favorable occasion. He thought the time had come late in 1916 and prepared an appeal to all the warring nations. Just before he issued it, Germany, speaking as a victor, called her opponents to a peace conference, using terms which made it likely that they would not come. In this way she discounted in advance in German minds the effect of Wilson's proposed step. He did not give up his plan but on December 18 had Secretary Lansing send identical notes to all the belligerents asking each to state terms of peace with a view to calling a peace conference to discuss them. England spoke for the Entente, making it clear that no peace would be made until Germany was beaten. Wilson had asked the nations to be content with "peace without victory."

UNRESTRICTED SUBMARINE WARFARE

AT the end of the year, 1916, the military situation in Germany was serious. Two and a half years of war had not brought the promised victory and the people were complaining of the burden. It was believed that too much consideration had been shown to the United States in regard to the use of submarines, and a popular demand arose for the unrestricted employment of this weapon, regardless of what America might do. The result was the announcement, made January 31, 1917, that unrestricted submarine operations would begin on February 1. With this announcement some rules were promulgated permitting neutral ships to go into the war zones under very narrow and humiliating restrictions. This assumption that our ships could exercise their legal rights only through the Kaiser's permission produced a storm of resentment.

609   The sinking of the American ship *Illinois*, from a photograph in the possession of the Navy Department, Washington

THE RECALL OF AMBASSADOR GERARD

THE German note of January, 1917, was a breach of the German promise of May 4, 1916, and Wilson promptly ordered intercourse with Germany suspended. Ambassador Gerard in Berlin was directed to demand his passports. Though he made the request immediately of the German Foreign Office, he was kept waiting several days without permission to depart and meanwhile was subjected to irritating annoyance. While thus detained he was asked to sign a treaty promising that the United States and Germany would not in time of war seize belligerent property. The bad diplomatic manners of this episode heightened the anti-German feeling in the United States. The suggestion was inspired by the desire to save from seizure German property in our limits.

610   James W. Gerard, 1867–, from a photograph by Underwood & Underwood, New York

611 Count Johann von Bernstorff, 1862–, from a photograph by Harris & Ewing, Washington

DISMISSAL OF AMBASSADOR VON BERNSTORFF

WHEN Gerard was recalled, the German Ambassador, Count von Bernstorff, was handed his passports and informed that facilities would be available for his departure His dismissal was attended by such politeness as the situation demanded. He had played an able game in Washington, and if he had had a free hand it is probable that the United States would not have been involved in the war; but he was hampered by the men above him who did not understand the American people. They thought we were soft with money-making, that we could not fight if we tried, and that the distance from Europe made it impossible for us to send a great army thither.

612   Wilson reads his war message to Congress, from a photograph by Underwood & Underwood, New York

WILSON GOES BEFORE CONGRESS

SUSPENSION of intercourse made war all but inevitable. It only remained for news to come saying that the submarines had done what they had been authorized to do. Such news arrived in March, and Congress was called to meet in extra session on April 2. The President appeared before it, his heart heavy with the responsibility upon him. To lead the country into a war in whose origin we had no part was, he told Congress, a fearful thing to do. But he felt that the time had come when we must fight to prevent liberal Government from being overwhelmed by autocratic Government. He called for war. He gave a rallying cry for the struggle about to begin when he stated his purpose—"To make the world safe for democracy."

Sixty-fifth Congress of the United States of America;

At the First Session,

Begun and held at the City of Washington on Monday, the second day of April,
one thousand nine hundred and seventeen.

JOINT RESOLUTION

Declaring that a state of war exists between the Imperial German Government
and the Government and the people of the United States and making
provision to prosecute the same.

Whereas the Imperial German Government has committed repeated acts of
war against the Government and the people of the United States of
America: Therefore be it

*Resolved by the Senate and House of Representatives of the United States
of America in Congress assembled,* That the state of war between the United
States and the Imperial German Government which has thus been thrust upon
the United States is hereby formally declared; and that the President be, and
he is hereby, authorized and directed to employ the entire naval and military
forces of the United States and the resources of the Government to carry on war
against the Imperial German Government; and to bring the conflict to a
successful termination all of the resources of the country are hereby pledged by
the Congress of the United States.

Champ Clark,
Speaker of the House of Representatives.

Thos. R. Marshall
Vice President of the United States and
President of the Senate.

Approved 6 April, 1917

Woodrow Wilson

613   From a photograph by the United States Signal Corps, War Department,
of the original document in the Department of State, Washington

THE DECLARATION OF WAR

ON April 6, four days after Wilson made his
eloquent appeal, Congress by joint resolution
declared that the issue of war forced on the
country by Germany was accepted by the
American nation; to the successful conduct
of the war all the resources of the United
States were pledged. The resolution passed
the House by a vote of three hundred and
seventy-three to fifty and the Senate by
eighty-two to six. The course of Germany
had united the people. All party conflict now
disappeared in the face of the conviction that
here was one overwhelming duty binding on
every citizen. Wilson expressed the common
feeling in saying, "Politics is adjourned."
Already the *New York Times* had expressed
a general conviction: "Do we know what a
German victory means for us here in the
United States? We know it with full entirety
and conviction. It means either that we buy
freedom from molestation by perpetual pol-
troonery, or that within a few years we shall
be engaged in a new war for independence
against an incomparably more formidable
foe." The war had begun without our will or
responsibility but it had reached a state which
made it impossible for us to stay out of it, and
this situation arose from the close interrela-
tion of the nations in economic and political
matters.

614   Claude Kitchin, 1869–1923, from a photograph
by Harris & Ewing, Washington

OPPONENTS OF WAR

UP to April 6, 1917, a considerable number of the members of
each House of Congress were opposed to war, but at the last
moment many of them came over to the side of the majority.
Claude Kitchin, of North Carolina, administration leader in the
House, and James R. Mann, of Illinois, Republican leader, were
both for peace. At the last, Mann gave in, accepting the war
because the country was determined to have it; but Kitchin
remained unshaken and voted with the minority. He did not
believe in war as a means of settling disputes, and he believed
that we should have accepted Germany's humiliating conditions
rather than fight. Few of the people accepted this view; and
most of the German-Americans were soon to show that they
patriotically accepted the cause of the United States. There
were many German-Americans in the armed forces of the United
States, and they fought as well as any others.

HALT the HUN!

BUY U.S. GOVERNMENT BONDS
THIRD LIBERTY LOAN

615 From a Liberty Loan poster by Henry Raleigh in Albert E. Gallatin, *Art and the Great War*, E. P. Dutton & Co., New York, 1919

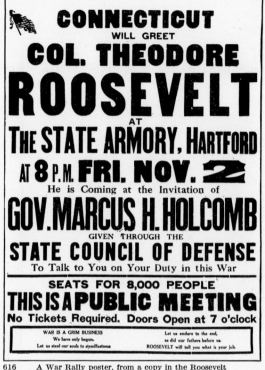

CONNECTICUT
WILL GREET
COL. THEODORE
ROOSEVELT
AT
THE STATE ARMORY, HARTFORD
AT **8 P.M. FRI. NOV. 2**
He is Coming at the Invitation of
GOV. MARCUS H. HOLCOMB
GIVEN THROUGH THE
STATE COUNCIL OF DEFENSE
To Talk to You on Your Duty in this War

SEATS FOR 8,000 PEOPLE
THIS IS A PUBLIC MEETING
No Tickets Required. Doors Open at 7 o'clock

WAR IS A GRIM BUSINESS	Let us endure to the end,
We have only begun.	as did our fathers before us.
Let us steel our souls to steadfastness	ROOSEVELT will tell you what is your job.

616 A War Rally poster, from a copy in the Roosevelt Memorial Association Museum, New York

THE APPEAL TO THE PEOPLE

IN all wars efforts are made to arouse the people of a warring nation against the enemy; for men do not kill until they hate. Germany's course in Belgium had given her enemies a ready weapon to be used against her in this respect. The transportation of non-combatants from Belgium into Germany, many of them women and girls, raised feelings of horror in the United States. With such incidents as these at hand the organs of public opinion heightened popular feeling. America decided to "Smash the Hun." It was a period of exalted national determination.

A PEOPLE UNITED FOR WAR

THE call to war found the nation ready for the sacrifices involved. Besides the fighting men, the women, old men and children were full of enthusiasm. Having observed the European struggle for nearly three years, they were adjusted in spirit to the duty now thrown upon them. Much interest was shown when a large number of the leading business men offered their services for a dollar a year. Among these men one of the most important was Bernard M. Baruch, who took a large part in conducting the work of the Council of National Defense. His wide business experience and his knowledge of the industrial situation in the United States made him a valuable Government agent. The vigor with which these dollar-a-year capitalists gave themselves to their country's service softened for the time the old popular suspicion of the capitalist class, which had been fostered by the long struggle against "Big Business." Perhaps, also, the war spirit had lessened somewhat the high pride of the very rich.

617 Bernard M. Baruch, 1870–, from a photograph by Harris & Ewing, Washington

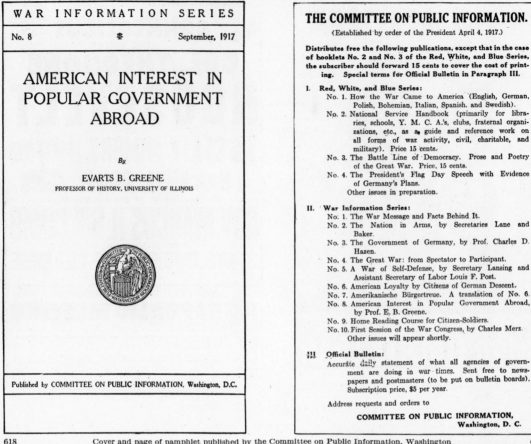

WAR INFORMATION SERIES

No. 8   ☙   September, 1917

AMERICAN INTEREST IN POPULAR GOVERNMENT ABROAD

By

EVARTS B. GREENE

PROFESSOR OF HISTORY, UNIVERSITY OF ILLINOIS

Published by COMMITTEE ON PUBLIC INFORMATION, Washington, D.C.

THE COMMITTEE ON PUBLIC INFORMATION.

(Established by order of the President April 4, 1917.)

Distributes free the following publications, except that in the case of booklets No. 2 and No. 3 of the Red, White, and Blue Series, the subscriber should forward 15 cents to cover the cost of printing. Special terms for Official Bulletin in Paragraph III.

I. Red, White, and Blue Series:

No. 1. How the War Came to America (English, German, Polish, Bohemian, Italian, Spanish. and Swedish).

No. 2. National Service Handbook (primarily for libraries, schools, Y. M. C. A.'s, clubs, fraternal organizations, etc., as a guide and reference work on all forms of war activity, civil, charitable, and military). Price 15 cents.

No. 3. The Battle Line of Democracy. Prose and Poetry of the Great War. Price, 15 cents.

No. 4. The President's Flag Day Speech with Evidence of Germany's Plans.

Other issues in preparation.

II. War Information Series:

No. 1. The War Message and Facts Behind It.

No. 2. The Nation in Arms, by Secretaries Lane and Baker.

No. 3. The Government of Germany, by Prof. Charles D. Hazen.

No. 4. The Great War: from Spectator to Participant.

No. 5. A War of Self-Defense, by Secretary Lansing and Assistant Secretary of Labor Louis F. Post.

No. 6. American Loyalty by Citizens of German Descent.

No. 7. Amerikanische Bürgertreue. A translation of No. 6.

No. 8. American Interest in Popular Government Abroad, by Prof. E. B. Greene.

No. 9. Home Reading Course for Citizen-Soldiers.

No. 10. First Session of the War Congress, by Charles Merz. Other issues will appear shortly.

III. Official Bulletin:

Accurate daily statement of what all agencies of government are doing in war times. Sent free to newspapers and postmasters (to be put on bulletin boards). Subscription price, $5 per year.

Address requests and orders to

COMMITTEE ON PUBLIC INFORMATION,
Washington, D. C.

618   Cover and page of pamphlet published by the Committee on Public Information, Washington   619

THE MOBILIZATION OF THOUGHT

FEW aspects of the war-time activity of the Government were more significant than its deliberate plan to guide the thought of the country. A unique system of free Government publications distributed far and wide became the daily reading of millions. They aimed to make every American familiar with the causes and the issues of the war as well as its purposes. These publications were chiefly small tracts. Their authors included a great number of very distinguished scholars, journalists and authors.

THE "WAR AIMS COURSE"

THE colleges and universities were drawn into the general system of intellectual propaganda. Many of the said institutions were taken under the direct oversight of a new branch of the War Department with Frank Aydelotte at the head of it. The curriculum was revised so as to put chief stress on what was called the "War Aims Course" devised by the Government with a view to preparing the whole country for the problems that would arise in making peace. It was thought that the United States would be called upon to play a large part in the process of reconstruction.

620   Frank P. Aydelotte, 1880–, from a photograph in possession of the publishers

CULTIVATING THE WAR SPIRIT

By way of promptly breaking up possibilities of foreign propaganda an elaborate system of espionage was established. Not a telegram passed over the American wires without close scrutiny to detect inner meanings. Groups of informal confidential observers were formed at many places under Government supervision for the purpose of closely watching the trend of thought in the locality. One of the things necessary for the successful conduct of a war is the support of public opinion in the country at war. This result was obtained in the United States in the World War by setting up a Committee on Public Information, of which Mr. George Creel, a clever newspaper man, was made the chairman. His activities extended to many kinds of writings, all intended to stir up enthusiasm for the great national effort that was to be made. His warm imagination made him a man suited to the task; but he frequently went further than men of sober judgment approved. His most glaring error was the creation of the opinion that rapid progress was being made toward the completion of a vast program of airplane construction. When, at last, the public discovered that only one airplane had been sent to Europe at a time when Creel allowed it to think many had gone, there was a violent shifting of opinion to the discredit of the work of Creel's committee, most of which was excellently planned and carried out.

621 George Creel, 1876–, Chairman of the Committee on Public Information, 1917–19, from a photograph by Underwood & Underwood, New York

622 Interned German ships, the *Prinz Eitel Friedrich* in the foreground, courtesy of the Navy Department, Washington

SEIZURE OF ALIEN PROPERTY

The property of enemies was promptly seized. This began with the German ships in American ports. Foreseeing what would happen, their commanders in some cases succeeded in sinking them just as war was declared. German crews were interned. The American possessions of German subjects were turned over, under act of Congress, to a new officer, the Custodian of Alien Property. Internment camps were immediately established in which many Germans within the United States were confined. They were held until the end of the war. In this way many agents who might otherwise have rendered effective service to the enemy were made powerless. The German ships in American harbors were repaired by the United States and used for the transporting of troops and supplies to the war zone. The disposal of the seized property was to become a matter of vexatious dispute after the war ended.

623   McAdoo signs the order for a loan to France, from a photograph by Underwood & Underwood, New York

LENDING MONEY TO THE ENTENTE ALLIES

WHEN we declared war it was generally said that we should not be expected to send a considerable army to Europe but should only be asked to lend money and supplies. With this in view, a British commission soon arrived in Washington to negotiate a loan from the United States to the British Government. The request was granted in a spirit of generosity, and a short time later a French commission obtained a similar loan. Other nations warring against Germany received like aid. The United States was then the only nation whose condition permitted the extension of financial help. Through two years of hard fighting they had sold Europe supplies she sorely needed, and now they lent her vast sums to buy other supplies. The terms of the loans were not hard, and nobody thought of pressing for payment of interest while the conflict went on.

WAR FINANCES

To Secretary of the Treasury McAdoo fell the task of raising the immense sums necessary to equip and sustain our forces, and also to enable the Government to advance the money promised to the nations in Europe. In reality, the purses of the American people were paying a very large part of the expenses of the total cost of the war against Germany. Instead of issuing bonds to the bankers who would in turn sell them to the people, McAdoo went directly to the public. He established an extensive organization for making financial appeals. Parades, newspaper notices, posters and speeches were some of the means employed. In four Liberty Loans and one Victory Loan, he raised a sum of $19,581,-201,450 to carry the war through to a successful issue. This method was in marked contrast to that used by the Government in the Civil War, when the bonds sold through the banks. McAdoo's success was due chiefly to the high spirit with which the country hailed the decision to enter the war, and to general coöperation of all classes.

THAT LIBERTY SHALL NOT PERISH FROM THE EARTH BUY LIBERTY BONDS
FOURTH   LIBERTY   LOAN

624   A Liberty Loan Poster, from Albert E. Gallatin, *Art and the Great War*, New York, 1919

CONSCRIPTION ADOPTED

Soon after war was declared General Pershing was appointed commander of the forces to be sent across the Atlantic and repaired to France at once. He found that the need on the other side was great and called for an immense army. Congress had already taken up the task of creating such a force. Many people favored raising it by the voluntary system which had been employed in the beginning of all our previous wars. Wilson, however, asked for a general conscription, and Congress after some debate adopted the plan. No discrimination was to be made between individuals, and all who were able were to be required to take due part in the national defense.

THE DRAFT

The process of holding the draft for such a great nation was interesting. First, all the men of military age were enrolled by districts and each given a number in his own district. Then, on a given day, a blind-folded boy in the War Department in Washington drew out numbers from a large vase and the men in each district were considered drawn for military service in the order in which their numbers were taken out of this vase. After this they went before boards for physical examination and to determine whether or not they were exempt from service by provisions in the conscription law. Camps were constructed rapidly and

625   From a cartoon by Marcus in *Cartoons*, June 1917, reproduced from the *New York Times*

in the early autumn two thirds of a million men were in training. These things put a heavy demand on all forms of industry but it was met by careful organization. The desired results were met without interfering with the stream of supplies going abroad. In addition we loaned vast sums to Europe.

626   Secretary Baker drawing the first draft number, from a photograph in the possession of the United States Signal Corps, War Department, Washington

627   Herbert C. Hoover, 1874–, from a photograph by Harris & Ewing, Washington

FOOD CONTROL

IN the stress of war the Entente Allies depended on the United States for a large part of their wheat and meat. To see that our resources in this respect were not wasted, a food controller was created and Herbert C. Hoover, noted for his able management of relief among the suffering people in Belgium, was appointed to the office. His services consisted in careful distribution of food, in the restriction of some kinds of food, and in arousing the people to a keen purpose to increase production. His motto, "Food will win the war," caught the imagination and was a strong incentive to effort. By creating a Government corporation to buy and sell wheat, he kept it out of the hands of speculators and kept its prices within the reach of the poorer consumers. By guaranteeing the farmers a fixed price for wheat he got them to plant large crops to meet the emergency.

CONTROL OF THE RAILROADS

THE railroads did all they could to enable the Government to carry on the war successfully. They established a Railroads' War Board, with Fairfax Harrison as chairman. It aimed by means of effective coöperation to avoid such waste as duplicated efforts and needlessly long hauls, and to obtain the most economical use of empty cars. At the end of 1917 it was seen that the best efforts of the Board could not save the situation, and at their suggestion the Government took over the roads. On December 26, the President appointed William G. McAdoo, Secretary of the Treasury, Director-General of Railroads, and in the following March Congress passed a law regulating Government control of railroads during the war. This step increased in a material way the efficiency of the service and was accepted as a war necessity. The Government took over the railroads with the agreement to guarantee dividends, keep the roads in efficient condition, and return them without depreciation to their owners. Advocates and opponents of Government control watched this experiment with equal interest.

628   McAdoo takes over control of the railways, from a photograph by Clinedinst, Washington

THE GOVERNMENT AS SHIPBUILDER

To get ships to transport to France the immense army we were raising and the vast quantity of supplies they needed was another severe task. The Government met it by buying ships in the coastwise trade, by repairing the seized German ships, by taking over neutral ships in the United States ports, and by building a large number of new ships, steel and wooden. Congress authorized the creation of the United States Shipping Board to carry out this expansion of the merchant marine. When it was found that the Board favored steel rather than wooden ships, a sharp controversy arose, stimulated by the friends of wooden ships. It was allayed when Edward N. Hurley was placed at the head of the Board. Under his wise and tactful management three hundred and eighty-four steel ships were built with a total tonnage of one million five hundred and forty-seven thousand eight hundred and twenty-four; also, two hundred and eighty-nine wooden ships with a total tonnage of five hundred and four thousand one hundred and eight. Without these efforts it would have been very difficult to give the Allies the necessary assistance.

629 Edward N. Hurley, 1864–, from a photograph by Harris & Ewing, Washington

630 Charles M. Schwab, 1862–, from a photograph by Harris & Ewing, Washington

THE EMERGENCY FLEET CORPORATION

To operate the Government ships, Congress created the Emergency Fleet Corporation, and Rear-Admiral Capps was placed in charge. In the days of organization some mistakes were made and delays occurred, and a serious state of dissatisfaction appeared in the public mind. Senator Lodge voiced this feeling in March, 1918, in a speech attacking the efficiency of the Shipping Board. Chairman Hurley issued a quick and complete refutation. President Wilson to satisfy the public placed Charles M. Schwab, president of the Bethlehem Steel Company, at the head of the Emergency Fleet Corporation. Schwab's prominence in the business world created public confidence in the Corporation. Its work, under his direction, reached a high state of efficiency.

FUEL CONSERVATION

The distribution of coal to industrial plants, as well as to householders, also necessitated Governmental control. To supervise the process, Harry A. Garfield, president of Williams College, was appointed Fuel Administrator. He had authority under the act of Congress to fix the prices of coal and to decide to whom it should be distributed. In January, 1918, when the coal situation in the Atlantic states was desperate, he issued an order closing for five Mondays all manufacturing in the region east of the Mississippi. This drastic order was enforced amid much complaint. It was perhaps the most extreme Government action in the war; but it gave the desired relief.

631 Harry A. Garfield, 1863–, from a photograph by Harris & Ewing, Washington

632 Henry P. Davison, 1867–1922, from a photograph
by Harris & Ewing, Washington

633 Miss Mabel Boardman, from a photograph by
Underwood & Underwood, New York

THE AMERICAN RED CROSS

THE American Red Cross, noted for its services in relieving distress under all sorts of conditions, became active everywhere soon after the war began, collecting in the United States large sums of money for its work

in the Entente countries of Europe. When we entered the war it enlarged its operations, mostly in behalf of our own armies. In America, the Secretary of the Red Cross was Miss Mabel Boardman. Wilson was its head, ex-officio. To reinforce the work of Miss Boardman he created a special council with H. P. Davison as chairman. In June, 1917, a nation-wide campaign for funds yielded more than one hundred million dollars for its support, and in five years its membership increased to five million. Its important work was to prepare hospital supplies, operate trucks, prepare hot meals and relieve refugees. Similar aid was given to the soldiers by the members of welfare organizations including the Young Men's Christian Association, the Knights of Columbus, Young Women's Christian Association, the Jewish Welfare Association and the Salvation Army.

AN INFORMAL SERVICE OF SUPPLY

LONG before we went into the war an extensive system of voluntary aid to France was carried on by many groups of American women under the general lead of Miss Anne Morgan. These groups now became equally active, giving indirect aid to the American army; sometimes by raising funds, sometimes by distributing the various forms of Governmental propaganda, sometimes by forming training classes for army nurses, often by making garments for the soldiers.

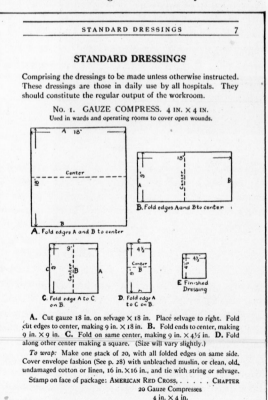

634 Facsimile of page from Red Cross Manual of Standard Dressings

WAR TIME RENUNCIATION

A SENTIMENT of renunciation swept the country. Among other things it caused the institution of the "gasless Sunday." Practically universal consent made it a social offense to run an automobile on Sunday except to serve definite public needs. There was also a widespread voluntary renunciation of the use of alcohol. This strengthened the prohibition movement, already strong in many parts of the community, and led eventually to the Eighteenth Amendment prohibiting the manufacture and sale of alcoholic beverages in the United States. The spirit of renunciation was a manifestation of the unity of the American people in support of the war. Never in their history had Americans been so united in the face of a great emergency. The voluntary savings which were effected in food and fuel were of considerable consequence in bringing the war to a successful conclusion. The saving of food, in particular, made it possible to supply food for England in the winter of 1917–18 when the submarine campaign was threatening the British people with starvation. The attitude of Americans in this respect was surprising even to themselves for, as a people, they tended to be wasteful. Their renunciation, however, did not reach that of the warring nations in Europe, who set us the example which in the world's necessity we were advised to follow.

Sixty-fifth Congress of the United States of America;

At the Second Session,

Begun and held at the City of Washington on Monday, the third day of December, one thousand nine hundred and seventeen.

JOINT RESOLUTION

Proposing an amendment to the Constitution of the United States.

Resolved by the Senate and House of Representatives of the United States of America in Congress assembled (two-thirds of each House concurring therein), That the following amendment to the Constitution be, and hereby is, proposed to the States, to become valid as a part of the Constitution when ratified by the legislatures of the several States as provided by the Constitution:

"ARTICLE —.

"SECTION 1. After one year from the ratification of this article the manufacture, sale, or transportation of intoxicating liquors within, the importation thereof into, or the exportation thereof from the United States and all territory subject to the jurisdiction thereof for beverage purposes is hereby prohibited.

"SEC. 2. The Congress and the several States shall have concurrent power to enforce this article by appropriate legislation.

"SEC. 3. This article shall be inoperative unless it shall have been ratified as an amendment to the Constitution by the legislatures of the several States, as provided in the Constitution, within seven years from the date of the submission hereof to the States by the Congress."

Champ Clark
Speaker of the House of Representatives.

Thos. R. Marshall
Vice President of the United States and President of the Senate.

635   Facsimile of the Eighteenth Amendment, from the original in the Department of State, Washington

636   Lee S. Overman, 1854–, from a photograph by Harris & Ewing, Washington

THE OVERMAN BILL

WHEN the Food Bill was before the Senate in July 1917, that House passed an amendment creating a committee with large power to direct war expenditures. At Wilson's protest, this amendment was dropped when the bill was in conference. By the following winter considerable criticism arose because of the slowness with which war measures proceeded. After a while a bill was introduced in Congress to create a special war cabinet, and it began to be whispered that Roosevelt would be a good man to place at its head. Wilson objected to the bill as an expression of lack of confidence, and got Senator Overman to introduce a bill to enable the President, as Commander in Chief of the Army, to redistribute power among various executive officers and make other sweeping innovations. The bill produced a violent protest from many Senators, but nevertheless it was passed with the provision that it should apply only to the war period. Thus Wilson escaped the humiliation of being set aside and acquired large additional power in the conduct of the war.

637   Newton D. Baker, 1871–, from a photograph
        by Harris & Ewing, Washington

SECRETARY OF WAR BAKER

SECRETARY BAKER became the storm center of the complaints against the administration. He was held responsible for the slow arrival of clothing in the camps, the delay in building airplanes, the delay in furnishing an adequate supply of machine guns, and various other things for which, in fact, the responsibility lay chiefly on the inability of the nation to shift at once from the habits of the times of peace to war activities. Several Democratic Senators joined with the Republicans in an investigation of his department. The examination continued for several weeks and attracted much attention. It was the usual thing to say that his department had broken down. The Government could not meet these charges by showing just what was being done, for that would convey important information to the enemy. Probably, through these reports the Germans were led to think that we would give no effective aid in the war, a conclusion that eventually cost them dear.

THE PEACE COMMISSION

WHEN the German armies were crumpled up by the combined offensive of the Allies, in 1918, a desperate Germany appealed to President Wilson in the hope of securing advantageous terms of peace. Wilson had announced his famous "Fourteen Points" on January 8, 1918, and with four additional "Points" they were accepted by the Allied Powers as the basis of peace. Germany, beaten back in the field and beset with revolution at home, could make no effective resistance and November 11,.1918, she accepted the armistice, the military features of which were dictated by Foch.

Five Commissioners went from the United States to represent their country at the Peace Conference. At the head was President Wilson himself. The other members were the Secretary of State, Lansing, who had followed with great care the preliminary steps that had resulted in calling the Conference; Colonel E. M. House, who as Wilson's personal representative in Europe had been in close relations with Britain, France, and Italy throughout the war; General Tasker H. Bliss, who as a military man was able to speak of the military features of the treaty about to be made; and Henry White, selected as a representative of the Republican party, a man whom Roosevelt had pronounced one of the country's best and most useful diplomats.

638   United States Peace Commission, courtesy of the United States Signal Corps, War Department, Washington
LEFT TO RIGHT: Col. E. M. House; Robert M. Lansing; President Wilson; Henry White; General Tasker H. Bliss.

ARRIVAL OF THE COMMISSION IN FRANCE

The steamship *George Washington*, with the commission and many assistants of one kind or another on board, sailed from New York on December 4, 1918, and reached Brest on the thirteenth. Paris, resplendent in sunlight, received them brilliantly. Her streets were crowded with two millions of people who had come out to see the man who some thought had ended the war and who was going to establish an era of permanent peace. One of his Fourteen Points, accepted by all the Entente nations as a basis of peace, was the creation of an "association of nations" to afford "mutual guarantees of political

639   President Wilson and Party landing at Brest, Dec. 13, 1918, from a photograph in the possession of the United States Signal Corps, War Department, Washington

independence and territorial integrity to great and small States alike." Realizing that a peace conference tended to become a place of selfish national bargaining, he had come to Paris to see that this feature of the agreement was not forgotten in the play of national interest. For this journey he was much blamed by his opponents, but he heeded them not, being used to criticism.

640   President and Mrs. Wilson with King George V and Queen Mary of England in the Victoria Railway Station, London, from a photograph in the possession of the United States Signal Corps, War Department, Washington

WILSON ACCLAIMED IN EUROPE

Wilson's reception by the people of Paris expressed the feeling entertained for him by the people of many European nations. He visited Great Britain and Italy in response to urgent invitations sent him from those countries. In England he was received with great applause; the King and Queen entertained him in Buckingham Palace, and his speeches revealed the gratification he felt. In Italy he received similar testimonials of public approval. These outbursts of friendliness were taken as intended to bring public opinion to bear on the diplomats who were about to gather in the Peace Conference in Paris.

IX—21

641   Hotel Crillon, Paris, from a photograph in the possession of the United States Signal Corps, War Department,
Washington

THE WORK OF THE PEACE COMMISSIONERS

THE United States Commission made active arrangements at Paris to perform its duties. The celebrated Hotel Crillon, in the center of the city, was taken as headquarters, and its many apartments became the scene of lively activity. The United States had lost no territory in the war and had no desire to acquire any. On the other hand, each of the European nations at the Conference had territorial problems to solve. Believing that acquisitions might sow the seed of future wars, the Americans endeavored to minimize them and to induce the other Powers to be satisfied with such terms as could be accepted by all as fair and just.

642   Intelligence Section Division Chiefs, from a photograph in the possession of the United States
Signal Corps, War Department, Washington

LEFT TO RIGHT, Seated: James T. Shotwell, George L. Beer, Allen A. Young, S. E. Mezes, Isaiah Bowman, Charles H. Haskins, Clive Day, Mark Jefferson. Standing: W. L. Westermann, S. A. Hornbeck, W. E. Lunt, E. C. Favabee, Charles Seymour, R. B. Dixon, D. W. Johnson, R. H. Lord.

THE AMERICAN HISTORICAL EXPERTS

BEFORE the war actually ended, it became known that the European nations were setting experts to work on the historical facts that could be used to support their boundary claims. To be able to meet these arguments wisely, Wilson took to Paris a large number of experts of his own, consisting mainly of historians and geographers, as well as persons who understood the economic condition of Europe. Many times the negotiators, bent on accomplishing their nationalistic objects, ignored the facts offered by the American experts, but on the whole the views of the Americans modified in important ways the decisions finally reached by the Conference. For this work and for other efforts to the same end our historians and other experts rendered without compensation much service to the country and to the progress of humane ideals.

ORGANIZED LABOR AND THE CONFERENCE

ORGANIZED labor in Europe and the United States realized that the Peace Treaty might have an important effect on the future of labor. The burden of war falls heavily on the working men, who furnish a large part of the private soldiers. When economic disaster follows in the wake of armed conflict, it is the family of the working man that suffers most — sometimes the extremity of distress. With a sense of the importance of the crisis, Samuel Gompers, head of the American Federation of Labor, went to Paris. He supported Wilson's demand for a League of Nations. He was one of a group of labor leaders from other nations who were instrumental in writing into the Treaty several clauses that gave labor what it was believed would lead it to take a new standing in international relations.

WILSON AND THE "BIG FOUR"

THE Peace Conference contained delegates from all the Powers that had declared war against Germany or her Allies. Four of them dominated the selection at the close of the fighting in Europe — France, Great Britain, the United States and Italy. If it became necessary to enforce the treaty with armies, the burden would fall on these Powers. Naturally, therefore, they assumed the controlling part in treaty-making. Clemenceau, Prime Minister of France; Lloyd George, Prime Minister of Great Britain; and Orlando, Prime Minister of Italy, were all present. Each in his own country was head

643 Samuel Gompers, 1850–1924, in Paris, from a photograph in the possession of the United States Signal Corps, War Department, Washington

of the existing Government and knew that his parliament would sustain him; otherwise he would not have gone to Paris. Because of our peculiar Governmental system Wilson had no such assurance. Even when he had finished the task of hammering out the last agreement he could obtain, he would still have to get it ratified by a Senate in which his political opponents had the majority. These four men assumed the treaty-making task, and the Conference in plenary session approved what they accepted. They were known as the "Big Four." Their decisions settled European affairs. The Japanese representative sat with them when Asiatic affairs were under consideration.

644   Orlando, Lloyd George, Clemenceau, and Wilson (from left to right, seated), from a photograph in the possession of the United States Signal Corps, War Department, Washington

645 President Wilson in Paris, from a photograph in the possession of the United States Signal Corps, War Department, Washington

WILSON'S BATTLE FOR THE LEAGUE IN PARIS

WILSON went to Paris resolved to fight for a League of Nations to make future wars impossible. He found the other members of the "Big Four" bent on arranging boundaries in accordance with the interests of their respective nations. They did not, on the whole, think highly of a League, but Wilson's popularity in Europe was so great that they did not dare override him. They agreed that he should head a Commission to prepare a plan for a League. It was made public on February 14, 1919, and therefore Wilson left Paris for a month to be present when Congress adjourned on March 4, 1919. When he returned to Paris he found that the others had agreed to postpone the adoption of the League until boundary questions were settled. Wilson's anger flared up. He demanded that the League Covenant should be made an integral part of the Treaty, and he ordered the ship *George Washington* to be ready to take him home if this should be refused. Therefore, his opponents gave way, and the Covenant became a part of the treaty. Wilson's battle for a League was won so far as the Peace Conference was concerned. But the fight of the League itself for existence had yet to be made. Accepted in Europe and rejected by the United States it had to begin a slow upbuilding of strength out of the desire of the people of the world for some relief against war.

THE TREATY COMPLETED

THE Treaty as a whole was completed and signed in a plenary session of the Conference on April 28, 1919. On territorial matters Wilson had tried hard to lessen the grasping of the Powers for German or Austrian territory, thinking that such policies only sowed the seed of future discord. In none of these attempts was he entirely successful. He could not get Japan to agree in writing that she would withdraw from Shantung, or induce Italy to give up her claim to Fiume. On the questions relating to the future of the Saar coal fields and the boundaries of Poland he had to accept compromises. The Treaty was offered to the German representatives on May 7, 1919, the fourth anniversary of the destruction of the *Lusitania*. On June 28, in the great hall at Versailles where the German Empire was proclaimed in 1871, they signed this instrument, protesting that some

of its terms were impossible. Immediately Wilson sailed for New York to begin a fierce battle for adoption against a strong opposition in the United States Senate. The Treaty of Versailles proved to be only the first step in the long and difficult process of bringing peace to Europe. It was prompted by fear and hatred deeply engulfed in the minds of the victors. Few of the negotiators realized how difficult it would be to enforce it.

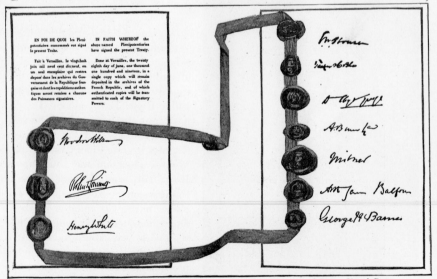

646   The Treaty of Peace, from a photograph in the possession of the United States Signal Corps, War Department, Washington

OPPOSITION TO THE TREATY

In the elections of 1918 the Republicans had carried Congress. Some of their leaders were already opposed to forming a League of Nations, while many favored it. A large number thought Wilson should not have gone to Paris and he was sharply criticized for not taking with him a truly bipartisan commission including perhaps a prominent member of the Senate. When the draft of the Covenant of the League was published, February 14, 1919, it was criticized in broad terms.

647   Senators Borah, Lodge, and Smoot, from a photograph by the Keystone View Company, New York

A group of Senators, notably Senator Borah, opposed it in principle, objecting to the idea that the United States should give up any of its absolute control of foreign affairs in order to enter a League. Others professed to approve of a League in general but declared the proposed plan was bad. Gradually it became apparent that a good deal of public opinion was against a League. Just before Congress adjourned on March 4, 1919, a number of its members issued a round robin declaring against the Covenant as announced. Some leaders welcomed the League as a political issue. The party was badly divided on domestic policies, and it was expedient to keep them in the background if the breach were to be healed. The League and the consequent doctrine of nationality was a promising issue on which both conservatives and Progressives could unite. Senators Borah, Lodge, and Smoot were active leaders in the program thus mapped out. Under the influence of such leaders the sentiment among the Republicans for a League of Nations gradually subsided and men who had once welcomed the League idea came to consider it a dangerous and insidious enemy to Americanism.

648   Elihu Root, 1845–, from a photograph by Harris & Ewing, Washington

THE PRO–LEAGUE REPUBLICANS

Wilson knew that many liberal-minded Republicans desired a League, and he asked some of the most prominent to suggest amendments to the first draft of the Covenant, hoping thereby to meet the objections to it. The request was complied with by Elihu Root, Ex-President Taft and Charles E. Hughes. The most important suggestion referred to the Monroe Doctrine. The critics had suggested that the League, by taking over international disputes leading to war, would take cognizance of violations of the Monroe Doctrine and thus supersede it. At the suggestion of Root, Taft and Hughes, Wilson brought the matter before the Commission on the League in Paris and was able to get it to insert in the Covenant a clause to the effect that the Monroe Doctrine was not weakened by the Covenant. The acceptance of the clause was only obtained by Wilson's persistent urging; for European nations had ever been loath to accord to us a privileged position in the western hemisphere. In the main, most of the suggested amendments were accepted by the Commission.

649 Henry Cabot Lodge, 1850-1924, Chairman of the Senate Committee on Foreign Relations, from a photograph by Underwood & Underwood, New York

THE SENATE COMMITTEE ON FOREIGN RELATIONS

THE key to the situation in the Senate was the Committee on Foreign Relations. The opponents of the League in the Senate organized the Committee so that their friends controlled it. Of its seventeen members nine were Republicans opposed to the Covenant, one a Republican favorable to it, and seven Democrats. The chairman was Senator Lodge. When the Treaty containing the Covenant was laid before the Senate it was referred to this Committee, which reported in favor of ratification but only if the Covenant should be modified by certain reservations. Wilson objected to these modifications as destroying the life of the plan. The vote on the amended Treaty was thirty-five Republicans and three Democrats for ratification, with the reservations, and forty-two Democrats and thirteen Republicans against ratification. This was in the extra session of 1919. In the regular session that followed Lodge contrived to lay the Treaty before Congress with still stronger reservations, and again it was rejected March 19 1920.

WILSON AGAINST THE SENATE

WHILE the Foreign Relations Committee was debating the Treaty, Wilson made a journey through the country defending the League. During the war the people had rallied with enthusiasm to his appeals in behalf of humanitarian ideals, and he believed that they would likewise respond to his call for help to restrict war in the future. He did not realize the quick reaction of the popular mind after the war strain was over. The long struggle in Paris had weakened his physical power, and on September 26 he had an attack which made it necessary to give up the journey. A week after reaching Washington he was stricken with paralysis, and throughout the most intense days of the Senate debate on the Covenant he lay near death. In this condition he was not able to make decisions wisely about the strenuous struggle then in progress. His recovery was never complete and he was still a bedridden invalid when the Treaty came to its final vote in March, 1920. Despite shattered nerves he had to decide whether or not it would, be wise to accept the Senate reservations. His decision to reject them was based on a belief, improperly formed through the reassurance of some of his associates, that the people in the election of 1920 would support him with their votes. He thus lost the opportunity to save the major part of his League. The idea of a League was not a thing that was likely to be understood by the average citizen, and on that account it was not good political strategy to submit it to the verdict of an election.

650   Woodrow Wilson in 1919, from a photograph by Wide World Photos, New York

651   The Republican Convention of 1920, from a photograph by Underwood & Underwood, New York

THE SITUATION OF THE REPUBLICANS

To the Republicans the supreme necessity was the reunion of the divided wings of the party. Dissension had caused their defeat in 1912 and in 1916. Leaders in each wing were equally willing to see the restoration of harmony. Roosevelt had been working for this until his death in 1919, and had he been alive in 1920 he would have been a promising candidate for the nomination. His passing left his friends without a strong leader. Hiram Johnson, of California, essayed to take his place, but the popular response was unfavorable. His weak boom collapsed and the Progressives having no man strong enough to bend the bow of Roosevelt, left the field to the conservatives. For all that, the conservatives feared to raise issues that would start again the resentment of the Progressives of 1910–12.

THE NOMINATION OF HARDING

THE conservative leaders played a skillful game. When the convention had reached a deadlock, no one of the candidates before it being able to get the prize, they united on Warren G. Harding, of Ohio, and obtained his nomination as a "dark horse." He was a man without antagonisms, and it was believed that he was suited for the restoration of party harmony. For Vice-President the convention, breaking away from the hands of the Harding leaders, selected Calvin Coolidge of Massachusetts. The platform did not declare for a League of Nations with the Republican reservations of the preceding March. Anyone could see that opinion was running against that ideal, and the platform kept up with this opinion. It only suggested an international court to settle disputes that might lead to war.

652   Warren Gamaliel Harding, 1865–1923, from a photograph by Underwood & Underwood, New York

653   Homer S. Cummings, 1870–, from a photograph by
            Underwood & Underwood, New York

THE DEMOCRATIC FOG OF 1920

ROBBED by disease of its strong leader, the Democratic party faced the election of 1920 in a sadly unpromising condition. Bryan was still living, but his avowal of pacifist doctrines had gone far to weaken his influence. The portion of the party that had followed him as a Progressive in 1912 and thus obtained the nomination of Wilson was still strong. William G. McAdoo essayed to lead it, but he was stoutly opposed by the wing which in 1912 had rallied around Champ Clark. Strong in this group was a combination formed by Murphy, of Tammany Hall, and composed of the delegations from New York, Illinois, Ohio and Indiana. The friends of Wilson were also well represented in the Convention. Homer S. Cummings, of Connecticut, presented his cause in an eloquent speech which aroused great enthusiasm, and the party expressed its loyalty to the League of Nations. For all that, it was not inclined to take an out-and-out Wilson man for its nominee. There was some foolish talk of nominating Wilson again, but a moment's consideration of the state of his health was enough to dispose of the suggestion. Against him had arisen a peculiarly bitter state of feeling for no other apparent cause than general partisan dislike, and his nomination would have been most unwise.

NOMINATION OF JAMES M. COX

IN the final contest of forces, the New York-Illinois group proved strongest and brought about the nomination of Governor James M. Cox, editor of a newspaper in Dayton, Ohio. Because of the support of Tammany, this choice produced a bad impression on a large portion of the party, the portion that had followed Cleveland and Wilson under the banners of reform. But those who knew Cox intimately had confidence in him. He was called to run on a platform that had the League for its chief feature. He fulfilled the task with

much ability and entire loyalty; but he had not been known as a national figure before his nomination and he could not in one campaign reveal himself convincingly to the whole country. The nation did not quite relish the sight of a Tammany nominee running on a Woodrow Wilson platform. It considered the combination as unnatural and deceptive. In this campaign we see two men brought before the country of whom neither had before this time played a considerable part in national politics. Each of them had been formed in the shrewd but unimpressive life of provincial editors. Neither was known, when nominated, for any policy that had challenged the attention of a large portion of the people. What was it that had brought our politics to the choice of candidates so little known beforehand? The answer is, two things that rarely happen at the same time. One was the reaction of the popular mind after a great war together with the fact that through concentration on war aims the public mind loses for the time its flair for political disputations. The other was the fact that each party, in the death of Roosevelt and the physical breaking of Wilson, had just passed from the rule of a strong personality under which strong leaders are not developed.

654   James M. Cox, 1870–, from a photograph by
                 Harris & Ewing, Washington

THE ELECTION OF 1920

The election of 1920 was apathetic. Though the Democrats were committed to the defense of the League of Nations, many of their leaders did not understand its nature. Such speakers were not likely to convince the average man that the League ought to be accepted. In the country at large popular opinion ran strongly against it. The Republicans found themselves encumbered

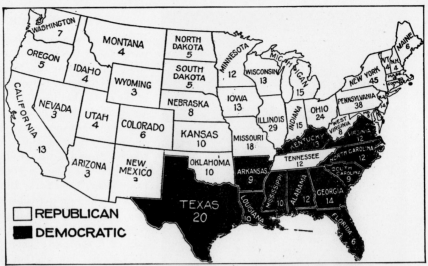

655   Election Map, from the *American Monthly Review of Reviews*, Dec. 1920

by a division on the question. While the majority of them opposed, a considerable minority favored adoption. Thirty-one leading men in this minority, after consulting with Harding, issued a statement in which they declared that the best way for the United States to enter the League was to elect him President. This announcement heartened many Republicans who did not wish to vote against their party. Harding managed to balance between the two sides without ever declaring what he would do about a League. Under this process two important things happened to the Republicans: the threatened split over the League was avoided, and by never mentioning domestic issues the Progressives became, in the main, good Republicans again. The result was the election of Harding by an electoral vote of four hundred and four to one hundred and twenty-seven for Cox. In this election the North and West remained Republican in general and the South Democratic.

OUR DWINDLING MERCHANT MARINE

The war had seen a sharp revival of the American merchant marine. The accompanying graph sums up the history of this once prosperous part of our economic life prior to the World War. It is interesting to note the relation of the tonnage-line to the rise and fall of the protective tariff. In this respect the palmy days of the merchant marine began when the compromise tariff of 1833 came to its fruition in the early 'forties and continued until the restoration of high duties in the days of the Civil War; since then the merchant marine broadly speaking has tended to disappear. Its sharp rise during the World War was due to the reigning crisis in ocean transportation. (See Vol. IV, Nos. 433 and 437.) The shrinkage of this form of industry without the artificial stimulation of war necessities has led to frequent suggestions of subsidies from the National Government. They have been tried, for the most part under the guise of appropriation for carrying the mail. But the experiments have not been popular and were generally short lived.

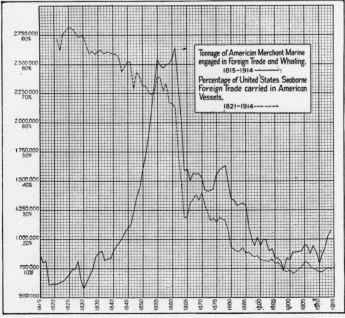

Tonnage of American Merchant Marine engaged in Foreign Trade and Whaling, 1815-1914 ———
Percentage of United States Seaborne Foreign Trade carried in American Vessels, 1821-1914 - - - - -

656   Drawn expressly for *The Pageant of America* from data compiled by David M. Matteson

657 President-elect Harding (third from left) with Senators Fall and Frelinghuysen, Henry P. Fletcher, Dr. Arthur H. Ely, and Harry M. Daugherty, at St. Augustine, Fla., Jan. 1921, from a photograph by Wide World Photos, New York

HARDING AND HIS SUPPORTERS

HARDING was one of our few Presidents who have been members of the Senate when nominated for the Presidency, but he had not been a leader in that body. He could not impose his will on other men by virtue of a strong personality; and it was evident that he would not dominate his own administration as Roosevelt and Wilson had dominated theirs. His election pleased the party men who surrounded him, and they looked forward to an era of party politics rather than of Presidential leadership. Among those who stood closest to him in the interval between election and inauguration, when he was selecting his Cabinet, were Senator Albert W. Fall, of New Mexico, and the manager of his political fortunes. Harry M. Daugherty, of Ohio.

HARDING'S CABINET

FOR Secretary of State, Harding chose Charles E. Hughes, who enjoyed the confidence of those who wanted the United States to enter the League of Nations. For Secretary of the Treasury he chose Andrew W. Mellon, a very wealthy banker and manufacturer, of Pennsylvania, who had the confidence of the business men of the country; and for Secretary of Commerce, Herbert C. Hoover, whose executive ability and broad knowledge of international relations recommended him to everyone. The other members of the Cabinet were not as eminent as these three and seem to have been selected on political grounds. Harding frequently asked the Vice-President to attend the sessions of the Cabinet.

658   Harding's Cabinet, from a photograph by Wide World Photos, New York

LEFT TO RIGHT, *Back Row:* President Harding; Andrew Mellon, Secretary of the Treasury; Harry M. Daugherty, Attorney-General; Edwin Denby, Secretary of the Navy; Henry C. Wallace, Secretary of Agriculture; James J. Davis, Secretary of Labor; Vice-President Coolidge. *Front Row:* Charles E. Hughes, Secretary of State; John W. Weeks, Secretary of War; Will H. Hays, Postmaster-General; Albert B. Fall, Secretary of the Interior; Herbert C. Hoover, Secretary of Commerce.

THE DISARMAMENT CONFERENCE CALLED

HARDING's promises during the campaign created the expectation that he would do something to promote international peace. Moreover, Secretary Hughes was so clearly pledged to the same cause, that it was thought that he would lead the administration in that direction. Even before the inauguration, Senator Borah introduced resolutions in the Senate for calling a conference of leading nations to consider the question of disarmament. Out of these circumstances came, August 11, 1921, Harding's call for a conference to meet in Washington on Armistice day, November 11, 1921. Invitations were sent to Great Britain, France, Italy, Japan, China, the Netherlands, Portugal and Belgium. The object was to consider disarmament and matters relating to the affairs of the Pacific and Far Eastern countries.

659   William E. Borah, 1865-, from a photograph by
Harris & Ewing, Washington

MEETING OF THE CONFERENCE

THE Washington Conference assembled in the Memorial Continental Hall in Washington on the appointed day and sat until February 6, 1922. During its sessions it was the most important event then attracting the world's attention. At the head of the United States delegation was Secretary Hughes, at the head of the British delegation was a former Prime Minister, the Earl of Balfour; while Prime Minister Briand led the French and Admiral Kato led the Japanese delegation. No more distinguished company has gathered in our National Capital. The two questions it was called to consider were of great importance. Disarmament was on the minds of the people of all civilized nations. The relations of the nations owning territory in the Pacific had for some time been strained through undue suspicion that would not be moderated. It was desirable that a treaty be made to establish more confidence between the United States and Japan.

660   Heads of Delegations to the Washington Conference, from a photograph by Keystone View Company, New York
LEFT TO RIGHT: Dr. H. A. Van Karnebeek, Holland; Dr. Sao-Ke Alfred Sze, China; Arthur J. Balfour, Great Britain; Charles E. Hughes, United States; Aristide Briand, France; Carlo Schanzer, Italy; Baron de Cartier, Belgium; Prince Iyesato Tokugawa, Japan.

661   Signing of the Naval Pact, Aug. 18, 1923, from a photograph by Underwood & Underwood, New York
LEFT TO RIGHT, *Seated around table:* Augusto Rosso, Italy; Henry O. Chilton, Great Britain; Charles E. Hughes, United States; Capt. André de la Boulaye, France; Masanao Hanihara, Japan.

THE LIMITATION OF NAVAL ARMAMENTS

ONE of the first decisions was that the Conference could do nothing to limit land armaments. France insisted that she could not reduce her army until it was evident that Germany would carry out in good faith the reparation clauses of the Treaty of Versailles. So difficult was the military problem that the Conference left it unsettled and turned its attention to the limitation of naval armaments. On this point Secretary Hughes astonished the world by proposing the immediate scrapping of some of the largest ships of war in the American, British and Japanese navies. The point was carried after some discussion. Hughes also proposed that in

building capital ships of war in the future the ratio followed should be five for Great Britain, five for the United States, three for Japan, one and three fourths for France and one and three fourths for Italy. This provision was also carried. Finally, these arrangements were embodied in the Five Power Naval Pact. It did not apply to light cruisers, submarines and other minor ships of war. This program was to be binding until the end of 1936.

JAPAN AND CHINA

ALTHOUGH Japan had promised at Paris to withdraw from Shantung, in China, she had not yet shown any intention of putting the promise into execution. She was protected by a treaty in which she and Great Britain had guaranteed the possessions of each other in Asiatic waters. After much discussion, Japan was induced to promise to withdraw from Shantung at once. Together with Great Britain, the United States and China, she signed a new agreement guaranteeing the island possessions of each power in Asiatic waters. The obvious significance of this pact was that the Anglo-Japanese treaty was expanded into a four-power treaty through which neither Japan nor Great Britain lost anything, but which yielded great advantage to the United States by removing the ever present fear that Japan might seize the Philippines. This treaty was perhaps the most valuable of all the agreements made in this Conference.

662   Baron Suteni Chinda, from a photograph by Harris & Ewing, Washington

663   The Washington Conference in session, from a photograph by Harris & Ewing, Washington

SIGNIFICANCE OF THE CONFERENCE

BESIDE the pacts to regulate naval armament and to limit Japan's aggression in China, a number of other agreements were made in the Washington Conference. They covered a wide range of subjects, including gases and submarines, the rights of the United States in territory held by other powers under "mandates," the definition of certain terms in the four-power pact, the future policy of the powers respecting the status of China, and the conditions under which China might conduct her custom houses and post offices. These agreements seemed a great achievement in the interest of world peace, and the Conference dispersed with the acclaim of the world.

THE FORDNEY–McCUMBER TARIFF

THE Underwood tariff, 1913, had hardly gone into operation when the World War checked temporarily the efforts of European manufacturers to compete for markets in the United States. When the war was over, many people predicted that under the existing tariff Europe would "dump" great quantities of merchandise on our market and thus ruin our manufacturers. It was soon seen that Europe, distressed by the war, was in no condition to "dump" commodities anywhere. Under these circumstances, the impulse to change the tariff gathered force slowly. Another restraining force was the conviction, largely held by international bankers, that American capital was needed to restore European industry and that the interest on such loans would have to be paid in commodities. The great bankers, therefore, used their influence against tariff changes. Although Fordney's bill for higher rates passed the House in 1921, it lay in the Senate, unacted upon, for many months. Finally, the small manufacturers gathered their strength, and in 1922 Congress was forced to action. Thus protection rallied its forces and the country rebuilt the high wall, which the Democrats had lowered in 1913.

664   Joseph W. Fordney, 1853–, from a photograph by Underwood & Underwood, New York

665   Immigration Commission, from a photograph by Keystone View Company, New York

A NEW IMMIGRATION LAW

ONE of the results of the World War was a determination in the United States to stop the migration to this country of vast numbers of European laborers. Efforts in this direction had several times been made with the support of organized labor, but they had been opposed by the employer class, on the ground that restriction of immigration would mean higher wages. The spread of communism among the workmen of Europe now seemed an additional reason for restriction, and a bill was passed in 1921 to limit arrivals from any foreign country to three per cent of the immigrants from that country who were residents in the United States in 1910. This law did not seem to go far enough and in 1924 an epoch-making immigration act was put on the statute books. It fixed the annual quota of each nation at two per cent of its immigration to the United States in 1890. By this means the number to be received from Southern Europe was greatly reduced; for only a few immigrants were received from that region in 1890. The new law by superseding the "gentlemen's agreement" and excluding Asiatics aroused against the United States the fierce anger of the people of Japan.

THE CENTRAL AMERICAN CONGRESS IN WASHINGTON

ALTHOUGH Harding's administration was careful to avoid any kind of coöperation with the League of Nations, it was willing to promote a better understanding among the Central American States. It gave encouragement to such a movement by bringing about a Central American Conference in Washington, attended by Nicaragua, Guatemala, Costa Rica and Salvador. The Conference accomplished the limitation of armaments for five years and fixed the number of men each state should have in its standing army. It adopted other measures looking to the establishment of peace between the states in attendance, and in two of the pacts the United States was a signatory power. The Conference sat from December 4, 1922, to February 7, 1923. It was violated in Nicaragua by Chamorro in 1925 when he set up a military dictatorship. President Coolidge, following Wilson's course with Huerta, refused to recognize his authority, which led to the landing of marines and participation in the local elections.

666   Members of the Central American Congress, from a photograph by Clinedinst. Washington

667   President Harding's body lies in state, from a photograph by Underwood & Underwood, New York

THE DEATH OF PRESIDENT HARDING

On August 2, 1923, the country was shocked to hear that President Harding had died in San Francisco after a brief illness. He had started a few weeks earlier on a journey through the West, going as far as Alaska; and it was on his return, while traveling by train from Seattle to San Francisco, that he was seized with the fatal attack. His death brought forth a great wave of sympathy and the play of party feeling ceased in the contemplation of his sudden passing. Thinking of the collapse in office of two successive Presidents, Americans began to consider the difficulties of the position held by their Chief Executive. America has become a vast and complex nation, its problems at home and abroad demanding for their solution statesmanship of the highest order. The task of a President has become too great for one man's strength. The tragic collapse of Wilson and Harding caused a firm conviction in the minds of the American people that something should be done to ease the burden under which the President labored.

PRESIDENT COOLIDGE

Upon the shoulders of the Vice-President, Calvin Coolidge, devolved the burden of the Presidency. His brief public life in Washington had revealed him as a man of simple ways and a taciturn nature, and there was at first much speculation over his capacity to meet the situation before him. Time revealed him as a man of good sense and great political judgment, a friend of economy in public expenditures, and an exponent of what the country had long been in the habit of calling New England simplicity. In this way he gradually won the confidence of the public and in 1924 was elected as his own successor.

668   Calvin Coolidge, 1872–, accepts the Republican nomination for President, Aug. 14, 1924, from a photograph by Underwood & Underwood, New York

NOTES ON THE PICTURES

1. Matthew B. Brady, a noted New York photographer who made a great reputation in the Civil War and later, going to the Union front at times, besides making portraits of most of the notables of his day. He was born in Cork, Ireland, in 1823, and in his youth was employed by A. T. Stewart, the New York merchant.

4, 5. The palmetto flag was hoisted in Charleston after the ordinance of secession was passed, and the palmetto cockade, made of blue silk with a palmetto tree on a button in the center, was worn by the Charleston ladies in public.

6. From 1855 until June 21, 1894, this weekly was known as *Frank Leslie's Illustrated Newspaper*, then for one issue as *Frank Leslie's Illustrated Weekly*, and from June 28, 1894, to the date of its discontinuance in 1922 as *Leslie's Illustrated Weekly*. Many illustrations from it appear in this volume.

15. For Thomas Nast as a caricaturist, see Vol. XII.

17. For a discussion of Currier & Ives' caricatures, see Vol. XII.

18, 19. The files of *Harper's Weekly* and of *Frank Leslie's Illustrated Newspaper* (see 6) for the period of the Civil War and the decade thereafter are invaluable to the student who would study the pictorial side of that conflict. Each reflected political opinion in its cartoons, and each maintained artists at the front.

23. The cartoons in *Punch*, published in London, very clearly represent the political views of the British Government at the beginning of the war. This view was later modified in the cartoons as the Government became more friendly to the North. Many Civil War cartoons in *Punch* were drawn by John Tenniel, often without his initials. See 46, 70, 71, 166, 171, 174, 175.

39. The artist lived for a considerable time in the White House, making observations preparatory to painting this picture.

51. See 1.

56. See 17.

59. One of Winslow Homer's early sketches reproduced as a woodcut. See Vol. XII.

64. Besides working as a caricaturist, Nast was frequently employed upon sentimental or inspirational pictures. This is one of many drawn by him at this time.

67. This enlargement of the original makes apparent the wart on Lincoln's right cheek.

69. Ritchie was born in Glasgow, Scotland, and became an N.A. in 1871. He was a painter, and engraver of many mezzotints, some after his own paintings.

70. Tom Taylor at this time was editor of *Punch* and this picture made amends in America for that journal's political leanings toward the South in the early part of the war. See 23.

76. Frank Bellew was an English illustrator and caricaturist in America at the time of the Civil War and later.

79. The artist, Cincinnati-born, studied under James H. Beard and was illustrator for *Harper's Weekly* during the Civil War. Later he worked as a painter abroad. See Vol. XII.

80, 86, 87. William Waud and his brother A. R. Waud were illustrators who came from England in the Civil War period and drew many sketches for wood-block engravers of the day.

88, 89. Davis, a well-known illustrator, many of whose sketches were "drawn on the spot."

104. Alfred Wordsworth Thompson, born at Baltimore, was an illustrator before he became a painter chiefly of scenes of southern life. See Vol. I.

105. Sheppard, a Virginia illustrator and painter chiefly of southern life. See Vol. III.

113, 115, 120. Taylor, an illustrator who had a wide experience of public events of the 'sixties.

121. Jean Paul Laurens, a well-known French painter of the last century, noted for his tendency toward dramatization.

123. Most of the illustrations in King's book are by J. Wells Champney.

126. See 113.

146. "Nast supplemented the work of the *Times*," writes James F. Rhodes, in his *History of the United States*, Vol. VI, pp. 406–407, "with one of his most effective cartoons. The four conspirators are in front and eleven other men complete a circle. The question is as put by the *Times*, 'Who stole the People's Money?' ''Twas him,' is the reply, and Hall indicates Connolly with his thumb, Connolly points to Sweeny, and Sweeny to Tweed and so on round the circle, the plasterer, the carpet manufacturer, the carpenter, the furnisher of gas pipes, the dealer in awnings, and the seller of furniture point each to his neighbor. Finally 'John Smith' points to 'Tom, Dick and Harry,' and the Old Board to the New, who completes the circle with the forefinger pointed at Hall. 'Let's stop these pictures,' exclaimed

Tweed on seeing this cartoon. 'I don't care so much what the papers write about me — my constituents can't read; but they can see pictures.' "

160–165. See 15.

166. See 23.

167. See Vol. XII.

185. See 17.

195. For Keppler as a caricaturist, see Vol. XII.

203, 205. A. B. Frost also famous for his pictures of rural life. See Vol. III.

209. The scene of this painting is the Supreme Court chamber, where the Electoral Commission sat, and the portraits are from life.

213, 215, 220, 239. Wales was also one of the leading caricaturists of the 'eighties.

214. Reinhart, besides occasional cartoons, published many illustrations on American life and history for *Harper's Weekly*. See 217, also Vols. VIII and XII.

229. The lettering accompanying this cartoon reflects the vindictiveness of politics of this period as manifested by this caricaturist, especially the allusion to Grant having accepted a free pass on his famous tour around the world, when he was received with distinguished honor in many countries. See 195, also Vol. XII.

230, 231. See 229. In 230 the Democratic leaders, as Israelites, are given a dusky hue.

248, 253. For Opper's caricatures for *Puck*, see Vol. XII.

291. Louis Dalrymple was a disciple of Joseph Keppler and in the opinion of some superior to him. See 294, 295, 314, 345, 350.

326. Graham, a facile and accurate illustrator of the day, chiefly for *Harper's Weekly*. See Vols. III and V.

349. W. A. Rogers, cartoonist for *Harper's Weekly* and later for the *New York Herald*. See 356, 436, 441, 446, 483, 485, 500.

369. Homer C. Davenport, a noted early newspaper cartoonist. Much of his work appeared in the *New York Journal* in the 'nineties. See 378, 379, 383, 386, 396.

388. Childe Hassam, American luminist painter and etcher. See Vol. XII.

410, 414. Nelan, a leading caricaturist of his day, chiefly on independent lines.

423. Bush, a noted cartoonist for the *New York Herald* and *The World*, New York. See 450.

455. Drawn by Keppler's son, signed by him Kpp. He was christened Udo, but changed his name to Joseph, Jr. See 469.

491. C. R. Macauley, well-known cartoonist for *The World*, New York. See 560, 569.

545. Césare, cartoonist whose work appeared during the World War in *The Sun*, New York. See 598, 604.

576. Rollin Kirby, whose work in *The World*, New York, has roused interest. See 584.

593. J. N. Darling, cartoonist whose work under the name of "Ding" appears in the *Des Moines Register-Leader* and is syndicated in other papers throughout the country.

INDEX

Titles of books under author are in italics, titles of illustrations under producer are in quotation marks.